FOURTH EDITION

Anatomy, Dance Technique & Injury Prevention

Justin Howse and Moira McCormack

methuen | drama

D1382978

Methuen Drama

1 3 5 7 9 10 8 6 4 2

First published in 1988 by A & C Black Publishers Ltd
Second edition 1992
Third edition 2000
Fourth edition published with a new title by Methuen Drama 2009

Methuen Drama
A & C Black Publishers Ltd
36 Soho Square
London W1D 3QY
www.methuendrama.com

A CIP catalogue record for this book is available from the British Library

ISBN 978 0 7136 8532 9

Typeset by Margaret Brain, Wisbech

Contents

Section Four • *Strengthening Exercises* 158

Section Four contains a series of exercises, illustrated by 256 specially modelled photographs

---

Section Five • *Technical Faults and Anatomical Variations: Their Causes, Consequences and Treatment* 202

Foreword

Dame Ninette de Valois

This book gives us the opportunity to indulge in some serious reflection. It is full of highly technical observations on movement as related to the world of ballet and is accompanied by helpful illustrations. A great deal of it should be rewarding to students, dancers, teachers, repetiteurs and ballet staff in general. I dare to add that, in my opinion, it is also food for thought for choreographers. Today it is not customary for choreographers to give either scientific or practical thought to their choreographic demands. Let us recall that a composer has to remember to keep within the range of a singer's voice. It therefore seems right for a choreographer to study more carefully not only the limitation of dancers' limbs but also the limitation of their general stamina.

Introduction

For anyone associated with dance, either as a performer or a teacher, a good knowledge of anatomy and physiology is essential both in the prevention and in the treatment of an injury. A teacher, particularly of the young, must be aware of the limitations of the body and the variations in ranges of movements between different pupils. Asking a student to assume positions which are not within his range will cause injury. Attempting to force a student into a position which it is impossible for him to obtain will cause an injury if the attempts are persisted with. Equally, dancers must realise their own limitations and work intelligently within them. Students must also realise that every body has its limitations and they in their turn must not cause damage to their own bodies.

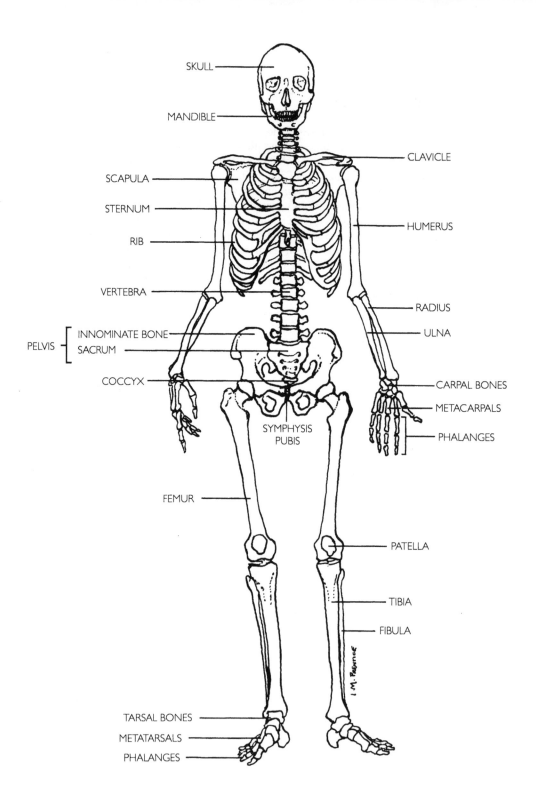

SKULL

MANDIBLE

CLAVICLE

SCAPULA

STERNUM

HUMERUS

RIB

VERTEBRA

RADIUS

ULNA

INNOMINATE BONE

PELVIS

SACRUM

COCCYX

CARPAL BONES

METACARPALS

PHALANGES

SYMPHYSIS
PUBIS

FEMUR

PATELLA

TIBIA

FIBULA

TARSAL BONES

METATARSALS

PHALANGES

1.1 The skeleton

Anatomy and Physiology

1.1 The Skeleton

The skeleton forms the scaffold upon which the other tissues are built and it forms the basis of the shape of the human body. The majority of the skeleton is made of hard, relatively incompressible bone tissue but some parts are made of the more flexible material, cartilage. As a foetus develops, the skeleton is first laid down as cartilage, most of which is gradually replaced by bone during growth and development. This process is called ossification. By the time the baby is born, most bones are completely ossified except for an area at the ends of the bone, a collar of cartilage called the growth or epiphyseal plate. It is the cartilage here that allows the bones to grow as the child grows. Once the skeleton reaches maturity the bones are fully ossified but cartilage remains covering the ends of the bones at moveable joints and is called articular cartilage.

Cartilage

- Cartilage is softer than bone, less rigid and slightly elastic.
- Cartilage can be regarded as a kind of water gel, made up of 75 per cent water and 25 per cent protein. It is made up of chondrocytes (cells which produce an extracellular matrix known as chondrin) and proteoglycans and strengthened by varying amounts of tough collagen fibres and yellow elastic (elastin) fibres, and by proteins.
- Blood vessels do not penetrate cartilage and therefore it receives its nutrients via diffusion from surrounding tissue fluids.
- **Hyaline** (from the Greek word meaning glass) cartilage is found in the costal cartilages of the ribs, the cartilage rings of the respiratory tract, and the nose, where a degree of form and flexibility is required. It is also the cartilage which forms the growth plates already mentioned.
- **Articular hyaline** cartilage covers the ends of bones where they articulate against each other at synovial joints (see p. 7). This cartilage is hard and glassy and provides a tough, enduring layer which protects the bone ends, reduces friction and withstands compression. It receives its nutrition from the synovial fluid that fills the enclosed joint space.
- **Fibrocartilage** has more collagen content than hyaline cartilage and can therefore withstand further compression and resist pulling or tearing forces. It is found in the intervertebral discs and symphysis pubis where these properties are required.
- **Elastic cartilage** contains more elastin and is able to recoil to its original shape when deformed. It is found in the external ear.

Bone

Bone is similar in make-up to cartilage but is impregnated with calcium salts, chiefly phosphate and carbonate. These give it its hardness, rigidity and high compressive strength. Its organic component, collagen, gives it its high tensile strength – its ability to withstand strong pulling forces.

The skeleton is made up of two types of bone tissue – **compact** and **cancellous** bone. Compact bone makes up the outer layers or cortex of the bones forming a tough, hard shell, accounting for 80 per cent of bone in the body. The microscopic structure of compact bone shows a dense, close packed arrangement of circular canals each of which is surrounded by concentric layers (lamellae) of bony tissue or matrix. These are called Haversion Systems. Each contains osteocytes (bone cells) within the lamellae and nerve and blood vessels within its canal. The inner part of the bone is made up of cancellous (trabecular or spongy) bone, which consists of interconnecting rods or plates of bone called trabeculae. Filling the spaces between the trabeculae is red bone marrow – a fatty substance in which blood forming cells are suspended. Each tabecula or beam is made up of layers of bone containing osteocytes and its blood supply is drawn from the surrounding marrow by diffusion.

New bone is laid down by osteoblasts but living bone is a constantly changing tissue. At any one time 5 per cent of the bone mass is being remodelled. Osteoclasts are another group of cells that constantly erode and absorb previously formed or damaged bone. There is a balance between the osteoblasts building new bone and osteoclasts eroding bone. They work in conjunction to ensure that bone retains its strength. This process also allows the structure of bone to be altered if need be, for example to respond to new stresses if its owner takes up a new exercise, or to repair damage. Importantly, bone responds to nutrition, developing strength and density with sufficient calcium and calorie intake, but weakening with dietary and hormonal imbalance.

Bone mass is maintained by normal exercise and any increased physical activity leads bone to adapt its material and geometric properties to best withstand future loads of the same nature (Wolff's Law) i.e. bone will remodel in order to accommodate new stresses. This is commonly seen in the normal stress thickening seen in of the dancers' 2nd and 3rd metatarsals.

DIFFERENT SHAPES OF BONES

- **Long bones** such as the femur, tibia, fibula, humerus and ulna have a shaft and two epiphyses. The metatarsals and phalanges are miniature long bones (Fig. 1.2).
- **Short bones** are usually cube shaped, for example the carpal bones in the wrist and the tarsal bones in the hindfoot.
- **Flat bones** such as the shoulder blade and the skull bones.
- **Irregular bones** as their name described are irregularly shaped such as the innominate bone of the hip.
- **Sesamoid bones** such as the two under the joint to the great toe.

FUNCTIONS OF BONE

- **Support:** the skeleton forms a framework suspended by muscles giving the body its form.
- **Blood cell production:** red blood cells are manufactured by red bone marrow contained within certain bones.
- **Movement:** the bones serve as levers operated by muscular forces.
- **Protection:** the skull protects the brain, the ribcage protects the heart and lungs, the pelvis protects the reproductive organs and the spine protects the spinal cord.
- **Storage:** calcium, phosphorus and magnesium are stored within bone and can be mobilised at any moment into the blood circulation for specific needs.

The diagram (Fig. 1.1) shows the human skeleton and names the more important bones. The skull, which contains and protects the brain, is supported on the vertebral column; the vertebral column also contains and protects the spinal cord. Part way down the vertebral column lies the thoracic cage, within which are the heart and lungs. At the lower end of the vertebral column is the sacrum, a column of five vertebrae which, as a result of evolution, have become fused to form one bone. At the tip of the sacrum there is the coccyx, made up of four tiny vertebrae which are usually movable, although only passively, and represents a rudimentary tail. The sacrum forms part of the pelvis, the sides of the pelvis being made up of two large bones called the innominate bones. These join at the back to the sacrum at the sacroiliac joints

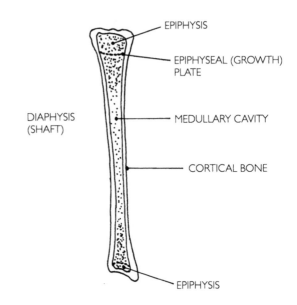

1.2 Diagrammatic representation of a long bone

and at the front they form the symphysis pubis. Both of these joints allow a very small amount of movement. At the sides of the pelvis are the hip joints from which the legs extend downwards. As far as the upper limbs are concerned, the attachment of the shoulder girdle to the rest of the skeleton is far less secure and definite. At the inner end of the clavicles, or collar bones, there is a joint with the breast bone, the sterno-clavicular joint, but apart from this the sole connection with the rest of the body is by the various groups of muscles around the shoulder girdle.

The Parts of the Skeleton

The skeleton can be considered in two parts:
a) the axial skeleton, which is composed of the skull, vertebral column, sacrum and rib cage;
b) the appendicular skeleton, which is composed of the shoulder girdle and upper limbs and the innominate bones and lower limbs.

THE AXIAL SKELETON

The skull, which encases the brain, together with the jaw bone or mandible forms the heaviest part of the body. It sits at the top of the cervical spine. The cervical spine comprises seven separate vertebrae. The first and second cervical vertebrae are highly specialised and totally different from all the others in the body (Fig. 1.3 and Fig. 1.4). The first cervical vertebra is also called the atlas, the name being derived from classical mythology. Atlas had to support the whole world upon his shoulders; the atlas takes the whole weight of the skull. It is the shape of a ring

1.3 The skull and cervical spine

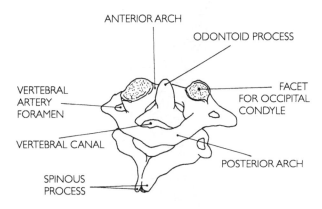

1.4 Atlas and axis from above

1.5 Lateral view of the spinal column

without the normal vertebral body. Only a nodding movement takes place between the skull and the atlas. The second cervical vertebra is known as the axis because it allows rotation to take place between the atlas and the axis. Just over 50 per cent of cervical spinal rotation takes place here with the rest of rotation occurring in the cervical spine. The movement is made possible because of a peg which extends upwards from the vertebral body of the axis. This goes up into the ring of the atlas and is kept in place by a very strong transverse ligament. It is known as the odontoid peg and developmentally represents the body of the atlas. The remaining five cervical vertebrae are similar to the others in the rest of the spinal column. As will be seen

from the diagram of the spinal column (Fig. 1.5), the vertebrae tend to become gradually larger as they descend. There are slight variations in the shape and structure of the vertebrae in the cervical, thoracic and lumbar regions. The diagram (Fig. 1.6) shows a typical lumbar vertebra from above and from the side and the various parts have been named. Some of these areas will be referred to in later sections of the book.

As will be seen from the drawing of two adjacent vertebrae from the back (Fig. 1.7), the articular processes or facet joints hook over each other. These are little synovial joints (vide-infra) which glide over each other, allowing some movement between each vertebra. Between the vertebral bodies are the intervertebral

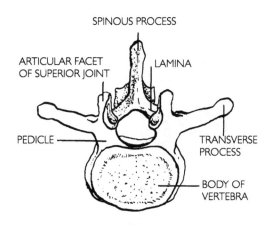

SPINOUS PROCESS

ARTICULAR FACET OF SUPERIOR JOINT

LAMINA

PEDICLE

TRANSVERSE PROCESS

BODY OF VERTEBRA

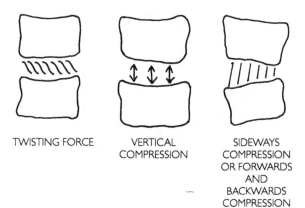

TWISTING FORCE

VERTICAL COMPRESSION

SIDEWAYS COMPRESSION OR FORWARDS AND BACKWARDS COMPRESSION

1.8 Intervertebral discs

ARTICULAR FACET OF SUPERIOR FACET JOINT

BODY

TRANSVERSE PROCESS

PARS INTERARTICULARIS

SPINOUS PROCESS

ARTICULR PROCESS OF INFERIOR FACET JOINT

1.6 Parts of a vertebra. The third lumbar vertebra is typical but the shape differs slightly at various levels. The lumbar region is of greatest interest to the dancer

ARTICULAR SURFACE OF SUPERIOR FACET JOINT

INTERVERTEBRAL DISC

SPINOUS PROCESS

TRANSVERSE PROCESS

INFERIOR ARTICULAR FACET

1.7 Posterior view of two lumbar vertebrae

SECONDARY CURVE

PRIMARY CURVE

SECONDARY CURVE

PRIMARY CURVE

1.9 The spinal column showing the primary and secondary curves discs. These discs are made up of tough fibro-cartilage. They act between the vertebral bodies very much like a piece of india-rubber, permitting some compression and some stretching to take place as the vertebral bodies move, one in relation to the next (Fig. 1.8) It is, however, important to remember that only a little movement takes place between each individual vertebra and its adjacent neighbour. It is these small amounts of movement which, when added together, produce the degree of flexibility which is obtainable in the spine as a whole. However, there are differences between the various areas of the spine. The cervical and lumbar regions are relatively mobile whereas the dorsal or thoracic region is relatively immobile.

As will be seen from the lateral diagram of the vertebral column (Fig. 1.9), this does not form a straight line. There are four distinct curves. In the thoracic and sacral regions this curve is convex towards the back or posteriorly, whereas in the lumbar and cervical regions the curve goes in a forwards direction. Initially, in foetal life, the whole spine is curved in the same direction, like the thoracic and sacral areas. These two areas are known as primary curves; later, secondary curves in the

opposite direction take place at the cervical and lumbar regions with the strengthening of the neck and vertical postures. The points of greatest stress are where the curves change direction and these areas are more liable to sustain injury. This is particularly so in the lower regions where the weight of the upper part of the body is being transmitted downwards, e.g. in fractures of the spine the most common area is in the lower dorsal/upper lumbar region, and for soft tissue and disc damage this occurs most commonly at the lower lumbar area between the 4th/5th lumbar vertebrae and the 5th lumbar vertebra and the first sacral vertebra at the top of the sacrum. The sacral vertebrae are fused (joined) together to make, in effect, one bone – the sacrum.

The vertebral column ends with the sacrum. This forms part of the pelvic girdle together with the two innominate bones.

The rib cage (see Fig. 1.1) is made up of twelve ribs on each side. At the back there are joints between the ribs and the thoracic vertebrae. At the front the lowest two ribs, the 11th and the 12th, have no attachment to the sternum or breast bone. The remaining ten ribs are

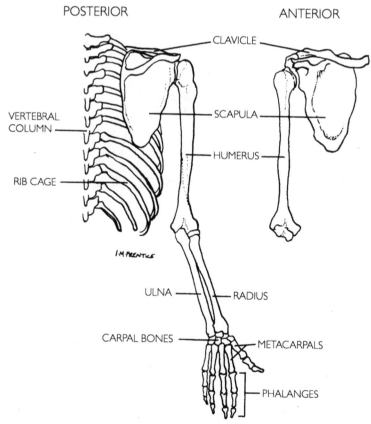

POSTERIOR   ANTERIOR

CLAVICLE

VERTEBRAL COLUMN

SCAPULA

HUMERUS

RIB CAGE

I·M·PRENTICE

ULNA — RADIUS

CARPAL BONES — METACARPALS

PHALANGES

1.10 The right upper limb and shoulder girdle. In the diagram on the right the rib cage has been omitted as it would have obscured the front (anterior) surface of the scapula which lies against the back of the rib cage joined to the sternum with short lengths of hard cartilage, known as the costal cartilages, the 8th, 9th and 10th ribs having long pieces of costal cartilage which combine with that of the 7th rib and then meet the sternum. This combination produces the curve that one sees at the lower end of the rib cage from the bottom of the breast bone curving away and downwards towards the side, where the rib cage at that point forms the upper part of the abdomen.

THE APPENDICULAR SKELETON

The Upper Limbs (Fig. 1.10)

The upper limbs start at the shoulder girdle. The collar bone, or clavicle, is the only bone which has an actual joint with the central part of the skeleton. This occurs

at the inner end where it meets the sternum. At the outer end of the clavicle there is a joint between it and the acromion process of the scapula or shoulder blade. These joints give little strength to the attachment of the shoulder girdle to the rest of the body and the shoulder girdle is in reality suspended by powerful muscles which are attached at one end to the spinal column and rib cage and at the other to the clavicle and the scapula. The bones of the upper limbs comprise the clavicle and scapula which together form the shoulder girdle, the humerus, radius and ulna, carpal bones, metacarpals and phalanges. Of the carpal bones the scaphoid is the only one deserving special mention. It is a common site for a fracture in adolescents and younger adults following a fall on the outstretched hand. These

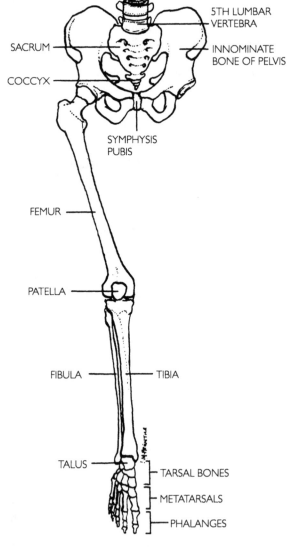

1.11 The right lower limb and hemi-pelvis from the back (posterior)

1.12 The right lower limb and the pelvis from the front (anterior)

fractures are notoriously difficult to show on an X-ray taken during the first two weeks following the injury.

The Lower Limbs (Figs 1.11 and 1.12)
The pelvis is formed by the sacrum and coccyx, which is the lowest portion of the vertebral column, and the two innominate bones. These latter join anteriorly to form the symphysis pubis (a cartilaginous joint) and posteriorly to the sacrum at the two sacroiliac joints (very strong, of fibrous tissue and cartilage). The bones of the lower limbs comprise the innominate bone, the femur, the tibia and fibula, the tarsal bones, metatarsals and phalanges. The innominate bone is made up of three bones which have become joined together to form one bone – the ilium, the ischium and pubic bones. Two tarsal bones in particular need recognition – the talus, which forms part of the ankle joint and the calcaneum (or os calcis) which is the heel bone.

1.2 The Joints

The function of a joint is to allow movement to take place between two bones and it is the presence of joints which allows the skeleton as a whole to be flexible. There are several types of joint and these various types possess different degrees of mobility, from the fully mobile joint to the joint which is fixed without an appreciable degree of movement.

Types of Joints

The first type of joint that we have to consider is the synovial joint (Fig. 1.13). This type allows a free movement range. The ends of the bone are covered with hyaline cartilage. This is extremely smooth and shiny and allows movements to occur with very little

friction. The joint is lubricated by synovial fluid and is surrounded by a layer of tissue called synovial membrane. Synovial membrane produces the joint fluid and also helps to absorb any debris that might form within the joint. Outside the synovial membrane is a strong capsule made up of fibrous tissue. In addition to the capsule which extends completely around the joint, there are various ligaments present. These may be a local thickening of the capsule to give a band of much thicker stronger tissue, or they may be separate from the capsule forming a very strong fibrous band. The ligaments are present to help limit the movement of a joint and to give stability to the joint. In limiting movement of the joint it prevents dislocation by stopping a movement going further than stability will allow.

The other important type of joint is that which has cartilage or fibro-cartilage between the bones. The chief example of this is the intervertebral disc lying between the bodies of adjacent vertebrae (Figs 1.14 and 1.7). This type of joint allows a little movement as the fibro-cartilage is elastic and can be slightly stretched and slightly compressed. Additionally, as it has a certain amount of elasticity, it acts as a shock-absorber between the bones. Thus, in jumping, all the intervertebral discs help to absorb the shock of the landing which would otherwise be transmitted up to the skull and the brain with a very much more serious jarring effect.

The final type of joint is the truly fibrous joint which allows little or no movement. An example of a fibrous joint which allows no movement is that between the flat bones forming the vault of the skull. An example of one which allows a little movement is that between the lower end of the tibia and fibula.

Joint Movements

Only the synovial joints have any significant degree of movement and this includes all those joints which the

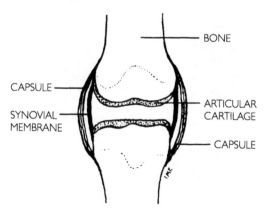

1.13 Diagrammatic coronal section of a typical synovial joint

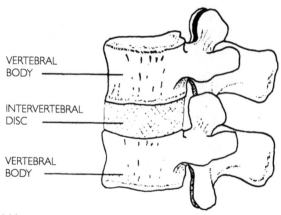

1.14 Intervertebral disc

layman would look upon as being actual joints. In order to avoid misunderstandings, the proper term must be used for each plane of movement (Figs 1.15–1.22).

- *Extension* is straightening out a joint so that the bones forming the joint will tend to come into a straight line with each other.
- *Flexion* is bending a joint so that you produce an angle between the two bones forming the joint.
- *Abduction* is a movement taking the limb, or part of the limb, away from the mid-line.
- *Adduction* is bringing the part towards the mid-line.
- *Rotation* is a movement at the joint where the part can rotate upon the axis going through the joint.
- *Circumduction* is the ability to move the part around in a circle and is usually a combination of flexion, extension, abduction and adduction.

There are various types of synovial joint giving different possible ranges and planes of movement. The ball and socket allows a free range in all directions, e.g. the hip joint. The hinge joint allows only flexion and extension, e.g. the interphalangeal joints of the fingers and toes.

There are various limiting factors when considering the range of movement in any particular joint. Starting from within and working outwards, the first factor is when bone comes up against bone from the two sides of the joint when it is being moved in any one particular direction. However, in the majority of joints, before that takes place the capsule and ligaments will limit the range of movement. These give the second limiting factor. With early training ligaments can be stretched to a certain extent, thus increasing the range

1.15 Flexion of spine, upper and lower limbs (plantarflexion of the ankle and foot)

1.16 Extension

1.17 Abduction of upper and lower limbs

1.18 Side flexion of the spine

1.19 Rotation of the spine

1.20 External rotation of the hips

1.21 Internal rotation of the hips

1.22 The lower limbs are adducted here

of movement above that normally expected from that particular joint. The next factor is tension in the muscles controlling the joint movement; these can be relatively easily stretched and the muscles can be actively lengthened. Finally, apposition of soft parts may prevent further movement taking place, e.g. someone with fat thighs and fat calves will be unable to flex the knee as fully as if they did not have this excess tissue. Activity at the limits of the range of movement of a joint will gradually stretch soft tissues, particularly before the age of puberty, thus increasing the range of available movement. There is, however, a considerable variation from one person to the next in their natural range of movement in any particular joint. This is in part due to a variation in actual anatomical shape of the joint but also some people have, as part of their congenital make-up, very lax ligaments and very stretchable soft tissues and it is these people who in lay terms are often referred to as being double-jointed. They fit into a spectrum of hypermobility, and, in extreme cases, can become contortionists.

Medically it is important to use the correct terminology in order for complete accuracy, but in the dance studio a different vocabulary is used. In classical ballet French terms describe movements, but dancers will talk about 'high extensions'. They mean the ability to lift the leg high in relation to the trunk. The movement to the front is flexion of the hip joint and to the side is a combination of abduction, external rotation and flexion. In this book the authors have tried to accept dancers' terminology as well as anatomical vocabulary, we hope without ambiguity.

Important Joints

THE UPPER LIMBS

The joint between the scapula and the humerus is a ball and socket joint (Fig. 1.23). The socket is very flattened and more like a saucer. It is known as the glenoid cavity. As a result of the shallowness of the joint a very wide range of movement is possible between the upper arm and the trunk. However, this range of movement does not take place entirely between the scapula and the humerus; much of it, particularly elevation of the arm, is made up by the scapula itself sliding over the chest wall. At the lower end of the humerus there is the elbow joint (Figs 1.24 and 1.25) which gives an articulation the upper ends of the radius and ulna. The joint between the ulna and the lower end of the humerus is a straightforward hinge joint but at the upper end of the radius the joint is rather more complex as it allows the radius to hinge up and down in relation to the humerus and also allows the radius to rotate in relation to the ulna and the

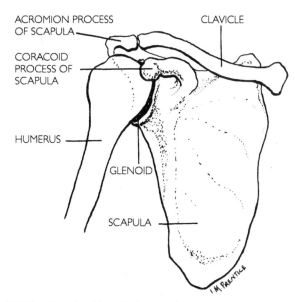

1.23 The right shoulder joint

1.24A (left) The elbow joint. Antero-posterior X-ray view
1.24B (right) The elbow joint. Lateral X-ray view

humerus. A similar rotatory movement takes place at the lower end of the radius and ulna. This allows the movement of pronation and supination where the hand can be held either palm down or palm up with this rotation taking place entirely within the forearm. As will be seen from the skeletal diagram (Fig. 1.25) the bones of the wrist and hand are complex. Most of the wrist movement is an up and down hinge action but there is a certain amount of sideways movement of abduction and adduction available (condyloid joint). The joints in the fingers between the metacarpals and the phalanges are also all of a condyloid type. Those

FOREARM SUPINATED   FOREARM PRONATED

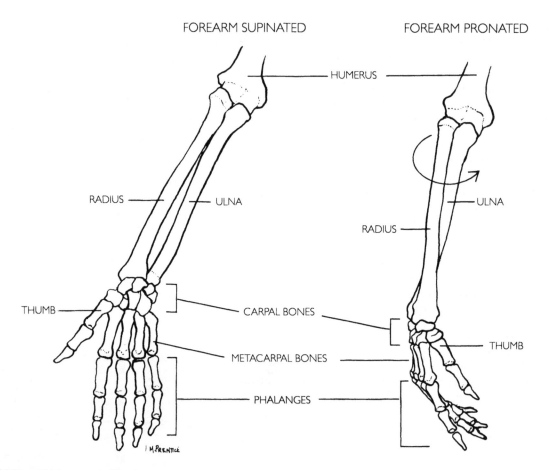

1.25 The right forearm and hand

between the phalanges themselves are purely hinge. However, at the base of the thumb the joint between the metacarpal and the carpal bones does allow some sliding and rotation so that the thumb can not only be flexed and extended but also abducted, adducted and circumducted to enable it to be brought across the hand in opposition to the various fingers. Without this movement the grip which we use in the hand would be non-existent and the extremely fine precision movements and uses of the hand would be impossible.

THE LOWER LIMBS

The pelvis is formed by the sacrum, which is part of the axial skeleton, and the two innominate bones at the front (Fig. 1.26). There is a joint between the sacrum and the innominate bones at each side. This joint is extremely strong with many ligaments crossing within the joint and also some fibro-cartilage. Very little movement takes place at the sacro-iliac joint. Anteriorly the innominate bones come together at the symphysis pubis, and once again very little movement takes place at this joint where there is fibro-cartilage between the

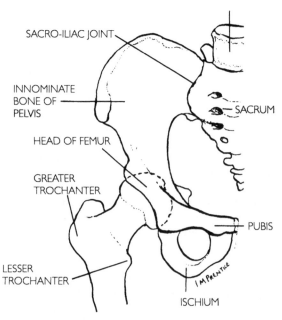

1.26 The right hemi-pelvis and hip joint

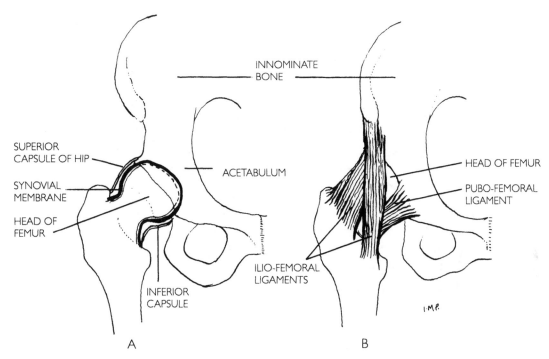

INNOMINATE BONE

SUPERIOR CAPSULE OF HIP

ACETABULUM

SYNOVIAL MEMBRANE

HEAD OF FEMUR

HEAD OF FEMUR

PUBO-FEMORAL LIGAMENT

INFERIOR CAPSULE

ILIO-FEMORAL LIGAMENTS

I·M·P·

A   B

1.27A Section through the right hip joint (diagrammatic)
1.27B Ligaments at the front of the right hip joint

bones. During pregnancy the fibro-cartilage and ligaments soften, giving far greater mobility and allowing delivery to take place. Delivery is also made very much easier for the female by a difference in the shape of her pelvis from that of the male.

The Hip Joint

At the sides of the innominate bones are the hip joints (Fig. 1.27). These are very large ball and socket joints but, unlike the shoulder joints, the acetabulum, which is the socket or cup part of the joint, is very deep. The head of the femur forms a ball which sits inside the acetabulum. As a result the joint is very strong and extremely stable. You will see from the diagram that the head of the femur is joined on to the shaft of the bone by a neck of bone called the femoral neck. As result of this the shaft of the femur stands out a little way from the pelvis, giving a far greater range of movement in all directions than would be possible if the ball was directly at the top of the shaft.

The Knee Joint

At the lower end of the femur is the knee joint. As far as its action is concerned this is mainly a hinge joint but as will be seen from the diagram (Fig. 1.28) it is potentially an very unstable joint because the upper end of the tibia, which forms the other side of the joint from the femur, is almost completely flat. Structurally it

is a condyloid joint but functionally a hinge joint. If it were not for the ligaments the lower end of the femur would be able to slide around in all directions on the tibia. In addition to the hinge movement there is a small amount of rotation possible when the knee is partly flexed but not when it is fully extended.

The diagrams (Figs 1.29 and 1.30) show the ligaments which stabilise the knee. The lateral collateral ligament runs from the lower end of the femur laterally to the upper end of the fibula and is cord-like. The medial collateral ligament runs from the lower end of the femur medially to the upper end of the tibia and is strap-like. Within the joint are the cruciate ligaments, so-called because they cross over. They extend from the notch between the condyles of the lower end of the femur to the front and back of the plateau at the upper end of the tibia. They can be seen in the diagram. The knee is different (but not unique) in possessing two menisci or semi-lunar cartilages as they are commonly called (Fig. 1.31). These are composed of fibro-cartilage and are attached at the outer edges to the capsule of the joint. The inner margins are free. They help to deepen the joint at the upper end of the tibia producing two shallow saucers. In addition they move very slightly when the joint is flexed and extended during normal activities and as a result help to circulate the synovial fluid around the inside of the joint. The cartilages themselves take no weight in the normal

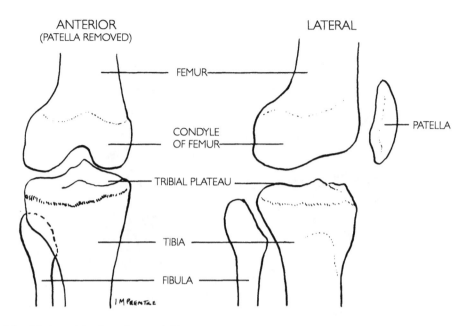

1.28 The bones of the right knee joint from front and side

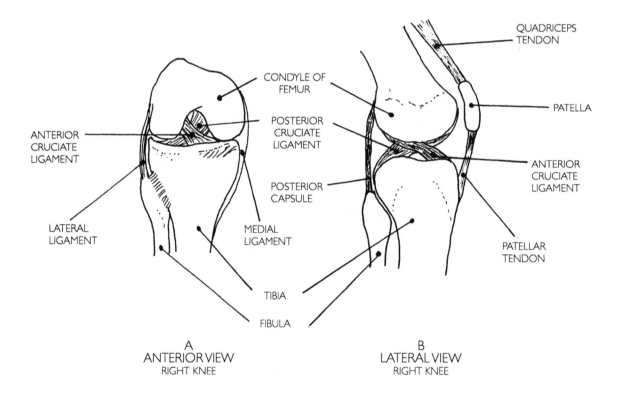

1.29A The right knee joint – view from the front with the knee flexed, looking at the end of the femur and the upper end of the tibia

1.29B Diagrammatic view of the knee joint from the side

1.30 The right knee joint (lateral view)

QUADRICEPS MUSCLE

QUADRICEPS TENDON

FEMUR

PATELLA

LATERAL LIGAMENT

PATELLAR TENDON

TIBIA

FIBULA

The Ankle and Foot (Fig. 1.32)

The ankle joint is made up of a stable syndesmosis of the tibia and fibula forming an adjustable mortise into which the convex articular surface of the talus inserts. The tibia on the inside forms the medial malleolus – the ankle bone on the inside, and the lateral malleolus is the outside ankle bone formed by the fibula. The body of the talus is wedge-shaped – wider at the front than the back. The main movement possible at the ankle joint is plantarflexion (flexion or the dancer's 'pointing') and dorsiflexion (extension or the dancer's 'flexing'). As the ankle plantarflexes the talus moves forwards in the mortise where there is a slight release. As the ankle dorsiflexes, as in a demi plié, the talus moves back in the mortise with its wider anterior part of the wedge locking and stabilising in the mortise. Depending on the shape of the tibia and talus, and tightness of ligaments there is more or less flexibility here. It is known as a hinge joint but there is some 'play' within the joint of side-to-side movement and rotation. The two collateral ligaments maintain congruence of the hinge joint. These are the medial triangular deltoid ligament from the medial malleolus to navicular, talus and calcaneum (Fig. 1.33), and the lateral ligament which is composed of three bands of fibres. These are the anterior and posterior talofibular,

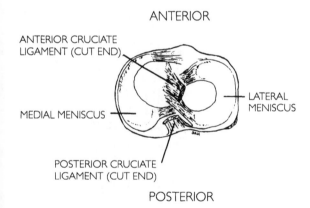

ANTERIOR

ANTERIOR CRUCIATE LIGAMENT (CUT END)

LATERAL MENISCUS

MEDIAL MENISCUS

POSTERIOR CRUCIATE LIGAMENT (CUT END)

POSTERIOR

1.31 Upper end of the right tibia. Viewed from above to show the menisci (cartilages)

function of the knee. However, if a partly flexed knee is twisted whilst weight-bearing, a cartilage can be trapped between the femur and the tibia and the twist can produce a tear in the cartilage.

Anteriorly lies the quadriceps muscle which leads into the quadriceps tendon, the patella and the patellar tendon. These together help to give anterior stability. Posteriorly the posterior capsule, aided by the hamstrings, gives stability.

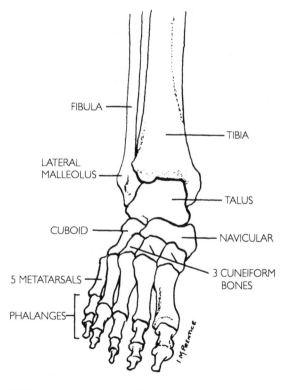

FIBULA

TIBIA

LATERAL MALLEOLUS

TALUS

CUBOID

NAVICULAR

5 METATARSALS

3 CUNEIFORM BONES

PHALANGES

1.32 The right ankle joint and foot

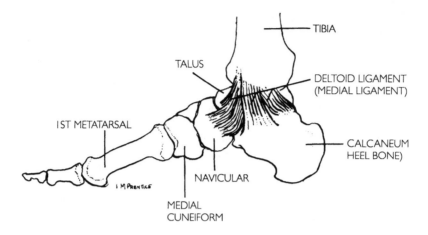

1.33 Ligaments of the medial side of the right ankle

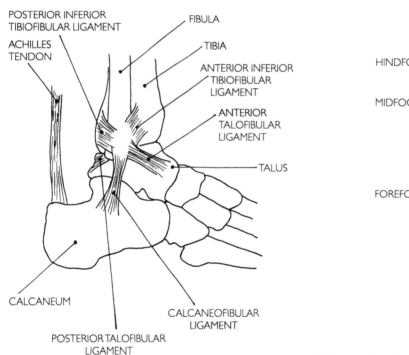

1.34 Ligaments of the lateral side of the right ankle joint

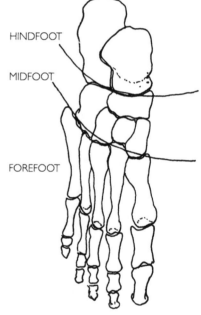

1.35 Bones of the foot

and calcaneofibular ligaments (Fig. 1.34). The long, thin fibula on the lateral side of the leg is bound to the tibia just below the knee at the proximal tibiofibular joint – a synovial gliding joint. The lower end forming the fibrous joint with the tibia is called the distal tibiofibular joint. While the fibula bears no more than 10 per cent of the transmitted body weight, movements of the fibula at both of its joints contribute to normal ankle function.

The bones of the foot are divided into the hindfoot, composed of the talus and calcaneum (heel bone); the midfoot, composed of the navicular, cuboid and the three cuneiforms, medial, middle and lateral; and the forefoot composed of the metatarsals and the phalanges (Fig. 1.35). The foot is constructed in arches. There are two longitudinal arches, the high medial one and the lateral lower one (Fig. 1.36). The medial longitudinal arch is composed of the calcaneum,

POSTERIOR TRANSVERSE ARCH

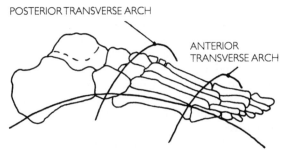

ANTERIOR
TRANSVERSE ARCH

LATERAL LONGITUDINAL ARCH

MEDIAL LONGITUDINAL ARCH

1.36 Arches of the foot

MIDFOOT ARCH
POSTERIOR TRANSVERSE
ARCH AT LEVEL OF
CUNEIFORM AND CUBOID

FOREFOOT ARCH
ANTERIOR TRANSVERSE
ARCH AT LEVEL OF
METATARSAL HEADS

1.37 Transverse arches of the foot

navicular, the three cuneiforms and the medial three metatarsals. On the lateral side are the calcaneum, the cuboid and the lateral two metatarsals. There are two transverse arches across the foot – the posterior one lies over the arched structure of the tarsal bones while the anterior arch can be visualised at the heads of the metatarsals (Fig. 1.37). The bones of the foot can be regarded as half a dome with the talus at the top. Standing in parallel, both feet form the full dome. This adaptable structure functions as an ideal elastic shock absorber, but can also become a rigid weight-bearing system for forward/upward propulsion. The sole of the foot must meet the ground efficiently, and so this flexible structure must be able to adapt to surface irregularities below and the changing position of the leg above.

Although mentioned that there is some 'joint play' in the ankle, most of this side-to-side motion comes from the subtalar joint below the ankle, required in normal function. The talus acts like a ball bearing, part of the ankle or talocrural joint above and part of the subtalar joint below. The subtalar joint is made up of anterior and posterior articular facets between the talus above and the calcaneum below. The subtalar joint functions to convert rotations of the pelvis, hip and knee joints into lateral motion during movement. The subtalar joint in weight bearing is said to pronate and supinate – composite movements involving eversion (sickling

out/fishing) and inversion (sickling in) of the calcaneum, and reciprocal movements of the talus. However, the subtalar joint is well aligned when it is in neutral and there is a perpendicular line running through the Achilles tendon, the talus and bisecting the calcaneum to the floor.

The next articulations to consider are those of the transverse tarsal joint (also known as the midtarsal joint). This is composed of the talus and navicular medially, and the articulation of the cuboid and calcaneum laterally. When the subtalar joint is well aligned these joints follow suit with both the longitudinal and transverse arches of the foot preserved. This is the transitional link between hindfoot and forefoot. This joint allows the forefoot mobility to adapt to hindfoot position so that the sole of the foot can always meet the ground. The movements here of abduction/adduction, plantarflexion/dorsiflexion and eversion/inversion are considered together as pronation and supination.

Intercuneiform movements are gliding in plantar-flexion and dorsiflexion. The three cuneiforms articulate with the bases of metatarsals 1 to 3 at the 1st, 2nd and 3rd tarsometatarsal (TMT) joints and metatarsals 4 and 5 articulate with cuboid. The 2nd TMT joint is different in that the base of the 2nd metatarsal articulates with a mortise formed by the middle cuneiform and the sides of the medial and lateral cuneiforms. The joint is set further back, is stronger and more restricted in its motion. There are also articulations between the metatarsal bases allowing motion between them. The metatarsal bone, with its corresponding toe, forms a functional unit, or ray.

The heads of the metatarsals articulate at the metatarsophalangeal (MTP) joints with the bases of the proximal phalanges. The phalanges are the bones of the toes. The MTP joints are condyloid joints which dorsiflex, plantarflex, abduct and adduct. The heads of the metatarsals weight bear as do the pads of the toes. The first toe or hallux has two phalanges with one interphalangeal (IP) joint, and the other lesser toes 2 to 5 have three phalanges with two IP joints, proximal and distal.

The metatarsals, their TMT and MTP joints function most efficiently when the foot and ankle are worked within a range of normal alignment. Any habitual and excessive flattening of the arches will impose a strain on bones, joints and soft tissues that will eventually result in injury. The integrity of the arches is dependent on bones, ligaments and muscles. The shape of the interlocking bones, bound by ligaments, form the arches and are further supported by muscle. Underneath, the longitudinal arches are supported by the short and long plantar ligaments, and the strong plantar fascia composed of dense connective tissue fibres from the calcaneum to the MTP joints. Both extrinsic and intrinsic muscles serve to tighten and support the arches. The tibialis posterior pulls on the navicular, medially tightening the longitudinal arch. The flexor hallucis longus and the abductor hallucis add medial support. The peroneus longus which runs obliquely anteriorly and medially under the foot, tightens all the arches. The foot is multifunctional. In the ballet dancer the foot and ankle must be flexible enough to enhance the line of the leg. This flexibility allows weight bearing on three-quarter pointe and pointe, but for this, strength and rigidity are required. Jumping requires propulsive power and great eccentric strength to shock absorb sufficiently to protect the rest of the body from landing forces. Unlike the 'normal' foot, the dancer's foot requires enhanced strength and control of the toes. Jumping requires the last push-off to come from the toes and MTP joints plantarflexing the foot and ankle in the air. The pads of the toes are the first to meet the ground on the descent, resisting and silencing the landing, lowering the foot to the floor into the plié. The dancer's foot is not assisted by supportive, cushioning footwear. It must rely on its own intrinsic strength and efficient control from above in order to minimise damaging stresses.

In classical ballet the dancer uses 'turn-out' – external rotation of the hip taking the lower limb into the familiar classical positions. If turn-out is not taught carefully, strengthening the muscles of the hip over several years of training, rotational stress within the knee and foot will take its toll. If the structure of the hip restricts external rotation no amount of training will allow pure classical positions. However, while professional classical dancers will from time to time suffer from turn-out-related foot injuries, there is no excuse for building faults in young students by encouraging an angle of turn-out at the feet which cannot be controlled and where good foot alignment is lost.

If the feet are planted at an unrealistic angle in a demi plié (so often dancers find their 'perfect' position this way) and then the knees are straightened, the feet are seen to absorb the rotational stress with altered biomechanics. The foot remains in position due to friction on the floor. The foot unlocks and abducts at the transverse tarsal joint, the subtalar joint pronates and the tibia is internally rotated in relation to the foot, which is seen to be 'rolling in'. The medial arch flattens and the metatarsals splay, everting relative to the floor. The heels become everted (Fig. 1.38) The first ray dorsiflexes, becomes hypermobile and can no longer support the medial longitudinal arch. The rotation of the hallux (big toe) is plain to see with associated valgus adaption. In this disadvantaged position the weight-bearing function of the foot is reduced, the muscular support of the arches is weakened, bones are stressed and ligaments are strained.

CORRECT ALIGNMENT   EVERTED HEEL

1.38 Foot alignment

1.3 The Muscles

General Considerations

Muscles are the meaty parts of the body and are responsible for all movements that take place within the body.

TYPES OF MUSCLE FIBRE

There are three different types of muscle (Fig. 1.39) and they have very specific and different functions.

STRIATED (SKELETAL)
VOLUNTARY MUSCLE

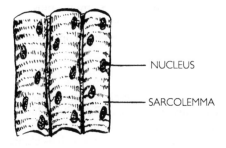

NUCLEUS

SARCOLEMMA

UNSTRIATED (BOWEL WALL, ETC.)
INVOLUNTARY MUSCLE

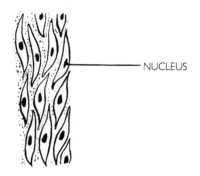

NUCLEUS

CARDIAC (HEART) MUSCLE

NUCLEUS

1.39 Diagram of the three types of muscle fibre

Striated or Skeletal Muscle

This muscle is also referred to as voluntary muscle because it can be controlled at will by the brain and nervous system. It includes the muscles controlling the limbs, muscles of facial expression and the muscles of respiration. It is known as striated muscle because when sections of the muscle are examined under a microscope the cells have the appearance of possessing striations or stripes. It may also be referred to as striped muscle (Fig. 1.39). A skeletal muscle is made up of many bundles of fibres surrounded by connective tissue which run longitudinally the length of the muscle belly. Each muscle fibre is made up of many myofibrils also running the length of the fibre. It is within the

myofibril that the contractile mechanism of skeletal muscle operates. Each myofibril is divided longitudinally into compartments called sarcomeres. Each sarcomere contains an arrangement of two types of protein filaments – actin and myosin. The muscle as a whole contracts as the thin actin filaments slide into the thick myosin filaments and each sarcomere becomes shorter. This takes place through neural stimulation when a nerve impulse activates the fibres it supplies. The connective tissue surrounding the muscle fibres and enclosing the bundles of fibres converges at the ends of the muscle to form a tendon which makes a strong attachment to bone. Where muscle attaches directly to bone a large surface attachment is necessary to withstand traction forces. However, a tendon composed of dense connective tissue can attach to a small area allowing muscles to act from afar, as is seen in the lower leg where muscle bellies contract to flex or extend the toes via tendons passing through the ankle.

Groups of muscles are in their turn surrounded by dense inelastic fibrous tissue which is known as fascia. In the diagram of the cross-section of a limb (Fig. 1.40), in this case the leg, about a third of the way down from the knee, it is possible to see how these layers are made

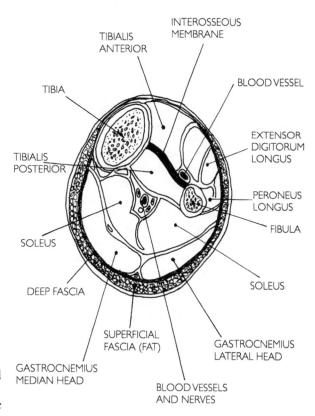

INTEROSSEOUS MEMBRANE

TIBIALIS ANTERIOR

BLOOD VESSEL

TIBIA

EXTENSOR DIGITORUM LONGUS

TIBIALIS POSTERIOR

PERONEUS LONGUS

FIBULA

SOLEUS

SOLEUS

DEEP FASCIA

SUPERFICIAL FASCIA (FAT)

GASTROCNEMIUS LATERAL HEAD

GASTROCNEMIUS MEDIAN HEAD

BLOOD VESSELS AND NERVES

MID LOWER LEG

1.40 Cross-section of the leg (upper third)

up. The skin surrounds the limb as a whole. Beneath this is a layer of fatty tissue which is called the superficial fascia. Then comes the deep fascia which is inelastic dense fibrous tissue enveloping various muscles. At this level there is also a dense band of fibrous tissue connecting the two bones of the leg, the tibia and fibula; this is known as the interosseous membrane. Not only does it help to hold to the two bones together, but it also gives an additional area for the attachment of the muscles.

The whole muscle is attached at each end, one called the origin and the other the insertion. The origin is that end which generally remains static and the insertion is at the end which is pulled and moves. Also the origin, as far as the limbs are concerned, is usually the proximal end, i.e. the end nearer to the trunk. However, their roles can be reversed; for example, if an object is grasped by the hand either the object can be pulled towards a stationary trunk, or the trunk can be pulled towards a stationary object.

The action of each muscle is controlled by one or more nerves. Many muscles have their nerve supply from several different nerves; when these nerves enter the muscle they gradually divide down until an individual nerve fibre reaches an individual muscle fibre. A motor unit consists of the motor neurone, its axon or nerve fibre, the motor end plate (neuromuscular junction) and the muscle fibres supplied. When the nerve fibre is stimulated it will in its turn stimulate the muscle fibre to contract completely. It cannot stimulate the muscle fibre to contract partially. This is known as the all-or-nothing law. This contraction shortens the muscle fibre. Depending upon the number of muscle fibres stimulated so will depend (a) the power or strength exerted and (b) the amount the whole muscle will shorten. By a very highly developed and sophisticated neuro-muscular control system the human being (and other animals, of course) can achieve amazingly delicate control of actual movements. In those areas of the body where very fine control is required a relatively small number of muscle fibres are controlled by each motor unit (e.g. those concerned with the use of the hand) than in areas where less fine control is required such as the large back muscles.

The stimulation down the nerve fibre is electrical but the stimulation between the nerve ending and the muscle fibre is chemical in nature with resulting mechanical action. Even at rest a few fibres are being constantly stimulated in turn and this maintains what is known as muscle tone. There are two types of voluntary muscle fibre and these are referred to as fast and slow fibres. The proportion of different fibres in an individual muscle determines whether the muscle as a whole is more suited to a prolonged supporting role or to quick, rapid response action. The soleus muscle in

the lower calf is more a postural muscle required to maintain stance for long periods and therefore is composed of more slow fibres. The gastrocnemius however, is a more dynamic muscle required for quick, explosive jumping action and is therefore composed more of fast fibres.

Unstriated or Involuntary Muscle

This is the name given to the muscle which controls various internal organs of the body (Fig. 1.39). This type of muscle is in the whole of the alimentary tract and also around much smaller structures such as glands and blood vessels. The conscious portion of the brain has no control at all over the action of these muscles, hence the name involuntary muscle. It is also known as unstriated muscle because on microscopic examination there are no striations or stripes as were found in the skeletal muscle.

Cardiac Muscle

This is the third type of muscle and is only found in the heart (Fig. 1.39).

Cardiac muscle will contract without stimulation, but the rate and rhythm is under the control of nervous impulses. The control of cardiac muscle will be dealt with later.

ACTION OF MUSCLES

Before passing on to the individual muscles it is important to consider how muscles themselves produce movements.

Muscles and Levers

It must be emphasised that muscles can only contract and therefore pull, they can never push. Movements are therefore brought about by using the bones as levers; there are three types of orders of levers, a first-order lever being like a see-saw (Fig. 1.41), with the balancing point referred to as the fulcrum. At one end of the lever is the 'load' and at the other end is the muscle action producing 'effort'. If no movement is taking place the part is in equilibrium and the force applied by the 'load' and the force applied by the 'effort' are balanced out, though this does not mean that the actual number of kilograms being exerted at these two points is necessarily the same. Anyone using a lever in order to try to move something heavy will realise that the longer the lever, the less force needs to be applied to move the object. This can be very simply worked out and expressed as an equation: the 'effort' multiplied by the distance of the 'effort' from the fulcrum equals the 'load' multiplied by the distance of the 'load' from the fulcrum. As the diagram shows (Fig. 1.42), if the 'load' is two units and the distance of the 'load' is three units, these figures multiplied together give the figure of six.

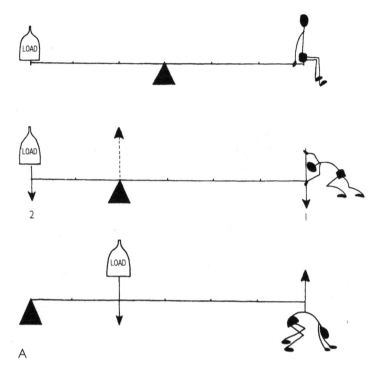

1.41 First-order lever – balanced, with equal arms and equal weights

1.42 First-order lever – balanced, with unequal arms and weights. Distance x load = distance x effort. In this case 2 x 2 = 4 x 1. This may be found where the skull joins the cervical spine. The pull of the muscles in he back of the neck balances the weight of the front of the skull, the face and the mandible

1.43A Second-order lever. The load is nearer to the fulcrum than the effort. The force applied by the load will be greater than that required by the effort

1.43B (below) Second-order lever, as occurs at the foot and ankle with the dancer on demi-pointe

On the other side of the fulcrum, if the distance of the 'effort' is six units from the fulcrum then the 'effort' required to move the 'load' will only be one unit because the 'effort' and distance multiplied together will also produce a six. An example of a first-order lever is the head, on the spine, where the weight of the face is counteracted by the muscles in the back of the neck.

In the limbs the other two types of lever are very much more common. In a second-order lever (Fig. 1.43) the 'weight' or 'load' will lie nearer to the fulcrum or point of movement than the 'effort' – in this case the muscle contraction. This is well seen in the foot when a dancer rises onto half pointe; the fulcrum is at the ball of the foot, the weight of the body is being transmitted down through the shin bone and ankle and the lifting force is by means of the calf muscle which is inserted through the Achilles tendon into the back of the heel. Once again, because of the levers the distance from the fulcrum at the ball of the foot to the ankle joint is less than the distance from the fulcrum to the back of the heel, so the effort in the calf muscle is slightly less than the actual weight of the body. It is only slightly less because the differences in the two distances from the fulcrum is only small.

Finally in the third-order lever (Fig. 1.44) the 'effort' or muscle contraction lies between the fulcrum and the weight or 'load'. This is seen at the elbow joint, where the biceps and brachialis muscles are inserted just in front of the elbow but the weight that is being lifted is situated further from the elbow, usually in the region of

TIBIA

TIBIALIS ANTERIOR

TIBIALIS POSTERIOR

DIRECTION OF PULL OF THE CALF MUSCLE THROUGH THE ACHILLES TENDON

CALCANEUM

FLEXOR HALLUCIS LONGUS TENDON

WEIGHT OF BODY

I M PRENTICE

A

1.44A Third-order lever. The effort is nearer to the fulcrum than the load. The force of the effort therefore has to be greater than the force of the load

1.44B (below) Third-order lever. In this instance the force of the effort has to be very much greater (about seven times) than the force of the load

B

DIRECTION OF PULL THROUGH

BICEPS

AND

BRACHIALIS

I.M. PRENTICE

LOAD

the hand. Because of the great difference in distances from the fulcrum between the 'effort' and the 'load' the actual force that is required to do the lifting is very much greater than the actual weight of the 'load'. This is because the distance between the fulcrum and the insertion of the muscle is very short, whereas the distance from the fulcrum to the hand, which may be carrying the weight, is about seven times greater; hence if the weight being lifted in the hand is only one kilogram, the force of contraction in the biceps muscle to lift this must be in the order of seven kilograms. If measurements are done in other areas of the body, particularly the lower limbs, it will be seen that the actual force required in the contracting muscle can be several times the body weight and, when jumping, this may reach between a half and three-quarters of a ton (500–700 kilograms).

A further important aspect of the use of levers is the difference in distance moved by the 'effort' and the 'load'. In first-order levers this can be either the 'effort' or the 'load' having to move further. In second-order levers the 'effort' has to move further than the 'load', because the 'effort' is further from the fulcrum. Thus the muscles producing the movement have to shorten more than the distance the 'load' will move. In third-order levers, which are the commonest type in the body, the 'effort' moves a much shorter distance than the 'load'. This has the great advantage of allowing a large movement to be made with only very slight shortening of the muscles producing the movements.

Muscle Contraction

A muscle contracts as a whole by the separate contraction of its individual muscle fibres. At rest, a few nerve impulses are constantly being supplied to the muscles so that some fibres are always contracting and maintaining what is known as 'tone' in the muscle. In other words, the whole muscle never relaxes completely. During a voluntary movement, depending upon the power required, an increasing number of muscle fibres will contract at the same time, and then in succession, in order to maintain the muscle contraction and to control its speed.

The muscle groups do not act singly but always in concert with other muscle groups; if this were not to happen the movement would be largely uncontrolled. For example, when picking up a cup of tea to carry it to the mouth, if the muscle groups initiating the action contracted by themselves the tea would be thrown into the face of the drinker! All movements are carefully controlled. The most important initiating group is known as the 'prime mover' or agonist. The groups of muscles acting in the opposite direction are known as antagonists. During a movement the antagonist group will also be maintaining some contraction and will 'give' gradually to allow the prime mover to direct the movement. In a grand battement devant the hip flexors are the prime movers and the hamstrings are the antagonists.

There are three types of muscle action. Contraction implies a shortening action and so the terms muscle work or muscle tension could equally be used. When analysing muscle action the force of gravity must be taken into account.

Isotonic contraction is when the muscle changes length, either shortening or lengthening. A **concentric** contraction (isotonic) is when the muscle shortens causing movement at the joint as in rising from a plié when the quadriceps contract to extend the knee. An **eccentric** contraction (isotonic) is when the quadriceps muscles lengthen with tension, opposing the descent in a plié when **gravity** is the main force directing the movement. The landing from a jump requires eccentric control from the intrinsic muscles of the foot, the calf muscles, the quadriceps and the gluteal muscles.

Isometric contraction (static contraction) is when a muscle contracts, maintaining the same length in the prime mover muscle and holds a position.

In addition, the prime mover or the antagonist may receive help from other groups of muscles which are known as synergists. These tend to act as co-ordinators of movements. They also help to counteract any unwanted directional force in the prime mover. As an example: the pectoralis major, when contracting to move the humerus in relation to the scapula, also exerts a dislocating force on the shoulder joint (the gleno-humeral joint). The coraco-brachialis is a synergistic muscle for this movement and by contracting, not only aids the movement of the arm, but also by acting at a different angle to the pectoralis major counteracts the dislocating component of the force exerted by the latter.

During different movements, first one group and then another will be prime movers, antagonists or synergists. It is because of this combined action of the muscle groups that, during regimes of strengthening exercises, not only do the prime movers have to be exercised, but also the antagonistic and synergistic groups. It is the action of the various groups which produce a well balanced and controlled movement. Although the groups of muscles are all composed of voluntary muscles, the antagonistic and synergistic actions are controlled reflexly. So just as they can be made to contract reflexly they can also be inhibited reflexly, as may occur with injury and pain.

NEURO-MUSCULAR CO-ORDINATION AND ENGRAMS

Individual muscles can rarely act alone. There is a prime mover or agonist. There are synergistic groups which assist the prime mover. There are antagonist groups which oppose the prime mover. There are stabilisers which fix joints in order to allow the movement to take place. Co-ordination training develops pre-programmed automatic multi-neuromuscular patterns. These are known as engrams. Constant, exact repetitions or practice will produce an engram, a condition where individual muscles or movements are not consciously considered. Proprioceptive feedback gives sub-conscious and conscious monitoring of the movement and shows whether it was successful or not. These automatic engrams can only be developed by voluntary repetition of the precise programme. This must be followed accurately otherwise the input of information will vary each time and the engram cannot be developed. It follows that initially the pattern must be slow enough to be accurate.

An engram allows a complicated movement to be performed far more rapidly than would be possible if conscious thought of each part of the pattern were required. At the same time as the movements are occurring, the engram will also produce inhibition of unwanted movements. This inhibition is an essential part of the regulation of co-ordination. Inhibition cannot be produced directly and consciously and is achieved by regular and accurate repetition of the pattern of desired movements. Co-ordination of the most rapid, complex and skilful actions is automated by engrams rather than by a voluntary controlled series of movements. The activation of the *engram(s)* is voluntary and under conscious control. In learning exercise patterns and, of course, far more importantly in learning dance technique, or for that matter any other technique, accuracy is absolutely vital in order to develop the correct engram. If inaccuracies are allowed during the development of a technique, this will produce 'bad habits' and these very inaccuracies or bad habits will themselves become an engram. Once this has taken place, the modification of the faulty engram will be extremely difficult and may call for that portion of the technique to be learned again from scratch. Hence the importance of learning any complex series of movements accurately from the start. As already stated, in order to achieve accuracy the pattern will have to be learned slowly. The number of repetitions required to produce a really well-developed engram numbers in hundreds of thousands or millions and not just hundreds or thousands. However, this is not as bad as it sounds because an action is usually made up of a series of engrams. It is the sum of the engrams which produces the final result. As already mentioned, the initiation of an engram is under voluntary and conscious control although the constituent parts of the engram are themselves not by that stage under voluntary control. What the mind does is to select the stored engrams, put them together and produce the desired result.

The use of engrams is probably seen and appreciated best when one considers a musician such as a pianist or organist. In this case, the symbols on a page will initiate engrams which allow the fingers, and in an organist the feet as well, to perform the complex series of manoeuvres.

It has to be admitted that some old proverbs certainly appear nowadays to have a scientific basis, e.g. practice makes perfect (the formation of the engram); you cannot teach an old dog new tricks (the difficulty in trying to change an engram).

RED AND WHITE MUSCLE FIBRES

It might be felt that this subject is too abstruse to be included in a book of this type at all. However, the excuse for including a few sentences on the subject is that dancers frequently ask about this as they have either read about it or heard about it and feel that they should be doing something about red and white fibres in order to improve their own performance.

Because of the presence of red meat and white meat in fowls, it has long been thought that there might be a difference between types of muscle fibre. However, in mammals there is not this overall appearance of red meat and white meat. Nevertheless, within muscles themselves there have been shown to be variations in the type of muscle fibre, some being dark and some being light.

The 'red' fibres are also known as slow twitch fibres and are also called Type 1 fibres. They tend to proliferate in endurance training.

'White' fibres are also known as fast twitch fibres or Type 2 fibres and they tend to proliferate in sprint-type exercise.

Both fibre types are normally extremely stable and do not change from one type to another.

Type 1 slow twitch fibres metabolise by oxidative phosphorylation and thus are high in aerobic capacity. They have a slow speed of contraction (hence the name slow twitch) and they are also slow to fatigue. These fibres are small in diameter. They have a low threshold of recruitment (i.e. they respond early to electrical stimulation from the nerve fibres) and they generate low forces but because of the low threshold and early recruitment they contract more frequently than Type 2 fibres.

Type 2 fast twitch fibres metabolise by glycolysis. They have a fast speed of contraction (hence fast twitch) and are also fast to fatigue. These muscle fibres are large in diameter. They have a high level of recruitment (i.e. they need much more electrical stimulation to make them contract) and they generate high forces. However, they contract less frequently than the Type 1 fibres.

To complicate matters a little further, there is also an intermediate fibre which is a sub type of Type 2. It is a fast oxidative glycolytic fibre (FOG fibre). These FOG fibres have a fast speed of contraction and an intermediate rate of fatigue.

Having said all that, the best advice to the dancer is that he forgets about his red and white fibres and that he contents himself with carrying out his proper exercise programmes, allowing his various types of fibres to look after themselves.

Individual Muscles

TRUNK MUSCLES

The trunk is symmetrical and if split down the centre into left and right halves each side would be a mirror image of the other as far as the muscles and skeleton are concerned. The muscles therefore occur in pairs

with one on either side of the body. When both sides act together the spine will be either flexed or extended. If one side alone acts, then it will either side flex the spine or rotate it or carry out a combination. The spine as a whole is capable of flexion, extension, lateral flexion in each direction and rotation in each direction. The most mobile portions of the spine are in the cervical and lumbar regions. The dorsal (thoracic spine) has a very much more limited range of movements. In the neck, flexion is brought about by the sterno-mastoid and extension by the splenius and the semispinalis capitis. In the rest of the spine extension is brought about by the **sacrospinalis** (erector spinae) and the **quadratus lumborum**. Flexion is brought about largely by the abdominal muscles, the **rectus abdominis** and the **external** and **internal obliques**. Flexion is helped by the **psoas major** which crosses the front of the hip joint and the psoas minor. All these muscles when acting on one side alone will laterally flex and/or rotate the spine and trunk. The quadratus lumborum in particular has the added function of steadying the 12th rib which, through the additional action of the various muscles of the rib cage, has the effect of steadying the whole rib cage.

THE RIB CAGE

The external and internal intercostal muscles, which are the equivalent of the external and internal oblique muscles of the abdominal wall, both help to raise the ribs. This action is assisted by the **serratus posterior superior**. This latter muscle can play an important part in creating tension in dancers if they are breathing incorrectly. It runs from the 2nd to the 5th ribs upwards and backwards across to the mid-line to the large ligament (the ligamentum nuchae) at the back of the neck and to the spinous processes of the upper three thoracic vertabrae. The intercostals, as their name implies, lie between the ribs. There are eleven pairs, corresponding to the intercostal spaces between the twelve ribs, and the muscles run from one rib to the next. They play an important part in respiration because by raising the ribs they increase the capacity of the rib cage thus helping to draw in air. This combined with the action of the diaphragm produces inspiration.

STABILITY

When considering injury prevention in dancers several factors must be taken into account. These are listed:

* age
* stage of growth
* physique – pattern of flexibility/restriction
* muscle balance
* stability
* strength
* fitness.

Posture and Stance

Before considering movement, the dancer's static posture must be as correct and as mechanically efficient as possible. 'Good' posture is when there is equilibrium in the body, with a balance of muscular control around each joint. The classical dancer's turned-out posture is a position of balanced muscular control that requires careful coaching. Muscle imbalance is a common cause of injury in dance and arises from a misunderstanding of classical posture and incorrect mechanics in technique. In dance students, if the beginning and end of every exercise is well placed, the movement itself is more likely to be well controlled.

Trunk stability is the basis of good posture and accurate movement patterns. **Stability** implies steadiness and immovability, and an object with stability has balance. Stability is dynamic and the trunk must be able to transfer load effectively in subtle movement as well as huge jumps. In training the dancer, the teacher is schooling the body to move efficiently and economically, with fine control. Skeletal balance is the starting point. Muscles will engage in a balanced manner and more readily if the skeleton is well aligned.

The trunk is comprised of the spine, rib cage and pelvis. It can be likened to a cylinder with the spine and back extensors behind, the abdominal muscles forming the sides and front; the diaphragm forms the top/lid and the pelvic floor, the base. If initially the trunk is aligned and stable, the hip joints will function more efficiently below and the shoulder girdle will function well over the top.

The pelvis is shaped like a bowl, which can tilt forwards and backwards; it can hitch to the side and can rotate. The rib cage can do the same over the pelvis but, if the spine is perfectly placed, the trunk and its component parts fall into alignment.

The spine is formed in a series of four adjustable curves. The vertebrae, discs, facet joints and supporting ligaments are designed in these curves which, if exaggerated or straightened posturally, result, over time, in strain. In the dancer the spinal curves are lengthened and held with adequate abdominal and spinal extensor muscle activation. The pelvis is held in neutral with the lumbar spine also in neutral – a natural forwards curve. The pelvis must neither tilt forwards as in an overarched position nor tilted backwards as in a 'tucked-under' position which straightens out the lumbar spine. The pelvis position can be measured from the side. The anterior iliac spine (ASIS) should be about 3 cm lower than the posterior iliac spine (PSIS). The exaggerated forwards tilt leaves the spine unsupported by slack abdominals and shortened back extensors. The 'tucked-under' position strains the spine, the hips weight-bear in a disadvantaged position and the body loses height. In the turned-out, tucked-under position, the gluteal and outer thigh muscles overwork and tighten, and the abdominal muscles work less efficiently.

Recognising the neutral lumbar spine and pelvis, or being able to correct spinal posture, still appears to be difficult for teachers. The tucked-under position of years ago is long out of date and teachers do need to keep up with current research in biomechanics, applying those concepts with confidence. Faults can be subtle. However, unless correct spinal positioning is instilled early on in students, problems are created for later.

The first muscles to be considered in terms of the control of the trunk and its contribution to posture, are the abdominals (Fig. 1.45) The abdominal muscles are arranged in layers and are divided into right and left by the linea alba, a dense connective tissue band stretching from the sternum to the pubis. The right and left rectus abdominis muscles on either side stretch like bands from the pubis to the 5th, 6th and 7th costal cartilages in vertical bundles of fibres, divided by connective tissue interdigitations giving it its 'six pack' appearance. Bundles of short fibres are more powerful than one unit of long muscle fibres. This muscle is a dynamic spinal flexor – important for moving the pelvis in relation to the rib cage or vice versa, but not for stability. The rectus abdominis is the prime mover in a sit-up exercise or a contemporary contraction. In a backbend it lowers the upper body backwards eccentrically. On each side of the rectus abdominis are the external obliques which attach from the ribs passing downwards and inwards (imagine putting your hands over your lower abdomen – the angle of the forearms is the same as the angle made by the external obliques) towards the linea alba. They interact with the internal obliques which pass upwards and inwards at 90° to the external obliques. Together these muscles control rotation and sideflexion of the rib cage on the pelvis or the pelvis on the rib cage. They are classed as global stabilisers, eccentrically controlling the pelvis as the dancer uses the legs. In movements as small as battement tendu and en l'air positions where alignment of the trunk is all important they control the pelvis which has to 'give' to allow the lower limb its required range of movement in the dance vocabulary.

The deepest muscle in the group is tranversus abdominis. Its muscle fibres pass around the trunk horizontally from the linea alba to attach via the thoracolumbar fascia to the transverse and spinous processes of each of the lumbar vertebrae. The thoracolumbar fascia is a diamond-shaped section of connective tissue composed of three layers which arise from the lumbar vertebrae, surround the muscles of the lumbar spine and provide attachment for several muscles important for strength and stability. When the

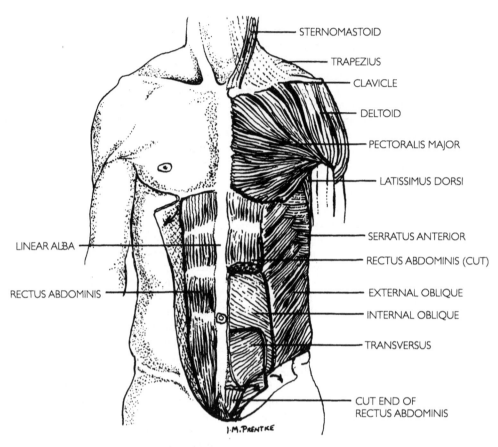

STERNOMASTOID

TRAPEZIUS

CLAVICLE

DELTOID

PECTORALIS MAJOR

LATISSIMUS DORSI

SERRATUS ANTERIOR

RECTUS ABDOMINIS (CUT)

EXTERNAL OBLIQUE

INTERNAL OBLIQUE

TRANSVERSUS

CUT END OF
RECTUS ABDOMINIS

LINEAR ALBA

RECTUS ABDOMINIS

J·M·PRENTICE

1.45 Muscles of the front of the trunk

transversus contracts it tightens the waist and flattens the abdomen, very much like a corset. There should be minimal spinal or rib cage movement and the 'drawing in' action should be specifically across the lower abdominal wall. This muscle is classed as a local stabiliser and has a particular role in maintaining segmental stability. When the transversus is activating, tension is transmitted via the various layers of the thoracolumbar fascia to the lumbar vertebrae, thereby stabilising both forwards/backwards (sagittal) and rotatory segmental movement. Therefore movement of the pelvis is also minimised.

The command 'pull up!' produces a lifting of the rib cage and extension of the thoracic spine, with the shoulders held too far back and resultant tension in the neck. Instead it is a mild 'pull-in' force of the transversus abdominis which elongates the lumbar spine and makes you feel taller – indeed you *are* taller, with the crown of the head lengthening away. In this position the dancer is more likely to be controlling turn-out with weight placement through the forefoot.

There are also deep local stabilisers within the spinal extensors. Multifidus is the largest of the deep back

muscles and is arranged segmentally in a repeating series of fascicles from the base of the skull to the sacrum. The lumbar spine carries the weight of the body above, is relatively flexible and is extensively used in the classical vocabulary. Here these muscles, situated close the facet joints, oppose undue excursion of the vertebrae and stabilise the spine with transversus abdominis.

It is the function of the muscular system to provide protection to articular structures. Minimising unnecessary joint displacement and absorbing a proportion of joint forces decreases stress on cartilage and prolongs its health. Various authorities talk about prolonging 'cartilage serving time' in relation to joint stability. (The concept can be applied throughout the body.) It has also been observed that transversus is the first abdominal muscle recruited to stabilise the lumbar spine during arm movements, suggesting that timing of muscle activation is important for effective stabilisation.

It is necessary to understand the importance and role of the pelvic floor – the base of the cylinder. The pelvic floor is not a structure ever referred to in ballet class for obvious reasons. It is composed of muscles and fascia which form a sling attached from pubis to coccyx. The structure is separated by the visceral outlet through which pass the urethra, vagina and anorectum. Voluntary contraction of the pelvic floor muscles constricts these openings to prevent the leakage of urine and faeces. Involuntary contraction occurs during coughing or holding one's breath, when intra-abdominal pressure is raised. It may be surprising how many young dancers at some time during training feel a lack of pelvic floor control with an element of stress incontinence, especially in jumps.

In females these muscles surround the vagina and help support the uterus. (During pregnancy these muscles can be stretched or traumatised and result in stress incontinence whenever the intra-abdominal pressure is raised.) The muscles of the pelvic floor and transversus abdominis coordinate in activation. Exercises for the pelvic floor subtly tighten the pubococcygeus muscle, tightening around the anus towards the back or urethra towards the front. Holding for a count of ten seconds or pulsing accesses fast and slow twitch fibres.

There are many mat exercises and Pilates exercises to activate these deep stability muscles. They are useful to isolate and stimulate sensory feedback, but it is even more important to feel these muscles working while dancing. It has also been suggested that the more dominant the rectus abdominis is, the less effective is tranversus activation. The rectus abdominis is a dynamic trunk flexor muscle, not a stabiliser. Traditionally abdominal exercises meant 'sit-up exercises' but the concept of specificity should be considered. If you train a muscle with sit-ups, it will give you great sit-up control – useful for contemporary dance, but not directly useful in the classical

vocabulary. Gym exercises using equipment and weights have their place, but only if stability (good activation of the deeper local muscles) has been established. Functional exercises relating to the needs of the technique should first be favoured.

Another muscle important to the stabilising of the trunk is the latissimus dorsi. This muscle arises also from the thoracolumbar fascia and the lower six vertebrae. Its muscle fibres span upwards and outwards with an attachment to the lower angle of the scapula, to converge in a tendon which passes under the arm to attach to the front of the humerus. This muscle links the pelvis to the shoulder girdle and gives support to the back of the trunk. Posturally this muscle depresses the shoulder girdle and holds the scapula down during ports de bras. As it arises from the thoracolumbar fascia along with the transversus, these muscles with the multifidus activate together providing reinforcement to the lumbar spine. However, if the spine is not well aligned, this muscle cannot activate well and instead the muscles above the shoulder girdle (i.e. upper trapezius) and other neck muscles tense, lifting the shoulders and freezing the neck.

UPPER LIMB MUSCLES

In addition to the shoulder girdle muscles shown in previous diagrams, Fig. 1.51 shows various other groups around the shoulder girdle. The deltoid muscle and the other short muscles arising from the scapula which are inserted into the upper end of the humerus are all responsible for the various movements between the humerus and the scapula. Shoulder movements take place at this joint between the humerus and the scapula and also at what has been termed the scapulo-thoracic joint. This is not a true joint in the proper

1.46 A well-placed position of balance

1.47 Incorrect position. The thoracic spine is arched with tension

1.48 The weight is back with tension in the neck

1.49 This jumping position shows perfect balance and dynamic posture

1.50 Line is lost in this jumping position as the spine arches with no stability control

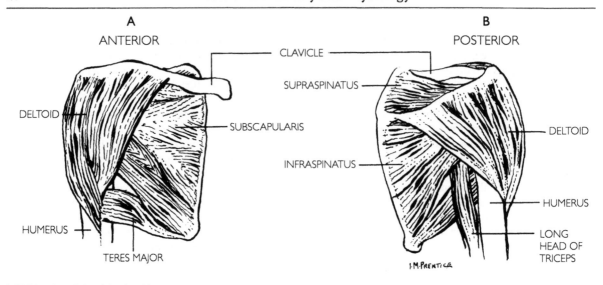

1.51 Muscles of the right shoulder.
1.51A View from the front with the rib cage removed (vide (Fig. 1.10)
1.51B View from the back

meaning of the word but the scapula is only connected to the rest of the trunk by the joints between the two ends of the clavicle; otherwise it is held and suspended by all the muscles that run from the trunk into either the scapula or the upper part of the humerus. As a result, the scapula is free to move around the chest wall and elevation of the arm is a combination of movements at the joint between the humerus and the scapula and between the scapula and the chest wall.

Below the shoulder joint the muscles can be considered entirely as groups; in the arm there are the flexors and extensors of the elbow, in the forearm the flexors and extensors of the wrist and the muscles which rotate the hand and wrist in relation to the elbow and then flexors and extensors of the fingers. When strengthening muscles for use, such as lifting in the pas de deux work, consideration has only to be given to the strengthening of groups of muscles rather than individual muscles.

THE SHOULDER JOINT

This as a whole is an extremely complex joint. The muscular control is therefore equally complex.

Movement of the shoulder takes place at two sites:
1. At the ball and socket joint between the humerus and the scapula.
2. By the scapula sliding over the chest wall at the so-called scapulo-thoracic joint. This is not a genuine joint but as the scapula is only attached to the trunk by muscles it is able to move relatively freely in relation to the rib cage.

Movements of the shoulder are usually enabled by a combination of movements at these two sites. As a result the range of the shoulder is very free. Flexion (to

the front) and abduction (sideways) both have a range of 180°. It is possible to elevate the arm from hanging vertically at the side to vertically above the head, either by bringing the arm forwards and upwards or by moving it sideways and upwards. Flexion and abduction both end up with the arm in the same position. Extension (backwards) and rotation are very much more limited. In the use of the arm in heavy work, e.g. for the boys when they are lifting in double work, stabilisation of the scapula itself is extremely important. The muscles which move the scapula are also responsible for stabilising it. The largest of these muscles is the **trapezius**. This muscle takes origin from the base of the skull and all the thoracic vertebrae and is inserted into the spine of the scapula and the clavicle. The **serratus anterior** is also a large muscle that passes from the ribs anteriorly around the rib cage and deep to the scapula to be inserted into the medial (or spinal) border of the scapula. If it is weak it allows winging of the scapula, that is, the medial border of the scapula stands out away from the rib cage, particularly when the arm is used to push something. The **rhomboid major** and **rhomboid minor** are also important in stabilising the scapula. All these muscles as well as stabilising the scapula do, of course, play a part in actual movements of the scapula. Stabilisation is achieved by a balance of forces between the different muscles contracting and pulling in their various directions.

Around the actual shoulder joint are what is known as the short rotators. These are the **subscapularis**, **teres minor** and **infraspinatus** muscles, all of which play a part in rotating the arm. The **supraspinatus** does not rotate the arm but plays a small part in abducting it. However, the most important action of all these four muscles is in stabilising the head of the humerus in the glenoid cavity, since the glenoid cavity or socket is, in fact, very shallow, like a saucer, and has little or no inherent stability of its own. Therefore, during movements of the humerus in relation to the scapula, these four muscles act in order to steady the head of the humerus in the glenoid. They have been referred to as adjustable ligaments and their action is far more like this than the action which is generally associated with muscles. Of the larger muscles, that which actually flexes, abducts and extends the humerus in relation to the scapula is the **deltoid** muscle. The front portion of this muscle will flex the arm forwards, the middle portion will abduct the arm sideways and the back portion will extend the arm backwards.

The **latissimus dorsi** is an important muscle. It takes origin from the lower six thoracic vertebrae and indirectly from all the lumbar vertebrae and from the iliac crest. It is finally inserted into the humerus where it acts as an adductor, internal rotator and extensor of the arm but, on the way, it passes a very significant slip to the inferior angle of the scapula. This plays a very important role in the stabilisation of the shoulder girdle. As an adductor of the arm it is helped by the **pectoralis major** and **teres major**. The pectoralis major also pulls the arm forwards and medially. The pectoralis major and latissimus dorsi are the most important muscles when lifting the body, for example when the body is being lifted by the arms or when pulling the body up when climbing.

THE ELBOW

The elbow is essentially a hinge joint, although rotation of the head of the radius against the lower end of the humerus takes place in order to give pronation and supination of the forearm. Normally, full extension occurs when the arm and forearm are in a straight line. However, hyperextension or swayback elbows are not particularly uncommon and when excessive can amount to as much as 25°. Flexion is from the fully extended position to approximately 140°. It is limited by the forearm coming up against the upper arm. As a result, an increase in muscle bulk or fat will decrease the possible range of flexion by the interposition between forearm and arm of the soft tissues.

Extension of the elbow is achieved by the **triceps** muscle, so called because it has three heads of origin. It is the only muscle lying at the back of the arm and is the main extensor of the elbow. Extension is helped by a small muscle, the anconeus, which lies just at the back of the elbow. Flexion is achieved by the **brachialis**, which lies deeply in the front of the arm and the **brachioradialis**, most of which lies below the elbow and extends along the forearm. More superficially in the arm lies the **biceps** (biceps brachii is its correct

name, to distinguish it from the biceps femoris which is the lateral hamstring muscle) which stands out so obviously when the supinated forearm is braced in flexion. As well as flexing the elbow it has the additional function of supinating the forearm. The muscle also helps to flex the arm in relation to the scapula as it takes origin from the scapula.

Lower down and lying in the forearm the **supinator** muscle helps the biceps to supinate the forearm. Pronation is carried out by the **pronator teres** and the **pronator quadratus**. The muscles lying more distally in the forearm need not really concern dancers greatly. They are responsible, of course, for flexion and extension of the wrist and flexion and extension of the fingers. The movements of the fingers are also aided by the small intrinsic muscles of the hands.

LOWER LIMB MUSCLES

The muscles of the hip joint are arranged in layers. Closest to the joint are the six deep external rotators which help with turn-out. In the erect posture the adductor group of muscles (Fig. 1.52) also participate

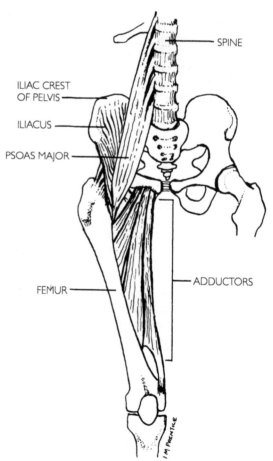

1.52 Muscles of the right hip (view from the front)

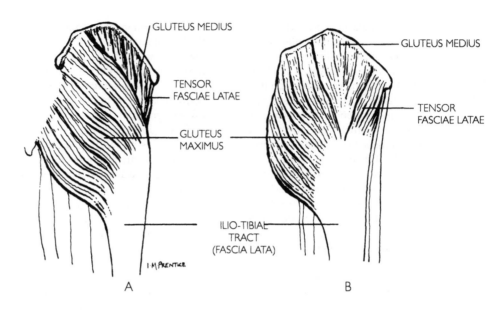

1.53 Muscles of the right hip A From behind B From the side

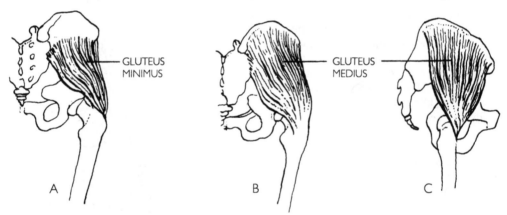

1.54 Muscles of the right hip
1.54A From behind, showing gluteus minimus with gluteus medius removed
1.54B From behind, showing gluteus medius
1.54C From the side, showing gluteus medius

in holding turn-out. The gluteus maximus (Fig. 1.53), a very large muscle, extends and externally and rotates the hip. Abduction of the hip is carried out largely by the tensor fasciae latae and the gluteus medius and gluteus minimus (Figs 1.54, 1.55 and 1.56). Flexion of the hip joint is largely carried out by the ilio psoas (Fig. 1.57), with some help from sartorius. In the thigh, additionally, the rectus femoris, which is part of the quadriceps muscle, also crosses the front of the hip joint and will help to flex the hip (Fig. 1.58). The quadriceps muscle which comprises the rectus femoris, the vastus medialis, vastus intermedius and vastus lateralis extends the knee powerfully (Fig. 1.59).

For the dancer and all athletes the vastus medialis portion of the quadriceps muscle is particularly important and contracts powerfully during the last fifteen degrees of extension of the knee. After any injury the medialis is the first part of the muscle which tends to waste and is usually the most difficult to build up again. Flexion of the knee is carried out by the hamstring muscles which lie at the back of the thigh (Fig. 1.60). These also pass behind the hip joint and therefore act additionally as hip extensors. When the knee is semi-flexed the biceps femoris portion of the hamstrings can rotate the tibia externally. Internal rotation of the tibia is brought about by the popliteus muscle, which lies

PIRIFORMIS

GEMELLUS
SUPERIOR

OBTURATOR
INTERNUS

GEMELLUS
INFERIOR

OBTURATOR
EXTERNUS

QUADRATUS
FEMORIS

1.55 Small external rotator muscles of right hip

GLUTEUS
MEDIUS

GLUTEUS
MINIMUS

TENSOR
FASCIAE
LATAE

ILIO-TIBIAL TRACT
(CUT EDGE)

1.56 Muscles of the right hip
– view from the side to
show gluteus medius and
minimus, tensor fasciae latae
and the ilio-tibial tract

PSOAS MAJOR

PSOAS
MINOR

ILIACUS

ILIACUS

SARTORIUS

1.57 Muscles of the
right hip – the main
hip flexors

PELVIS

SACRUM

RECTUS FEMORIS

PATELLA

PATELLAR
TENDON

TIBIA

1.58 The right rectus femoris
muscle. This is a part of the
quadriceps muscle and is the
only portion to cross the front
of the hip joint. It acts as a hip
flexor as well as a knee extensor

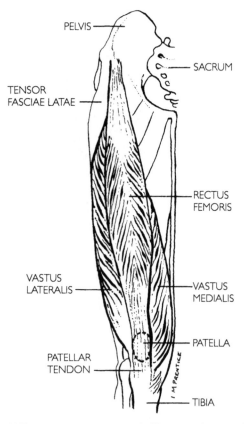

PELVIS

SACRUM

TENSOR
FASCIAE LATAE

RECTUS
FEMORIS

VASTUS
LATERALIS

VASTUS
MEDIALIS

PATELLA

PATELLAR
TENDON

TIBIA

1.59 The right quadriceps muscle. The vastus intermedius is hidden by the rectus femoris

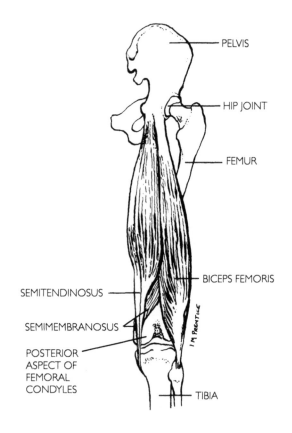

PELVIS

HIP JOINT

FEMUR

BICEPS FEMORIS

SEMITENDINOSUS

SEMIMEMBRANOSUS

POSTERIOR
ASPECT OF
FEMORAL
CONDYLES

TIBIA

1.60 The right hamstring muscles

FEMUR

TIBIA

TIBIALIS
ANTERIOR

GASTROCNEMIUS

CALF MUSCLES

EXTENSOR
DIGITORUM
LONGUS

SOLEUS

EXTENSOR
HALLUCIS
LONGUS

1.61 The right leg, from the front

GASTROCNEMIUS

SOLEUS

ACHILLES TENDON

1.62 The right leg, from the back. Note that the gastrocnemius muscle has two heads which cross the back of the knee and therefore help flex the knee as well as plantarflex the foot and ankle

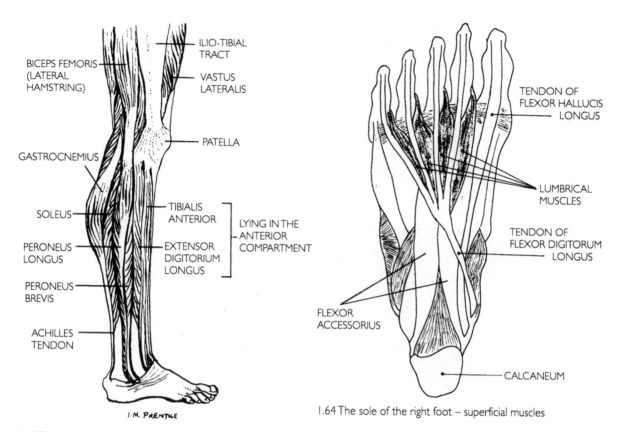

BICEPS FEMORIS
(LATERAL
HAMSTRING)

ILIO-TIBIAL
TRACT

VASTUS
LATERALIS

PATELLA

GASTROCNEMIUS

SOLEUS

TIBIALIS
ANTERIOR

LYING IN THE
ANTERIOR
COMPARTMENT

PERONEUS
LONGUS

EXTENSOR
DIGITORIUM
LONGUS

PERONEUS
BREVIS

ACHILLES
TENDON

I·M. PRENTICE

1.63 The lateral side of the right leg

TENDON OF
FLEXOR HALLUCIS
LONGUS

LUMBRICAL
MUSCLES

TENDON OF
FLEXOR DIGITORUM
LONGUS

FLEXOR
ACCESSORIUS

CALCANEUM

1.64 The sole of the right foot – superficial muscles

deeply behind the knee along with semitendinosus and semimembranosus. Neither external or internal rotation of tibia is a strong movement. When the knee is fully extended, no rotation is possible between the tibia and the femur in the normal knee.

Below the knee (Fig. 1.61) in the anterior compartment or front of leg are the muscles which extend or (as is more commonly called) dorsiflex the ankle, foot and toes. At the back of the leg are the calf muscles (Fig. 1.62), consisting of the gastrocnemius and soleus muscles. These join together at their lower ends to form the Achilles tendon. This is responsible for the powerful plantarflexion of the foot. The gastrocnemius muscle has two heads proximally which pass behind the knee joint to take origin from the the back of the lower end of the femur. It also helps to flex the knee. The soleus muscle lies deep to the gastrocnemius muscle and its origin is in the leg below the knee joint. Twisting the foot into inversion is carried out by the combined action of the tibialis posterior and the tibialis anterior, lying respectively, as their name suggests, at the back and the front of the leg. In simple dorsiflexion and plantarflexion they help to reinforce these movements, tibialis anterior dorsiflexing and tibialis posterior plantarflexing the ankle and foot.

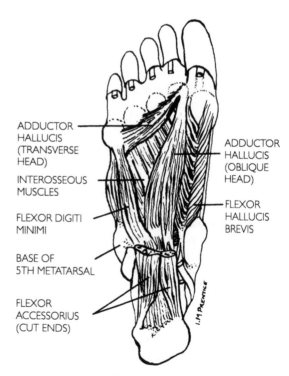

ADDUCTOR
HALLUCIS
(TRANSVERSE
HEAD)

INTEROSSEOUS
MUSCLES

FLEXOR DIGITI
MINIMI

BASE OF
5TH METATARSAL

FLEXOR
ACCESSORIUS
(CUT ENDS)

ADDUCTOR
HALLUCIS
(OBLIQUE
HEAD)

FLEXOR
HALLUCIS
BREVIS

I.M. PRENTICE

1.65 The sole of the right foot – deep muscles

1.66 A well-pointed foot. The toes are stretched so that there is maximum stretch at the front of the ankle

1.67 A badly pointed foot. The intrinsic muscles are weak, so the toes become curled by the unopposed long flexors. As a result there is increased tension along the Achilles tendon and the curled toes prevent the front of the ankle being stretched. Note also the absence of a contraction in the soleus muscle which in Fig. 1.66 is visible below the marked bulge of the contracting gastrocnemius muscle

In the lateral part of the leg (Fig. 1.63) the personeal muscles are responsible for twisting the foot outwards (eversion). The long extensors and long flexors of the toes as they cross the front and back of the ankle also assist in ankle movements.

Within the foot itself are the intrinsic muscles of the foot (Figs 1.64 and 1.65); these are made up of the interosseous muscles and the lumbrical muscles. Although small, they are of the utmost importance to the dancer as strength there helps to maintain the transverse metatarsal arch across the foot. They are responsible for keeping the toes straight when the foot is pointed hard (Fig. 1.66); without the action of the intrinsic muscles the long flexors cause the toes to curl when the foot is pointed (Fig. 1.67).

Principal Muscle Groups

In this section will be described the more important muscles in the lower limbs which move joints and which are of particular interest to dancers. It would be totally unrealistic to describe all the muscles in the body and their actions and it would be equally unrealistic in considering any particular joint to mention or expect any readers to memorise the names of all the muscles concerned. We are, therefore, going to consider only the main muscles.

THE HIP

The hip is a very stable synovial ball and socket joint. Unlike the freely mobile shoulder joint, the hip is built for weight bearing. The cup-shaped acetabulum (socket) on the pelvis is directed sideways, downwards and slightly forwards, and receives the spherical head of femur. This position enhances stability. Both articular surfaces are covered and protected by a layer of articular hyaline cartilage. Further deepening and stabilising the joint is the acetabular labrum, a ring of cartilage attached to the margin of the acetabulum. It helps to spread the weight bearing load within the joint.

The head of femur is offset by a neck of bone holding it away from the shaft. This allows the joint a far greater range of movement. The head and neck of the femur are directed upwards, inwards and slightly forwards into the acetabulum. At the junction of the neck and shaft is the greater trochanter. Several strong gluteal muscles are attached here, but when they are relaxed this large projection of bone can be felt on the outside of the top of the thigh.

The joint is stabilised by its fibrous joint capsule which is a ligamentous sleeve of strong, dense tissue attached above to the rim of the acetabulum, surrounding the neck of femur and attaches below to its base. Also the acetabulum is deepened by an extra cartilaginous wedge-shaped rim called the the acetabular labrum. This helps to stabilise and maintain congruence of the femoral head in the socket. Anteriorly the iliofemoral ligament (the name explains its attachments and therefore function) stabilises the hip joint, restricting extension. This ligament is shaped like an upside-down Y with a lateral band which diverges towards the greater trochanter and medial portions. The lateral trochanteric portion restricts external rotation of the femur. Medially the pubofemoral ligament is tensioned by abduction of the joint and posteriorly the spiral fibres of the ischiofemoral ligament stabilise the back of the joint, limiting internal rotation. The ligament of the head of the femur – ligamentum teres – attaches from the centre of the head of the femur to the acetabulum. Although not considered a major stabilising force it brings the blood supply to the head of the femur. As in every synovial joint the capsule is lined with synovial membrane and the articular surfaces are bathed in synovial fluid.

Flexion of the hip (flexion of the femur in the acetabulum) is usually limited only by the thigh coming up against the trunk and approximately 100° is possible. Following this the sacroiliac joint becomes involved and the intervertebral joints of the lumbar spine. With the knee extended the length of the hamstrings is the limiting factor. Extension is limited by the iliofemoral ligament, mentioned above, and the length of the hip flexors with about 20° possible. Approximately 45° of pure femoral abduction is possible, but with external rotation of the femur can abduct freely limited by the length of hamstrings and adductors. Without the external rotation the greater trochanter approximates the outer surface of the ilium where it blocks, therefore mechanically the hip joint of the dancer has a wider range of movement when externally rotated. Adduction is limited to 30° and after this the pelvis has to tilt laterally involving the lumbar spine.

Medial and lateral rotation can take place through-out the flexion/extension/abduction/adduction range of movement. However, with the hip in standing position approximately 30–40° of medial rotation (turn-in) and up to 60° of lateral rotation (turn-out) are possible. This hip measurement helps determine the potential facility for classical ballet in pre-vocational orthopaedic assessment. When examining the pathol-ogy of the hip joint it is important to consider the movements of the head of the femur within the acetab-ulum. In flexion the head of the femur rotates about a coronal axis but also glides posteriorly in its socket. In extension it glides anteriorly. In the neutral position the head of the femur points slightly anteriorly. In external rotation it moves forwards even more towards the anterior of the joint and its capsule. In hip abduction the head of femur glides downwards and inwards in the acetabulum.

The hip joint is surrounded by layers of muscles that co-operate to produce its wide but complex range of movement. The kinematics of the hip continue to be researched and explored, but here it is possible only to explain in simplified terms with a few suggestions, its movement and control in dance.

Over the back of the joint are layers of gluteal muscles. The deepest are the six small external rotators – obturator externus and internus, the gemelli superior and inferior, quadratus femoris and piriformis – all of which externally rotate the femur. Following the rules of muscle function, the deepest muscles surrounding a joint, although small, are designed to stabilise, align and compress articular surfaces. As the femur moves from extension to flexion, the axis of joint motion changes and these muscles together operate a relay system to control external rotation of the femur as the hip joint moves through its full range.

The abductors lie in the next layer. The deepest is gluteus minimus which is also a medial rotator balancing the deep external rotators. It lies under gluteus medius and they originate from the lateral surface of the ilium and insert on the greater trochanter. The posterior fibres of gluteus medius contribute to external rotation of the femur, the middle fibres abduct and the anterior fibres medially rotate. These are important muscles to the dancer in that on the supporting side they balance the pelvis horizontally with the tensor fasciae latae when the dancer is standing on that leg. Without their activation the dancer 'sinks in the hip', destabilising the pelvis, lumbar spine and hip joints.

The most superficial of the gluteal muscles is the gluteus maximus. It is a large, powerful muscle and can be regarded as having two parts. The upper part has an abductor and external rotation function while the lower part has an extensor, adductor and external rotation function. It is a large muscle originating from the posterior surface of the ilium and sacrum and inserting into the iliotibial band, the greater trochanter and the posterior aspect of the femur.

The hamstrings work with gluteus maximus as primary extensors of the hip. They are two joint muscles in that they originate from the ischial tuberosity (often referred to as the 'sit' bones) on the pelvis and insert below the knee, thus both extending the hip and flexing the knee.

The adductor muscles on the inside of the thigh are important to the dancer. The crossed positions of classical ballet require strong adduction forces. In closed positions the adductors exert a pull on the back of the femoral shaft, assisting with external rotation of the thigh. While they cannot be regarded generally as turn-out muscles, in classical ballet dancers they can be seen to be contributing to the control of the turned-out thigh in standing crossed positions, as well as stabilising the pelvis over one leg. If used well, hyperextension of the knee is controlled.

Psoas major has anterior attachments to all the lumbar vertebrae transverse processes, the bodies and interposing discs T12 to L5. The muscle fibres pass downwards to the pelvic brim, posterior to the inguinal ligament, anterior to the hip joint, and converge into a tendon with iliacus which inserts into the lesser trochanter. The psoas major has primarily a stabilising role in the lumbar spine, providing axial compression to resist displacement along with the multifidus. At the hip joint it acts as a deep stabiliser of the hip joint, pulling the head of the femur into the acetabulum.

The iliacus is an important hip flexor and arises from the inner surface of the ilium. It should activate strongly in all flexion movements and after 90° becomes the main flexion force.

The tensor fasciae latae originates from the outer lip of the iliac crest and inserts into the strong iliotibial band (ITB) of fascia on the lateral thigh. This muscle is considered to flex, abduct and medially rotate the thigh. Most importantly it tensions the ITB which reinforces the weight-bearing function of the femur, steadying the pelvis over the femur and the femur over the tibia. The secondary flexors are the sartorius and the rectus femoris.

As with all major joints, alignment and muscle balance promote strength and prevent injury. The deeper muscles stabilise and their timing and activation are fundamental to joint health.

THE KNEE

The knee joint is, in practice, a hinge joint. When it is fully extended there is no rotation possible between the lower end of the femur and the upper end of the tibia. With the knee slightly flexed there is some rotation possible between the femur and the tibia but this only amounts to about 15° in either direction. Extension of the knee, although normally occurring fully when the thigh and leg are in a straight line, is very frequently greater than this, giving a certain amount of hyper-extension producing the familiar swayback knees. Flexion is, in most people, limited by the calf muscle coming up against the back of the thigh. Strong collateral ligaments prevent any abduction or adduction of the knee.

The movement of extension is achieved by the **quadriceps** muscle. As its name implies this is made up of four parts. The **rectus femoris** takes origin from the pelvis above the acetabulum and crosses the front of the hip joint to be inserted via the combined quadriceps tendon, patella and patellar tendon into the upper part of the front of the tibia. Therefore as well as extending the knee it will help to flex the hip. The **vastus lateralis**, **vastus intermedius** and **vastus medialis** all take their origin from the shaft of the femur. They do not cross the hip joint. They, together with the rectus femoris, join together at their lower ends to form the quadriceps tendon. This is inserted into the patella, which at its lower pole gives origin to the patellar tendon which is inserted into the front of the upper end of the tibia. The vastus medialis is particularly important in dancers and other athletes. It is largely responsible for the final 15° of extension. It also opposes the lateral tracking of the patella which would otherwise take place by the action of the vastus lateralis and the tensor fasciae latae, the latter through the intermediary of the fascia lata itself. In any knee injury the vastus medialis is the first portion that weakens and wastes and in rehabilitation is the most difficult to build up again. Its importance is referred to on many occasions in **Section 3**.

Flexion of the knee is brought about by the hamstrings. These are the **semitendinosus** and **semimembranosus** lying on the medial side of the

back of the thigh and the **biceps femoris** lying on the lateral side of the back of the thigh. As well as flexing the knee they also act as hip extensors as they cross the back of the hip joint taking origin from the pelvis, apart from the short head of the biceps which takes its origin from the back of the femoral shaft. When the medial (semitendinosus and semimembranosus) hamstrings and lateral (biceps femoris) hamstrings are not balanced up in strength, either following an injury or due to incorrect working, they can produce uneven rotational forces at the knee when the joint is anything other than fully extended. In the semi-flexed situation injury is more likely to occur.

Flexion of the knee is aided slightly by the gracilis and the **sartorius**. The latter also acts as a flexor of the hip. It helps to abduct the hip and rotate the femur externally. As a result of these actions if the dancer is straining to over-turn the feet, pushes back on the knee and gets into the weightback situation, a great deal of strain occurs at the upper end of the sartorius and this muscle then becomes a frequent site of the so-called groin strain. As will be seen in **Section 5**, groin strains are usually a result of incorrect weight placement.

At the back of the knee is a small muscle called the popliteus, which helps to flex the knee and it also will rotate the tibia medially (internally). When the knee is flexed the medial and lateral hamstrings will also aid in rotating the tibia at the knee, the medial hamstrings (semitendinosus and semimembranosus) helping to rotate the tibia medially, and the lateral hamstrings (biceps femoris) helping to rotate the knee laterally. However, as has been mentioned earlier, when the knee is fully extended there is no rotation possible at the knee joint. The ligaments lock it in order to prevent rotation, therefore any excessive rotational force will produce damage within the knee. As the knee starts to flex, then an increasing amount of rotation is available between the tibia and the knee but this only amounts to about 15° in each direction at the maximum. It is not until the knee reaches about 45° of flexion that significant active rotation of the tibia in relation to the femur occurs. At less than this amount of flexion, the movement is extremely weak, although this is not to imply that the rotational movement even at 45° of flexion and greater, is particularly strong.

THE ANKLE, FOOT AND TOES

These joints are considered together because many of the muscles concerned will act on all the joints. The **gastrocnemius** is the superficial muscle at the back of the calf and leads us into this section from the knee, because it takes its origin from the lower end of the femur above the back of the knee. It therefore acts as a knee flexor assisting the hamstrings. As it passes through the leg it joins with the **soleus**. These two together form the Achilles tendon which is inserted into the back of the os calcis or heel bone. The gastrocnemius and soleus together act as plantarflexors of the ankle. The **plantaris** is a small muscle which also arises from the back of the lower end of the femur. It has a very long tendon and is also inserted into the os calcis. It acts in a similar fashion to the gastrocnemius by helping to flex the knee and to plantarflex the ankle. Plantarflexion is helped by the **long flexors of the toes**.

Due to the arrangement of the bones in the hind foot and foot as a whole, when the ankle is plantar-flexed it takes with it the whole of the foot, because the mobility of the foot within itself in the direction of dorsiflexion and plantarflexion is not very great. Therefore, when one considers dorsiflexion and plantarflexion of the ankle, one can consider the movement of the whole foot in those two directions.

Dorsiflexion of the ankle and foot is carried out by the actions of several muscles, the **tibialis anterior**, the **extensor hallucis longus**, the peroneus tertius and the **long extensors of the toes**. However, all these muscles have other actions in addition.

Inversion and eversion of the foot take place in the tarsal bones or hind foot. Essentially, the talus remains fixed in the ankle joint as far as inversion and eversion are concerned, merely moving as a hinge in dorsi-flexion and plantarflexion. Inversion and eversion take place along a line through the axis of the talus, the movement occurring mainly in the sub-taloid and talo-navicular joints, although to a certain extent there is some inversion and eversion in the mid-tarsal joints in the middle of the foot. Inversion of the foot is obtained by a combined action of the **tibialis posterior** and the **tibialis anterior**. Eversion of the foot is carried out by the action of the peroneal muscles. The long extensors of the toes, as they cross in front of the ankle, do have an action as mentioned in dorsiflexing the ankle and at the same time in extending the toes. Extension at the foot and ankle is synonymous with the expression dorsiflexion, the latter expression being more commonly used when applied to the ankle and foot. The long flexors of the toes cause them to curl as they flex at both the metatarsophalangeal and the interphalangeal joints. Additionally, the long flexors of the toes will help to plantarflex the ankle and foot, plantarflexion here being synonymous with flexion when applied to the ankle and to the foot.

Additionally, in the foot as in the hand, there are many small muscles which are known as the **intrinsic muscles**. These are responsible for opposing the clawing effect of the long flexors of the toes, so that when the toes are flexed at the metatarsophalangeal joints, the intrinsic muscles by their action will help to keep the interphalangeal joints straight. Thus in a well pointed foot, we see the plantarflexors of the ankle and

foot working and assisted by the long flexors of the toes but the actual flexion effect of the last group of muscles on the toes is counteracted by a strong action of the intrinsic muscles, keeping the toes straight in the pointed foot. Some of the intrinsic muscles also have an effect in maintaining the transverse arch across the forefoot. If the transverse arch drops due to weakness of the intrinsic muscles, then pain can develop under the heads of the metatarsals (known as anterior metatarsalgia).

1.4 The Nervous System

The nervous system comprises the brain, the spinal cord and perpheral nerves. The nervous system is further sub-divided into two parts:

1. that part associated generally with the muscles moving the body and limbs and the associated sensory perceptions, and
2. the other part, known as the automonic nervous system, which supplies the nerves to involuntary and cardiac muscles and to glands.

However, these two systems are closely related; reflex arcs are involved in both systems and the higher senses of control of each are in the brain. The nervous system, as all other systems, is based upon individual cells known as neurones and, unlike other cells, they have extensions from the cell (Fig. 1.68). One type of extension is called the dendron; this may be single or multiple and passes impulses towards the cell body. The other type of extension known as the axon conducts impulses away from the cell body. The voluntary nerves and those associated with sensation are surrounded by a fatty sheath and are known as medullated nerves or white fibres; whereas the autonomic nerve fibres do not have this fatty layer and are known as non-medullated or grey fibres because of the actual colour difference. The neurones all have a specific function; sensory neurones are those which receive stimuli and pass them centrally to the spinal cord and from there, where necessary, to the brain. Motor neurones are those which pass impulses from the brain and from the spinal cord to the muscles.

The sensory nerves not only receive and perceive what we would consider sensations, such as hot, cold, pain, etc. but also they are responsible for transmitting messages concerned with tension within muscles, tendons and ligaments and information regarding co-ordination and special relationships. It is the combi-nation of these mechanisms which enable you, for instance, to place the tip of your finger on your nose or any other part of your body without the necessity of watching it in motion.

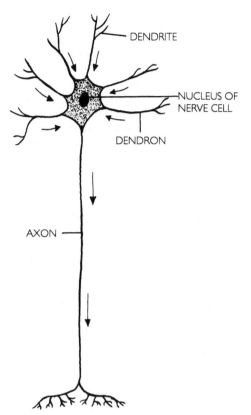

1.68 A typical nerve cell. The arrows show the direction of the electrical impulses in the nerve

The Voluntary or Somatic Nervous System

The term voluntary, although commonly applied, is not a particularly satisfactory name for this portion of the system but it is used to distinguish the major part of the nervous system from the autonomic nervous system (vide infra). Somatic nervous system is a better though less used name.

It is probably easier when considering the action of the nervous system to start peripherally, rather than centrally. If we consider a case where an individual nerve is divided, this will cut through both sensory and motor nerves; the result will be that no sensation of any sort can reach the spinal cord or the brain. The part will feel numb and there will be no appreciation of where it is in space. Division of the motor nerve will prevent any movement at all in the distribution of that divided nerve; the muscles supplied by the nerve will lose all tone as no electrical impulses can travel across the division in the nerve. This therefore will produce what is known as flaccid paralysis, in other words the muscle will be completely soft and toneless to the observer's touch.

Now take a case of a division across the spinal cord itself; the spinal cord will be normal, both above and below the level of division, but there will be no conduction in either direction across the division. We have therefore intact nerves going from the spinal cord to the muscle and from the muscle, skin and other tissues back to the spinal cord. Within the spinal cord there are some nerve connections directly between the sensory nerves and the motor nerves. These three pathways between them produce what is known as a reflex arc. In primitive creatures where there is little or no brain, the entire organism functions by means of these very simple reflex arcs. Taken at its simplest a reflex arc consists of

a) a sensory receptor;
b) a sensory neurone;
c) a synapse (which is where one nerve ending makes contact with another nerve ending);
d) a motor neurone, and
e) an effector cell.

The drawing (Fig. 1.69) shows a simple reflex arc from a sensory receptor (e.g. pain appreciation) to the spinal cord, via an intermediate neurone known as an

1.69 Illustration of a reflex arc in the nervous system

internunicial neurone to the motor neurone which will supply a muscle fibre causing a contraction. In the simplest reflex arc the internunicial neurones may be missing.

There are reflexes within the spinal cord, passing impulses up and down to leave at higher or lower levels, as well as those going in and out at the same level. There are also more highly developed reflexes going up and down the spinal cord to and from the brain.

Reflex actions play a vital role in
a) control of the internal organs;
b) controlling the tone in voluntary muscles;
c) producing controlled inhibition of antagonistic groups of muscles;
d) causing protective reactions.

In the division of the spinal cord in a higher animal such as a mammal, the animal is reduced below the level of the division to a primitive type of state. Although the brain cannot receive or transmit any messages, certain functions still occur below the level of division. Muscle tone, for instance, is actually increased in these reflex arcs, because of the lack of modification from the higher centres. Although voluntary movement has been abolished and the muscle is paralysed in that sense, the increased tone produces what is known as spastic paralysis because the affected muscles tend usually to be in spasm because of the increased tone. Various reflex arcs can be initiated by stimuli. For example heat, cold or pain will produce a withdrawal reflex without the brain perceiving anything. In the absence of injury these primitive reflexes are modified by nerve impulses transmitted from the higher centres. In the normal animal there are innumerable reflex arcs not only from the periphery to the spinal cord and brain but also within the different sections of the brain itself, continually modifying, altering and controlling all aspects of function.

The neurological system as a whole is extremely complicated, but in what is possibly an over-simplification, it might be considered that development from primitive life to the human state has progressed from below upwards, starting with a reflex arc and proceeding with the development of the portion of the brain nearest the spinal cord, the hind-brain, the cerebellum and mid-brain and finally to the cerebral hemispheres or fore-brain. The brain and cerebellum have a very wrinkled or convoluted surface in order to increase the available surface area of the brain. With the higher mammals, and particularly with primates, increasingly complicated series of movements can be learned consciously, and once mastered can be reproduced without obvious conscious thought about each individual part of the total complex action. This does not, however, mean that once learnt, these complex actions are then brought about in the lower

levels of the spinal cord. These actions are still initiated and controlled within the brain and it is a misnomer to refer to these complex actions as reflex actions.

The Autonomic Nervous System

Once again this is not a very satisfactory name as it implies by the name autonomic that it is self-controlling, whereas it is in fact closely linked with the somatic system and its highest centres are in the brain.

This is the system that controls the involuntary and cardiac muscles and the glands. The autonomic system itself is divided into two parts – the sympathetic system and the parasympathetic system. The two systems act against each other and are therefore called antagonistic. The sympathetic system is a stimulatory system and acts with adrenalin to prepare the body for action. Initially this was, of course, to either fight an enemy or flee from him, but in the more modern situation it will produce the keyed-up feeling required for social confrontations such as examinations, performances or arguments with other people. It is the sympathetic system and the adrenalin which increase the pulse rate and blood pressure on these occasions and produce a feeling of 'butterflies' in the stomach by diverting the blood supply, from the alimentary tract in particular, to other areas which are needed for the 'figurative fight'. The parasympathetic system is inhibitory in type and tends to produce rest and relaxation in the body and aids digestion by increasing the blood supply to the abdominal organs. The sympathetic and parasympathetic systems have their main nerve supplies outside the spinal cord, starting in what is know as ganglia and then running up and down inside the trunk. Parasympathetic and sympathetic nerve fibres travel with the ordinary motor and sensory nerves to the limbs and muscles.

The Sensory System

There are three types of sensory endings:
1. Those which can detect stimuli coming from outside the body. These are known as exteroceptors.
2. Endings which sense stimuli from within the body, particularly the internal organs, such as the alimentary tract. Known as enteroceptors.
3. Those which can detect the tension in the muscles and tendons. These are known as proprioceptors.

Stimulation of the exteroceptors produces a conscious awareness of the type of stimulus. However, we are not normally aware of the stimulation of enteroceptors and proprioceptors except for a feeling of hunger or unless it reaches the point where the stimulus is so great that it is interpreted as a feeling of pain. The extero-ceptors are responsible for producing a variety of conscious effects; these are sight, taste, smell, touch, temperature, pain, hearing and balance. The latter two are both detected within the ear.

Over-stimulation of touch, temperature and even of hearing may be interpreted as pain.

SKIN SENSATION

Temperature and pain are protective types of sensation. Touch is largely connected with the use of the limbs and movement. A person with a numb hand or even a numb finger finds that the use of the hand in picking things up and particularly in fine and skilled uses is seriously imparied. They will not know that they are holding something or how tightly they are holding it and they therefore tend to drop objects. They will frequently be under the misapprehension that the hand is weak, although this is not in fact the case. Loss of sensibility to touch in the feet produces a stamping gait because the person cannot feel the feet touching the ground and therefore the necessary stimulation to initiate the reflex arcs is absent. As far as the dancer or athlete is concerned we can pass over the taste and smell modalities.

AURAL SENSATIONS: SOUND AND BALANCE

Although the appreciation of music in both pitch and rhythm is important to a dancer, hearing problems are not something upon which we need dwell in a work such as this. Balance is, however, extremely important. The organs of balance are situated in the inner ear: there are three semi-circular canals lying in different planes to each other (Fig. 1.70). The cells inside the canals have hair-like processes and the canals themselves are filled with fluid. Hearing appreciation takes place in the cochlea.

The movement of fluid within the canals stimulates the hair-like processes and it is this interpretation of the stimuli which produces a sense of balance. Diseases of the inner ear can produce a sensation of falling or dizziness, known as vertigo. This is often temporary in nature and frequently associated with a cold and possibly a middle ear or inner ear infection. The ability to balance is a combination of the information

received from the inner ear, the information received from the proprioceptors in the muscles and also the information received from the eyes. The eyes are the least important as the normal person has no difficulty in walking or standing in total darkness. However, if there is damage to the inner ear, then the visual reflexes can take over to a certain extent. In these circumstances if the person then closes his eyes there will be a tendency to fall over.

VISUAL SENSATION

Visual defects with which one is born are most commonly caused by too long or too short an eye ball and these defects can be corrected by spectacles or by contact lenses. As there is a small distance between the eyes, the actual field of vision in each eye is slightly different and it is this slight difference in field of vision which the brain can interpret to produce a stereoscopic or 3-D effect.

This gives an accurate judgment of distance, allowing objects to be touched or picked up extremely accurately. In a person born with monocular vision the brain compensates extremely efficiently for this defect and such a person is usually only at a disadvantage in rapid ball games. However, if vision is lost in one eye later on in life the individual has far greater difficulty in compensating. As a result there can be problems picking up objects and driving vehicles.

PROPRIOCEPTION

The word 'proprioception' arises from the Latin word *proprius*, meaning one's own or self, and receptor, meaning something that receives. Proprioception is the body's ability to sense the position of the body as a whole, and its individual body parts, in space. It is the central nervous system (CNS) that orchestrates all movement. Before it can do this, it must receive information from joints, muscles, tendons, the soles of the feet, the fingertips and the balance mechanism in the ears, to name but a few sites of sensory receptors.

Proprioception is a term that refers particularly to the recognition of kinaesthesia (sense of joint movement) and of joint position. It is this accurate

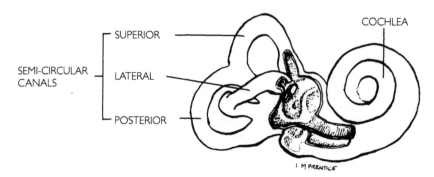

SEMI-CIRCULAR CANALS — SUPERIOR — LATERAL — POSTERIOR   COCHLEA

1.70 The inner ear

sensory (or afferent) input that gives the experienced dancer such superiority of motor control over other athletes, and it is this that ballet teachers with a clear understanding can train in their students.

In joint capsules and ligaments there are sensory receptors called mechanoreceptors which are sensitive to deformation and therefore inform the CNS of position, change of position and movement of joints. In muscle it is the muscle spindles that inform the CNS of muscle length and stretch, and are sensitive to velocity of stretch (see p. 99). The Golgi Tendon Organs, another receptor located at the musculo-tendinous junction, also send proprioceptive feedback to the CNS. Here they monitor the force transmitted through the tendon by the muscle during movement. Exteroreceptors in the skin respond to pressure and in the sole of the foot, for example, are highly refined, promoting balance control in weight bearing.

Along with visual information and the balance mechanism of the inner ear (vestibular apparatus), proprioceptive information allows the CNS to integrate and respond, producing smooth, co-ordinated movement. Closing the eyes during an exercise forces the body to rely on proprioception, and allows the body to explore and intensify sensory appreciation. The child will follow and copy a teacher's demonstration, then attempt to reproduce it, learning over time the exact and precise pathway and placing of a battement tendu. All the above mentioned sensory receptors will be accessed at conscious level with the child watching, listening to corrections and physically interpreting them. Gradually the movement becomes more automatic, less and less conscious, and the battement tendu movement is stored in the nervous system to be instantly accessed when required. We call this cognitive programming.

The proprioceptive system can be challenged by exercises balancing on an unstable surface such as a wobble board. Even attempting a battement fondu exercise on a foam mat will consciously recruit the balance mechanisms and all the proprioceptors to control the movement that was so easy before. Practice will perfect the exercise with less effort, and back on a firm surface the control of supporting ankle and knee and co-ordination of the gesture leg will be even more assured.

Overusing the mirror in a dance studio makes the dancer too reliant on visual feedback to place and control movement and shape. Performance and expression require instead, a finely tuned proprioceptive system. Holding on too tightly to the barre can detract from the body's stability and balance, leaving the body less prepared for centre practice.

Accidents happen when the proprioceptive system fails. A sprained ankle results in a failure of the mechanoreceptors in the ankle to reflexly save the alignment of the joint, and a ligament is overstretched. Of course pain is then registered from pain nerve endings. With the resultant pain, swelling and obligatory rest required, the proprioception of the ankle joint is dampened, and one of the first requirements of rehabilitation is to recover that acuity with simple exercises to begin with, to the final quick, dynamic changes of direction in the final stages. Wearing an ankle support when first returning to class can remind the dancer (through sensory input) to be careful with otherwise normal movements, but prolonged use of a joint support is thought to counteract full proprioceptive acuity. It is worth noting that an ankle with significantly overstretched ligaments can still recover full control if the proprioceptive system is effectively rehabilitated.

An understanding of proprioceptive training can be applied to every part of the body. The lumbar spine and pelvis are targeted early on in training when posture is addressed. A fine control and appreciation of the neutral lumbar curve and pelvic tilt sets the spinal position and develops the spinal stabilisers (the deepest muscles nearest the spine, responsible for control of facet joint position). 'Tucking under' (tilting the pelvis backwards) causes too much tension in the more superficial muscles which must necessarily be released in movement. The opposite is the more inexperienced tilt forward with arched lumbar spine and lack of control. The spine is destabilised and in both situations an adequate proprioceptive sense from muscles and joints is never developed. Proprioceptive deficits here are associated with lower back injuries.

The weak, hyperextended knee also needs proprioception training due to its deficient joint position sense. A young student with hyperextended knees often locks back to extend without balanced use of the quadriceps muscles. In the weight-bearing position this upsets the foot below, the muscle balance of the thigh and the equilibrium of the body above. This type of knee requires neuromuscular control to achieve dynamic awareness and find stability in a neutral position when supporting the body.

Proprioceptive sense has also been found to be affected by fatigue. Accidents and injuries are more frequent at the end of the day when dancers are tired. Stamina training and maintenance should be part of every professional dancer's and student's week.

Supplementary balance and proprioception exercises can be given in and out of class to all students to enhance ankle and knee control, stabilise the pelvis and position the shoulder girdle. Just as training the cardiovascular system increases fitness and training, the musculoskeletal system increases strength; training the proprioceptive and balance systems increases co-ordination, and technique building can then proceed

more successfully contributing to proprioceptive
awareness, control and co-ordination.

The muscle spindle (under the microscope, shaped
like a spindle) is made up of specialised fibres called
intrafusal fibres, which are sensory in action,
monitoring the muscle shortening. They lie parallel to
the extrafusal fibres, which are the fibres which
contract to shorten the muscle. Nerve fibres relay
messages from the spindle to the spinal cord and brain,
on stretch. The stretch reflex is the quick response to
sudden stretch. The CNS, if alerted to any sudden or
harmful stretch, relays a message to the muscle
(extrafusal fibres) to contract and the muscle is saved
from overstretch.

A body with a refined sense of proprioception can
balance well and move with great control and ease. In
other words – it belongs to a dancer.

1.5 The Skin

The skin comprises two layers of tissue (Fig. 1.71): the
epidermis, which is the superficial or outer part and the
dermis which is the deeper part. The dermis contains
nerves and blood vessels; the epidermis has neither
nerves nor blood vessels. In the deeper layers of the
epidermis are living cells which proliferate, pushing the
more superficial cells towards the surface. As they get
nearer to the surface they become flattened and then
die, giving layers of dead, horny cells. The epidermis is
being constantly renewed by growth from the deeper
layers and the superficial horny cells are constantly
shed. This is particularly well demonstrated when a
part has been encased in plaster of Paris and the dead,
horny cells are then only too apparent where they have
not been worn away but are still lying in place, giving

the appearance of a scaly reptile-type skin. Friction and
pressure both stimulate the growth of the cells of the
deeper part of the epidermis, thickening up the
epidermal layer. This is normal on the soles and the
palms, particularly in those who walk bare-footed or
who do heavy manual labour. In certain areas this
thickness may be localised, producing a callosity.

The skin is not permeable to water. This is not to
prevent the rain from getting in but to prevent water
being lost from the body. The epidermis is also a
protective mechanism that prevents the entry of germs.

The skin contains two types of glands (Fig. 1.71):
1. the sweat glands – the chief function of which is to
   help cool the body. When the temperature of the
   body rises the sweat glands secrete sweat; this covers
   the skin and evaporates. In order to be turned from
   a liquid into a gas, i.e. evaporate, energy has to be
   absorbed; this is done in the form of heat absorption
   from the body and thus the production of the
   cooling effect. The sweat contains various types of
   salt and some waste materials from the body. The
   sweat can be looked upon as playing a minor part in
   the excretion of these materials. However, in a hot
   climate where sweating is profuse the body is able to
   regulate the amount of electrolytes or salts in the
   sweat and decrease the loss to practically nil. Were
   this not the case there would be a serious depletion
   of essential electrolytes in the body.
2. the sebaceous glands, which produce an oily
   secretion known as sebum which lubricates the
   horny epidermal cells and the hairs to prevent them
   from becoming brittle. (Mammary glands which
   produce milk are specialist forms of sebaceous
   glands.)

The skin contains nerve endings which perceive
temperature and touch. Pain endings are at a deeper
level.

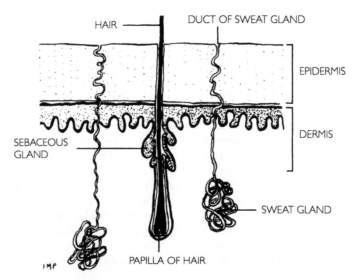

1.71 Cross-section of the skin

1.6 The Cardiovascular System

This system comprises the blood which circulates around the arteries, veins and capillaries, the heart which pumps the blood through the blood vessels, and the arteries, veins and capillaries themselves.

The Blood

The blood consists of two portions: there is a liquid part which accounts for just over half the volume of the whole blood and a cellular part which accounts for just under half.

The cells themselves are of two main types – the red cells and the white cells. The red cells do not have nuclei by the time they enter the blood stream. They are responsible for carrying the oxygen and give the blood its red colour. There are about four and a half to five million red blood cells in each cubic millimetre of blood. The red pigment in the red blood cells is haemoglobin; this can combine very easily with oxygen and equally easily can shed the oxygen again and it is by this method that oxygen is transported around the body, taking it from the air in the lungs to release it where required in the tissues. The red blood cells only exist in the blood stream for three to four months before being broken down. They are mainly produced in the red bone marrow which contains what is known as erythropoietic tissue – the red marrow in adult life is largely confined to the flat bones, e.g. the pelvis and the scapula, and the ends of the long bones. In childhood most of the bones contain red marrow but this quantity decreases in adult life. In these inactive sites, the red marrow becomes yellow marrow which does not contain erythropoietic tissue. However, if demand suddenly becomes great, even in adult life the yellow bone marrow can revert to red bone marrow and start producing the red corpuscles once more. This may be stimulated by chronic blood loss, e.g. when blood is lost gradually over a long period as in a bleeding ulcer, etc.

When the cells are broken down after three to four months the iron is retained in the body and is stored in the liver to be used again for making further red corpuscles. The other products from the breakdown of the haemoglobin are excreted in the bile which passes into the alimentary tract and hence out of the body in the faeces. The white blood corpuscles, which are also known as leucocytes, are fewer in number than the red corpuscles. There are four thousand to ten thousand per cubic millimetre of blood, but various diseases can produce a very marked increase in the number of white cells. The white cells themselves are divided into two types: polymorphonuclear leucocytes or granulocytes 60–75 per cent and mononuclear leucocytes or non-granulocytes 25–40 per cent. The granulocytes have large irregular nuclei which are lobulated. They are subdivided by their staining characteristics when examined microscopically: neutrophils 60–70 per cent, eosinophils 2–4 per cent and basophils 0.5–2 per cent. The neutrophils are those most concerned with the attack on bacteria and foreign particles. They rapidly collect at any site of infection or invasion by foreign matter, where they act by surrounding these particles or organisms by what is known as amoeboid movements. In this action the individual cells come up against the foreign body or particle and then surround it – the cell membrane breaks down and the foreign particle is taken into the cell itself and the cell membrane reforms. The eosinophils increase in numbers as a result of allergic reactions. The basophils manufacture heparin, which helps to prevent blood clotting in the blood vessels and histamine which causes the small blood vessels to dilate, usually as a result of local injury. The basophils are, however, by no means the sole source of either heparin or histamine.

The other group of white cells are the mononuclear leucocytes, each having a large round nucleus. They form some 25 per cent of the white blood cells; the majority of these are lymphocytes which are associated with immunological responses.

There is a third non-liquid component to blood. These are the platelets; they are very small and are not cells. The blood platelets are associated with the clotting of blood. The mechanism of blood clotting is extremely complex and there are a large number of factors involved; it is the interaction of these various factors which produces clotting at the proper time. If one or more of the factors is missing then blood clotting may not occur. This happens in diseases such as haemophilia. In a greatly over-simplified scheme, clotting is produced by the production of thrombokinase from blood platelets and injured tissue, this then acts with a substance called prothrombin in the plasma, forming thrombin. This action can only take place if there is calcium present in the blood as is the normal state of affairs. The thrombin then acts with a protein in the blood known as fibrinogen producing fibrin. This fibrin will form a net which gradually becomes denser with the formation of more fibrin. The red and white corpuscles get caught up in this net and form the clot. Serum is the liquid that remains after a clot has formed, i.e. when all the clotting factors and cells have been removed.

The blood is the transport system of the body and as such has a variety of different functions:

1. It carries gases around the body. Oxygen is carried mainly in combination with haemoglobin in the red blood cells and is required by the tissues as part of their metabolism. A small amount of oxygen is

actually dissolved in the plasma. Carbon dioxide is returned from the tissues to the lungs in both the red cells and the plasma. Nitrogen is also carried around the body dissolved in the plasma. This is an inert gas and forms the bulk of the air that we breathe. It is this nitrogen in the blood stream which causes the problems with deep sea diving; with an increased air pressure being breathed, a far greater amount of nitrogen becomes dissolved in the blood. If the diver is brought to the surface and therefore to a reduced pressure too rapidly, the nitrogen will no longer remain dissolved in the blood because of this decrease in pressure and it will form bubbles in the blood stream. These bubbles can block the small capillary vessels and this results in death of the tissues which would normally be supplied by these capillaries.

2. Food products are carried to the tissues of the body and waste material from tissue metabolism is carried either as carbon dioxide to the lungs or as other waste products to the kidneys where it is excreted in the urine. Various salts and electrolytes are carried around the body in the plasma. Many of these are required by the cells although they cannot be looked upon as a true food item.

3. White blood corpuscles are constantly transported around the blood stream so that they can be readily available as part of the defence system against infection or the penetration by any foreign material.

4. Heat is carried to the skin for removal by a combination of sweating and radiation.

Circulation of the Blood

Obviously in order to perform the functions that have been described the blood has to travel around the body. The heart pumps the blood down through the arteries into gradually decreasing sizes of vessels until the capillaries are reached. The arteries and the smaller arteries (arterioles) have muscular walls which stretch and contract (Fig. 1.72). The capillaries have extremely thin walls which are only one cell thick, so that salts, electrolytes, food substances and gases can pass through the walls into the tissues and waste substances can pass back again. The capillaries then gradually join together to form venules and veins. These have rather thicker walls than the capillaries but are very much thinner than arteries (Fig. 1.72). The veins have very little muscle in their walls and are far less elastic than the arteries.

As can be seen from the schematic diagram (Fig. 1.73) of the circulation, the heart (Figs 1.74–1.75) is a double pump. Each pump is divided into two parts, an atrium which receives the blood which it then passes through to a ventricle which gives the powerful

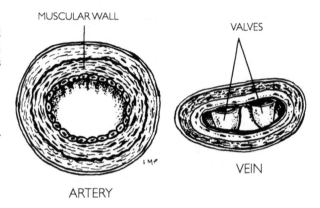

1.72 Cross-section of an artery and a vein. Note the muscular wall in the artery which is absent from the vein

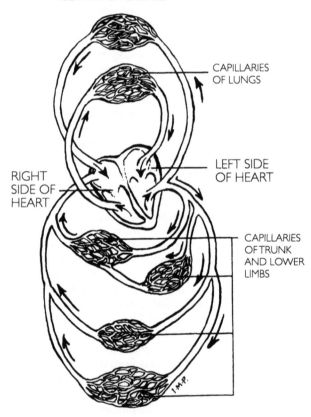

1.73 Diagrammatic representation of the circulation

contraction to push the blood around the circulation. Blood returning from the main part of the body enters the right atrium and passes from there to the right ventricle; from the right ventricle it is pumped to the lungs via the pulmonary artery and then around the capillaries of the lungs where it can get rid of the carbon dioxide and absorb oxygen. The blood going to the lungs is de-oxygenated and full of carbon dioxide; the blood leaving the lungs has lost most of its carbon dioxide and is loaded with oxygen. From the lungs, via the pulmonary veins, it enters the left side of the heart in the left atrium, passes from there to the left ventricle and is then pumped around the systemic circulation, as it is known. The circulation going through the lungs is known as the pulmonary circulation. Far greater effort is required from the heart to pump the blood round the very much larger systemic circulation, so the left side of the heart has thicker muscle than the right side. In its pumping action the atria first contract, filling the ventricles which expand to accept the blood. The ventricles thereafter immediately contract, giving the familiar heart sound of 'lub-dup', these being the contractions of the atria followed by the ventricles. There are valves at the entrance to each of the four chambers of the heart in order to prevent the blood being pushed back in the direction from which it came by the contraction of the heart muscle.

The rate of the heart beat is controlled by a special area of cardiac muscle known as the sinu-atrial node. This produces a rhythmic contraction and it acts completely in isolation. The wave of contraction of the muscles spreads through the atrial muscles causing a complete contraction of each atrium; it does not spread

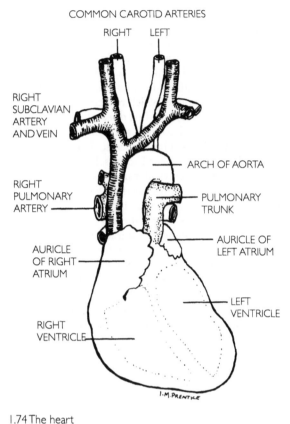

COMMON CAROTID ARTERIES

RIGHT   LEFT

RIGHT SUBCLAVIAN ARTERY AND VEIN

RIGHT PULMONARY ARTERY

AURICLE OF RIGHT ATRIUM

RIGHT VENTRICLE

ARCH OF AORTA

PULMONARY TRUNK

AURICLE OF LEFT ATRIUM

LEFT VENTRICLE

I.M.PRENTICE

1.74 The heart

LEFT COMMON CAROTID ARTERY

LEFT SUBCLAVIAN ARTERY

ARCH OF AORTA

TO LUNG

PULMONARY VEIN

SUPERIOR VENA CAVA

PULMONARY ARTERY TO LUNG

PULMONARY VEINS

RIGHT ATRIUM

LEFT VENTRICLE

I.M.PRENTICE

INFERIOR VENA CAVA

AORTA

1.75 Diagram of the circulation of the blood within the heart and great vessels directly to the ventricle but the impulses go via another special node of cardiac muscle, known as the atrio-ventricular node, and then down a special bundle called the atrio-ventricular bundle. This causes the stimulation of the ventricular muscle which begins at the apex of the ventricle, squeezing the blood up into the aorta and on into the arteries. Although the sinu-atrial node has its own completely independent rhythmic contraction this is modulated by stimuli from the sympathetic and para-sympathetic nerves. Para-sympathetic stimulation causes a slowing in the rate of the heart beat and sympathetic stimulation causes an acceleration of the heart rate.

From the left side of the heart the blood is squeezed into the major artery which is known as the aorta; this then sub-divides into the lesser arteries and arterioles and then the capillaries, as described earlier. As the ventricle contracts the pressure in the aorta rises and this pressure is, of course, transmitted down through the rest of the circulation. To accommodate the blood the aorta and arteries expand; when the ventricle ceases to contract, valves between the aorta and the ventricle close due to the pressure of the blood in the aorta. Following this the muscles in the walls of the arteries contract as a direct result of the stimulus of the stretching of the vessel walls. This then acts as a secondary pump, squeezing the blood further out to the periphery. It also has a secondary effect of maintaining a pressure in the arteries in between the ventricular contractions. If this did not occur the pressure would rise during the ventricular contractions and then drop away to nothing when the ventricles ceased to contract.

It is this combined mechanism which gives the two readings which are obtained when the blood pressure is taken with a sphygmomanometer during a medical examination. The top pressure of about 120 millimetres of mercury, which is the average in a healthy adult, is the pressure which is reached at its maximum when the ventricle is contracting. When the ventricles relax pressure falls to about 80 millimetres of mercury and it is the combination of elasticity and muscular contraction in the walls of the arteries which maintains the pressure from falling below this level at the time of the heart muscle relaxation. The wave of pressure passing down through the arterial tree is detected as a pulse at various sites in the body where an artery can be compressed between an examining finger and some firm, but deeper structure. The pulse rate corresponds to each contraction of the heart muscle, so in this way the heart rate can be measured very simply.

In the normal, undiseased heart the pulse rate, that is the heart contractions, are completely regular and only the rate changes. The rate is increased by the sympathetic nervous system or the release of adrenalin into the blood system and is a natural response to an increase in demand by the rest of the body for oxygenated blood. The increase in heart rate is particularly apparent on exercise but everyone has been equally aware of an increase in heart rate during periods of stress and nervousness. This latter increase is produced by sympathetic nervous stimulation. Irregularity of the pulse, which reflects irregularity of the heart beat, occurs only in a diseased heart, notably in those people who have suffered from heart attacks or coronary thrombosis. This can cause damage to the very special portions of cardiac muscle, the sinu-atrial node and the atrio-ventricular node and the conducting pathways, thus interfering with the normal stimulation of the cardiac muscle.

In normal, healthy people there is a variation in heart rate corresponding to inspiration and expiration during respiration. On inspiration the heart rate will increase slightly and on expiration it will decrease a little. It is possible to detect this very easily in oneself by breathing deeply and slowly with a finger on the pulse.

The circulation through the lungs via the pulmonary arteries and capillaries and back by the pulmonary veins is mechanically very similar to the systemic circulation through the aorta, arteries and major veins. However, the pressures within the pulmonary circulation are less than those on the systemic side.

In the systemic circulation the blood flows from the aorta, arteries and arterioles to the capillaries which form what is known as the capillary bed, a gigantic mesh-work of minute vessels where the actual exchange of oxygen, carbon dioxide, food and waste products occurs.

From the capillaries the blood passes into tiny veins or venules and from there into gradually larger veins, and so back via the vena cava to the right side of the heart. During the heart beat the pulse wave is lost in the capillary system. Therefore the pressure within the veins remains at a far more constant level. There are, however, three totally separate factors which affect the pressure within the veins; the first is gravity – in the standing person from the level of the heart downwards there is the height of the column of blood above the level at which it might be measured in any one particular vein, thus in the veins of the feet there is a column of blood about four feet high in a six-foot person. Quite a lot of pressure is therefore required to push this column of blood up towards the heart. This is aided by valves within the veins preventing the blood from flowing in the wrong direction along the veins. If the valves become incompetent and fail to hold the blood back the veins become very distended and it is this factor which produces what is known as varicose veins. Above the level of the heart there is of course negative pressure as the blood drains downhill from the head and neck towards the heart.

The second factor which aids the flow of blood along the veins is muscular contraction; many veins pass in between muscles in the limbs and trunk and as these muscles contract and tighten they will squeeze the blood along in one direction, i.e. towards the heart. This one-directional flow is brought about by the presence of the valves in the veins, as already mentioned, which only allow the blood to pass in one direction. This effect of the body muscles in aiding the circulation is sometimes referred to as the peripheral pump.

The third factor associated with the circulation is respiration: when inspiration takes place, that is breathing in, the contraction of the diaphragm and the contraction of the muscles between the ribs increases the size of the chest cavity, this produces a negative pressure within the chest cavity, sucking air into the lungs; at the same time this negative pressure will also affect the large veins within the chest producing a slight negative pressure within them, helping to draw the blood up from the peripheral circulation.

The Lymphatic System

While not strictly part of the cardio-vascular system the lymphatic system may be considered in this chapter as the lymph finally drains into the general circulation.

In the capillaries of the general circulation the walls are extremely thin so that some of the liquid portion of the blood can pass through. Once outside it forms tissue fluid, or interstitial fluid, lying between the cells in tissue spaces. Much of this passes back into the blood stream but the lymphatic system serves to drain any excess. It will also remove any particulate matter and large molecules, such as protein, which cannot pass directly into the blood because of their size. These particles or molecules are carried in the lymph. The lymphatic system starts as very fine capillaries which open directly into the tissue spaces so there are no walls for the tissue fluid and small particles to pass through. Once gathered into these capillaries the fluid is known as lymph. The lymph capillaries join together to form lymphatic vessels which, like veins, have valves, though they are far more numerous. The lymph vessels will join together and along their course will pass through lymph glands or nodes. These lymph nodes tend to become grouped together in various parts of the body notably the groins, axillae, inside the trunk along the base of the vessels coming from the alimentary tract and in the central part of the chest. These lymph nodes act as filters to prevent unwanted matter, such as bacteria, from gaining access to the blood stream. If they intercept a significant amount of infected material containing a large number of bacteria the lymph glands themselves can become painful, swollen and inflamed. This is particularly well shown in tonsilitis because the tonsils themselves are little masses of lymph gland tissue. After passing through the lymph nodes in the lymph circulation the lymph vessels converge and gradually produce larger lymph vessels which finally drain into the large veins before they reach the heart.

1.7 The Alimentary Canal and Digestion

The Alimentary Canal

This runs from the mouth as a continuous tube to the anus (Fig. 1.76). Food is taken into the mouth, where the particle size is broken down by chewing before the ball of food, or bolus, is swallowed. When this happens the back of the nasal cavity is closed by the soft palate. The roof of the mouth is made up of two portions, the front half being the hard palate which is fixed, and the back half being the soft palate, which is movable. This latter palate can be lifted up, closing the nasopharynx so that food cannot enter this area. At the same time the larynx, which lies at the beginning of the respiratory tubes or trachea, is pulled upwards and forwards and is closed by a fold of tissue known as the glottis. This prevents food entering the trachea. From the pharynx the bolus enters a tube known as the oesophagus which extends from the oro-pharynx (mouth and throat) down through the chest cavity and through a hole or hiatus in the diaphram to enter the stomach. The stomach acts mechanically as a large receptacle to contain the mass of food from a meal before it is passed on for further digestive processes, as well as initiating some of the chemical digestive processes. Following the stomach there is a short length of small bowel known as the duodenum. Leading into the duodenum is a duct (or tube) which is made up of two other ducts which have joined together just before entering the lumen of the duodenum. These are

a) the bile duct coming from the gall bladder and the liver to bring bile and bile salts, and

b) the pancreatic duct which brings digestive enzymes from the pancreas.

Following the duodenum there is the remainder of the small intestine comprising the jejunum and then the ileum. The latter leads into the caecum, which is the beginning of the large bowel and from which the appendix arises. The remainder of the large bowel is made up of the ascending, transverse and descending parts of the colon which lead into the rectum. The rectum is another reservoir, this time for the residue of the food which forms the faeces.

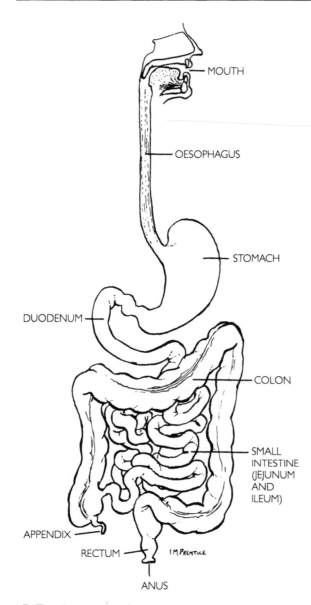

1.76 The alimentary canal

Digestion

Digestion commences in the mouth. The contents of
the alimentary tract are propelled along by waves of
muscular contraction known as peristalsis. This
peristaltic wave starts at the beginning of the
oesophagus and is not under voluntary control. If the
peristaltic waves become excessive as in an infection
such as gastro-enteritis, they are perceived as severe
spasms of pain or colic. At other times the peristaltic
wave is not normally felt.

During the mechanical breakdown of food by
chewing, saliva is mixed with the food. This helps to
lubricate the food bolus so that it can be swallowed

more easily and it also contains the first of the digestive
enzymes – ptyalin. Ptyalin is the only digestive enzyme
acting in the mouth and its role is to start the breakdown of starch, although its effect is not very significant in the overall process of starch digestion. If some
starchy food such as bread or potato is chewed and
moved around the mouth for a short period the breakdown of starch can be detected by the slight sweetening
of the chewed material as the starch is changed to
simple sugars. An enzyme is a complex chemical and
acts as a biochemical catalyst. Digestive processes are
brought about by various enzymes in order to break
down the large complex food molecules into much
simpler molecules which can be absorbed through the
wall of the digestive tract and pass via the blood stream
to the liver. Various enzymes enter the alimentary tract
at different levels.

Each enzyme is very specific in its action and can
only initiate or control one chemical process. Individual
enzymes can only act in a very narrow range of pH
(the measure of acidity or alkalinity). They all act
optimally at body temperature and are destroyed by
heat, thus cooked foods have all the enzymes that they
may contain destroyed by the cooking. Food substances
all have to be absorbed through the wall of the
alimentary tract in order to give any benefit and large
complex molecules cannot pass through. Without the
necessary enzyme this molecular breakdown cannot
occur. For example, human beings, although omni-
vorous (eating flesh and vegetables), have no enzyme to
break down cellulose which as a result passes straight
through the bowel as roughage. Therefore humans
could not live off grass, whereas herbivores do produce
such an enzyme and can break down cellulose to
produce usable carbohydrates.

In the stomach the food is temporarily stored and at
the same time mixes with further secretions from the
wall of the stomach. Part of the secretion is acid in
order to adjust the pH of the contents and allow the
gastric enzymes which are also secreted to work at the
correct degree of acidity. There is little absorption of
food substances through the stomach wall apart from
possibly some simple sugars and alcohol. Food
substances are passed in small quantities at a time from
the stomach into the duodenum. Separating these two
areas is a muscular valve or sphincter which opens
periodically in order to allow further food to pass into
the duodenum from the stomach.

In the duodenum further enzymes are introduced to
the food. Intestinal juice containing a variety of
enzymes is produced by the glands in the duodenal
wall. Bile which is produced in the liver enters via the
combined biliary and pancreatic ducts. The bile
contains bile salts and bile pigment. Bile salts are
concerned with the emulsification of fats and they

assist in the absorption of the breakdown products of the fat, particularly fatty acids. The bile pigments are waste materials which have been produced by the liver, largely from the breakdown of red blood cells. Their injection into the small bowel at the duodenum is one of the methods by which they are removed from the body. Through the same combined opening in the duodenal wall, pancreatic juice is introduced into the duodenum. This contains enzymes which help further with the digestion of fat and enzymes which aid in the breakdown of sugar and proteins.

The function of the pancreas does not cease with the enzymes which are introduced into the bowel; within the substance of the pancreas are what is known as endocrine glands. These are glands which produce substances which are secreted directly into the blood stream. In the pancreas the endocrine glands are present in what is known as the Islets of Langerhans. These islets produce two hormones, insulin and glucagon. The insulin lowers the level of sugar in the blood and helps the body cells to store it as glycogen. Glucagon raises the level of sugar in blood by stimulating the breakdown of glycogen back into simple sugars. It is the lack of insulin due to a fault in the pancreas, which causes diabetes mellitus.

In its passage through the rest of the small bowel, enzymes continue to act on the food products, gradually breaking them down. When this breakdown has progressed sufficiently the nutrients are slowly absorbed into the intestinal wall. Most of this absorption has taken place by the time the food has reached the caecum and most of what remains then are waste products in a semi-liquid state. The main function of the large bowel is the absorption of water from the food residues in order to prevent too much being lost from the body. This also reduces the bulk of the waste matter to a solid form so it takes up less space. Only a very small amount of absorption of remaining nutrients from the digested food takes place through the large intestine walls. The amount absorbed is relatively insignificant.

Functions of the Liver

The liver is extremely complex and has many functions which can be considered under three main headings.

SECRETORY

Bile is produced by the liver and contains bile pigments and bile salts. The bile pigments are largely produced by the breakdown of aged red blood cells. They enter the duodenum and are then largely removed from the body in the faeces, but a small quantity is re-absorbed through the wall of the small intestine and enters the general blood circulation from which it is removed in

the kidneys and excreted in the urine. Bile pigments are largely responsible for the yellow colour of the urine.

The bile salts also reach the duodenum along the bile duct and their role is to emulsify fats to aid further breakdown and absorption. Once bile has been formed in the liver, most of it is concentrated and stored temporarily in the gall bladder which is a pouch formed as an off-shoot of the bile duct. It is in the gall bladder that stones can form. These may comprise an excess of bile pigments or they may be crystaline deposits of bile salts.

Heparin is also produced by the liver but passes directly into the blood stream. Its function is to help prevent clotting of blood as it passes round in the normal circulation of the body.

STORAGE

a) Glycogen is stored in the liver. It is formed from glucose and is the chemical form in which it is stored. It can be made extremely quickly and broken down to glucose again equally rapidly when required. Glycogen is also stored in the muscles. When glucose is required as a result of exercise or fasting (both of which will produce a fall in the blood-sugar level) glucose is very rapidly formed by the re-conversion of glycogen. After a meal, glucose which is produced from the digestion of carbohydrate and is not immediately required for metabolism is stored as glycogen. This replenishes the glycogen stores which may have become depleted between meals.

b) The liver is a storage site for vitamins A, the B complex and D. Originally the vitamins are absorbed from the food as they cannot be manufactured in the human body. From the storage depots in the liver the vitamins can be released as and when required.

c) Iron is stored following the breakdown of old red blood corpuscles; it is then released for the synthesis of haemoglobin which is required for new red corpuscles.

METABOLIC

The liver is responsible for the utilisation of proteins, fats and carbohydrates for the general nutrition of the body. These substances, which are mainly in a very complex form when they are taken as food, have to be broken down into far simpler substances to make them suitable for utilisation by the body. Following the breakdown of proteins into amino acids which are very much simpler chemical chains, the liver will then synthesise new proteins as and when required for the various physiological functions of the body. Although the human liver can also synthesise many of the necessary amino acids from basic simple molecules, there are certain amino acids which it cannot produce. These are known as 'essential amino acids'. They must be present in the diet either as amino acids or as more complex protein forms, otherwise the body will come deficient in them and will not function.

If too much glucose is present and the glycogen stores are full, the excess carbohydrate is converted into fat by the liver and is then stored elsewhere in the body. Most poisonous substances which are taken with the food are detoxicated by the liver. Detoxication means that the liver changes the chemical structure of these substances so that they are no longer poisonous. Following that they may be passed back into the blood stream to be removed by the kidneys or they may be excreted in the bile and through the bowel. In addition there are some potentially poisonous substances which are produced as a result of normal protein metabolism in the body. For example, ammonia is immediately converted into urea by the liver. The urea then passes into the circulation and is excreted by the kidneys in the urine. During the process of detoxication the liver cells can be damaged by various poisonous substances which have been ingested. Although new cells can be produced sometimes this does not always take place and the dead liver cells are replaced by fibrous tissue, thus gradually destroying the functional capabilities of the liver and leading to liver failure. Probably the commonest substance which can cause these problems in the liver is an excess intake of alcohol. Various drugs and some industrial chemicals also cause liver damage.

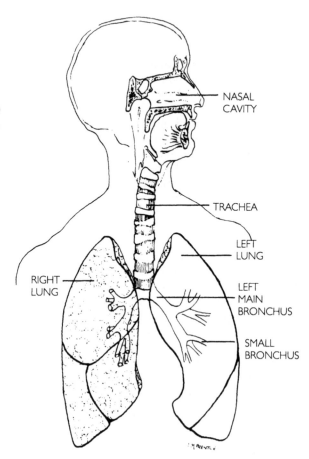

1.77 The respiratory passages

1.8 The Respiratory System

Breathing

Breathing ensures an adequate intake of oxygen for the oxidative processes of the body, and also ensures the removal of sufficient carbon dioxide to maintain a constant acid/alkali concentration in the blood (the acid/base balance). In the lungs oxygen is extracted from inspired air and quickly absorbed by red blood cells to be transported around the body. Also in the lungs carbon dioxide leaves the circulatory system to re-enter the lungs and is removed on expiration. This is called gaseous exchange. Air is drawn in through the nose where it is warmed and filtered by small hairs in the nostrils (Fig. 1.77).

The lungs are two large, thin-walled elastic organs located in the thorax. They can be expanded or compressed by movements of the thorax in such a way that air is repeatedly drawn in and expelled. We breathe through the mouth or nose, into the pharynx and then inspired air passes into the trachea or windpipe. From there the oxygen-rich air passes into the lungs via the two bronchi.

These airways branch into smaller and smaller passages called bronchioles, ending in millions of tiny bubble like sacs called alveoli. These are thin-walled sacs lying in contact with the capillary network of the circulatory system. Across the thin alveolar and capillary walls, oxygen and carbon dioxide pass (Fig. 1.78).

The lungs are enclosed in the thoracic cavity and therefore changes in the shape and size of the thorax results in changes in air pressure within the lungs. The respiratory muscles are responsible for changes in the shape of the thoracic cavity that cause air movement involved in breathing. In inspiration the thorax enlarges with inspiratory muscles controlling the ribs and the diaphragm descends. The lungs expand with the thorax, increasing their volume and reducing pressure within them. Air is then drawn in to balance the pressure.

The lungs are enclosed in a double-walled sac called the pleura. The parietal pleura lines the walls of the thoracic cavity and the visceral pleura covers the lungs.

1.79 Rib movement

1.78 Alveolus in lung. This shows the terminal part of the air passage (the alveolus) with the mass of capillaries in close proximity which allows the interchange of gases between the air in the alveoli and the blood in the capillaries

The intrapleural space lies between the two pleural membranes. It contains a very small amount of fluid which makes both portions of the pleura moist and slippery and able to glide easily against each other as the lungs expand and deflate with each breath.

The two lungs are shaped like cones. The apex of each reaches just above the clavicles and the bases lie on the diaphragm at the level of the 6th rib at the front and 8th at the side. The lungs are divided into lobes. The right has three lobes – upper, middle and lower divided by fissures. Each lobe is independently supplied by a bronchus or airway. Each lobe is further sub-divided into segments, supplied by a segmental bronchus. The left lung has two lobes – upper and lower. Thus if a lobe or segment of a lobe is incapacitated, remaining lobes or segments compensate to continue oxygen supply.

The thorax is made up of twelve ribs which articulate with the thoracic spine posteriorly and the sternum anteriorly. At the spine the ribs form synovial joints with the bodies of the thoracic vertebrae (costovertebral joints). Ribs 2–9 form a demifacet with the body of the vertebra above and below. In addition the tubercle of the rib articulates with the transverse process of the lower vertebra (costotransverse joint). Ribs 1, 10, 11 and 12 each articulate with one vertebra at the costovertebral joint and 11 and 12 have no costotransverse joint.

Anteriorly the ribs are formed of cartilage which gives them flexibility for the movements of respiration and shock absorption. Ribs 1–7 are termed true ribs and articulate with the sternum at gliding synovial joints (costosternal joints). Ribs 8–10 articulate with the costal cartilage of the seventh rib, and ribs 11 and 12 are floating with no anterior attachment.

Both lungs and chest wall contain elastic elements in their structure. The elastic tissue of the lungs tends towards shrinking down, while the rib cage tends towards the opposite direction, providing an opposing force.

Rib Movements

The ribs slope downwards from their attachment to the vertebral column, and their costal cartilages ascend to reach the sternum. The lowest point on the rib is laterally placed while the anterior ends of the ribs are lower than the posterior ends. The 1st and 2nd ribs move only slightly while ribs 3–6, when elevated, can move in two ways. The ribs can be elevated anteriorly lifting the costal cartilages and with them the sternum. This is called the 'pump handle action' – as in the way a pump functions. This increases the front to back dimensions of the rib cage (Fig. 1.79). The second pattern of rib movement is when the rib pivots around its anterior and posterior ends and the shaft elevates, increasing the transverse diameter of the thorax. This is called the 'bucket handle action'. Ribs 7–10 move more in a bucket handle action and also with an opening out 'caliper' action which considerably expands the thorax and lower lung capacity. The two floating ribs 11 and 12 are capable of slight movements in all directions, but when the ribs above are elevated, 11 and 12, which have attachments for the diaphragm, are depressed and stabilised by quadratus lumborum.

Muscles of Breathing

The diaphragm is the main muscle of breathing. It is dome-shaped, lying within the thorax, with circular attachments from the lower six ribs, the xiphoid process of the sternum and the bodies of the upper two lumbar vertebrae. From here radiating muscle fibres ascend to a flat central tendon. The diaphragm divides the thoracic and abdominal cavities, lying under the lungs and over the liver, spleen, kidneys and stomach. When the muscle fibres contract, as in inspiration, the central tendon descends and the dome flattens. The vertical dimension of the thorax therefore increases compressing the abdominal organs. When the diaphragm becomes stationary over the liver, it continues to contract elevating the lower ribs which expands the transverse dimension of the thorax.

It is the main muscle working in quiet breathing. When we are asleep breathing continues due to neural and chemical control.

The intercostal muscles lie between the ribs filling the intercostal spaces. The most superficial are the external intercostals whose fibres pass downwards and forwards from the lower border of one rib to the upper border of the one below (similar to the external oblique muscle). Deep to these lie the internal intercostals muscles. These lie at 90° to the external intercostals and run downwards and backwards. These two muscles interact in inspiration when the lower rib is pulled upwards toward the next as in a bucket handle action. Expiration is largely passive elastic recoil of the lungs, but in forced expiration, they come into play.

Patterns of Breathing

While in sport efficient breathing patterns are necessary, the effort is primarily to inspire the highest volume of air and use the highest percentage of oxygen. Stamina rises and the cardiovascular system functions at its best. In dance the same efficient physiological function is required but aesthetically the effort in difficult moves should not show. The most challenging moves must look effortless and the flow of movement undisturbed.

In exercise, and particularly dance, the body's demand for oxygen rises, but as movements become more challenging so does the need for stability and control of the spine and shoulder girdle. Dance, at its most strenuous, demands an increase in both rate and depth of breathing, but should still look effortless and smooth. The abdominal corset still needs to be engaged to control posture and provide a stable pelvis from which the lower limbs can operate. Therefore the pattern of breathing in the dancer needs to be carefully observed and anything affecting it corrected if necessary.

Good technique requires the relationship of the shoulder girdle, spine and pelvis to be under control at all times, whether it be a renversé or battement tendu.

Tension carried in the shoulders and neck will affect breathing and is often a result of incorrect spinal posture with rib movement, lungs and breathing adversely affected. The tendency is often to breathe too high in the lungs with a shallower less efficient pattern. If a child is anxious or attempting too difficult a step, the shoulders tense up, breathing is shallow, the weight goes back and movement becomes less co-ordinated.

LATERAL OR COSTAL BREATHING

Good static posture ensures that the spinal curves are balanced (see Stance, p. 56). The shoulder girdle is stabilised over a well-aligned pelvis. The ribs are free to move upwards and outwards sideways with the abdominal muscles activated, especially the transversus abdominus. The latissimus dorsi supports the back and anchors the shoulder girdle. The ribs are able to move in a bucket handle action, the diaphragm can function well, the trunk is stable and the shoulder girdle is free. The larger, lower lobes can be well used and the dancer can 'breathe into her back and sides'. The intercostal muscles can be used efficiently. If good posture is established from the beginning, breathing patterns and control of more complex movements develops naturally.

APICAL BREATHING

This type of upper lung breathing is less efficient. As mentioned above this is often a result of incorrect posture. Over-turning out the feet pushes the weight back, destabilises the posture and tension develops in the neck. Misunderstanding the command 'pull up!' can do the same. The rib cage rises at the front, the thoracic spine extends losing its natural curve and the pump handle movement of the ribs takes over. Returning to the apprehensive child who takes tension in the neck, the importance of teaching in a positive, supportive and nurturing atmosphere cannot be more emphasised. If this is not carried out correctly, the accessory muscles of breathing come in to 'lift' the shoulders in order to fill the lungs. The sterno-cleidomastoid, scalenes and upper trapezius muscles of the neck come in to lift the clavicles and therefore sternum. The pectoral muscles tense and the deeper muscles around the thoracic spine tighten, further inhibiting movement in the costovertebral and costotransverse joints of the ribs.

If the muscles above the scapula are tense, the port de bras and use of the head is restricted. The audience sees facial, neck and arm tension rather than flowing, expressive arms and epaulement. In challenging allegro all breathing patterns will be employed but if stamina is less than it should be, breathing becomes laboured earlier and movement is compromised.

In correcting posture especially the rib cage, care must be taken not to simply drop the rib cage down at the front. The spine must be repositioned and the weight brought forwards. The ribs must be shown how to expand laterally, with the shoulders dropping and the core activated. To simply ask for the ribs to be put down or to correct from the front leaves the child unable to breathe properly, confused and no better off.

ABDOMINAL BREATHING

This pattern of breathing facilitates good expansion of the lower lobes of the lungs. However, relaxation of the abdominal muscles is necessary so that the diaphragm descends and the abdomen distends and the ribs are also free to expand. This is an efficient way to fill the lungs and is effectively used by singers who can plant themselves in a stable position before using breath and lung control to achieve sustained notes or complex phrasing. It is not so practical for dancers who require stamina and control of movement.

Exhalation is firstly an elastic recoil of the lung tissue and the diaphragm rises. In more energetic breathing the lungs must expel carbon-dioxide-rich air in order to take on more oxygen. The intercostals muscles and the abdominal muscles come in more forcefully.

Exploring the use of the lungs makes a dancer appreciate the importance of volume, depth, rhythm and stamina. In yoga the use of breath is intrinsic to the exercise and the psychological as well as physical benefit of yoga can be a revelation to the more experienced dancer.

For further reading: Calais-Germain, B., *Anatomy of Breathing*. Seattle: Eastland Press, 2006.

Respiration

Respiration may be considered in two parts:
1. external respiration;
2. internal or tissue respiration.

EXTERNAL RESPIRATION

External respiration takes place in the lungs. Air which contains the oxygen required for tissue metabolism is carried to the lungs through the respiratory passages, ending up in the alveoli (Fig. 1.78). The walls of the alveoli have a large number of capillaries containing blood and the separation between the blood stream and the air in the alveoli is about two cells thick. At this point oxygen passes from the alveoli into the deoxygenated blood which is being brought from the right side of the heart. At the same time the carbon dioxide from the blood passes in the opposite direction from the blood stream through into the alveoli. The expired air therefore contains a decreased amount of oxygen and an increased amount of carbon dioxide compared with the inspired air.

INTERNAL OR TISSUE RESPIRATION

Internal or tissue respiration takes place in every living cell of the body. It is the mechanism which provides the energy which is required for all bodily activity. The commonest energy-producing material to be oxidised is carbohydrate in the form of glucose. The glucose combines with oxygen to give carbon dioxide, water and energy. This reaction is aided by an enzyme. Substances other than the carbohydrates may also be oxidised. These require different enzymes as all enzymes are extremely specific in their action. If fat is oxidised, rather more oxygen is required than if carbohydrate is oxidised.

Transport of Oxygen and Carbon Dioxide

In the alveoli in the lungs the oxygen in the air becomes dissolved in a thin film of moisture on the cell walls. It then passes by diffusion through the cells into the blood plasma. Most of the oxygen which diffuses through combines with the haemoglobin in the blood to form oxyhaemoglobin with a very small amount remaining dissolved in the blood plasma. The presence of the haemoglobin allows about seventy times as much oxygen to be carried around the blood stream as oxyhaemoglobin than would take place by a simple solution of oxygen in the blood plasma. At the cells where the oxygen is utilised carbon dioxide is produced. This carbon dioxide dissolves to form carbonic acid, which is carried mainly as bicarbonate in the plasma. There is also a small amount of dissolved carbonic acid and some of the carbon dioxide will combine with the haemoglobin once the oxygen has been displaced in order to produce carbaminohaemoglobin.

When the deoxygenated blood returns to the lungs the carbaminohaemoglobin breaks down to liberate carbonic acid. Some of the bicarbonate will also break down to liberate further carbonic acid which diffuses across the cell membrane into the alveoli of the lungs and hence to the outside air.

Control of Respiration

The control of the rate of respiration is largely reflex although it can be modified to a certain extent voluntarily. The main controlling factor is the acidity of the blood as determined by the level of carbonic acid. The greater the amount of carbon dioxide being produced in the tissues, the higher the level of blood carbonic acid and the more acid the blood. This alteration in acidity is detected by the respiratory control centres and the depth and rate of inspiration and expiration will be increased to allow the extra carbon dioxide to be removed through the lungs. A decrease in the oxygen level of the blood will also stimulate reflex centres and cause an increase in rate of depth of respiration, but a fall in oxygen level is much less of a stimulus than an increase in carbon dioxide in the form of carbonic acid. By far the most important factor is the acidity as reflected in pH level of the blood.

Incidentally, there are two forms of oxide of carbon. Carbon monoxide is produced by exhaust gases and when carboniferous fuels are incompletely oxidised. Carbon monoxide is extremely poisonous because it combines with the haemoglobin in the blood, preventing the combination of oxygen, and thus kills by depriving the tissues of the oxygen they require. Carbon dioxide is formed when carboniferous fuels (which of course includes glucose and other foods) are completely oxidised.

It is not itself poisonous as it is easily displaced by oxygen at the haemoglobin molecule. However, inhalation of very high levels of carbon dioxide will produce very rapid and severe changes in the pH of the blood. This increase in acidity due to the increase in carbonic acid totally upsets the acid base balance in the body and death may follow very rapidly.

Smoking cigarettes produces a significant amount of carbon monoxide. This combines as described with the haemoglobin, interfering with oxygen transport. Therefore the smoker will be less able than the non-smoker to provide the muscles with the necessary increase in oxygen demanded by any athletic activity, including dancing. As a result performance will be a little less good than a non-smoker's would be.

1.9 The Excretory System

The excretory system is made up of two kidneys, two ureters, a bladder and an urethra (Fig. 1.80). From each kidney there is a ureter which goes down to the urinary bladder, from which the urethra carries the urine to the outside. The kidneys lie within the upper part of the abdominal cavity behind the liver and stomach. However, they are surrounded by fat and are not free-floating within the abdominal cavity. The ureters run down the posterior abdominal wall to enter the bladder which lies within the pelvis. The actual excretory functions only take place in the kidneys. The ureters, bladder and urethra are there to transport and store the urine and allow intermittent discharge externally. Without the storage capacity of the bladder there would be a constant drip of urine occurring.

Blood is carried to each kidney by a large renal artery and is returned from the kidney by a renal vein on each side. Within the substance of the kidney the arteries divide to form smaller vessels. The point where

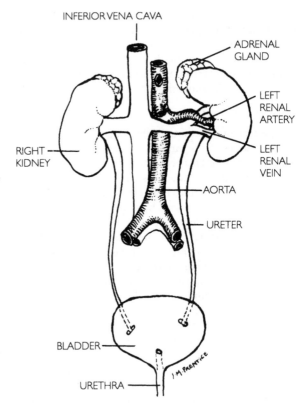

1.80 The execretory system

excretory activity occurs is known as the glomerulus (Fig. 1.81). This is a knot of capillaries. The vessel supplying this knot is wider in diameter than the vessel carrying the blood away. As a result the blood within the glomerulus is under increased pressure. At this point some of the fluid component of the blood is filtered through the cells walls into a collection portion known as Bowman's capsule. The cell membranes between the blood stream and Bowman's capsule are such that the blood corpuscles and the blood proteins

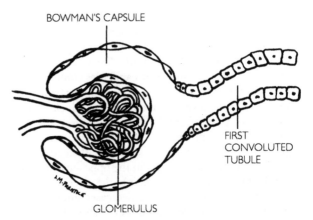

1.81 A glomerulus and Bowman's capsule

are unable to pass through and so remain within the blood. The fluid which passes through to Bowman's capsule is made up of water with small amounts of various salts and nitrogenous waste products produced by the breakdown of proteins. This latter is largely in the form of urea. At this point there is also some sugar, water-soluble vitamins and various other substances that are normally present in the blood stream.

The liquid passes from Bowman's capsule to the first convoluted tubule where all the sugar, vitamins and some of the other substances and some water are absorbed again (Fig. 1.82). From there it passes through the Loop of Henle where further water is absorbed. It is at this point that the amount of water which is absorbed will vary in order to adjust the osmotic pressure of the blood correctly. Following the Loop of Henle is the second convoluted tubule where the pH is adjusted. Urine is normally on the slightly acid side. Following the second convoluted tubule is the collecting duct. This will join with other collecting ducts from other convoluted tubules. Finally all joining together they form the pelvis of the kidney, leading into the upper end of the ureter at the point where it leaves the kidney. The

kidneys are extremely efficient at stabilising the water and electrolyte balance in the body, which is only able to tolerate very small variations from the normal ratio between the various electrolytes and the water. The control is via hormones. The pituitary gland produces a hormone which encourages water retention while the hormones of the adrenal cortex encourage the retention of sodium and an increased loss of potassium. If a great deal of fluid is taken by mouth the urine increases in quantity and becomes very dilute. This is achieved by a decrease in the absorption of water from the Loop of Henle. However, in hot climates when there is a considerable amount of perspiration the urine output decreases in quantity and becomes very much more concentrated. The sensation of thirst is brought about by a very small increase in the osmotic pressure of the blood affecting certain cells in the brain.

The kidneys have an additional function inasmuch as they produce two hormones, renin and erythropoietin. Renin affects the maintenance of blood pressure. If pressure within the renal artery decreases then some quantities of renin are released in order to stimulate an increase in the blood pressure. Should the blood pressure fall below a certain level, as may occur in states of surgical shock where there has been a considerable loss of blood, then filtration from the glomerulus into Bowman's capsule ceases and the person enters a state of renal failure. Unless this is corrected, death will follow because of the steady increase in the nitrogenous waste products and the total upset of the salt and water balance of the body.

The second hormone, erythropoietin, helps to control the production of red blood cells.

1.10 The Endrocrine System

The endocrine system comprises a number of endocrine organs. These are glands which pass their secretions, known as hormones, directly into the blood stream. The glands have no ducts in which to collect the secretions, unlike those glands which lie in the walls of the alimentary tract. A hormone is a compound formed within the gland. It is carried from the gland via the blood and its action is to influence the activity of another organ or organs. The two regulating systems of the body, i.e. the nervous system and the endocrine system, are very closely linked. In some instances the production of hormones is controlled directly by nervous impulses. The main function of the endocrine system as a whole is to maintain homeostasis, i.e. the constancy of the internal environment of the body. The mode of action of hormones is biochemically extremely complicated and outside the scope of this book.

1.82 Diagram of a renal tubule

The actual endocrine glands are: the pituitary gland, which has anterior and posterior lobes with separate functions and which lies in the base of the skull, closely associated with the brain; the thyroid and parathyroid glands, which are anatomically intimately associated, lying in the front of the lower part of the neck; the adrenal glands, composing the cortex and medulla, with separate functions and lying like little caps on the superior poles of each kidney. Apart from these well localised glands there are scattered areas of cells in various other organs, in particular the so-called Islets of Langerhans in the pancreas, the interstitial cells in the testes and the follicular cells in the ovaries. There are also some cells in the walls of the stomach and small intestine. In pregnancy some cells of the placenta can have a temporary endocrine effect.

The anterior lobe of the pituitary gland is sometimes said to be the conductor of the endocrine orchestra. This lobe is regulated by hormones produced in the hypothalamus of the brain. The hormones secreted by the anterior lobe of the pituitary then in their turn regulate the activities of the various other endocrine organs. Normally it is the concentration of hormones in the blood circulation which will regulate the stimulation or otherwise of the further production of hormone. In other words, if the hormone level is high, this will tend to suppress the stimulatory effects which would encourage the production of further hormone (Fig. 1.83). Conversely, if the level of hormone in the blood stream falls to a low level, this will then stimulate the activity of the endocrine glands to produce more hormone. In most hormones their life in the blood stream is relatively short, sometimes only a few minutes, before being destroyed. This enables the equilibrium to be very accurately and constantly adjusted. The hormones in the blood stream are either de-activated by the liver or excreted through the kidney.

The endocrine glands themselves can be the subject of disease and this may result in either the over-production or under-production of the relevant hormone. Probably the common condition that is seen and with which most people will at least be acquainted, is that of thyrotoxicosis, when the thyroid gland produces an excess of hormone, one of the side effects of which is to produce the staring, pop-eyed appearance of a patient who is thyrotoxic. Additionally, the patient tends to be very overactive, lose weight, and feel hot and sweat freely. In general the over-action or under-action of an endocrine gland also produces changes in the production of hormones from other endocrine organs due to the close relationship that there is between one endocrine gland and another. This means that when there is, for instance, an over-production of hormone by a diseased gland, the clinical picture becomes complicated because of the other endocrine effects which also become manifest, even though the other endocrine glands themselves are not the subject of disease.

The symptoms which are caused by the alteration in hormone level from the diseased gland are known as primary symptoms. Secondary symptoms are those which are produced by the variation in hormone level at the other endocrine glands which are not themselves the seat of the disease. It is this widespread upset in the endrocrine pattern produced by an excess or lack of hormone that makes the administration of steroid drugs such as cortisone a potentially hazardous process and not a treatment that should be undertaken lightly and without proper consideration of the potential and grave side effects. It must be emphasised that this only applies when cortisone is given by mouth. The steroid which is used for injection to control local effects during the course of treatment of various local injuries or inflammations does not have these side effects. This

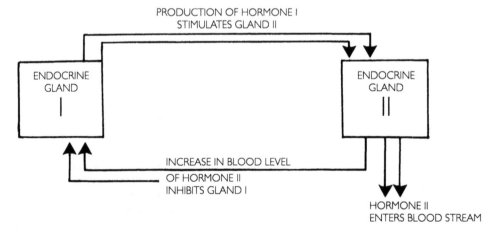

1.83 Diagrammatic representation of the interaction of hormones between two endocrine glands

preparation of the steroid (usually hydrocortisone acetate) is not absorbed generally into the circulation as it is a suspension and remains where it has been placed. It does, however, have its own complications which are of a local nature and these will be considered later in the section on injury and the treatment of injuries (see **Section 2.5** Medical and Surgical Treatments, p. 106).

Actions of the Endocrine Glands

These will be dealt with very briefly as any great detail would be irrelevant to the probable requirements of the reader.

THE PITUITARY GLAND

The anterior pituitary gland produces six hormones. The growth hormone is secreted in greatest quantity during childhood but there is some secretion during the rest of adult life in order to maintain normal body structure and function. Occasionally it is administered clinically in a child who is very small and under-developed. However, like the use of any other hormone, its administration is fraught with undesirable side effects and dangers and its use should not be undertaken lightly.

The thyrotrophic hormone stimulates the thyroid, helping to control the level of thyroxin which is produced by the thyroid gland. The adrenocortico-trophic hormone stimulates the cortex of the adrenal gland to produce its hormones. These hormones from the adrenal cortex are associated with the regulation of carbohydrate metabolism and, less importantly, make sex hormone production.

The follicular stimulating hormone, the luteinizing hormone and prolactin all have activities on the gonads (ovaries and testes), are responsible for the maturation of the ova and spermatozoa, and are associated in part with the development and regulation of menstruation and the post-pregnancy regulation of milk production.

The regulation of the production of anterior pituitary hormones is through the hypothalamus in the brain, which produces stimulating or inhibiting hormones acting on the anterior pituitary. The regulation is also controlled by the level of hormone produced by the other endocrine glands on which the anterior pituitary itself has an effect.

There are two hormones from the posterior pituitary. The most important hormone produced is vasopressin, the chief action of which is as an anti-diuretic hormone. In other words, it acts on the kidney, increasing the amount of water which is absorbed from the collecting tubules, thus preventing excessive water loss from the body. Additionally, it has a very minor effect on the maintenance of arterial blood pressure by causing contraction of the smooth muscle in the blood vessel walls. This latter effect was the first one discovered by researchers, hence the name given to the hormone. The other hormone which is produced by the posterior pituitary, oxytocin, only has an effect in the female during childbirth and lactation. Like the anterior pituitary, the posterior pituitary secretions are controlled by the hypothalamus in the brain.

THE THYROID GLAND

The thyroid gland produces thyroxin and an associated hormone, both of which stimulate cell metabolism. Additionally, the gland produces calcitonin (thyro-calcitonin), which prevents the transfer of calcium from the bones to the blood stream. It thus brings about a lowering of calcium in the blood stream as it still allows the transfer of calcium from the blood plasma into the bones. The control of production of the hormones from the thyroid is by the anterior pituitary.

There are four parathyroid glands, which lie closely applied to the back of the thyroid gland. They produce a parathyroid hormone which is responsible for an increase in the concentration of calcium in the blood. The action is by increasing the absorption of calcium from the urine while still in the kidneys. It increases the breakdown of calcium in the bone, thus pushing it into the circulation, and it also increases the absorption of calcium from the intestine in the presence of adequate quantities of vitamin D.

THE ADRENAL GLANDS

The adrenal glands consist of the cortex and the medulla. The cortex produces hormones which regulate the electrolyte and water balance in the body, sexual function and carbohydrate metabolism. The adrenal medulla produces two forms of adrenalin. The effect of adrenalin is to increase the rate of the heart and increase the capacity of the heart to push the blood through the circulation and therefore raises the blood pressure. It also constricts the blood vessels supplying all the alimentary tract and constricts the blood vessels of the skin. This is the reason why people go pale with fright or in other situations of stress, caused by blood being diverted to the heart and skeletal muscles so as to deal with the emergency which may have arisen. It also has a general arousal function so as to make the person more alert. It is sometimes referred to as the fight or flight hormone because in more primitive conditions it was to prepare someone to either fight the attacker or run away. Under present day conditions, it is the hormone which produces the feelings of apprehension, increased pulse rate and butterflies in the stomach before examinations, performances or times of modern stress. The action of the adrenal medulla is stimulated by nerve impulses through the sympathetic system.

The testes and ovaries are responsible for the production of sex hormones, testosterone in the male and oestrogen and progesterone in the female. At puberty the levels increase greatly and the balance alters. This produces the secondary sex characteristics, the general maturation of the body and the onset of menstruation in the female. In particular, after the onset of puberty and maturity it becomes difficult and probably impossible to stretch fibrous tissue such as there is in the ligaments and capsules.

The Islets of Langerhans in the pancreas produce two hormones, insulin and glucagon. These two hormones are responsible for regulating the transport of glucose and its storage by changing it into glycogen and also the breakdown of glycogen to produce glucose when required (see **Section 1.7** Digestion, p. 47). It is the lack of production of insulin which produces the well-known condition of diabetes mellitus.

1.11 Functional Anatomy Relevant to Ballet

The overall use of the muscles is directed at attaining correct stance and weight placement. To this end the muscles can be considered in groups rather than as individuals. Correct use of these various groups starts at the head and shoulder girdle and encompasses all the groups down through the trunk and legs to the feet. It is only when all groups are *working correctly and in balance with each other* that correct stance and weight placement will be obtained and the dancer will be completely stable in all the many and varied positions required during the execution of ballet technique.

Stance (Fig. 1.84)

Trunk stabilisation is achieved by the spine extensors, i.e. the long back muscles assisted by the short muscles between the individual vertebrae, and the trunk flexors which are made up largely of the abdominal muscles. The trunk has to be balanced on the lower limbs. This is achieved by the balance between the hip extensors (the gluteals) and the hip flexors, which between them control the tilting of the pelvis.

The knees in many people are relaxed when standing still and stabilisation is achieved by the ligaments alone. However, in most dancers there is usually some degree of hyperextension of the knees (swayback knees) which varies from mild to very marked and in these instances the knee has to be stabilised in neutral by contractions occurring in the quadriceps and hamstring muscles. Of course, it is perfectly possible for a person even with very marked

1.84 The main muscle groups controlling posture when standing. A and B From the side. C and D From the front

swayback knees to allow them to drop into hyper-extension and stand thus, which unfortunately one frequently sees happening in dancers. However, this position in dance pushes the weight much too far back and leads to technical faults and injuries. The rectus femoris muscle, which is part of the quadriceps complex, and all the hamstring muscles, cross in front of and behind the hip joint respectively so they also play a role in stabilising the pelvis in relation to the thighs.

Below the knee, stability depends upon a constant interaction between the calf muscles which plantarflex the foot (i.e. a movement in the direction of pointing the foot) and the muscles in the front of the leg which dorsiflex the foot. In the foot itself the intrinsic muscles are maintaining the longitudinal and transverse arches as well as the general foot posture. Note also that the superficial calf muscle – the gastrocnemius – crosses behind the knee, taking its origin from the back of the lower end of the femur, so it also plays a part in knee posture.

As will be seen when standing correctly on one foot, the line of the centre of gravity is moved sideways so it falls through the supporting foot (Fig. 1.85).

Note that the trunk and pelvis do not alter. The hip on the supporting leg is adducted and stability is achieved by the interaction between the adductors and the abductors (gluteus medius, gluteus minimus and tensor fasciae latae. Gluteus maximus is a hip extensor).

Unfortunately and only too often the adjustment of the line of centre of gravity is made totally incorrectly and the subsequent rather bizarre posture remains uncorrected (Fig. 1.86).

In the turn-out position the stance remains basically the same but the area of weight bearing on the floor is much narrower from front to back so the postural muscles have to be even more finely and accurately tuned to maintain correct balance with the minimum of effort.

USE OF THE BARRE

There is much information about why a pre-class warm-up and post-class cool-down is beneficial for the exercising body and the establishment of those therapeutic additions to dance training must be retained at all costs. However, the traditional classical class is a well-nigh perfect design of rising and falling physiological and technical demand.

Most teachers will probably set two exercises facing the barre to begin the articulation of foot and ankle and ease the hips into turn out. Standing sideways at the barre, exercises progress in demand using speed and intricacy of footwork, and then height of leg both sustained as in adage and thrown as in grand battement.

Moving to the centre, the process begins again progressing to jumps and grand allegro. However it is the use of the barre in the context of the classical class that is in question here.

It does depend on what is wanted out of the barre in the first place and it is important to be clear about its particular function for each individual dancer. Generally if too much support is gained from the barre with gripping to sustain balance, the dancer is not initiating the trunk stability and use of the floor required to develop the classwork and progress to centre practice. If the barre is used to enable a more extreme turn-out or sustain a higher leg with a less than perfect placement, the dancer will not be

1.85 Standing correctly on one fooot, showing the line of centre of gravity falling through the supporting foot. The pelvis and trunk remain aligned correctly

1.86 Standing on one foot incorrectly. The pelvis and the trunk are misaligned and crooked

1.87A Correctly balanced pelvis in turn-out

1.87B Incorrectly balanced pelvis in turn-out

sufficiently ready to exercise in the centre without a struggle to re-establish balance or more likely a great deal of cheating technique. If the barre is relied upon to hold you up, you will fall about in the centre! It will also be obvious that the work at the barre was not within your capabilities. Gripping the barre produces a one-sided tension reaching the neck and a rise in that shoulder. If the barre, however, is used for reassurance only and postural stability sought from the first tendu with realistic technical demand, work can progress in the centre having established sufficient balance and muscular control.

The more inexperienced the dancer, the more dependent on the barre he or she will be. However, using the barre to explore the sensations of intricate footwork or pointe work in particular exercises can be extremely helpful to the young dancer. The more experienced dancer may use more or less support at will, to achieve the desired result – developing increased control or working on height of leg etc.

In general it is recommended for all age groups to use the barre for confidence only in the first portion of the class. The arm is held in a gentle slope forwards at waist height with fingers resting on the barre without the thumb gripping underneath it. The barre should feel almost absent with the dancer presenting to the front using epaulement and changes of direction as if it were not there. In this way the dancer retains placement and balance of each side of the body.

Turn-out (Fig. 1.88)

The constraints which limit the possible range of turn-out at the hip are:
(1) bony
(2) capsule and ligaments and
(3) muscles.

1.88 The turn-out position correctly held

BONE SHAPE

a) Depth of the acetabulum (socket). The deeper the joint, the more stable but also the more restricted.
b) Orientation of the acetabulum. The more forwards the direction, the more restricted is the external rotation of the femoral head.
c) The angle of the head and neck of the femur in relation to the shaft. The head and neck are angled upwards, inwards and slightly forwards into the acetabulum. The angulation forwards is the important variation. The forwards angulation is termed anteversion and restricts the external rotation of the femur. In this configuration internal rotation is far greater. The opposite, when the angulation is less, external rotation is free and internal rotation is reduced, the term is retroversion.
d) The length of the neck of the femur must be taken into account. The neck holds the shaft away from the joint and if it is longer the joint is given more freedom.

CAPSULE AND LIGAMENTS

The joint capsule holds the articular surfaces of the synovial joint together. Ligaments can be thickenings in the capsule or extra capsular and further stabilise the joint. They are composed of connective tissue and are strong and relatively inelastic. In the tight, strong physique the iliofemoral and pubofemoral ligaments will restrict external rotation of the femur. After puberty when ligaments establish length in the maturing body it is difficult to stretch them. Late starters, unless naturally endowed with flexibility and the appropriate bone structure, find classical technique difficult to master.

MUSCLES

The muscles that hold external rotation of the hip must be strong to hold the possible range. Control of turn-out is an interaction between the internal rotators and external rotators and so exercises that internally rotate the hip joint help to retain range of movement and preserve the integrity of the joint.

The hip joint is a ball and socket joint. In classical ballet, external rotation is used in the full range of flexion, extension and abduction of the joint. The six external rotators work in relay to control turn-out. The six deep rotators are piriformis, gemellus superior and inferior, obturator internus and obturator externus and quadratus femoris (Fig. 1.54).

A different combination of external rotators will activate in throughout the range of movement in the hip.

In first position standing, all six external rotators will be active. The posterior fibres of gluteus minimus and medius will activate along with gluteus maximus, sartorius and the adductor group (a closed or adducted position) all assisting external rotation.

In retiré and second position en l'air all the deep rotators activate strongly to hold the abducted position and therefore the lateral rotation.

The adductors are limited in their external rotation capability. It is true that the more anterior fibres, from their origin on the pubis through to their insertion on the linea aspera on the posterior aspect of the femur, may exert a rotatory force while adducting the femur. In closed positions it appears to be beneficial to teach good activation of the adductors, as this promotes a more balanced use of the hip muscles in turn out, and helps control the hyperextended knee.

Working at an angle of external rotation within the limits of the hip joint, and at a neutral pelvis position, allows for a balanced control of turn-out at the hip and stabilisation of the rest of the lower limb. Working beyond the capabilities of the physique produces a muscular imbalance about the hip that precipitates injury locally, and instability in the knee, foot and trunk. The 180° turn-out quoted in old ballet texts is long outmoded and, in reality, anatomically impossible without strain, even for the most gifted physiques. As in the illustration, working at 180° is actually over-turned, working at 160° is 'flat' turn-out and 140° is a realistic angle for most dancers, even professionals. It is rather naïve to believe otherwise (Fig. 1.89).

The test is from a fifth position: release the back foot to coup de pied and hold the turn-out on the supporting leg. If the pelvis remains square and the supporting side unaltered, the correct angle and control are being used and there is no 'cheating' going on. On the other hand, if the feet are over-turned the pelvis will rotate inwards towards the supporting side. Having said that, the aesthetics of classical ballet often require some subtle adjustment to produce an acceptable 'look'. You will see professional dancers subtly slipping the heel back from fifth position in centre adage, as the working leg is released. This allows balance to be preserved over the supporting leg with no loss of control. This is not something that is mentioned in technical rules, but is rather technical 'licence'.

Children need to be introduced to turn-out safely by gradually training the correct balance of muscular control. Each child is encouraged to work within his/her capabilities. It must be remembered that the overturned-out student will rely heavily on the barre for stabilisation. Once in the centre, the lack of control will be evident. Therefore the barre should be used for reassurance only, with the correct hip and lower limb control activated in preparation for more complex centre practice and eventually, allegro.

An overturned-out foot will pronate and abduct. At the knee the tibia is externally rotated in relation to the

1.89A A 'flat' turned-out first, if measured along the medial border of the foot, is an over-turned position that is physically impossible to control

1.89B A first position placed at an angle of 160°

1.89C A first position placed at a more realistic 140°, which a flexible, strong hip would be able to control

femur with resultant distorted forces through the patellar tendon and maltracking of the patella. This causes instability within the lower limb, and outer hip muscles that grip to hold position. In order to achieve as much external rotation as possible in the hip joint, the pelvis will anteriorly tilt to release tension within the iliofemoral ligament. This ligament restricts extension and external rotation and if the hip is slightly flexed, slightly more turn out is possible within the joint. With the pelvis anteriorly tilted, the lumbar spine arches and the abdominals deactivate. The trunk becomes unstable.

At the foot and ankle over-turning will produce flattening of the longitudinal arch. This can progress to eversion of the heel with the line of weight bearing falling inside instead of through the ankle (Fig. 1.38)

If incorrect movement patterns are built up, eventually an injury will result, either from overuse or trauma.

There is no *active* external rotation (turn-out) possible at any level of the leg below the hip joint in the standing position. A small amount of extra turn-out can be obtained when standing because of friction between the foot and the floor which can be used to give a *passive* external rotation force to the whole leg and this can produce a rotation between the knee and the foot. This passive external rotation can produce very damaging results (see **Section 5.7**). When the knee is flexed there is some active and passive rotation possible within the knee joint but this does not occur when the knee is extended (see 'rond de jambe' p. 63).

Use of the Shoulder Girdle

Placement and use of the shoulder girdle is as important as that of the lower limb. The eye tends to fall upon the arms, head and neck of the dancer first. The teacher Vera Volkova suggested that the real talent was seen in the hands and arms. A tension-free neck with graceful, natural hands and fluid co-ordination of the arms relies on correct biomechanics below, and contributes to the stability of the trunk.

The girdle of bones is composed of the sternum providing attachment to the thorax, clavicles articulating with sternum medially and acromion process of the scapula laterally, and the humerus making up the shoulder or glenohumeral joint. The triangular scapulae lie flat against the chest wall with the shoulder sockets (glenoid cavity) angled 30° forwards (see Fig.1.10 p. 5). The scapula is suspended in muscles that hold it in place and rotate it outwards to allow range of movement for the shoulder. The shoulder girdle also elevates, depresses, protracts and retracts. It is built for mobility and therefore must rely on muscle balance and proprioception for stability rather than ligamentous restriction.

In classical ports de bras the shoulder girdle is held down at all times and although the arm traverses a wide range of movement, taking with it the scapula and clavicle, the length of the neck is undisturbed. The muscles below the shoulder girdle hold the scapulae down – latissimus dorsi and lower trapezius. The latissimus dorsi spans and supports the back of the trunk linking the lumbar spine to the upper body. With transversus abdominis it tensions the thoracolumbar fascia contributing to trunk stability.

The scapulae are held flat against the chest wall by the serratus anterior (protractor of the scapula i.e. pulling the scapula forward). It arises from the sides of the upper eight ribs and passes around the rib cage to attach along the medial costal border of the scapula. With balanced use of the muscles surrounding the scapulae the arms feel as if 'they come from your back'.

The shoulder joint alone can abduct to just below 90°, but after that the head of the humerus approaches the acromion which must rise with lateral rotation of the scapula to allow the humerus its range of movement. The glenohumeral joint is a ball and socket joint but unlike the hip joint in that it is non-weight bearing and far less stable. The rounded head of the humerus is three times larger than the shallow, pear-shaped

glenoid cavity. The joint capsule is relatively lax and therefore the shoulder joint relies on a set of four small muscles which are inserted into the thickened part of the capsule surrounding the humeral head called the rotator cuff, which operate as 'contractile ligaments'. These small muscles, supraspintus, infraspinatus, subscapularis and teres minor exert opposing forces on the joint, retaining the head of the humerus in its socket.

Young growing students may need correction and careful placement of the upper body with breadth at the front and 'flattened' shoulder blades at the back. Placement will depend on perfect spinal posture and efficient breathing patterns (see exs p. 50).

With a neutral lumbar spine and the thoracic spine balanced above, the rib cage will be well positioned. If the thoracic spine is over extended, the shoulders are held too far back, the ribs protrude and the shoulder girdle is weakened along with the rest of the posture. In this situation the port de bras will never be easy and controlled.

SECOND POSITION OF THE ARMS

Classical ports de bras follow the structure of the shoulder girdle. The arm in second position is held at an angle of 30° forwards, in line with the scapula and its glenoid cavity. The arm slopes slightly downwards in a gentle curve, with the latissimus dorsi stabilising the scapula. The internal rotation of the humerus at the shoulder but supination below the elbow, lifts the elbow but presents the palm of the hand to the front. If the spine and scapulae are well placed, the hands will be tension-free and natural. If the arms are held too high the muscles over the shoulders are overused. If the arms are held in line with the body rather than slightly forwards, the scapulae are drawn away from the chest wall, the weight goes back and the lumbar spine will overextend. Training like this will soon precipitate lower back problems.

FIRST POSITION OF THE ARMS

Again the arms slope downwards and forwards in a gentle curve. Different schools have different rules but classical lines are rounded with no breaks at elbows or wrists. Children are better able to control a lower line while learning trunk control and developing scapular stabilisation.

FIFTH POSITION OF THE ARMS

While the arms are elevated here, the shoulders are not. Anatomically the scapulae are laterally rotated and the clavicles are sloping upwards, but the dancer imagines that only the arms have moved into fifth. The neck is free and the spine remains unchanged. The hands are held forwards so that they can just be seen by the dancer. In this position there is no loss of abdominal control. This position is used in so many dynamic movements that it must be perfectly established early on.

Plié (Fig. 1.90)

At the start a plié in first position, for example, the feet should be placed at a realistic angle of turn out which is well controlled from the hips, with the pelvis and spine in neutral. The position of the pelvis and spine remains unchanged throughout the demi and grand plié – the descent and the ascent. The angle of turn-out at the feet should also not change.

Throughout the plié turn-out at the hip is maintained by the six deep external rotators. On the descent the flexion at the hip and knee are largely controlled by eccentric action of the quadriceps muscles with some contribution from the adductors which actively 'pay out', controlling the descent against gravity. In the demi plié the heels are in contact with the floor, the weight placement through the centre of the feet eliminates ankle tension and the patellae (knee caps) are in line with the second toes. Ankle dorsiflexion is controlled by the calf muscles eccentrically lengthening. In the descent into the grand plié the heels are gradually raised when the ankle dorsiflexion range of movement has been taken up.

When the depth of the plié is reached there is no relaxation of the thighs. Instead there is an immediate reversal of muscle action as the quadriceps and gluteal muscles (hip extensors) concentrically shorten to extend the knee and hip as the ascent begins. The heels reach the floor and from the demi plié upwards the adductors

1.90 Plié
1.90A From the front
1.90B From the side. Note that the knee is reasonably well aligned over the foot but is not quite perfect. If there is any degree of tibial torsion (which is very common in dancers) then it will never be possible to obtain exact alignment as the foot is externally rotated in relation to the knee

and hamstrings activate strongly to close the thighs in the first position, retaining turn-out. Rising from the plié is achieved by pushing down on the floor with the feet, returning the heels to the floor but retaining the weight placement forwards through the centre of the foot.

Care must be taken to ensure that the knees and feet remain aligned, particularly when going down as far as a grand plié, as it is easy to allow the the heels to swing forwards and the feet to roll, producing an over-turned situation when coming out of the plié.

On rising from a plié care must be taken to maintain the weight correctly over the feet otherwise there is a marked tendency to come up with the weight too far back. This can occur even if the position of the weight has been correct at the start and during the descent of the plié. The tendency is to push the weight back as the dancer comes up.

Another fault is to tuck the pelvis under on the descent. The spine must retain its position and therefore its strength, throughout the movement as the demi plié is the basis of ballet technique. Neither should the use of the port de bras interfere with the spine – the head and arm co-ordinate perfectly with the movement.

In order to maintain the correct alignment and weight placement throughout the plié, it is essential that the dancer feels the contact with the floor through the feet. The imagery at the beginning is one of lifting and growing taller as the body descends, and on the coming up he actually pushes down into the floor so that he has the sensation that he is pushing himself up from below.

The grand plié is considered a strengthening exercise for the knees, hips and spine and also challenges co-ordination and balance. When taught well on an able physique it is indeed strengthening. However, like all exercises, if executed in incorrect alignment a cumulative effect would be injury. The demi plié and fondu come into practically every ballet step and therefore alignment is paramount. If the physique is so limited in hip rotation that a visually and functionally acceptable demi plié is not possible, then the child should not progress to the grand plié. Further training in ballet is ill advised.

As far back as 1990 the grand plié was questioned as a 'safe' exercise. It has been generally accepted that as long as the knee position is well aligned and the knee is healthy to begin with (balanced quadriceps muscles, balance between hamstrings and quadriceps and no undue ITB tightness) then the plié is a good exercise. After all professional dancers have to be versed in Bournonville choreography as well as some of the most challenging contemporary moves. The risk is really in the young, growing dancer whose quadriceps are tight and knees ache after exercise. In this situation appropriate quadriceps and ITB stretches and vastus medialis exercises should be given. A temporary hold should be put on grand pliés with jumps in moderation. It is agreed that the number of grand pliés should be moderated when they are introduced in a syllabus and the grand plié in fourth crossed should be avoided. There is a knee rotation in most physiques in this position and to stress the knee in a deep knee bend is unnecessary. Where they are introduced in class has also been debated, and teachers have experimented. It is agreed that the thighs and knees must be well warmed up in preparation.

Tendu (Fig. 1.91)

This term means stretched and its main benefit when correctly carried out is its effect on the feet. It is very important that the correct placement in the trunk and supporting leg is maintained throughout, otherwise the exercise is totally useless. If the position of these other areas is incorrect and the weight is back the tendu becomes ineffective and the muscles in the feet are not stimulated and therefore do not benefit.

BATTEMENT TENDU À LA SECONDE

The battement tendu à la seconde is a movement of apparent simplicity, but is actually extremely complex. A perfectly placed degagé from first position (without the barre) demonstrates weight adjustment, balance and stability over one leg. Maintenance of spinal and shoulder girdle placement are also challenged. The turned-out starting position in first must be established at the correct angle for the individual physique or smooth control of the movement will not be possible. If the feet in turn-out are forced beyond that which the particular physique can control, the moment the working foot is disengaged control is lost. The pelvis will rotate either inwards towards the supporting leg at the expense of the working leg, or outwards towards the working leg

causing pronation of the supporting foot and rotation of the knee. Either way the pelvis cannot remain stabilised, the centre is lost and so is the base of support.

When the appropriate angle of turn-out is used, as the working leg is released the weight is subtly adjusted over the supporting side. Physics tells us that as the base of support (two feet) changes to one foot, the body weight must move over its new base to maintain equilibrium and allow the working foot to articulate, brushing the floor into the pointed, non weighted, a la seconde position. From fifth position the adjustment of weight required is less. From fifth where the weight is balanced over a more compact base, with each foot sharing the support, the weight 'settles' over the support foot, front or back, as the other is released.

Some schools of thought teach that the weight does not change but stays central as the working foot is released. This would require the working foot to weight-bear – lift it and you would fall over. Either that or the trunk becomes distorted or widespread imbalanced muscular tension manages to hold a simulated position. It should be remembered that the battement tendu is the basis of many more complex movements in the classical repertoire and therefore it should be learned as such – with control and smoothness that allows it to initiate and link movements. As an exercise in itself, it strengthens the working (moving) foot and ankle, sensitises its proprioception and establishes fine balance over the supporting side in preparation for more challenging movements.

The working foot slides to second at the same angle of turn-out at the hip and the toes should remain on the same line as those of the supporting foot. As much balance as possible between both sides of the body should be preserved with the spine in neutral and therefore the pelvis in balance and held squarely to the front. As the working foot releases there should be no sinking in to the supporting hip. The gluteus medius,

1.91 Tendu
1.91A Note that the stretch carries on to the tips of the toes, which remain straight
1.91B Incorrect tendu with toes curled

minimus and tensor fasciae latae on the supporting side hold the pelvis horizontal and the amount of weight adjustment sideways should be only enough to balance over the middle of the foot with forefoot and toes embracing the floor. (Lack of placement will be seen in the supporting foot. If the foot is pronated or the tendons at the front of the ankle are unduly tense, correct control has been lost.) There should be no weight through the pointed foot. Adjustment too far over is also a fault, is unnecessary and encourages sinking in the hip The return of the pointed foot to the closed position is a reversal of the degagé, with pressure and use of the floor as the foot closes.

Once this complex co-ordination is learned the use of arms and épaulement embellish the movement without disturbing control and balance further down.

SECOND POSITION EN L'AIR

As stated in the technique section on battement tendu, the starting of a movement from an unrealistic angle of turn out will lead to distortion and loss of balance.

The second position en l'air is a difficult position which is misunderstood by teachers mostly due to a lack of anatomical knowledge. Students do what they are asked to the best of their ability, and if faults are not picked up by their teachers, strain and injury ensue.

Very few physiques can stand in first with the medial borders of their feet in a straight line, with perfect control (see turn-out p. 58). The degagé to second from that position is difficult to achieve (without distorting the pelvis and supporting side) unless the hip joints allow that amount of flexibility. The position en l'air of course becomes far more challenging, requiring strength as well. The muscles used to hold the position are the hip flexors and the abductors. If the working leg is held slightly forwards, more external rotation can be utilised, the hip flexors can be fully engaged and the pelvis can be held down on that side. An extremely flexible hip joint may even feel a bony block in the 'flat' second position as the greater trochanter impinges on the posterior lip of the acetabulum and ischium. Holding the leg slightly forwards frees the femur to increase external rotation and employ the hip flexors to gain further height in the leg.

Most physiques, in order to build a basis upon which technique can be developed must be placed within their capabilities. In second position en l'air the pelvis cannot remain horizontal. Asking for this will encourage 'sitting' in the supporting hip and restriction within the working one. However, lifting the pelvis on the working side will encourage tension in the wrong muscles and will ultimately restrict the potential height of the leg. Compromise is the key to teaching technique along with a clear recognition of the limitations of the physique in front of you.

ROND DE JAMBE

The rond de jambe en l'air is often misunderstood by dancers.

This is a circling action of the lower leg where the foot begins and ends in second position at 45°. The en dehors movement involves the working foot tracing a straight line from second inwards to touch the top of the calf. From there the foot traces a circular movement forwards completing the semi-circle out to second. The circular movement comes from the hip joint where an increase in external rotation is demanded from the deep rotators of the hip. The knee should not be involved in any rotation of the tibia on the femur as is often believed. Repeated use of rotation within the knee, even non weight bearing, is to be discouraged.

The en dedans movement traces the inwards circular movement forwards of the supporting leg to the calf and then straight out to the second again. Again there is an increased use of rotation at the hip.

This is used in rond de jambe sauté and gargouillards.

(For the non-dancer: en dedans means the inward turning of the legs or arms, en dehors means the outward turning of the legs or arms. Rond de jambe may be more easily understood by the uninitiated by thinking of standing with the knee and hip bent to 90° and then swinging the foot and leg to the side [a pure hip movement] then bringing the foot and leg backwards [a pure knee movement] then swinging the foot and leg inwards [hip movement] then finally swinging the foot and leg forwards to the original position [a knee movement]. There is no knee rotation despite what some dancers believe.)

Arabesque

The arabesque line is one of the main classical positions in ballet and should be developed slowly and carefully in training to establish strength, flexibility, stability and correct control. It is a position of beauty and of flowing line which belie the flexibility and strength it requires. Although basic rules apply, each individual will produce a unique arabesque line in accordance with their particular physique.

The arabesque is made up of several components each of which require attention. If any component is neglected the equilibrium of the position is disturbed.

The supporting leg base is turned out, but with the movement necessary in the pelvis to release the gesture leg derrière, the supporting leg is compromised with turn-out reduced.

Extension of the hip joint is a movement restricted to about 20°, and so a 90° arabesque will demand an anterior tilt of the pelvis and extension in the lumbar spine to accommodate the gesture leg. The orientation of the acetabulum – sideways, downwards and slightly forwards – means that to achieve a complimentary line in the gesture leg derrière, the pelvis must rotate towards it – only as much as anatomically necessary. The lumbar spine is then extended and rotated with shoulders relatively unaffected. If the pelvis does not rotate but remains square, the gesture leg will appear turned in and the strain on the lumbar spine is increased.

The shoulder girdle remains more or less square depending on the style or type of arabesque. This means that the thoracic spine rotates in opposition especially with the same arm devant as leg derrière. The Ceccetti/RAD second arabesque will demand more opposing rotation between lumbar and thoracic spines and therefore more strength in the thoracic erector spinae muscles to control extension and rotation.

Biomechanically the extension should be spread throughout the spine with as little hinging at any one level as possible. The thoracic spine is the stiffest part of the spine in extension with the lumbar spine the most flexible. The area of most 'give' is where most extension will be taken unless carefully controlled by the abdominal muscles activating at the front. The deep transversus abdominis must activate protecting the lumbar spine from excessive extension. If the spine hinges at one level, usually L4/L5 or L5/S1, problems will arise eventually involving the facet joints or more seriously stress reaction in the pars interarticularis (p. 155). Wear and tear on the related disc when the career is in full swing results in serious problems, or post-career when the muscular support weakens. This precarious type of arabesque is seen in the dancer who pulls back in the upper body, strains the neck, retracting the head, and still manages a high leg derrière.

There should be a sweeping line through the spine to the tip of the toes. Enhancing the line is the fully extended knee of the derrière leg, with the ankle and

foot fully plantarflexed. The foot should follow the line of the leg with no overt eversion (fishing) which interrupts the line and increases tension in the muscles from the calf to the waist. The arabesque (derrière) leg should be held behind its the hip, rather than slightly abducted, which detracts from a purer line. Neither should the derrière leg be over crossed, which puts undue strain on the lower back.

The supporting leg should be fully extended without locking back into the knee and the weight falling back through the heel. Weight-bearing should be forwards through the foot with the toes actively meeting the floor.

Rise (Fig. 1.92)

The trunk and pelvis move as one and come slightly forward with the line of the centre of gravity, to lie over the toes when the rise is completed. This is achieved by pushing up from the floor with the forefoot in order to maintain correct alignment and weight-bearing. Anatomically, the calf muscles contract, lifting the heel and hindfoot against gravity. At the same time the tone is maintained in the gluteals, the adductors, the hamstrings and the knee extensors (quadriceps) giving the feeling of being lifted up from above and not pushed up from below. In the presence of swayback knees the balance between the quadriceps and hamstrings is exceptionally important in order to maintain correct knee control.

The rise can stop at either half pointe or three-quarter pointe.

Pointe (Figs 1.93 and 1.94)

Because of the constraints of the pointe shoe, and more importantly the anatomy and mechanics of the foot, the rise on to pointe progresses from half to full pointe with powerful use of the intrinsic muscles (flexors) of the foot as well as the calf complex. It

1.92 Rise
1.92A To quarter pointe
1.92B To half pointe (demi-pointe or à demi)
1.92C To three-quarter pointe (à trois quarts)

1.93 On pointe. This is reached by means of a relevé in which the dancer passes through the various levels of pointe to reach the full pointe position (sur la pointe)

1.95A An over-pointed foot. To come up pnto pointe with the foot in this position places an excessive strain on the capsules and ligaments of the dorsum of the foot as the line of the centre of gravity falls in front of the toes (i.e. in front of the dorsal aspect)

1.94 On pointe. X-ray of a dancer on pointe

1.95B The same foot in the correct position for on pointe

should be noted that attempting to pass through three-quarter pointe is not a functional movement in pointework, and demands unnecessary force to do. Slow rises to full pointe are a preparation for the faster relevé and therefore should employ similar mechanics in the ankle and foot recruiting the appropriate muscles. From half pointe the intrinsic flexors including the lumbrical muscles, powerfully lever the foot on to pointe with the calf muscles fully engaging.

Flexibility of the ankle and foot, stability and balance are the crucial factors required to maintain the pointe position. The weight placement through the smaller base of support en pointe requires fine control and accuracy. The hypermobile foot and ankle has the ability to overplantarflex which, when weightbearing, is mechanically weak, unstable and therefore easily injured. The correct position can be taught however, with exercises for strength and proprioception. Neither over plantarflexed with the line of balance falling in front of the base of support and sinking in the shoe,

nor holding back in a 'retracted' position, the hypermobile foot and ankle must find the intermediate position of balance. To fully activate the foot with strong, straight toes there should be a sensation of pushing into the floor but lifting out of the shoe. There should be a vertical line from mid-base through medial malleolus and knee. Balance between the calf and anterior extensor muscles and between the everters (peroneals) and the inverters (mainly tibialis posterior) is the key to a strong, controlled position. The hypermobile foot and ankle are regarded as aesthetically more pleasing, but it is a more difficult foot to teach. The less attractive foot with a passable range of movement can be easier to strengthen and if used well enhances the technique. However, a stiff foot and ankle that cannot achieve the line of balance, lacks the range to allow a position of equilibrium en pointe and may predispose to injury. Encouragement to progress to pointe with this physique is inadvisable (see os trigonum p. 222).

Lowering from pointe into the fondu requires the same chain reaction. For example, from a pose the foot eccentrically lowers to half pointe, as the hip and knee flex to silently shock absorb.

Skill and advanced technique in pointework do not only depend on the strength of the foot. Strength and stability of the knee, hip and spine, and co-ordination of the whole, are prerequisites. Therefore before a student progresses to pointework, there should be adequate control of turn-out at the hip, an understanding of pelvic alignment and an appreciation of dynamic foot alignment. Children mature physically at different rates and within a class there may be a wide range of physiques. It is the teacher's responsibility to care for and prepare each individual. Foot exercises (see p. 192) are commenced very early in the training and the teacher will have a clear idea of those who will progress to pointework and those who will be channelled to alternative classes. The gifted but immature physiques will progress more slowly in order to establish the correct movement patterns before more complex, faster exercises are set. In other words, there is no definite age when pointework should be started. In vocational schools intensive training takes place during the most formative years, when joints and bones are vulnerable. However, as long as the rules of joint alignment are obeyed and muscles activated in balance and training then consistent and individual development will continue uninterrupted.

AGE TO START POINTEWORK

It has been thought for many years that twelve was the year at which a child could start pointework. However to generalise like this is not to take into consideration the type of physique, the stage of physical development, the stage of technical development and the intensity of the training. To be dogmatic about an age does not make any reference to the child's maturity or immaturity.

From early on the teacher will recognise those with potential to progress further. The shape of leg and flexibility of foot and ankle are the first considerations. There must be the facility to trace a line through the middle of the knee, the medial malleolus (inside ankle bone) the first metatarsal to tip of the second toe. The stiffer ankle will not allow correct alignment of the body over the pointe base and therefore the pointework route should be discouraged.

A class of twelve-year-olds will vary in heights as growth rates and timing of growth spurts vary. At around this stage girls are starting a major growth spurt when stability, strength and acquired technical ability are challenged. Starting pointework training at this stage requires a careful and systematic approach, tailored for the needs of each child in the class. The preparation for this next phase of training is not only intrinsic foot strengthening (which can start at the age of seven), but adequate control of turn-out from the hips, good trunk control and core stability. Alignment of the spine and correct posture should be understood. The student must have achieved a good, strong three-quarter pointe with secure balance control on one leg. Again alignment of the foot and ankle, knee and hip should be routine. If this has yet to develop, the transition to pointework should be delayed. The hypermobile foot and ankle has the potential to achieve this but, to begin with, will not be strong enough to stabilise the various pointe positions. As a result, over-pointing will result with potentially serious consequences. Great caution is required when dealing with this type of foot. Although a pleasing line is achieved in open positions, it is at greatest risk once pointe has started. Sufficient proprioception must be developed to stablise within a functional range. This type of foot may be part of a hypermobile physique and will need a careful and slow preparation for vocational training (see p. 67).

Children who have been selected for vocational schools will have their intensive training planned and will be physically able to move on. (Nevertheless, each physique must be individually understood and managed.) It is doubtful whether the young student who is attending ballet classes fewer than three times a week will be advanced enough or have enough teaching to progress fast or safely enough to pointework.

There are certainly well-known dancers who were not strong enough to start their pointework until they were over the age of sixteen and this has proved no handicap in their careers. Conversely there are those who have lasting problems whose care was not conservative enough at a vulnerable time in their training.

POINTE SHOES

Professional dancers take their pointe shoes very seriously. Over the years of training and then performing they develop an intimate relationship with their shoes, each pair carefully prepared to take them through each different role and different demands. There are many different brands to choose from and the professional dancer will have experimented for years before settling on the perfect shoe.

Young dancers starting pointework require careful fitting. Appropriate length and width allow the foot to function well within the shoe. Intrinsic muscles must be able to function or the strength of the foot and toes is restricted.

The depth of the vamp must suit the flexibility of the foot and ankle. A deeper vamp will support the flexible foot and hold it back from over-pointing. A harder back will also give more support to the more flexible or weaker foot. A shorter vamp will allow a stiffer foot to use its full range of movement. Drawstrings should be above (proximal to) the MTP joints (knuckles) so as not to cause friction. The platform is a matter of preference, but the young dancer will benefit from a wider one to promote stability.

The foot must be fully active within the shoe, and must be taught to articulate in the pointe shoe. The foot musculature functions with the calf complex. If the shoe is too hard the foot articulation is restricted and the control of the calf too, is disturbed. The quality of the relevé must pull through the Achilles freeing the back of the ankle before it is closed up on pointe. The either 'up or down' positions without quality of movement between the two makes the ankle vulnerable to posterior impingements. The descent also requires quality of eccentric control for shock absorption and timing (and noise control).

Dancers these days have a huge choice of padding in their pointe shoes. Whatever is used for comfort and prevention of blisters, it should be kept to a minimum and it must not interfere with 'the feel of the floor' or the activity and strength of the toes. Padding should not lie between the toes and the sole of the shoe. Instead the padding should protect the tips of the toes and the dorsal surfaces where friction occurs. Sorbethane or gel toe caps can be very effective and certainly useful in helping the young dancer get started. Animal wool was the traditional choice but some dancers use simple tissue, plasters or various tapings for each toe – including masking tape as a cheap alternative.

The choices of shoe available are not always ideal and customising pointe shoes is sometimes, if not always, necessary. Shaving the sole with a Stanley knife will give it more flexibility and paring down the rim of the sole will help with balance. A side seam will take up extra satin if the sides are too deep. Slitting the interior canvas at the sides and leaving the shoe overnight in a shoe stretcher will give the forefoot extra width.

Using shellac in the blocks can prolong the life of a traditional shoe and this is widely done by professional dancers.

Hypermobility

Today's professional dancers are expected to possess extreme degrees of flexibility. Choreographers want it and so do audiences. We are bombarded with photos of, and advertisements for, dancers in extreme positions. Legs are required to be high and spines must bend. Dancers themselves admire extremes of flexibility and strive for it. Extra flexibility may be inherited or acquired, and joint mobility may be increased with training.

There is a whole spectrum of flexibility to consider. There is the tightly bound, limited physique which is unsuited to ballet (short muscles and bony limitation of joints) through to the extreme flexibility of the dancer who is 'bendy', weak and unco-ordinated, but 'full of potential'. Through sheer hard work stretching may increase range of movement and dancers with normal tissues will develop a hypermobile range in specific joints as required by the technique. Dancers with a natural (inherited) hypermobility are believed to have an abnormality of their connective tissue and many children are drawn to dance because of the ease with which they achieve more extreme positions, and the aesthetic appeal of the hyperextended knee and hypermobile ankle.

CONNECTIVE TISSUE

The type of connective tissue making up the body determines the flexibility. Connective tissue connects, binds and supports body structure. It is the living material that makes up ligament, capsule, tendon, cartilage, menisci, labra, fat pads, disc and bone. Each of these structures has different functions and therefore varied microarchitecture and biomechanical behaviour.

Generally connective tissue is composed of cells and fibres suspended in a matrix. In ligament the fibroblast cells produce dense, parallel-arranged masses of collagen and elastin fibres. These proteins give ligament and tendons their powerful resistance to axially loaded tension forces but allow some stretch.

In inherited joint hypermobility where there is a generalised joint laxity, there is a disorder in collagen synthesis. This is a genetic disorder affecting the genes which encode the various connective tissue proteins including collagen and elastin. Genetic defects distort the biochemical structure of these proteins and impair their tensile properties resulting in tissue laxity or hypermobility. Unfortunately tissue fragility, weakness and a tendency to mechanical failure accompany this. This is the downside of having a natural extra flexibility in dancers.

Joint hypermobility syndrome (a syndrome is a set of characteristics indicating the existence of a condition) has a place within a group of heritable disorders of connective tissue. The group is large and varied in severity. The commonest are Marfan syndrome, Ehlers-Danlos syndrome, Osteogenesis Imperfecta and joint hypermobility syndrome. Features are varied and can affect the joints (instability), the skin (thin, stretchy, easily bruised and scars abnormally), the heart (valve fragility), the veins (varicose), muscular (hernia), lung (pneumothorax) and the skeleton (osteoporosis) to name but a few. Over the last twenty years research has illuminated this group of pathologies and continues today to identify those at risk and those individuals with unrecognised pathology.

In dancers we see those in the middle of the spectrum who have stretched efficiently to develop enough range of movement for their dance genre. They will be blessed with a bone structure that allows for slight hyperextension of the knee, a good range of movement in the foot and ankle and a functional range at the hip and spine. Flexibility and strength will have been acquired by determination, intelligence and consistent work throughout the years of growth. Then there those who are naturally very mobile. They have hyperextended knees and elbows (often 15° past neutral), hypermobile wrists and fingers (untrained), stretchy skin, are injured frequently and struggle to keep up with the rest of the class, apparently hindered by their physiques. These are the ones who concern us. These can also be ones that are initially attractive in the audition process.

In 1973 Beighton and colleagues devised a quick five-manoeuvre test to score hypermobility. The nine-point score is not an accurate measure but is an interesting initial observation. Testing the 'untrained joints' gives an indication of the stretchiness of the ligaments involved, which may reflect a general type (see Fig. 1.96 A–E).

Apart from artistic development, ballet training aims to cultivate balance, proprioception, stability, spatial awareness and accurate motor control within a certain vocabulary. While the hypermobile physique is drawn to dance, the vulnerable skeleton is easily injured. A hypermobile joint has a lax capsule and ligaments which are less efficient at restricting its range, it is less stable and its ligamentous complex is weaker and more susceptible to injury, therefore it is reliant on muscular support and neural control for its integrity. Hypermobile individuals have decreased effectiveness of proprioception and therefore balance and co-ordination are affected. They tend to need more training

1.96 The nine-point Beighton Score. A Passively dorsiflex the 5th metacarpophalangeal joint > 90° right and left. B Oppose the thumb to the forearm right and left. C Hyperextend the elbow right and left 10°. D Hyperextend knees 10°. E Hands flat on floor without bending knees that is paced slowly to instil good posture and alignment throughout the body. Attention needs to be paid to the deeper stabilising muscles that support the joints of the spine, shoulders, hips and feet. In spite of their flexibility, hypermobile dancers appear to want and need to stretch, especially first thing in the morning. They need longer to warm up too. They will often relax in extreme positions and should not be advised otherwise – they have a different kinaesthetic sense and need only to be encouraged to keep up with stability exercises.

Hypermobiles tend to have lower pain thresholds and they often take longer to heal. Both of these facts are important for dancers, teachers and therapists to understand. The skin tends to be stretchy, noticeably on the back of the hands or the front of the knees. Stretch marks are visible after puberty, on the thighs and over the lumbar spine.

The very mobile foot is desirable in ballet because of its line in pointing, but it is a weak and unstable structure with a tendency to pronation on weight bearing (rolling in with collapse of the medial arch) especially in the turned out position. Until foot biomechanics are fully understood and sufficient strength is achieved not only within the foot but posturally too, pointework should not be attempted. Some of the first preparation exercises for ballet training should be intrinsic foot exercises to support its arches and strengthen dynamic work. (Professional dancers return to these throughout their careers.) If a teacher is concerned with a child's foot position, referral to a podiatrist for orthotics for outdoor shoes may contribute to promoting correct biomechanics. (There is no evidence that orthotics help except hearsay from podiatrists.)

The very mobile spine can eventually produce a glorious arabesque line but needs to build stability at the same time for true strength and injury prevention. No dancer should be left with an injury after training and some back problems once established can be difficult to deal with. In hypermobility there is an increased risk of stress fractures, spondylolisthesis and disc problems – typically affecting the lower lumbar spine that is flexible but insufficiently stabilised by deep local muscles. Correct posture is the starting point with a clear understanding of pelvic position, neutral lumbar spine and deep abdominal activation.

The shoulder girdle is another area where hypermobility can cause problems. The shoulder joint is already a loosely held together structure, built for mobility rather than stability. Good scapular patterns and activation of the small rotator cuff muscles that act like ligaments, stabilise it. The hypermobile shoulder is prone to instability and can sublux or dislocate more easily without rotator cuff strength. Pumping weights at the gym is, however, not the answer. The key is fine control of the scapula throughout the range of the shoulder and good core stability. As the hypermobile physique tends towards a lowered proprioception or kinaesthetic awareness, this can take time and patience with this fine position control also applied to the foot, knee, pelvis and spine.

The swayback knee continues to challenge teachers. Better hamstring strength, correct hip and pelvis control, a balanced use of the quadriceps and correct foot alignment will strengthen the hypermobile joint and prevent some of the common knee problems that are even more prevalent in this population.

Small children who are hypermobile are often delayed in walking and crawling. It has been reported that, in general, joint laxity declines with age. The most positive outcome would be a consistent increase in muscle mass, strength, motor control and stability in the young, hypermobile dancer.

It has been suggested that hypermobile physiques should not be trained vocationally because of the risk of injury, but it can be argued that they may make the most interesting and stunning dancers if they are understood, trained well at their own pace and prevented from injury. These physiques are different, therefore the nature of this condition and the implications of teaching should be fully grasped and respected.

Patterns of Growth and the Adolescent Growth Spurt

In early childhood boys and girls grow at a steady and similar rate. The three-year-old has a 'baby tummy' and pronounced spinal curves, which persist until the spine elongates enough, to contain the major organs with abdominal muscles engaged. Some children appear more 'streamlined' by six, and some not until nine. The liver in the young child is only minimally smaller than the adult size, taking up significant abdominal space. Therefore in any effort to 'pull in' the abdominal muscles at a young age, the shoulders and rib cage rise to make space for the abdominal contents. When corrected the shoulders lower and the tummy reappears, demonstrating the folly in attempting abdominal exercises and postural correction in the very young.

By the age of nine children should have gained some control of the lower abdominal muscles and pelvic balance. Floor exercises can be commenced as early as seven to raise awareness and isolate muscles.

The age of puberty in boys is around twelve and a half years (twelve to sixteen) and in girls, ten and a half (ten to fifteen). There is considerable variation. At this stage in females, changes occur due to the increased production of oestrogen and progesterone secretion by the ovaries. The breasts develop and fat is deposited around the hips. In boys the increased secretion of testosterone targets certain tissues: skeletal muscle mass enlarges, hair grows on the face and body and the larynx enlarges with a deeper masculine voice.

Peak growth rate, known as the major growth spurt, occurs approximately two years after puberty. During the adolescent growth spurt there will be a noticeable increase in height. It is advisable to measure height regularly at this time to fully understand the changes the body is undergoing. During this time girls can add 6–11cm to their height and boys 9–15 cm. By the age of fifteen most girls will have reached 99 per cent of their adult height, while boys can still be growing at twenty-one. It must be borne in mind that young men entering professional companies should still have their height screened and all partnering monitored, as the physique remains vulnerable at this time. This can be hard to gauge but appropriate upper body exercises and attention to any discomfort should ease the dancer into pas de deux roles with a suitably matched partner.

This increase will be due to longitudinal growth in the long bones – the femur and tibia – and also increased height in the vertebrae in the spine. However the growth of different body parts at this time is disproportionate, resulting in a rapid change in body shape and proportion. At the onset of the adolescent growth spurt the long bones grow first. The hands and feet appear to grow initially and the long bones of the limbs lengthen before the trunk. Some children do complain of aching in their legs, often at night, and these have been described as 'growing pains'. Although not clearly defined, these have to be accepted as such.

Bones in the foetus are miniature cartilaginous models of those in the adult.

Ossification begins at different times in different bones. This is the laying down of bone salts – calcium and other minerals – within the immature bones, beginning the strengthening and hardening process. In long bones the first centre of ossification begins in the diaphysis or shaft, followed by the secondary centres of ossification in the epiphyses or ends of the bones. The bones continue to develop throughout childhood increasing in girth with the increase in circumference brought about by the deposition of new bone by cells under the periosteum. They grow in length at the ends where a plate of cartilage (growth or epiphyseal plate) remains and bone cells (osteoblasts) are exceptionally active. An X-ray of the ankle of a twelve-year-old will show the black plate of epiphyseal cartilage present at the lower end of the tibia and fibula, indicating the immature physique. The long bone is fully matured when the epiphyseal plate closes and lengthening comes to a halt. In the adult the calcium in the dense bone tissue absorbs the X-rays and the bone is white on film with no cartilage present. This maturing is

directed by the increase in the production of the adult hormones – oestrogen in females and testosterone in males. The growth plates in the exercising adolescent are vulnerable and, if injured, can interfere with growth on that side, which can have serious consequences subsequently on the rest of the physique if the result is a length discrepancy in a limb.

A promising young dancer may be progressing well until she begins growing when the developing assurance slows down. Posture, balance, proprioception, flexibility and strength are all affected, as well as confidence. Clumsiness is common and tripping on the stairs, for instance, is easy to do if the feet or limbs have grown but the nervous system has not quite adjusted.

Longer legs mean longer, heavier levers to lift and height of legs will necessarily be compromised at this stage. Young dancers can commonly develop clicking hips and groin strains, very often from progressing technique at a time when the physique is slightly weaker. This is a time to pay more attention to correct positioning of the pelvis, maintain abdominal stability and lower the legs rather than allow compensatory loss of alignment.

Muscles cannot keep up with bone rate of growth and in the thigh the quadriceps are often compromised by the growing femur, disturbing strength and coordination. Strain is put through the patello-femoral joint resulting in anterior knee pain, and the patellar tendon insertion at the tibial tuberosity resulting in Osgood Schlatter's disease (see p. 144). Any movements which transmit increased forces through the knee joint should be well monitored. Misalignment in the knee joint in grand pliés or jumping will cause problems and any rotation here must of course be corrected. Repetition should be carefully monitored especially in centre practice. A similar situation develops with the rapid growth of the tibia and the calf muscles, and pain at the site of insertion of the Achilles tendon on the calcaneus, which may result in Sever's disease.

The vertebrae can also grow in spurts and transitory scolioses can appear during this period. With rapid growth of vertebral height in the lumbar spine the spinal extensors and thoracolumbar fascia tighten and the lumbar lordosis increases. The thoracic spine then develops a reciprocal kyphosis. If leg height, especially derriere, is not controlled and trunk stability is not maintained, there is risk of injury to the spine, for example stress fracture (spondylolisis, see p. 155). For the same reason boys should not be lifting at this stage either. With attention again to placement, posture and maintenance exercises for trunk and shoulder stability, this period of transition passes.

Good motor control relies on good sensory feedback but with altered limb length and higher centre of gravity there is a temporary loss of fine neuromuscular control. However, by the age of thirteen in girls, when the growth spurt is in full swing, technique becomes more demanding and pointework begins. Intrinsic foot strength should be well developed by now, but decreased balance mechanisms means that progress should be slower with, instead, attention to detail. Again with the progression of jumps, consideration must be given to weaker muscles, eccentric control, coordination and ground reaction forces. If there is any knee pain, jumps should be curtailed and stretching plus floor exercises carried out instead.

Important for normal development is, of course, a good diet balanced in the main elements with a sufficient number of calories not only to feed hard-working muscle but also to promote growth, menarche and regulate menstruation. The reproductive system is fragile at this stage and vulnerable to over-exercise and under-nourishment. First-class protein, high in iron, is recommended for the young dancer. The adolescent at this point needs to carry normal weight rather than be emulating the experienced professional dancer's physique. Bone density relies on balanced hormones and the years up to the mid-twenties are important for building towards peak bone density.

STRATEGIES FOR KNEE HEALTH

- Monitor the number of grand pliés which increase stress through the quadriceps/patellar complex.
- Adjust the fourth position for grand plié to make it less stressful on the knee joint (less rotation) or remove it for the time being.
- Decrease the jumping section and replace with exercises for inner quadriceps (vastus medialis), hamstrings, and gluteal muscles.
- Add stretches for quadriceps, hamstrings, ilio-tibial band, gastrocnemius and soleus.
- Leave out kneeling in choreography for the time being.
- Ensure that floors are sprung.

STRATEGIES FOR BACK HEALTH

- Exercises for lower abdominals – transversus abdominis.
- Lower back extensor stretches.
- Attention to pelvic position – neutral spine and pelvis.
- Limit the depth of the back bend and encourage optimum use of abdominal activation.
- Attention to arabesque line – lower, with alignment, rather than straining for height.
- Limit any serious lifting in boys until more skeletally mature.

STRATEGIES FOR HIP HEALTH

- Lower the height of leg devant and side as well as derrière.
- Employ internal rotation positions to counteract over emphasis on turn-out (p. 210).
- Piriformis stretches (p. 187).
- Less emphasis on the relevé.
- No 'tucking under' the pelvis.

FOOT AND ANKLE CARE

- Pointework should be progressed slowly.
- Foot alignment should be monitored throughout the jumping section with no undue pronation of the forefoot.
- Simple balance exercises should be included (see p. 175).
- Intrinsic foot exercises (see p. 192).
- Calf exercises (see p. 197) and stretches.

All forms of cross training should be encouraged for cardiovascular fitness, such as walking, cycling, swimming, gym work with care, yoga with care and Pilates exercises.

The psychological stresses and strains of trying to function in an adult world are enough for the adolescent to deal with, but add a hypercritical studio atmosphere and productive work will suffer. The often perfectionist tendencies of the young dancer are better controlled in a supportive atmosphere where strategies are discussed and explained.

Injuries: Pathology, Causes, Treatment, Prevention, Nutrition

2.1 Patho-physiology of Injury: Inflammation and Healing

Injuries to tissues can arise from a variety of causes: mechanical, burns, chemical, action of bacteria, action of viruses, etc. However, in this book we are really only interested in injury which is caused mechanically. These injuries include sprains, muscle tears, fractures, bruises and occasionally cuts and abrasions.

Inflammation

Any injury, whatever the cause, produces inflammation. Inflammation is a response which occurs in the surviving adjacent tissues at any injured site. There is a general view that inflammation is something which is undesirable and should be avoided, because the first thing that springs to mind when one considers inflammation is something very painful such as a boil, sore throat or similar infection which has produced an inflammatory response. As bacterial infection of tissue is one form of injury it therefore produces an inflammation, hence the feeling that the inflammation itself is undesirable. However, the opposite is the case, inflammation is a very beneficial thing. It is a natural protective and defensive mechanism which the body has developed in order to deal with any type of injury.

If the inflammatory response is absent dramatic and disastrous effects can arise. Everyone nowadays hears of patients who have been treated with special drugs to prevent inflammation, particularly following various organ transplant operations and also, of course, in a slightly different form in the conditions known as AIDS (Acquired Immune Deficiency Syndrome). Without the inflammatory response, there is a very high incidence of severe infections which can spread extremely rapidly and are frequently lethal. It is this inability of the body to control infections that renders patients so vulnerable when they have had immunosuppressive therapy, as it is known. It is important therefore that it is understood from the beginning that the inflammatory reaction is a desirable condition. Whatsoever the type of injury to the tissue the result in the normal person is an acute inflammatory response.

THE SIGNS OF INFLAMMATION

The signs of inflammation were described some 2000 years or more ago and have been taught ever since.

Until the current century they were always described in Latin as 'calor, rubor, dolor, tumor' and 'functio laesa' or in English 'heat, redness, pain, swelling and loss of function.'

Heat – calor
Heat accompanies the redness of the hyperaemia and is due to the increased blood flow. It is only appreciated at the skin surface because this is usually cooler than the internal body temperature, so with the increased blood supply the skin temperature is raised up to, or nearly up to, the inside of the body, i.e. 37°C. (98.4°F.) There is, therefore, a localised increase in warmth compared with the surrounding skin.

Redness – rubor
The redness appears early. It is due to the dilatation of the arterioles in the area. This allows the capillaries to fill up and become distended very quickly. It is sometimes known also as hyperaemia, which means an increased blood flow.

Pain – dolor
There are various causes for the pain which is associated with an inflammatory reaction as distinct from the pain which is produced by the actual injury, for example a sprain or a fracture, both of which are painful in their own right. The inflammatory pain may be produced by local stimulation of nerve endings due to an alteration in the local pH level (the acid alkali balance) or by the release of certain chemicals such as histamine which also stimulates the nerve endings. Swelling within the inflamed tissues causes pain due to the increase in pressure.

Swelling – tumor
Local swelling always occurs in the presence of inflammation and is due to the spread into the tissues of fluid and cells from the blood stream. This will be considered again shortly.

Loss of Function – functio laesa
Loss of or altered function occurs with inflammation. Pain may well inhibit muscular action and swelling will also limit movements of joints. However, apart from these very obvious causes of loss of function the underlying reason for the alteration in function in the presence of inflammation at other sites is not really

understood. The most likely explanation is that the function becomes inhibited to allow the part to rest.

TISSUE CHANGES IN INFLAMMATION

Fluid Changes

As mentioned above, the redness and heat are brought about by the dilatation of arterioles which leads to engorgement of the capillaries. With the dilatation of the capillaries there is an alteration in permeability of the walls of these tiny vessels.

Instead of retaining the large protein molecules within the circulation and not allowing them to cross the cellular barrier of the capillary walls, the permeability of the walls changes and some large protein molecules can pass out into the tissue fluid. As a result the osmotic balance between the tissue fluid and the blood alters and further amounts of water are drawn out into the tissue fluid, producing the local swelling. This increase in vascular permeability is the most important factor in the causation of the swelling. However, there is a less important factor in that the dilatation produces an increase in the pressure of the blood within the engorged vessels and this increased pressure will also aid the pushing out of water into the tissues.

The endothelial cells which line the small vessels and largely form the walls of the capillary vessels act in a physical sense as a semi-permeable membrane. A semi-permeable membrane is any sort of membrane or layer which allows water and small molecules to pass through but keeps back the larger molecules. It acts very much like a sieve. In normal circumstances the plasma proteins in the blood circulation are large molecules which cannot pass through the semi-permeable membrane. The concentration of large molecules on one side of the semi-permeable membrane exerts a force which is knows as an osmotic force, drawing fluid and smaller molecules, depending upon the permeability of the semi-permeable membrane, through into the blood in an attempt to dilute down the concentration of large molecules. This osmotic force is also known as the osmotic pressure. In inflammation, the permeability of the endothelial cells alters and as a result the large protein molecules can pass through so that they enter the tissue fluid. Therefore the difference in osmotic force between the two sides of the semi-permeable membrane alters and, due to the proteins which have been exuded into the tissue fluid, there is now a force there drawing more water out into the tissue spaces. The fluid which passes out into the tissues as a result of the inflammation is known as the exudate.

The lymphatic system also plays an important part in acute inflammation. The lining cells of the very small lymphatics separate a little, allowing material from the spaces in the tissues to drain into the lymphatics. There is thus a very great increase in the flow of lymph draining from an area of inflammation. This lymph is carrying not only normal tissue fluid with the extra plasma protein and blood cells but also various agents which may have caused the inflammation. In an injury, of course, these are only the products of tissue damage but if the inflammation has been brought about by infection or penetration by foreign material, this material or the bacteria will get into the lymph system and will be carried along in the lymphatics. They will then reach the regional lymph nodes which act as filters.

As was decribed in the first section of the book, the lymph nodes or lymph glands filter out any foreign material. As a result the regional lymph nodes themselves can become inflamed. Everyone will have experienced a sore, infected throat at some time in their lives and will have found that the glands at the angles of the jaw become enlarged and tender. This is because the glands at that site are acting as the filters for the lymph which has been flowing from the sore throat. As a result of the infection and the bacteria which the glands have filtered out, they themselves become the site of inflammation but, due to their capability to concentrate the white blood cells, they are able to deal with the bacteria or other materials and prevent them passing through into the rest of the blood stream. Occasionally, if the infection is severe, it can get through the lymph nodes. It then stands an excellent chance of being filtered out by more central nodes but if these nodes are also overcome it can reach the general circulation, producing a generalised infection throughout the body and severe illness in the person concerned.

As far as injury is concerned, there is usually at most some cell debris or breakdown products of blood which have to be filtered out, so any inflammatory changes which may occur in the regional lymph glands are only mild.

Cell Changes

In the early stages of the acute inflammation, the arterioles and capillaries are dilated and the flow of blood into the inflamed area is greatly increased. However, shortly after that, as the fluid passes out of the capillaries and very small vessels into the tissues, the concentration of cells left behind in the blood increases and the blood becomes more sticky, i.e. the viscosity increases. As a result of this, the circulation within the area slows down. With the slowing of the blood flow the white blood cells or leucocytes move to the periphery of the stream adjacent to the lining of the blood vessels. This phenomenon is knows as margination because the leucocytes are moving towards the margin of the blood stream in these small vessels. When the leucocytes reach the linings of the blood vessels, or the endothelium, they tend to stick to the endothelial lining. This is known as pavementing because under the microscope it has an appearance much like that of a cobbled street. The leucocytes then push their way through the walls of these tiny vessels. They penetrate the vessel wall in an amoeboid fashion by inserting a small portion of their tissue through the space between two cells in the lining wall and then gradually squeezing the rest of the cell tissue of the leucocyte through this space. It would be much the same if you picked up a jellyfish from the shore and then started to push it through a small knot hole in a piece of wood. As a jellyfish is so completely mobile, you would push a small portion through and as you went on pushing, the body would narrow down, the jelly fish would slowly go through the hole so that more and more of it appeared on the other side, which would get larger, until finally the last bit went through without any damage at all to the jellyfish (Fig. 2.1). This type of action is known as amoeboid movement because the very primitive cells, or amoebae, move

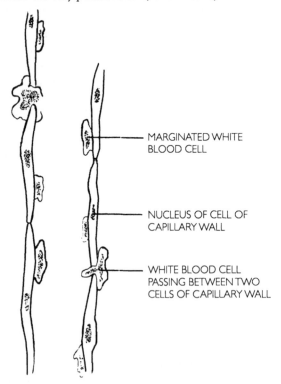

MARGINATED WHITE
BLOOD CELL

NUCLEUS OF CELL OF
CAPILLARY WALL

WHITE BLOOD CELL
PASSING BETWEEN TWO
CELLS OF CAPILLARY WALL

2.1 Diagram showing margination of the white cells along the walls of a capillary and two white blood cells passing through the capillary wall. The capillary wall is itself made up of cells each with its own nucleus. The white cell passes out between two cells forming the capillary wall and not through a cell body

along like this. The portion of cell they initially put out is known as the pseudopodium which, translated literally, means false foot.

Thus the leucocytes or white cells move from the capillaries into the tissue fluid so that they can deal as necessary with the cause of the inflammation. Once through into the tissue fluid, the leucocytes move very specifically in the direction required. This is brought about by chemical stimulation and the process is known as chemotaxis. The chemotactic signals which attract leucocytes can emanate from infectious agents, damage to tissues and substances produced by the proteins which have passed out from the blood stream by osmosis. There are several different types of leucocyte or white blood cell and they have different actions. The first cells appearing in large numbers within the exudates at inflammatory sites are the neutrophils, named thus because of their neutral staining character-istics. They are the commonest white cell in the ordinary blood circulation and have a very short life. There are large numbers kept in reserve in the bone marrow which can be released when required. At the site of inflammation, they are able to engulf bacteria or foreign materials by putting out pseudopodia and spreading around the particle and taking it within itself. This process is called phagocytosis. Once it has been enveloped within the cell, the particle or bacterium will be destroyed or digested by various enzymes within the cell. In an acute infection, if a sample of blood is taken and the white cells counted, there will be a greatly increased number of neutrophils per cubic millimetre of blood and this increase is taken as evidence of infection when a blood count is carried out.

The eosinophil is another type of blood cell. It is in much smaller numbers in the blood stream. It becomes dyed a bright red when the stain eosin is used, hence its name. Although it will respond in much the same way as the neutrophils and will kill some bacteria, it is basically a cell which gathers in much larger numbers when the inflammation is of the allergic type. Thus in allergic conditions, the count of eosinophils in a blood sample is increased.

The third type of white blood cell which comes in the group of granulocytes is the basophil. These cells are called granulocytes because the cytoplasm of the cell has large granules. In the basophil these granules stain a dark blue whereas in the other two types of granulocyte the neutrophil stains lavender and the eosinophil stains red. The basophils are only present in very small numbers in exudates. They are stimulated to release the contents of their granules into the surrounding fluid in non-specific and immunological reactions.

The monocyte is a different form of white blood cell and, unlike the granulocytes, the cytoplasm has very few granules. Its life is about four times longer than the granulocytes. Monocytes enter the exudate in small numbers and at a smaller rate than the neutrophils but with the passage of time their number increases steadily. When a monocyte is within the exudate it is usually called a macrophage and during normal circumstances it will often be wandering around through the connective tissue spaces in the body and it is sometimes then referred to as a histiocyte. Basically, these three names refer to the same type of cell. Its functions are very much like those of the neutrophils inasmuch as it is able to absorb particles and bacteria into itself and kill and digest them. When in the tissue, its life cycle is different from the neutrophil in that it can survive for very long periods. The neutrophil, as with the other granulocytes, cannot sub-divide and form new cells. The macrophage or monocyte is, however, capable of cell division when in the tissue fluid and it can also synthesise or build-up a variety of different enzymes within its own cell. Thus it is able to respond and deal with a variety of different noxious agents. Sometimes the macrophages will join together to form one large cell with several nuclei. These are known as multinucleated giant cells.

As mentioned, the macrophages are not only seen in the exudates at sites of inflammation but they are also normally distributed around the body and are not only in the blood stream as monocytes. They may also be fixed and line the vessels in the spleen, the liver and the bone marrow and also the walls of the lymphatic system. Their main function is phagocytic, i.e. the ingestion of particles which would otherwise be harmful to the body as a whole. They act as the street cleaners of the body. They are constantly working because in many aspects of daily life there is a release of a large number of bacteria into the blood stream, for example, eating and teeth cleaning will produce a lot of organisms in the blood stream. These rapidly get removed by the phagocytic activities of the macrophages. As a result, these episodes of what is known as bacteraemia are very short-lived and cause no harm at all.

The last type of leucocyte, which is the lymphocyte, is only present in very small numbers in exudates. However, if the exudate becomes old and the inflammatory reactions becomes chronic, the number of lymphocytes increases markedly. They are seen therefore in chronic infections such as tuberculosis. The functions of lymphocytes are largely in the production of various aspects of the immune reactions and are outside the scope of this book.

It will now have been seen that the inflammation is in fact a good or beneficial thing from the body's point of view. The increased blood supply has brought cells to clear up the tissue damage or infection. It has brought proteins and electrolytes to help with tissue repair and will also in various conditions have brought antibodies. The exudate can also start to form a clot, which is made up of fibrils of protein which work very much like a scaffold as the first stages of tissue repair. This will be mentioned a little later.

Types of Inflammation

There are three different types of inflammatory reaction. The normal one following an injury such as a cut or an infection such as a boil is known as an acute inflammation. The inflammation will develop rapidly with the various aspects which have been described. This will be followed by repair and healing all taking place over a relatively short period. If the infection is one which is known as chronic, then there is an advanced repair process going on but at the same time the inflammatory condition persists, so for a very extended period there is continuing inflammation with continuing attempts at repair alongside this. In chronic inflammation the aspects of acute inflammation are much less marked, i.e. there is less swelling and pain, although both these may persist to some extent as does also some degree of interference with function; heat is usually absent. A sub-acute infection is an intermediate between acute and chronic infection, where there is some evidence of repair but there is also some inflammation and exudation going on. It is often experienced by the subject as an area which does not seem to get really bad and yet does not seem to get better. When one refers to an inflammation of a particular part, it is usually named by taking the particular inflamed part and adding the four letters 'itis' as in tonsillitis or appendicitis. Arthritis is also well known and applies to an inflamed joint. If it is an injured joint which is painful and swollen, it will often be referred to as a traumatic arthritis, i.e. an arthritis which has been produced by trauma.

Inflammations are also sometimes further described by the type of exudate which is produced. While there is no need to go deeply into this as there are many different types of exudate, it is worth mentioning a serous exudate which is one composed largely of fluid and protein and has very few white cells. For the dancer the most common serous exudate that they will see is the fluid which is present in a blister. The swelling in a damaged joint may be a serous exudate with very few cells, or if the damage has been great and there has been actually some tearing, the fluid in the joint may contain a greater or lesser amount of blood, in which case it may be called an haemarthrosis. Another type of exudate which is well known is, of course, pus. In this the neutrophils are in such great numbers as to colour the fluid and make it white. The pus also contains products of digestion and disintegration of the damaged tissue.

Sequelae of Inflammation

Considering as we are in this book injuries rather than other conditions, we need to consider what happens after the initial acute inflammatory response to the injury. The result will depend largely on the degree of damage to the tissues. If there has been very little or no destruction of tissues, the inflammation will settle and what is known as resolution will take place and the tissues will return to normal. An example of this would be a small blister where the skin gets damaged. The exudate forms underneath the skin to give the actual blister, the skin over the blister breaks, the exudate is discharged, the area dries and heals with the dead epithelium slowly peeling off, leaving once again normal skin at that site.

If there has been a significant degree of tissue destruction then resolution cannot occur, i.e. the tissues cannot return to normal. In this case, the area where the tissue has been destroyed has to be repaired. Repair can occur in two different ways. The first and best way is by cell regeneration. This occurs when the neighbouring undamaged cells divide and reproduce and proliferate, replacing the damaged tissues with new cells which are identical to those which have been lost, thus replacing the whole area with the same kind of cell. The other method of repair is brought about by the proliferation of fibrous tissue, or connective tissue which produces a scar. Due to the differing abilities of the various kinds of cells and tissues to regenerate, repair is usually by a combination of regeneration and scar formation. The ability to regenerate depends entirely upon the ability of the cells in a particular tissue to sub-divide and produce new identical cells. Tissues such as the skin and the lining of the whole of the gastrointestinal tract can regenerate very well. Some of the internal organs such as the liver and kidney can also regenerate provided that the areas of damage are not too great. Unfortunately for the dancer, regeneration in muscle is normally very limited and healing is largely by scar tissue. Heart muscle cannot regenerate at all and heals entirely by scar tissue. Equally importantly, there is no regeneration at all of damaged nerve cells. Recovery after heart attacks occurs because neighbouring cells and the rest of the heart muscle take over the function. However, if the damage is too great the remaining heart muscle will be unable to cope properly and heart failure will occur. Similarly, in the brain, if cells have been destroyed by a stroke, which is either a haemorrhage or a thrombosis in the brain, they cannot be repaired or regenerate. Any function which does return is by adjacent cells taking over the actual neurological functions of the destroyed cells.

However, repair by scar tissue (fibrous tissue) is a very efficient and satisfactory repair process although obviously not as functionally good as the original tissue. The repair comes about in the following manner. Into the damaged area there is an ingrowth of proliferating connective tissue so that the damaged area becomes what is known as organised, the process being known as organisation. The ingrowing tissue is referred to as granulation tissue. This is made up of proliferating fibroblasts which produce fibrous tissue and proliferating capillary buds which form new capillary vessels, together with some white blood cells from the inflammatory process and the fluid parts of the exudate and loose connective tissue.

Organisation is already occurring within several days of the start of the inflammation. By the end of a week the granulation tissue is still loose so that the wound can be easily pulled apart. However, after about a week the fibroblasts in the granulation tissue produce substances which lead to the formation of the protein called collagen. The collagen appears as fibrils within the granulation tissue. As time passes the amount of collagen is gradually increased and becomes steadily more dense. It is the dense collagen which forms the actual scar and this process takes about two weeks to achieve sufficient strength to hold the wound together. Over the following weeks the collagen continues to increase in strength. The lines of the fibrils that have been laid down in the collagen gradually become more regular so instead of being higgledy-piggledy as will be the state to begin with, they become more arranged upon the lines of tension. In the early days this scar has a high vascularity and therefore looks pink. With the passage of time the scar loses the pink colour and becomes white, the length of time varying from person to person. Also varying in individuals is the amount of scar tissue which is laid down. Sometimes the scar becomes extremely thickened and this is then often referred to as a keloid scar. It may also be very irritating.

Healing of Injuries

There are two patterns of healing. The first is known as healing by first intention, or primary healing. The second type is referred to as healing by second intention. The most desirable form is healing by first intention.

HEALING BY FIRST INTENTION

If we consider a very simple injury such as a wound caused by a clean cut in the skin, where the edges have been brought together, we can see what happens in healing by first intention. Immediately after the wound occurs, there is bleeding, the wound edges are bound together by a blood clot, in which the stringy fibre acts as a binding material. At the edges of the wound an acute inflammatory reaction develops in exactly the fashion that has been described earlier. The various cells pass into the blood clot and the macrophages in particular begin to destroy it. As the demolition of the blood clot takes place, granulation tissue grows into the area and after a few days the wound is crossed completely by the granulation tissue. Obviously the length of time taken to bridge the wound depends upon the size of any gap. However, in primary healing, the gap should be minimal.

During this time, in a skin wound, the epithelium at the surface begins to regenerate and after some days there is a thin layer of epithelium across the wound surface. This epithelium gradually thickens and becomes mature so that it looks like the adjacent skin. In the deeper layers, the granulation tissue has matured to form a scar which is a dense collection of collagen or white connective tissue. In the skin, if the edges have been really well opposed, the final scarring at the surface may be practically invisible. In skin wounds which gape, the reason for putting in stitches is to hold the edges close together so that healing can take place by first intention.

HEALING BY SECOND INTENTION

Healing by second intention is largely similar to that which has already been described. However, it occurs in wounds or injuries where the edges cannot be brought together and opposed. This may happen at the skin level if there is tissue loss or if the wound is gaping and is not stitched up, or it can occur in deeper layers of tissue. In order to fill the gap, very much more granulation tissue is required and at the skin surface very much more regeneration of the epithelial cells. As a result, a very much larger scar is formed. Because the collagen is laid down in the granulation tissue and then matures, this leaves a dense mass of collagen or fibrous tissue. At the skin, this leaves a very obvious scar. It must be remembered that in deeper layers a similar mass of scar tissue will also form in order to fill a gap. As was mentioned above, different tissues have different powers of actual regeneration of cells. Therefore, in many areas where an injury occurs, the damaged area is repaired mainly or totally by fibrous scar tissue. This scar tissue can become adherent to adjacent structures. The presence of the mass of scar tissue in, for example a muscle, can impair the function of the muscle as a whole. It is therefore extremely important when an injury occurs to avoid further damage and hence the proliferation of scar tissue. If an injured part is exercised too early or unwisely, the the amount of scar tissue formed can be increased considerably.

Essentially, healing of any damaged tissue in the body is similar to that which has been described. Local variations occur because of different types of cells and

their ability or otherwise to regenerate. Even in bone, the actual healing process is similar. However, with the formation of the granulation tissue and accompanying the migration of the cells are two types of bone cell – the osteoblasts which are responsible for laying down new bone and the osteoclasts which are responsible for eating away the bone. Initially, in a fracture the broken bone ends are slightly eaten away by osteoclasts and the various minerals are released. This gives a very high level of concentration of the minerals required for bone repair. The healing takes place with the formation of granulation tissue and collagen and along this scaffold that has been laid down, osteoblasts will produce bone. This bone which is put down is done in a totally random manner. With the passage of time and the action of the osteoclasts, this new bone is eaten away and relaid so that the lines of the bony mesh are lying in the right direction. The bone slowly becomes mature and the outline becomes remodelled to a variable extent so that it tends to resume its old shape. This happens particularly well in children before they have stopped growing. The immature bone which is initially laid down during the process of healing of the fracture is relatively soft and springy. The hardness of bone that we recognise is brought about by the various mineral salts in the bone. As the new bone is formed, the mineral salts are gradually brought in and laid down and the bone hardens and becomes solid.

FACTORS AFFECTING HEALING

The most important factor associated with healing is the presence of a good blood supply to the damaged area. If the blood supply is very poor, the inflammatory processes do not take place adequately. This will lead to very slow or inadequate healing and also predisposes to infection because of the deficiency of the body's protective mechanisms, largely due to the inadequate number of white blood cells reaching the area. If the damaged part does not have adequate rest, the newly formed granulation tissue can be repeatedly damaged, which will again affect the blood supply to the area and also increase the amount of fibrous tissue which is laid down. Infection from the beginning, for example in a dirty wound, can also impair the healing processes as can other non-infected foreign material.

Even if healing has taken place normally, the scar tissue itself can cause problems. It may become stuck to local structures fixing them together, producing what are called adhesions. As scar tissue matures, it tends to shorten or contract. As a result, movements of a part may become limited resulting in permanent post-injury stiffness. A scar which contracts in the skin can produce a marked disfigurement and it takes little imagination to realise the limitation of movement which can occur by similar contractures occurring in the deeper tissues when they are damaged. Also, as already mentioned, at skin level an excessive amount of collagen may be formed leading to a very prominent scar which is known as a keloid scar. This is usually of cosmetic importance only, although at an area where rubbing can occur, the scar can tend to break down repeatedly and become sore. Occasionally, during the process of healing, small damaged nerve fibres can produce a lump of nerve fibres in the area of healing. This is known as a neuroma and a neuroma can produce a very painful or tender area within the scar.

The primary aim of any form of treatment is to obtain healing by first intention. This will produce the shortest recovery time, the minimum amount of scar tissue and hence the maximum return to full and normal function.

2.2 Types of Injury

Having discussed the patho-physiology of injury and how healing occurs we are now going to describe various types of injury with consideration of how the injury affects different parts and structures in the body. Although the general principles outlined above apply to all types of injury, because of differences in the structures in the body, the response to injury will vary between different structures and hence sometimes produce variations in the healing processes.

Joint Injuries

In considering the joints we will include not only the bony parts of the joint but also the capsule and any external ligaments that are supporting the joints, any internal ligaments of the joint, and the synovial lining of the joint. In addition, in the knee there are flaps of cartilage known as menisci or semi-lunar cartilages which stick out in the joint and are themselves subject to injury. The temporo-mandibular joint of the jaw is the only other joint to possess a meniscus.

The commonest injury to a joint is a sprain affecting one or more of its ligaments and usually the capsule and synovial lining in addition. A sprain occurs when the fibrous tissue of the ligament or capsule is stretched and this is accompanied by what are known as micro-tears within the substance of the ligament and capsule. In these micro-tears a varying number of fibres are actually torn. If the sprain is more severe there can be actual lengthening of the ligament as these torn fibres tend to pull out past each other. If the force continues the ligament can rupture and a gap occur.

The first structure to take the strain in an abnormal movement is usually one of the ligaments around that joint. If the stretch continues the adjacent capsule becomes involved and then the underlying synovial membrane lining the joint itself. A sprain produces local bleeding where the various fibres have been torn and this frequently shows superficially as discolouration beneath the skin, i.e. bruising. This particularly applies to joints which have little overlying tissue, such as the ankle. In deep joints (e.g. the hip) this bleeding is not usually visible in the subcutaneous tissues. If there is any damage or irritation of the synovial lining of the joint there will be an outpouring of fluid into the joint, causing the whole joint to become swollen. This fluid is produced by the synovial membrane and represents an attempt to flush away or dilute the irritant source. This is seen in anything more serious than a very minor sprain. Frequently the effusion is merely an excess of synovial fluid secreted by the irritated synovial lining. If there has been any damage to the synovial lining bleeding will occur into the joint, producing an haemarthrosis. An effusion or haemarthrosis is always painful, mainly due to the increase in tension in the joint although the blood itself is an irritant and causes pain. Both are indicative of serious injury. The only way to differentiate between an effusion and an haemarthrosis is to aspirate the joint with a needle and syringe. Sometimes an haemarthrosis is due to a fracture of the bone with the fracture line entering the joint. X-rays are required in order to exclude or to confirm a fracture.

It is very important to determine whether a sprain is relatively minor or whether it has progressed to the stage where there is a complete rupture of a ligament. This may be obvious on clinical examination but sometimes the examination causes too much pain for the patient to tolerate the proper testing of the ligaments. In these cases it may be necessary to administer an anaesthetic in order to test the stability of the joint. X-rays are taken at the same time in order to demonstrate whether there is any instability of the joint when it is strained in one or other direction (Fig. 2.2). In the case of damage to internal ligaments within a knee (the cruciate ligaments) or possible injury to a meniscus of the knee, then arthroscopy is invaluable. An arthroscope is a fine telescope which is inserted into the joint through a small wound, making possible direct inspection inside the joint. It is possible to carry out some operative procedures using the arthroscope; removal of portions of damaged meniscus can frequently be carried out with the help of the arthroscope and without opening the joint widely. However, for most conditions within the knee and certainly with injuries affecting other joints that require surgery, open operations are inevitable.

If significant ligament damage is undiagnosed early, the condition can progress to a chronic sprain or, if the

2.2A An X-ray of an ankle, showing that the talus is tilting during a forced passive inversion

2.2B The same X-ray without any inversion strain applied, showing that there is a normal appearance despite the presence of ligament damage

ligament has been greatly stretched, or ruptured, to chronic joint instability.

If there is any instability in the joint, the dancer feels very unsafe on that joint and it tends to give way frequently. This may or may not be accompanied by repeated swelling around the area as well as by pain. Late repair of undiagnosed ruptured ligaments is not very satisfactory and the results are far worse than repair of ruptured ligaments immediately after the injury. By immediate one means within the first twenty-four or at most forty-eight hours. Failure to institute surgery when necessary may result in a degree of instability sufficient to prevent the dancer getting back to full work with confidence. A late repair, although improving the situation, may still fail to give the required stability to enable the dancer to perform fully.

Sometimes a feeling of instability in the joint is due to damage to the nerve ends which lie in the capsule and ligaments. This can be improved by intensive physiotherapy in various forms. The ankle is the most common joint to be affected in this manner and here the balancing board is one of the most vital parts of the rehabilitation programme. (See Figs 3.3, 3.4 and 3.5 on p. 120.)

Within the joint itself there can occur occasionally what is known as an osteo-chondral fracture where a chip of the articular cartilage and a small fragment of the underlying bone is damaged and separates from the joint surface. This is uncommon in dancers as it usually follows a direct blow on the unprotected surface of a joint, such as the front of the flexed knee. However, in

certain types of inversion injury of the ankle, a fragment can be knocked off the dome of the talus.

Bone Injuries

ACUTE FRACTURES

In bones the common injury is a fracture when the bone is broken. A fracture is merely the medical name for a broken bone (Fig. 2.3). In children these fractures may be of the greenstick type where the fracture is only partial and is accompanied by some bending of the unfractured part of the bone. Sometimes fractures are accompanied by fragmentation of the broken ends and these are known as comminuted fractures. In compound fractures there is a break in the skin and sometimes the bone actually comes through the skin. Severe fractures are uncommon in dancers.

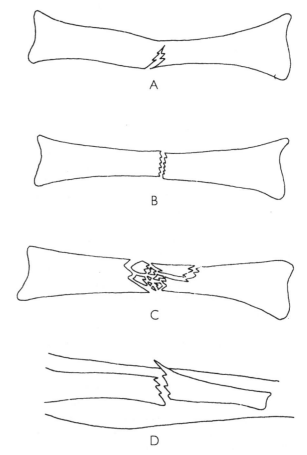

2.3
2.3A Greenstick fracture
2.3B Transverse fracture
2.3C Comminuted fracture where there are several fragments
2.3D Compound fracture where the bone comes through the skin

The commonest type of fracture is that affecting the 5th metatarsal. This is produced by a forcible inversion injury. Fractures can take from six weeks to many months to heal. Usually they are immobilised with a plaster of Paris cast. Occasionally internal fixation – plates and screws – is required. There are a few fractures which can be treated by simple strapping. During immobilisation the dancer should spend a great deal of time exercising all the other groups of muscles in the body that have not been immobilised by the plaster. Once the plaster is removed then time has to be spent strengthening up muscles which have become weak as a result of the immobilisation. Many fractures will be the site of aching even though the fracture has united satisfactorily. Although uncomfortable this is not of serious significance and in the long term gradually settles. Frequently the aching becomes more pronounced in cold or damp weather. It does not stop the dancer performing fully and certainly does not mean that there is anything wrong with the healing of the fracture.

Obviously it is of importance to diagnose a fracture early and to this end X-rays are usually required although a clinical diagnosis of a fracture is usually fairly straightforward and only requires X-ray confirmation.

STRESS FACTURES

These are particularly common in dancers and are more frequently seen than actual acute fractures. They occur as a result of repeated local stress on one area of the bone and come on gradually. If a bone is subjected to recurrent forces or stresses that are somewhat different from those experienced in everyday activities – walking, stair climbing, running relatively short distances, etc. or if these everyday activities are excessive – the area of bone that is being stressed will respond initially by gradually thickening up the hard cortex. This is well seen in dancers, especially in the 2nd metatarsal which, particularly if it is long, can often be seen to be very much thickened on an X-ray. When the stress ends, e.g. when the dancer retires, the stress thickening will gradually disappear and the bone will return to a normal X-ray appearance.

If the stress is more intensive and particularly if it is well localised, small cracks will develop in the bone. The local response is to invoke the inflammatory and healing mechanism. However, if the stress continues the cracking may proceed faster than the healing in which case a stress fracture or even multiple stress fractures (as often seen in the tibia) will occur. This produces a gradual increase in the amount of pain experienced by the dancer. Initially it will only trouble them while they are actually dancing, but as the stress fracture increases the pain becomes more continuous until eventually the pain is present all the time that

there is any type of activity, although it will usually disappear when the part is being rested completely. If the presence of a stress fracture is ignored it can progress eventually to a complete fracture of the bone. Additionally, the longer the dancer continues to work with a stress fracture, the longer it will take to heal. The history and examination should enable the diagnosis of a stress facture to be made without much difficulty. Persistent pain on activity, which is well localised to one area, is suggestive of a stress fracture. When examined, this area, if the bone is superficial, will reveal a local area of warmth, well localised tenderness and palpable thickening. These findings are highly indicative of a stress fracture. Early treatment in the form of rest from dancing activity should be undertaken.

Stress fractures usually do not show up if X-rays are taken in the early days. In the case of the metatarsal it may be two weeks before there is any evidence of a stress fracture. In the tibia (Fig. 2.4) or the pars interarticularis of the spine it may be several months before any X-ray changes are visible. It is most important that treatment is not delayed until there are positive X-ray findings otherwise the length of time for healing and recovery can be lengthened to many months. It is possible to confirm the presence of a stress fracture by a radio-isotope bone scan. The radio-active isotope is concentrated at the stress fracture site, producing what is known as a 'hot spot'.

As with other injuries, during the period of rest from dancing, the dancer can still do a whole series of exercises in order to keep the body in good physical trim. This programme of exercises should be worked out with the help of an experienced physiotherapist so as to ensure that no strain is put on the site of the stress fracture.

2.4 A stress fracture in the mid-shaft of the tibia

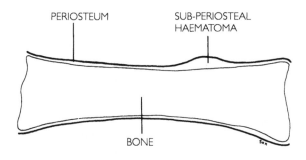

PERIOSTEUM   SUB-PERIOSTEAL HAEMATOMA

BONE

2.5 A sub-periosteal haematoma

Associated with bone but not an actual bony injury is a condition known as a sub-periosteal haematoma (Fig. 2.5). This results from a direct blow to relatively superficial bone such as the shin. Bleeding occurs between the periosteum and the bone, lifting the periosteum from the bone and producing an extremely painful lump. Treatment is symptomatic only. Very rarely the haematoma can become infected, producing an osteomyelitis. This is certainly more likely to happen if someone is injudicious enough to try to put a needle into it to aspirate the blood. An additional sequel to a sub-periosteal haematoma is that the blood may not be completely absorbed and some of this residual blood may be converted into bone, leaving a small bony lump at the site of the haematoma

Tendon Injuries

Tendons provide a strong connection between the contractile muscle belly and the part to be moved. They are composed of dense, strong, connective tissue and depending on the shape of the corresponding muscle and forces to be transmitted, can be thick and rope like, thin and wire like or a broad sheet. Tendons run from the muscle belly to the point of insertion on bone where they make a strong attachment to the periostium. They transmit large tensile forces generated by the muscle through constricted areas – the ankle, knee, wrist and elbow. They are strong, do not stretch much and have a limited blood supply.

They, like other structures, react to sudden overload, malalignment of joints and imbalanced forces with pain, thickening of the tendon and impaired efficiency. This collective term for injury to tendons is **tendinopathy**.

It is the jumping in dance that overloads tendons, as in other sports, and causes pain in the patellar tendon where it attaches to the kneecap (also known as 'jumpers' knee'). Pain in the mid portion of the Achilles tendon is the other main site. It is the more experienced or professional dancer who develops these serious and long-term pathologies and they must not be confused with the growth-related problems of the

young dancer. The tendon becomes thickened and painful in exercise and extremely sore to palpate. Ice, rest and anti-inflammatories may help short term but do not solve the problem and the dancer feels that he is losing strength in the area with persistent symptoms.

The last ten years have seen growing research in tendinopathies. Chronic pain in the (Fig. 3.33) proximal patellar tendon, the Achilles tendon and the hamstring tendon can seriously detract from training and performance and needs to be approached in the light of the most recent research. The term tendinitis refers to inflammation in the tendon but it is now accepted that long-term tendon problems are not inflammatory because they do not react to anti-inflammatory treatments and medication, and they do not heal. They have instead been described as degenerative, with a failure to heal.

Studies have shown that extra capillaries grow in an effort to supply the tendon with blood to aid healing (but the process is unsuccessful) and with the blood vessels nerve tissue also proliferates. The pain associated with the condition is thought to come from this. The tendon fails to manage the force demand and the dense organised collagen making up the tendon becomes disrupted and thickened with cellular-level changes. Tendinosis is the current term for this condition. The first line of action is to correct any biomechanical errors or technical problems. Rest, ice and gentle stretching should be carried out, but long-term problems need an evidence-based, planned rehabilitation.

Clinically, diagnosis is straightforward from the history of the problem, but ultrasound scanning and the use of a colour Doppler confirm tendinosis. Sound waves are passed into the tissues via a transducer and an image of the area is shown on a computer. The colour Doppler picks up blood flow and represents this in colour over the image. Therefore neovascularisation and increased blood flow is detected, and the condition confirmed.

There are many researchers at work experimenting with treatment of the condition. Various treatments involving injection have been and are being researched with successes reported. Sports physiotherapists will be informed of the latest treatment regimes and may well be working with researchers. The main conservative approach is using a carefully prescribed regime of eccentric exercise. This type of exercise maximally loads the tendon and when carefully prescribed, controlled and graded, can decrease pain. In patellar tendinosis unilateral, isotonic eccentric squats are prescribed. In Achilles tendinosis the isotonic eccentric ankle drop is prescribed with a programme of six to twelve weeks. Hamstring tendinosis can also be treated this way. Accurate diagnosis is vital and the conservative treatment regime of choice should follow the latest research guidelines and be monitored by a physiotherapist. In a case of debilitating pain that interferes with performance referral to a sports physician is advised for further treatment.

TENDON RUPTURE – PARTIAL AND COMPLETE

Partial rupture of a tendon is a more serious injury and is akin to the sprain which occurs in the ligaments. A dancer experiences sudden pain and may actually hear or feel something give way. A partial rupture results in the tearing of some of the fibres of the tendon while other fibres remain intact. There will be local bleeding at the site of the partial rupture and this will manifest itself as a local tender swelling. If the tendon is superficial, an increase in warmth can be felt by the examining fingers. Rest, with or without any immobilisation, is usually all that is required in order to allow healing of the partial rupture to take place. Occasionally however, surgical repair is indicated if it is considered that the partial rupture is fairly extensive or if there is doubt about whether there may or may not be a total rupture of the tendon. If adequate rest is not allowed for healing to take place, then the condition can progress to a chronic state where a combination of healing and further tearing is taking place at the same time. This normally occurs if a dancer does not take the necessary time off to allow complete healing to take place. After the period of rest an exercise programme is required in order to strengthen up the muscles which have been affected by the period of rest.

A total rupture of a tendon in dancers is fortunately very uncommon. In the population as a whole the commonest tendon rupture is where one of the extensor tendons is pulled off the distal phalanx of the finger, causing the phalanx to droop down into partial flexion; this is known as a mallet finger. This also occurs in ball games when the end of the finger is struck. Very occasionally in dancers the major tendons are ruptured, i.e. the Achilles tendon, the patellar tendon and the quadriceps tendon. Almost invariably this happens because of a sudden violent contraction of the muscle. This may take place because the dancer misses his footing or slips from a prop. More commonly it happens in the mature dancer or dance teacher who is demonstrating a large jump or unaccustomed routine which needs a sudden explosive burst of muscle power.

Immediate diagnosis is vital. Initially the diagnosis is fairly obvious but if some hours have elapsed the local swelling may be sufficient to disguise what was earlier an easily felt gap. Urgent repair in the first twenty-four hours is essential if a satisfactory functional result is to be obtained. Even so, the rupture of a major tendon will usually lead to the dancer failing to regain the same level of activity which was pertaining before the rupture. Apart from the immediate and skilful surgical repair, the post-operative physiotherapy plays a vital part in the satisfactory recovery of the patient. The treatment includes a full rehabilitation programme and a great deal of hard work by the patient.

TENOSYNOVITIS AND PERITENDONITIS

The tissues surrounding the tendon can be the site of inflammation and irritation. In those tendons which have a proper sheath the inflammation will affect this tendon sheath producing what is known as tenosynovitis. Some tendons, for example the Achilles tendon and the patellar tendon, do not have a sheath but the soft tissue around the tendon can become inflamed in exactly the same way as the tendon sheath. This is known as peritendonitis. In both tenosynovitis and peritendonitis the condition tends to be triggered off by over-use of the tendon. This can be caused by either faulty technique where the tendon is being repeatedly over-stressed or by too many repetitions of the same movement. Clinical examination usually shows that there is some swelling and tenderness along the line of the affected tendon and sheath. Movements are painful and frequently the examining finger can feel a crepitus or grating/creaking sensation over the moving tendon.

Treatment is by rest which usually produces rapid relief. In other cases ice, ultrasound and physiotherapy measures are required and some form of splintage may assist. In long standing cases, an injection of steroid will be helpful. Only on very rare occasions is an actual surgical decompression of the tendon sheath required. This is only necessary when the condition has become chronic and is not responding to conservative treatment. By then it has usually led to some thickening and scarring of the tendon sheath or the peritendinous tissues. Occasionally, there is a local cause such as pressure on a tendon. In dancers this is sometimes seen at the lower end of the Achilles tendon near its insertion, where badly fitting shoes can cause pressure. In sportsmen the high backs of the shoes or a shoe tab can cause great irritation of the Achilles tendon. Obviously where there is a local cause, this must be removed.

TENDON INSERTION INJURIES (ENTHESOPATHIES)

These occur at the site where the tendon goes into the bone and are usually in the form of a strain. Adequate rest is an essential part of treatment. Ultrasound, ice and occasionally steroid injections may be required. Frequently the response to treatment is slow and treatment may be prolonged.

Use of steroids in any type of tendon injury should be confined to chronic injuries only. Many authorities believe that steroid injections can pre-dispose to a total rupture of the tendon. Certainly injections of steroids should never be made into the tendon itself but only into the tissues around the tendon, either within the tendon sheath or in the peritendinous tissues. Repeated injections of steroids should be avoided as this is certainly more likely to lead to a tendon rupture. As at all other sites, steroid injections should not be looked upon as a quick cure to get the dancer back to full performance. After the steroid injection, even if the symptoms are relieved, a proper course of rehabilitation exercises must be instituted to prevent the condition rapidly recurring or progressing to a more serious injury.

Muscle Injuries

Fortunately, serious muscle injuries are not particularly common in dancers although minor muscle pulls and strains are quite frequent.

Muscles may be damaged by direct blows, such as an inadvertent kick or striking a prop or scenery. This can produce bruising with possibly some actual damage to a few of the fibres. A short period of rest accompanied by ice and ultrasound followed by some gentle graduated exercises and stretching usually produces a rapid resolution of the condition.

MUSCLE TEARS

Actual tears of the muscle may occur. Usually, these are only minor and partial, i.e. the tear does not extend right across the muscle and only involves a portion of the muscle belly. It is usually known as a pulled muscle and will occur in most circumstances because of an unco-ordinated contraction of the muscle or part of the muscle, frequently associated with an improper or incomplete warm-up or having to work in an environment which is too cold, possibly standing around between sudden bursts of activity. The tear may be centrally within the substance of the muscle or in the periphery of the muscle. The latter tends to cause less marked pain and interference with use than the former. In a central muscle tear the central swelling which occurs exerts pressure all around the periphery, whereas in a peripheral tear the bleeding is able to disperse and may track along the muscle, appearing at some distance from the site of the tear. However, having said that, it is frequently difficult or impossible to differentiate between the two types of tear. It is often only because recovery is taking very much longer than anticipated that one can come to the definite conclusion that it was a central tear which had taken place. If extensive bruising has appeared, this will be a peripheral tear so the dancer can be confident that recovery will be fairly rapid. A central tear will normally take three or four weeks to heal and allow recovery to take place. Treatment is initially by rest, in order to minimise the

amount of bleeding and to prevent any further tearing. Application of ice will help to decrease the amount of bleeding as will also compression by a firm bandage. Elevation of the injured limb will help to decrease the pressure in the injured area.

Early active and passive movements are instituted once it is certain that bleeding has ceased. The degree of exercise must be regulated by pain. Injudicious exercise can aggravate the situation. As the condition settles, a gradual increase in resisted exercises is required to build up the muscle. This is accompanied by regular, gentle stretching so that the scar tissue at the tear does not contract. The more time every day that the dancer can spend on the graduated exercises, the more rapid and satisfactory the recovery. A short period of exercise once a day with nothing in between is not conducive to a rapid recovery.

It is essential that the muscles return to full strength before the dancer is allowed to return to full dancing. However, with care, a gradual return to class can be used as part of the rehabilitation programme.

Occasionally, muscle damage can be complicated by formation of bone within the healing area of muscle. This is caused by damage to the periosteum at the same time as the muscle injury, leading to spillage of bone cells into the muscle haematoma. This bone formation produces a great deal of pain and there is marked limitation of movement. A very firm swelling can be felt deeply within the muscle and this swelling gradually becomes harder. X-rays will show that bone is starting to form in the muscle. The only treatment is to rest the muscle completely. Any sort of activity will aggravate the situation and increase the ossification. No form of physiotherapy helps and is certainly contra-indicated, as treatment is nearly always detrimental to recovery. Only when the bone has matured and there is no risk of it increasing can active physiotherapy start again. A satisfactory recovery usually occurs if these initial precautions are taken conscientiously. Only rarely is it necessary to remove the lump of bone. Unfortunately, this itself may lead to further spillage of bone cells and the condition can recur, so surgery should certainly not be undertaken lightly.

MUSCLE SORENESS AND STIFFNESS

Muscle stiffness usually follows unaccustomed exercise. It is therefore experienced most frequently when the dancer returns to work after a period of holiday. Grand pliés and jumping after a period of rest will register in the quadriceps and the calves. Occasionally it can occur if the dancer has to undertake a sudden increase in workload. The causes of the soreness may possibly be due to minute ruptures within the muscle fibres occurring in the muscle unprepared for heavy exercise, giving rise to local swelling and causing pain and inflammation. Another possible cause is the accumulation of various waste products which are not removed as rapidly in untrained as in trained muscle. However, neither of these theories has been proved.

This particular type of muscle soreness is called delayed onset muscle soreness – DOMS – and appears to be worst after unaccustomed eccentric exercise (muscle contraction while the muscle is lengthening). It is characterised by a dull ache 24–48 hours after exercise. This happens less in those who work consistently and train regularly. Regular cooling down after exercise with stretching and possibly massage can prevent this happening.

Whatever the cause of the stiffness, the treatment is to continue with regular classes and to gradually build up the work. It is important that classes are carried out in a warm atmosphere and that they are designed to give adequate warm-up with a graduated increase in the amount of work. Class should finish with an adequate cool/warm-down.

X-rays and Scans

Before any type of treatment can be started an accurate diagnosis must be made. It has always been taught that in 75 per cent of cases a diagnosis can be made at the end of the history which must be carefully and accurately taken. A further 10 per cent can be made at the end of the examination which is often merely confirming the initial diagnosis. A further 5–10 per cent can be finally diagnosed by special tests.

History taking and the skills of physical examination are taught during professional training and are outside the scope of this book. Similarly, blood tests and other pathological tests need not be considered. However, various scanning methods are frequently used in the diagnosis of problems in dancers and are of interest. It is important for the patient to know of the aims and the limitations of the different techniques. Dancers and other athletes probably have a much greater interest and insight in the physical functioning of their bodies than the average member of the population. Also to be able to actually see an image of, for example, a stress fracture will make the dancer (and the teacher or artistic director) more willing to accept an unwanted diagnosis and a possible recommendation to have a period off dancing than the unsubstantiated word of the physiotherapist or doctor.

X-RAYS

These were first discovered and described by a German, Wilhelm Roentgen, in 1895. He called them X-rays because a more accurate definition was not possible at that stage. However other scientists gave them the name of Roentgen rays and the pictures produced on photographic film, Roentgenograms. This name is still used at times in Germany and also in the USA. It is said that Roentgen himself disliked the use of his name.

Everyone will be familiar with the appearance of an X-ray picture. X-rays themselves are at the very short end of the electromagnetic spectrum. They have a very much higher energy than ultraviolet rays which themselves have a higher energy than visible light hence the burns which are caused by UV rays (sunburn). X-rays are ionising radiation, and are measured by their energy rather than by their wavelength. They are very much more dangerous than rays of much longer wavelength and much less energy. This was not realised by the early experimenters who frequently X-rayed themselves and their colleagues often causing permanent and sometimes fatal damage. Modern techniques and machines have made everything very much safer but even so unnecessary X-rays should be avoided, particularly in the case of young females.

X-rays are absorbed by tissues depending upon their density. As a result, bones or metal show up very clearly, whereas the soft tissues such as muscle and the internal organs are much less well delineated. In order to partially overcome this problem, for many years a contrast medium has been used. These were liquid iodine-containing products injected to show up kidney, spinal canal etc. or barium products used for the alimentary tract. Despite more sophisticated examinations now being available they still have a place. Most radiographs are now recorded digitally and viewed on computer sceens.

CT SCANS

CT is short for computerised tomography. It was invented by a British scientist, Sir Godfrey Hounsfield, who was awarded a Nobel prize. The patient lies in a wide, short tunnel and X-rays are sent from several directions through the body. The X-rays are absorbed to varying extents by tissues of different densities. Having been through the body they are picked up by detectors and the results computerised to give a cross-sectional image of that part of the body. In effect this is a slice across the body. As with plain X-rays, bone absorbs the most X-rays and the varying densities of the other structures allow the computer to produce pictures of the different structures. Various contrast media can be injected to enhance different tissues. As X-rays are used this is an investigation that should only be undertaken when there is a proper indication and not a 'well we might as well have it'.

MRI SCANS

Nuclear magnetic resonance imaging is the full name of MRI scans. Here nuclear refers to molecular cell components not nuclear radiation. The word nuclear has been dropped in the medical context to avoid any confusion or worry. MRI was originally discovered by Dr Raymond Damadian but he never produced any satisfactory images of the body parts. Those that were made took many hours. Sir Peter Mansfield of Nottingham University and Dr Paul Lauterbur of Illinois University produced the first rapid and satisfactory images. They were awarded a Nobel prize for their work. There were many other contributors to the development. At the University of Aberdeen Dr John Mallard and his co-workers are credited with producing early clinically useful scans. Unfortunately, unlike with X-rays and CT scanning, many people claim to have made important and original contributions to MRI scanning and indeed have probably done so. Ever-increasing refinements are still being made in relation to this technique, particularly in studies of the central nervous system. The authors must apologise to anyone who feels that they have been left out of the brief summary above.

The patient is placed in the narrow tunnel of the scanner in a very strong magnetic field. This aligns the protons of hydrogen in the water in the body. A second electromagnetic field at right angles knocks the protons out of alignment. They slowly drift back at varying rates depending on the tissue in which they lie, giving off different radiofrequencies. These are detected by the scanner and the computer converts them into visible images of the tissues and organs.

Unlike X-rays, the magnetic fields and the radio frequencies used in MRI scans are believed harmless to the patient, although it is still unknown whether there may be some harm from repeated exposures. As in X-ray rooms the radiographer retreats into another room for protection. There is a window and microphone to allow two-way communication with the patient.

From the patient's perspective the down-sides are that the examination can be extremely noisy from time to time and the tunnel is narrow and on current machines quite long. This can be claustrophobic for some people but this can be greatly diminished by listening to music with earphones and wearing an eyemask as handed out on long-haul flights. This prevents the patient looking at the tube which is only a few inches from the eyes. There are now 'open' scanners where the patient lies between two parallel interfaces and this is often acceptable to those with extreme claustrophobia in a tubular system.

Sometimes a contrast medium incorporating gadolinium is injected into a vein which helps to delineate various tissues.

MRI scans are much better for the study of soft tissues than CT scans whereas the latter are better for bone examination. The decision about the type of investigation must be left up to the professional concerned.

ULTRASOUND SCANS

These scans are produced by directing sound waves into the body from a hand-held scanner. A gel applied to the skin enhances contact between the scanner head and the body. The sound waves are reflected back by the body structures to varying degrees and are picked up by the scanner. A computer generated picture is produced on the screen which can then be printed as with the other scanning methods.

Ultrasound scans are usually better then MRI for the diagnosis of tendon and some other soft tissue injuries. They are very much cheaper and very much quicker to perform. Ultrasound scans have no harmful effects. Everyone has heard of their use in pregnancy.

Using Doppler techniques, blood flow especially that associated with inflammation can be evaluated.

ISOTOPE BONE SCANS

An isotope, also known as a radionuclide, is inserted into the body usually by intravenous injection. Various isotopes are used depending on the part to be screened. A technetium isotope is used for a bone scan. To scan a thyroid gland an isotope of iodine is used. The isotopes or radionuclides used diagnostically are produced artificially. They are unstable, having more neutrons than the stable or normal version. In the unstable state they give off energy as they break down. This is in the form of gamma rays and it is these rays that can be detected by a gamma camera. In the final form presented to the clinician they have an appearance similar to an X-ray. In bone, where there is an area of increased activity (i.e. an increase in the local blood supply), the isotope will be taken up in greatly increased amounts. On the film this is seen as a darkened area in the bone. The appearance is not in itself diagnostic but merely shows where the blood supply is increased. This change can be due to infection, tumour, fracture etc. However prior to requesting a scan the clinician will have the potential diagnosis in mind and the scan will confirm that there is pathology present. In dancers the investigation is usually requested because of a suspected stress fracture.

In bone scans the isotope is given by intravenous injection. This is followed by scan pictures which show the blood flow. There is then a break of three or four hours during which the isotope is taken up by the bone. During the waiting period it can be very helpful to drink plenty of fluids to wash out any excess isotope. At the end of this period the patient will be scanned again with the gamma camera.

The technetium isotope has a half life of six hours. This means that the isotope will have decayed to half its radioactivity in six hours. The amount of radiation in the very small dose of isotope is not dangerous and amounts to much the same as an X-ray. However until the isotope has decayed the patient is giving off small amounts of radioactivity and is usually asked to keep away from pregnant women and children. Very occasionally, patients may be allergic to contrast media and isotopes used in imaging, so it is prudent to report any known allergy before any investigation.

2.3 Causes and Complications of Dance Injuries

All dance injuries are caused by faulty technique.
Dance injuries are not an Act of God.

There is no doubt that this is the most important fact the dancer or dance teacher must understand. When trying to determine the cause of an injury the first question which must be asked by the professional dancer or student, by the dance teacher or by the medical attendant is 'What technical fault has led to this injury?' Once they have started asking this question they are at least part way to making the right diagnosis and instituting the correct treatment and remedial measures. The aim must be a full recovery as rapidly as possible and, equally importantly, the prevention of recurrences of the same injury.

Always remember that the cause or causes of injury may not be apparent except on detailed and meticulous observation and examination.

A small percentage of injuries are best called dance-related injuries and are not dance injuries as such. Under this heading would be included injuries which are sustained during the course of dancing but have extrinsic causes arising from environmental conditions – floors, costumes, shoes – rather than faulty technique.

There is also the dancer who is suffering from an injury which is neither a dance injury nor a dance-related injury. A bad fall downstairs can fracture a foot or ankle. Treatment will follow standard lines but, during rehabilitation, which should start from the early stages of treatment, consideration should and must be given to the fact that the patient is a dancer and will be required to return to a very high level of activity. Rehabilitation must be intensive and thorough.

Causes of Dance Injuries

INJURIES CAUSED BY FAULTY TECHNIQUE

Anatomical Causes
As most dancers are not anatomically perfect for dance,

there will be physical limitations and constraints which may play a part in preventing the development of a perfect technique. Certainly the commonest anatomical cause of potential problems and injuries is limitation of turn-out (external rotation) of the hips.

It is important for the dance student and the teacher of the student to realise and appreciate as early as possible the exact anatomical limitations present so that the student can learn to work within his true physical range. During their early years students must learn to make the best use of all aspects of their physical potential but should not attempt to go beyond that. Reference to **Section 5.7** will enable you to appreciate all the troubles and problems that can arise if dancers attempt to turn the feet out further than the hips allow, i.e. by attempting to exceed their physical potential or limits.

The hypermobile physique may have the range of movement but not the control which can be equally stressful on the joints. Strengthening, stabilisation and technical coaching will be the only way to prevent injury and further a career.

Lack of Technical Knowledge
During student years young dancers will be more prone to injury as they try to put into effect technique which they are in the middle of learning. Many injuries are seen during this phase of their career, usually minor, particularly if facilities are readily available for early diagnosis and treatment. If, however, these facilities are not available, it is also at this stage of their lives that the injury can become long-term and persistent. This is usually a result of a failure to appreciate the actual cause of the injury so that the young students do not receive the technical help which is needed to prevent the injury becoming recurrent or chronic.

Bad Teaching
Teachers can cause injuries as they commonly fail to appreciate the anatomical limitations of the student in front of them. They fail to recognise areas of weakness which may be exacerbated at some particular time by a growth spurt, by a medical illness such as glandular fever, or by some other extraneous problem. They can fail to notice technical faults which the child is developing and, even worse, they can be teaching technical faults which can cause injury or compound problems already present. Over-turning the feet in relation to the hips is probably the commonest single teaching fault, e.g. demanding a flat or 180° turn-out at the feet which is not matched at the hips. As a general rule the feet should not be turned out further than the available turn-out at the hips. Putting children on to pointe too early and before they are strong enough or pushing them into examinations or other situations

with which they are not ready to cope, can also produce very significant problems.

Non-application of Correct Technique
This situation includes professional dancers who are technically fully trained but who for various reasons may allow their technique to slip. This is particularly prone to happen when they become tired. It is seen frequently during the course of a long tour. In this situation, as the tour progresses, the injury rate gradually increases due to a combination of many performances, a great deal of travel with insufficient rest between performance venues and frequently, inadequate conditions for performance and of hotel facilities.

In this sub-section should also be included injuries which are produced by overtaxing choreography, where the choreographer may, during the never-ending search for something totally new, embark on a routine which is so awkward that good technique cannot be applied. In this situation dancers may become injured while they are trying to develop a technique in order to carry out the required routine, or injury may follow the unaccustomed use of the body. A new way of working requires gradual development.

ENVIRONMENTAL CAUSES OF INJURY

These causes will produce what might be termed dance-related injuries, although the environment may in fact contribute to genuine dance injuries themselves. Over most of these environmental causes the dancer personally will have little or no control, although the experienced professional should be able to recognise the potential dangers and at least make representations for an improvement or correction of whatever defect is present.

Among the environmental causes are inadequate facilities. This particularly applies to a lack of daily class opportunities as pertains in many stage shows which involve a great deal of dancing, as opposed to professional dance companies where the daily class is part of the routine working of the company. In a large town it may be possible for the dancer to go out and join an open class if one is available. However, in some areas adequate classes may not be held and it is in this situation that the management, if they fail to provide facilities for their dancers to carry out a daily class of their own, would be creating an environmental cause for the development of injuries among the dancers concerned. If the dancer has no access to a space large enough for him even to construct his own daily class, he will be in the situation where he has to go into the show each evening without any adequate preparation earlier in the day. It is at times such as this that injury rates can be seen to rise steadily. It is certainly in the

management's own interest either to provide the actual facilities for a daily class for all their dancers including, if possible, someone to take the class, or else to make arrangements for the dancer to have the opportunity to attend an outside class. This failure on the part of management and promoters is probably as much due to their lack of appreciation of the requirements of their dancers as any deliberate disregard of these necessities. From this point of view the dancers themselves, together with their representatives, must take some of the blame for not insisting on the provision of adequate facilities.

Among the genuine environmental causes which may predispose to injury are (a) temperature (b) floor.

Temperature
The ambient temperature in which the dancer is expected to take class, rehearse or perform must be such that they do not become chilled before, during or after any of these activities. The ambient temperature should not be allowed to fall below 68–70°F. As has been mentioned in the causes of injuries (**Section 2.2** Muscle Tears, p. 83), muscle injuries in particular are far more likely to occur if the dancer is inadequately warmed-up. Excessively high temperatures, although not predisposing directly to injury, have their own complications, notably the production of excessive sweating leading to loss of water and electrolytes (mainly salt). If this loss is adequately replaced then no harm will accrue. However, there is a tendency for the dancer to inadequately replace the fluid loss and this can lead to muscle cramps and spasms as well as more serious medical problems if it occurs over a longer period (see Water and Hydration, p. 114).

The Floor
This is an extremely important factor in environmental causes of injury. The actual floor construction is of the greatest importance to the dancer. Unfortunately, in many modern theatres and in studios which are not purpose-constructed the underlying foundation for the floor is reinforced concrete. The sight of a wooden floor should not delude the dancer into thinking the wood has been sprung. Only too frequently it has been laid directly on a concrete surface, or upon rolled steel joists. The lack of spring can produce many injuries, notably foot problems, injuries in the lumbar region of the spine, in the muscles which are associated with take off and landing and in the bones, mainly the tibia and the metatarsals, which can be the site of stress fractures. Floor construction is a complicated subject and outside the sphere of this book. However, it does appear that provided classes and rehearsals are carried out on a floor which is completely suitable for dancing, then occasional performances which are carried out on

inadequate floor constructions may be acceptable provided the inadequate floor is covered with two layers of special cushioned vinyl. Although this is the current thinking, further experience may indeed show that even this covering of a solid floor is, in the long term, inadequate, particularly if performances are regularly held on that type of surface as opposed to a short series in one particular theatre or television studio.

A second factor in floor construction applies to stages. Many touring companies will find that they have to work on a heavily raked stage. While this is eminently satisfactory for normal theatrical productions in giving the audience a far better view, it does pose great problems for dancers. The presence of a rake not only predisposes to the development of injuries but it can also delay recovery from minor injuries which are insufficient to stop the dancer from working. Predominantly, a raked stage will cause a weight back situation with all its associated problems (see Section 5). Additionally, moving *across* a rake poses different problems. Unfortunately, there is nothing that can be done about the presence of a raked stage but it is important that the dancer and therapist are aware of the possible dangers.

Finally, when considering the floor, the actual surface is important. The difficulties associated with a slippery surface are obvious. The lateral hip and thigh muscles tighten as they grip to stabilise, with all the ensuing problems. Less obvious, however, is the over-use of rosin. Unless the floor is cleaned regularly, the rosin can build up, frequently in irregular and uneven patches. This can result in a dancer suddenly finding that his foot is sticking to the floor with potentially disastrous consequences if he is in the process of a turn, when the transmitted twist between the fixed foot and the moving body can produce serious injury at the ankle or knee.

General Complications of Injury

EFFECTS ON THE WHOLE BODY

Decrease in Cardio-respiratory Fitness

As a result of the enforced decrease in activity fol-lowing an injury, the cardio-respiratory fitness of the dancer will decline. In other words, when he returns to exercise, he will get out of breath more rapidly, his pulse rate will increase to a higher level and he will feel his heart pounding for a given activity. These effects are largely brought about because the stroke volume of the heart will have decreased. In other words, the amount of blood pumped out on each contraction of the heart will be less, hence to get the same amount of blood to the various organs, in particular the muscles, the heart will have to beat more quickly. In the trained person,

the heart will on each stroke pump out a larger volume of blood than in the untrained heart, therefore the athlete can maintain an increased blood flow to the muscle by a combination of increased volume from the heart on each stroke as well as an increased stroke rate. In the untrained heart, the demand for more oxygen and a greater requirement for the removal of carbon dioxide will result merely in an increase in heart rate, with little ability to increase the volume of blood on each stroke. This at the limit will produce a situation where the heart will reach such a rate that inadequate time is given for the heart to fill between each contrac-tion so that a further increase in rate would be self-defeating. During the course of training the heart responds by a greater relaxation between each con-traction, which allows a greater volume of filling, thus increasing the quantity of blood pumped out on each contraction. On the respiratory side, the chest capacity and lungs will undergo a similar adaptation so that the volume of air which is breathed in and out on each occasion becomes very much greater.

Generalised Muscle Wasting

This comes about due to inactivity. As a result of the lack of demand the bulk of the muscles will gradually decrease (muscle wasting), the tone will go down, as will also the strength of contraction of each muscle. If the inactivity is prolonged, the muscles will become increasingly flabby. During this period they will also tend to shorten a little, thus slightly decreasing the available range of movement.

Increase in Body Weight

This is by no means inevitable. However, eating patterns are in general psychologically based rather than occurring as a result of demand. Therefore, although the calorie requirements are greatly decreased as a result of the decrease in activity, the calorie intake will probably remain very much the same. These extra and superfluous calories will inevitably be laid down as fat as they cannot be metabolised. If eating is controlled sensibly following an injury, then this weight increase need not occur, although at the same time an adequate balance of nutrients must be maintained in order to facilitate rapid healing (see **Section 2.7**).

Psychological Effects

These may be more or less noticeable depending upon the mental make-up of the individual dancer. However, if the injury is such that the dancer has to be off work, a general feeling of depression is not uncommon. This seems to reach its peak when dancers have been off about five weeks, at which time most of them will become very depressed, will sleep badly and generally feel that no progress is being made at all. If this is anticipated and the dancer is given the support from teacher and therapist he will usually get over this period without very much difficulty. An occupational psychologist can explain coping techniques and help the dancer put the injury and rehabilitation in perspective.

LOCAL EFFECTS

Persistent Swelling
Although swelling follows most injuries, it will normally settle fairly rapidly. Not unusually, the swelling may be such that it has disappeared when the dancer gets up each morning but then gradually recurs during the day. This type of swelling can be helped by elevation from time to time during the day but will gradually lessen and disappear during the course of treatment and the normal healing processes. The dancer merely needs reassurance. However, the swelling may become more permanent. If it is still present first thing in the morning, particularly if the dancer has been elevating the foot of the bed, it may have more serious significance. In the early days the swelling will be due to retention of fluid locally and this can drain away. If, however, drainage is for any reason inadequate, either because the part has not been elevated sufficiently or because there has been more local damage than had been realised, the swollen area may become invaded with fibrous tissue and permanent thickening and scarring can result, hence the importance of the early elimination of swelling as part of the initial and continuing treatment process.

However, this invasion with scar tissue will not take place if the situation is such that the swelling has always disappeared after a night's rest with elevation of the injured part. Permanent thickening, although it may be inevitable if the injury is serious with considerable soft tissue damage, can unfortunately occur just as commonly as a result of inadequate treatment and advice to the dancer. It is in these latter circumstances that it is totally avoidable and to allow it to develop is unforgivable.

Local Vascular Effects
These may play a part in the development of persistent swelling. There may be damage to the local small vessels, particularly the capillaries and lymphatics, which interfere with the resorption of tissue fluid. Elevation of the injured part becomes even more essential in order to aid the drainage of tissue fluid by the use of gravity. With the passage of time, damaged vessels will usually reform themselves and blocked channels will become reopened or new ones will develop. During this part of the healing phase, assistance can be given to the normal body processes by minimising swelling and aiding resorption of the fluid by ice and elevation and other local methods.

Less common are local aberrant vascular responses resulting in greatly increased blood flow with flushing or constriction of vessels with blanching. These effects may be caused by the nervous system but normally will settle spontaneously. At the periphery of the upper or lower limbs there is a rare vascular phenomenon (Sudek's dystrophy) where the bones of the hand and wrist or foot and ankle become partially de-mineralised. The skin becomes tense and shiny and the tissues tend to be swollen. The exact causes for the onset of this syndrome are unclear but there is no doubt that it can be aggravated by immobilisation. Unfortunately, because of persistent pain associated with the condition there is a tendency to prolong the period of immobilisation and this makes the situation very much worse. It can be helped by active movements and use and therefore activity of the part is to be encouraged provided that this is compatible with the healing of any underlying fracture. Fortunately, the condition is normally self-limiting and recovery will be spontaneous, though possibly slow.

Local Muscle Wasting
The causes of this are the same as described above for general muscle wasting. However, due to the local inactivity of the injured part, the muscle wasting in this area will be rather greater, particularly if the limb has had to be immobilised because of a fracture. The muscle wasting will occur rapidly and can be noticeable within two to three days of an injury. By the end of this time the decrease in tone of the muscle can be easily felt by the examining fingers and there can even be a measurable difference when compared with the other limb. Muscle wasting and weakness can be minimised by exercising as much as the injury or immobilisation will allow. It is very important to try to develop some sort of suitable exercise routine which can be initiated early and applied throughout the rehabilitation period (see **Section 2.5**).

Stiffness of Joints
Following inactivity the whole body will tend to feel rather stiffer. If there has been immobilisation of a joint or joints during the course of treatment then, once the immobilisation is discontinued, the joints will be found to have stiffened up to a greater or lesser extent. This stiffness occurs in the soft tissues around the joint, i.e. the capsule and the ligaments, in the soft tissue planes between the various structures and within the muscles themselves which may have very slightly shortened. Additionally, a weaker muscle is usually less able to relax and lengthen than a trained muscle, so this will also contribute to some loss of movement range. In the normal course of events, provided the joint itself has not been the site of damage, this post-

immobilisation or post-inactivity stiffness will wear off fairly rapidly and full mobility will be regained. Once again, exercise is the most important factor in the regaining of a full movement range, together with general strengthening of the muscle groups which control the joints. If, unfortunately, there has been some damage to the joint itself, particularly within the joint, then some restriction of movement may be permanent.

2.4 The Treatment of Injuries – General Principles

The most important fact to recognise is that treatment itself does not heal injuries. Injuries heal by the processes described in **Section 2.1** and are entirely brought about by the body alone.

Treatment can be considered as having primary and secondary aims.

The Primary Aim of Treatment

It must, in essence, be the provision of the optimum conditions so that the body's natural processes of healing can work in the most efficient and rapid manner. These optimum conditions are rest, maintenance of a good blood circulation and a ready supply of the necessary nutrients.

REST OF THE INJURED PART

The rest will allow healing to proceed unimpeded. Movement may cause damage to the granulation and other healing tissue, thus resulting in the end in a great increase in the amount of scar tissue that is formed.

Disadvantages of Rest
If the area rested is too widespread, for example involving the whole limb or even the whole person, then this will have a three-fold undesirable effect. First, there will be a decrease in stimulation of the circulation. Second, unnecessary muscle wasting will occur. Third, if rest is very prolonged the bones become de-mineralised. Ideally, therefore, the actual area of injury alone should have rest and all the other areas should be encouraged to remain active.

Effects of Immobilisation
The collagen and other tissues of the fibrous network, such as areola tissue, become hard and dense with loss of suppleness during periods of immobilisation. It will start to occur after a few days. The time taken to recover mobility depends on the length of the immobilisation. However, the recovery time to regain full

motion is not a simple arithmetical progression but a geometrical progression. This means that immobilisation for, say, four weeks, will not take merely twice as long to recover from as immobilisation for two weeks but will take four to five times as long.

MAINTENACE OF ADEQUATE CIRCULATION

A good blood supply is essential as has been explained in **Section 2.1**. The blood stream is responsible for bringing most of the necessary cells, proteins, minerals and other requirements for satisfactory healing to take place. Therefore, a good circulation of blood is to be encouraged and factors which can interefere with the blood supply have to be eliminated as far as possible. Probably the most important factor which intereferes with the blood supply to the injured part is local swelling. Following the injury there is a great out-pouring of blood and fluid into the tissues. This should become absorbed by the lymphatics and circulation. However, this reabsorption can become impaired and the swelling can become greatly aggravated by the effects of gravity and by local inactivity. The heart will have no difficulty pumping blood to the injured part in normal circumstances but drainage via the veins or lymphatics can be greatly hindered by increased pressure due to local swelling and by the effects of gravity. If the swelling increases too greatly it can actually restrict the flow of blood into the part and therefore interefere with healing. This can occur to such a degree that the areas adjacent to the damaged tissue can start to die from lack of blood supply and this produces what is known as tissue necrosis. Two important and relatively simple measures can be used to help to decrease this local swelling and maintain an adequate circulation.
a) *Elevation* If the injured part, usually the foot or some other portion of the lower limb in the dancer, is elevated, gravity can be used to advantage to help the swelling drain away from the injury.
b) *Ice* Local application of ice packs or cold packs help to reduce the swelling. NB. Care should be taken with the use of ice packs, particularly if they have been stored in a deep freeze where the normal temperature is 0°F (minus 18°C). (See **Section 2.5** Technique of Application, p. 93.)

The measures which are taken to minimise bleeding and swelling at the site of injury are not a contradiction of the statement that a good *circulation* must be maintained. Blood circulation implies that the blood is taken to a part and then removed again via the veins. If there is bleeding at a site of an injury this blood is lost to the circulation as well as increasing local swelling. The ideal is to ensure that there is minimum bleeding following the injury but also then to maintain the maximum circulation.

c) *Pressure bandaging* The purpose of this is to minimise bleeding at the injury site. The compression should aim to apply enough pressure to control the blood loss into the tissues but at the same time not to be so excessive that the circulation becomes impaired. Less pressure is required to impede or stop the venous return than to impede or stop the arterial inflow. If the venous return alone is impaired then the effect will be to increase rather than decrease swelling because the arterial blood will continue to be pumped into the area. Unless properly applied, compression is better avoided. It is only of value until local bleeding has stopped and should then be discontinued.

Elevation and ice are easily instituted by the patient or helpers and, if carried out immediately, can play a great part in the rapid recovery from an injury. These simple measures, accompanied by a short period of rest for the injured part, may be all that is required to allow satisfactory resolution to take place.

In achieving the primary aims of treatment (i.e. rapid healing with minimum scarring) the physiotherapist has a part to play by the use of ultrasound, etc. This will be described later.

ADEQUATE NUTRITION

This may sound a strange statement when applied as it is to a society affluent enough to afford to maintain dance companies and similar 'luxuries'. However, as will be described in **Section 2.7** on Nutrition, many dancers (as well as other athletes) have very bizarre ideas of what they should be eating. These faulty eating patterns are frequently associated with very undesirable attempts to achieve a weight far lower than is healthy. Without an adequate supply of nutrients the body cannot properly repair tissue damage from injury or even maintain tissues in the best condition following the normal cycles of cell breakdown and repair that constantly occur in all living organisms. During the whole of life various tissues in the body are in a state of change and replacement. There is a continuous change over of the constituent parts of cells. The various body proteins are being broken down and rebuilt, the minerals are being moved around and cells that die are being replaced daily by the million. This is one of the characteristics which makes a living organism as opposed to something like a lump of rock which, however chemically complex it may be, does not alter within itself.

The Secondary Aim of Treatment

This is so to arrange a rehabilitation programme that, while the primary aims of treatment are not jeopardised, the rest of the body can be kept in the best possible physical condition. This includes maintaining cardio-vascular and respiratory fitness as well as ensuring that all possible muscle groups are kept strong and active and are not allowed to waste or weaken. To this end the most important action is to construct an exercise programme for the particular dancer for his or her particular injury.

It must be recognised that rehabilitation, if it is to achieve the greatest success, should start immediately following injury and is not something which is commenced days or weeks later.

2.5 Specific Treatments of Injuries

Although most forms of treatment have to be administered by a physiotherapist or in the case of more sophisticated treatments, by an orthopaedic surgeon, there are certainly some measures which can be applied satisfactorily by the dancer himself. These are cold therapy or ice, elevation, rest of the injured part and exercise. The latter, of course, can only be carried out by the subject and no third party can do exercises for him.

First-Aid Measures

In most acute injuries, i.e. an injury which happens suddenly as opposed to a chronic injury which comes on very slowly and insidiously and is usually the result of recurrent minor traumas, there are certain measures which should be carried out as soon as possible by the dancer. If carried out immediately they can have a very beneficial effect in dramatically decreasing the time during which the dancer will be partially or wholly incapacitated.

ICE

As soon as the injury has occurred, ice should be applied to and around the injured area. The actual technique of application will be described a little later under the specific physiotherapy treatments (see p. 92).

ELEVATION

The icing should be accompanied by elevation of the injured part in order to discourage swelling. As most dancers' injuries occur in the lower extremities, gravity plays a very important part in increasing the amount of swelling. If the leg is elevated then gravity will assist in the drainage of fluid from the injured area.

REST

Rest will encourage early healing to take place without extra disturbance of the damaged tissues. In other words, don't carry on with the class or performance if the injury is anything other than of a trivial nature. Take a taxi home rather than walk a long distance or stand on public transport. Once home, continue with the ice and elevation. These simple measures promptly applied can frequently halve the length of time for recovery.

COMPRESSION

Firm bandaging to compress the injured area is often advised. The purpose is to arrest the local bleeding which occurs at the site of any injury. While theoretically advantageous it can have undesirable complications. In order to arrest the local bleeding the pressure must be sufficient to compress the vessels. If this compression is maintained for too long, or if too extensive, then interference with essential blood supply can occur and there may be local tissue necrosis (death). If used, it should be for a relatively brief period. Once bleeding at the site of injury has ceased, compression can no longer be of any benefit.

In the case of a mild strain it might well be possible to continue class or performing with the use of supporting bandaging or strapping. However, it is important to be certain that there is no serious underlying injury before this action is taken. Immediately after an injury the damaged part can rapidly become slightly numb and during this period the injured person may not be aware of the possible serious nature of any damage. To continue activity in the presence of a fracture can greatly prolong the actual recovery period or even do more significant damage.

In this short section on first aid measures, a cautionary word against the use of pain-killing tablets or even more powerful pain-killing injections would be in order. If the pain is sufficient to interfere with a performance then nine times out of ten disguising the pain with tablets or injections to allow the performance to continue is merely going to hide temporarily a significant underlying injury. To perform in that state is going very greatly to increase the period of recovery and may indeed cause such further damage that the dancer's career may be ruined – either because he will never be physically capable of returning to dance or because the recovery is so prolonged that he may lose his job.

Never forget that pain is a protective mechanism provided by nature in order to stop further damage taking place and to allow recovery to take place in the shortest possible time. Another protective mechanism which some people will try to abolish without due consideration of the consequences or of the next steps in the progress of treatment, is muscle spasm. Muscle spasm is nature's way of providing splintage to an injured part. The muscles around the damaged area will tighten up in order to attempt to immobilise the area. In other words, to provide local rest to the part in order to permit healing to take place as rapidly and successfully as possible. The abolition of muscle spasm by drugs or other methods without due regard to what is taking place underneath and without proper consideration of the next line of treatment can be almost as damaging as the injudicious use of pain-killing drugs. The abolition or relief of muscle spasm at the correct time, i.e. during the course of proper treatment, is highly desirable, but certainly not in order to allow the dancer to continue performance regardless of consequences.

The dancer should always remember that following injury the responses of the body that have been provided by nature have been developed by evolutionary processes to provide the optimum conditions for healing of the injured part. It is only when *adequate* treatment is provided that nature's own protective mechanisms can be removed. It cannot be over emphasised that far too many dancers and other athletes have had their convalescence unnecessarily prolonged by unwise treatment provided either by themselves or by their friends or by ignorant advisors.

It is obviously in the dancers' and their employers' greatest interest that the injury should cause the shortest possible time off work or classes and that recovery should be as complete as possible. An incomplete recovery can be very troublesome as it usually leads to recurrent injuries, either of the same part or elsewhere.

Physiotherapy Treatments

COLD THERAPY

This is usually loosely referred to as ice. However, the cold can be applied by various methods as described under the Techniques of Application in this section. The uses of cold therapy are for
a) relief of muscle spasm;
b) mechanical trauma;
c) pain relief;
d) arthritis;
e) burns.
The last two – arthritis and burns – are not relevant to this book.

In Muscle Spasm

The use of cold therapy in muscle spasm can decrease the actual tone in the muscle itself, provided that the muscle temperature is lowered. If the muscle temperature is not lowered then the tone is not decreased and the muscle spasm is not relieved. Cooling of the skin alone may, in fact, increase the spasm. It may take from ten to as long as thirty minutes, depending upon the amount of fat present, to produce a decrease in the temperature of the muscle.

However, the effect, once achieved, is long lasting due to the insulating effect produced by the vaso-constriction in the fat layer. The fat itself is an excellent insulator and the insulation effects are improved by the vaso-contriction of the blood vessels in the fat, i.e. the shutting down of the blood vessels.

Decreasing the spasm in an antagonistic muscle will free the protagonist and can enhance its performance by up to 50 per cent. The effect on the muscle can also help facilitation techniques.

In Mechanical Trauma
Cold therapy can be used advantageously in mechanical trauma. The trauma should be acute, i.e. of recent onset, but it should not be used in severe trauma. The cold works by vaso-constriction (shutting down) of the blood vessels which in turn reduces swelling and bleeding. To this end it is as well to remember the great benefits of applying ice as soon as possible after the injury and before there has been very much swelling or bleeding. The vaso-constriction is produced by its effect on the sympathetic fibres and also directly by lowering the temperature of the blood within the blood vessels.

In Pain Relief
Pain relief by the use of cold therapy is brought about by several pathways. The pain may be decreased by a direct effect on the sensory endings of the nerves and on the pain nerve fibres. It also works by relieving muscle spasm, which can itself be causing pain within the muscles. Additionally, pain can be relieved indirectly by decreasing swelling. The presence of swelling will cause pain because of increased tension (pressure) within the tissues. Finally, the relief by the use of cold can take place because the cold is acting as a counter-irritant. Pain relief by a counter-irritant has been used for thousands of years and is usually the basis for the various analgesic ointments, balms and linaments that are rubbed into the skin.

Technique of Application
Compresses can be used. These are usually of terry towelling which is soaked in melting ice and water. This mixture gives a temperature of 0°C. The terry towel-ling is wrung out and then placed on and around the affected part.

The part itself can be immersed in the ice and water mixture. Massage using blocks of ice can be carried out. Gel packs can be frozen in a freezer compartment of a refrigerator. They are particularly useful because, when frozen, they do not become solid and can be moulded around a part.

Note: Great care must be taken with massage with blocks of ice or with gel packs. The freezer compart-ment of a refrigerator or deep freezer is normally set at minus 18°C (0°F) for the adequate preservation of food. Therefore ice straight from a freezer will be at that temperature. Ice does not reach 0°C (32°F) until it starts to melt. Hence the great safety and value of a mixture of ice and water. The surface of a block of ice which is very cold may well adhere to the skin and cause damage unless the surface of the ice has reached the temperature of 0°C and has started to melt. Gel packs are just as dangerous because, as they are malleable, it can be very easily forgotten that they are at a very low temperature. They should not therefore be applied directly to the skin straight from a deep freeze. Before application they can be placed in a bowl of cold water, although this is an uncertain method of raising their temperature. When applied to the patient some terry towelling can be put on the skin first and then the cold pack applied on top of that. Alternatively, the skin can be oiled before the cold pack is applied. The oil will prevent any adherence and will also act as a very slight insulating layer. Over-cold packs can produce frostbite (cold burns). Once a cold pack has been applied it should be lifted from the skin every minute to make certain that the skin is not being blanched, indicating that cooling is excessive.

The skin itself cools rapidly but there is a very much slower reduction in muscle temperature. This rate of drop will depend largely on the thickness of the fat layer. It will take at least ten minutes in a thin person and up to half an hour in an obese person to begin to cool the underlying muscle.

When cooling is applied in trauma it should be carried out early before any considerable swelling has developed. It can with advantage be combined with elevation of the part and also sometimes with simul-taneous compression. Once swelling and bleeding are minimised and are not likely to recur, further cooling application of the part serves no purpose. (This, of course, does not apply when cooling is being applied for the relief of muscle spasms.) Cooling over an excessive period may retard healing because of the vaso-constriction of the blood vessels. It was seen in **Section 2.1** that one of the prerequisites of satisfactory healing was an adequate blood supply. Bleeding into an area must not be confused with blood supply. The bleeding produces no satisfactory purpose and merely increases the tension within the tissues. Blood supply implies that the blood is not only brought to the part with the necessary cells and nutrients but also that metabolites and other substances are being removed from the area, i.e. for a good blood supply you need not only an adequate arterial flow and supply but also an adequate venous drainage. Swelling and increase of pressure within the injured part will inter-fere more with the venous and lymphatic drainage than it will with the arterial supply which is coming in at a far greater pressure.

HEAT THERAPY: METHODS AND EFFECTS

Methods of application of heat are sub-divided into those that heat the superficial tissues only and those that heat the deeper layers. Hot packs, infra-red and similar radiant heat sources heat only the superficial tissues while shortwave diathermy, microwave and ultrasound all heat deeply. All these different modalities work by producing temperature elevation but the reasons for their individual choice comes from the fact that they will selectively heat different areas of the body and will produce a peak of temperature in different locations.

It is important to remember that none of these forms of heat is a cure in itself but it can be extremely valuable in association with other therapies.

The most important factors in determining the intensity of the reactions of the body are

a) *the level* of the tissue temperature attained. To obtain therapeutic benefit the range of temperature lies between 40° and 45°C;

b) *the duration* at which the temperature remains elevated to gain therapeutic benefit; this should be from three to thirty minutes;

c) *the rate* at which the temperature rises within the tissues being treated;

d) *the size* of the area that is heated.

The physiological responses to heat therapy are as follows:

1. A rise in temperature increases the extensibility of collagen. The heat will produce changes in the fibrous tissue which makes up tendons, joint capsules, ligaments and scars. This enables them to be stretched very much more easily. In order to attain this the heating needs to be by one of the deep methods of application; pure skin heating is useless. The heating has to be vigorous in order to produce an adequate rise of temperature in the area to be stretched. A steady stretch is very much more effective than intermittent stretching or short-term stretching. It is for exactly the same reasons that stretching should be done towards the end of a class when the body is warmed up rather than at the beginning of a class or before a class. Certainly stretching should never be carried out when the person or part is cold. In those circumstances, instead of stretching, the tissue will tend to become torn.

2. Heat will decrease joint stiffness, in part by its effect on the fibrous tissues around the joint and in part by its effects within the joint itself.

3. Heating produces pain relief by its effect on the peripheral nerves and nerve endings.

4. Heating will decrease muscle spasm by its direct effect on the muscle spindles which makes them less sensitive to stretch stimuli. This is also another reason for only stretching when the muscles are warm.

5. Heating will increase the blood flow by the direct effects of temperature on the blood vessels as well as by reflex mechanisms.

6. Heating assists in the resolution of the inflammatory swelling and exudates by its effect on the tissue and on cellular function.

Distant Reactions to Heating

If the skin in one area is heated an increase in blood flow is produced in other parts of the body, although this increase in blood flow will be less than in the heated area. If the underlying muscle itself is not heated its vessels may actually constrict because blood is being diverted from inactive organs to the skin for heat exchange and body temperature control. Of interest is the observation that has been made that when heat is applied to the abdominal wall the lining of the stomach blanches (whitens because of a decrease in blood supply) and there is a fall in acid level in the stomach. Heat on the abdominal wall also causes relaxation of the smooth muscle in the gastro-intestinal tract and in the uterus, hence the beneficial effects on pain by the use of a hot water bottle on the abdomen at times of abdominal pains from the gastro-intestinal tract and in dysmenorroea.

Heating may be vigorous or mild. In vigorous heating the tissue temperature in the deeper structures is elevated and it is particularly indicated when scar tissue is to be stretched. Although superficial heating tends to be mild, if it is applied to a very small part such as a finger, the temperature of the whole part can become very significantly elevated.

Contra-indications to the Use of Heat

1. In anaesthetic (numb) areas damage may be caused by heat because of the inability of the person being treated to detect any over-heating. In most instances the physiotherapist relies upon the patient to inform her if the part is becoming too warm.

2. Regions with an inadequate blood supply should not be heated because the increase in warmth will also increase metabolic demand. If there is an inadequate vascular response, as would be the case with poor blood supply, the increase in metabolic demand may in fact lead to ischaemic necrosis (death of the tissues due to inadequate blood supply).

3. Any bleeding tendency is increased by heating because of the increase in blood flow and vascularity.

4. If an acute inflammatory response is present, this will be aggravated by vigorous heating but may be helped by mild heating.

5. Heat is also contra-indicated in many acute mechanical problems. For instance, an acute

prolapse of an intervertebral disc, when the rise in temperature produced by an increase in heat will result in an increase in local swelling. If a nerve is already under pressure from the disc prolapse, the pressure on the nerve will be increased, possibly with serious results. However, in an acute mechanical problem, mild superficial heat may help by relieving secondary spasm.

While gentle superficial heat is unlikely ever to do any harm, none of the deep heat modalities should be applied except by a fully trained physiotherapist. Severe and lasting damage can be caused by any of the sophisticated deep heating methods, some of which also have non-thermal effects. In no circumstances should the dancer be tempted to use one of these machines either on himself or on a friend.

SELECTION OF MODALITY OF HEAT

Superficial Heating
This can be applied by hot packs, paraffin wax baths, infra-red or heat tunnels. However, it is as well to remember that a very small part such as a finger may, even with superficial heat, have a rise in temperature of the whole part, merely because of the small bulk of tissue.

Hot packs may be obtained by wringing out terry towelling in hot water and then applying to the part. However, they have the disadvantage of cooling rapidly. Gel packs can be used hot as well as cold and these have the advantage of retaining their heat for a very much longer period. Paraffin wax baths have traditionally been used for many decades for the treatment of hands and feet. They are particularly beneficial in the treatment of hand injuries and rheumatoid arthritis but have little application in the treatment of sports and dance injuries.

Infra-red or radiant heat is produced by special bulbs or heating elements. It uses the red end of the spectrum, going into the adjacent infra-red wavelengths. It has very superficial penetration, reaching the skin and only the most superficial parts of the subcutaneous tissues.

The Effects of Superficial Heating
Benefit can be derived for pain relief by being a counter-irritant. It can also produce some deep responses reflexly but these are of little value or significance although there can be some relief of muscle spasm. In the main, superficial heat will produce a feeling of comfort and relaxation in the patient and will help from that point of view.

Contrast Baths
These really fall in a section of their own, using as they do both hot and cold. They achieve their benefit by producing a hyperaemia (an increase in blood flow) by alternately submerging the part in hot water and in cold water. In sports and dance injuries they are particularly useful for feet and ankles. The hot water should be at a temperature of between 40° and 44°C and the cold water at between 15° and 20°C, although some authorities recommend a much lower temperature than this for the cold bath.

The contrast baths are used by immersing the part in the hot water for ten minutes initially and then transferring to the cold water for one minute. The cycles are then continued with four minutes in the hot bath and one minute in the cold bath for a period of half an hour. Contrast baths are something that can be very safely and satisfactorily carried out at home by the dancer. They are very effective and achieve their results by increasing the blood supply.

End with the cold bath.

DEEP HEATING

Diathermy is a name which covers a variety of different methods of heat production, all acting in the deeper layers. Energy is converted into heat at an interface, for instance between subcutaneous tissue and a muscular layer or between a muscle layer and bone.

The pattern of heating will vary between the different diathermy modalities. The temperature distribution is also modified by the different physical properties of the various tissues, e.g. by their specific heat (this is the amount of heat energy which is required to elevate that particular tissue by 1°C – tissues and all other matter have varying specific heats) or by their differing thermal conductivities (some substances, e.g. metals, conduct heat very quickly and effectively, whereas others such as wood conduct heat very slowly).

Microwave is rarely, if ever, used in the UK now. Short-wave diathermy in continuous mode has limited use but pulsed shortwave is still used frequently. Much of the criticism of electrotherapy may stem from misuse of or lack of understanding of the modalities. Research carried out by Professor Tim Watson of Hertfordshire University, England, does appear to reinforce the claims made by the protagonists of electrotherapy. There are important contra-indications for their use (as noted under their headings); also see Professor Watson's recommended website www.electrotherapy.org and his book and his many articles.

Short-Wave Diathermy (SWD)
This is the application of high frequency currents for therapeutic purposes. All SWD machines have three components, namely, a power supply, an oscillating circuit and the patient's circuit. The allowed oscillating frequencies are 13.66, 27.33, and 40.98 Megahertz

(MHz). The most commonly used frequency is 27.33 MHz which is equivalent to a wavelength of 11 metres. The patient's own electrical impedence (resistance to the passage of an electrical current) forms part of the patient's circuit. Therefore the machine has to be tuned for each individual patient. The actual current flow through the patient can then be regulated after tuning by varying the inductive coupling of the high frequency oscillating circuit and the patient's circuit. It is not possible to measure the high frequency current flow through the patient. The physiotherapist is guided by the feeling of warmth on the part of the patient. Low warmth indicates a low dose. A high warmth up to the limit of tolerance is required for a high dose, hence the importance of having normal sensibility in the part being treated. An anaesthetic area is a very definite contra-indication to the use of SWD.

Basically, the treatment is applied by the part being treated lying between two capacitor plates. These can vary in shape and flexibility.

There are certain precautions which must be taken. Metallic objects will undergo selective heating, so all watches, jewellery, etc. are removed before treatment starts. The patient must be treated on a wooden and not a metal couch. If the circuit is not tuned correctly, small movements of the patient may alter the impedence of the circuit, causing resonance. As a result, there may be a surge of increased current flow and possibly burns of the patient. Internal metal such as pacemakers or artificial joints (unlikely in dancers) and metal plates or screws used to fix bygone fractures (quite possible in dancers or athletes) are definite contra-indications to short-wave diathermy and must be reported to the physiotherapist before treatment starts, if the physiotherapist has not already made enquiries about their possible presence. However, surgical implants such as plates and screws, if far removed from the site of treatment, do not impose any particular risk. Contact lenses may cause hot spots and although normally nowhere near the area of treatment, it is advisable to remove them before treatment starts.

Microwave

These are very high frequency currents and are usually either 2456 MHz or 915 MHz in medical application. The latter are rather better and produce heating more deeply. These very high frequency currents are selectively absorbed by water and hence allow selective heating of certain tissues such as muscles which contain a lot of water, but relatively little heating of bone which contains very little water. (Hence the use of microwave in cooking, when the food – all of which has a high water content – is heated and cooked, while the dish remains cold until it is warmed by direct conduction from the hot food.)

Therapeutic Effects Microwave can selectively and easily heat the musculature and can also selectively heat a joint, provided it has only a little soft tissue covering.

Side Effects The eyes, which contain a great deal of water, can be selectively heated and must be carefully avoided. Microwave can produce a decrease in bone growth. It should not be used in anaesthetic areas or in the presence of buried metal.

Non-Thermal Effects Microwave may also have some non-thermal effects but these are not fully understood and must therefore be discounted for therapeutic purposes.

Ultrasound

The ultrasound machine produces a high frequency alternating current of 0.8 MHz to 1.00 MHz. This is converted by a crystal transducer into mechanical sound waves – acoustic vibrations. The sound beam produced by the ultrasound head is almost cylindrical in shape. The intensity is expressed in watts per square centimetre (watts/cm^2). The maximum that should be used is 4 watts/cm^2. Most commonly, the application is at less than 1 watt/cm^2. Like audible sound waves, ultrasound waves are propagated by compression waves. Therefore propagation depends upon the presence of a medium capable of being compressed. As the wave passes through the tissues it produces powerful mechanical forces, among the effects of which may be the production of small, gas-filled cavities from dissolved gases. These cavities then collapse, causing shock waves. As the sound is passed through the tissues it becomes absorbed and converted into heat. Remember a basic law of physics, i.e. that energy can neither be created nor destroyed. It is therefore converted from one form of energy to another form of energy, in this case from sound to heat, although initially it was electrical energy which was converted to sound.

The penetration of ultrasound into muscle is very satisfactory. The temperature distribution produced by ultrasound is different from the other modalities – short-wave diathermy and microwave. Ultrasound causes very little superficial temperature elevation and has a greater depth of penetration into the muscles and soft tissues than SWD or microwave. The ultrasound selectively heats interfaces between tissues of different acoustic impedance because of reflection, formation of sheer waves and selective absorption. Even the temperature in joints covered by a great depth of soft tissues can be raised therapeutically by ultrasound. (For example, in the hip, which is not greatly affected by either short-wave diathermy or microwave.)

Effects of Ultrasound These are due to the heating effects of ultrasound and are similar to the effects produced by the other agents, although as mentioned, ultrasound can penetrate far more deeply.

Non-Thermal Effects Ultrasound increases the permeability of tissue membranes. Cavitation can be produced and this can cause tissue damage. It is evidenced by petechial haemorrhages (small red spots on the skin) but these only occur at high intensities of ultrasound and a poor application technique. However, with a poor technique, cavitation can be produced at even one to 2 watts/cm². With good stroking technique, intensities of up to 4 watts/cm² are safe although usually quite unnecessary. In certain situations ultrasound can speed up healing processes but this mainly occurs in chronic rather than in acute lesions.

Side Effects Ultrasound can cause nerve damage due to a concentration of heat at the interface with the nerve and also within the nerve at the interfaces between the nerve fibres.

Ultrasound is, however, the only deep heating method that can be used safely with buried metal because although there is an increase in heat at the metal interface due to reflection, the metal carries away the heat more quickly than any effective or damaging rise in temperature that can be produced.

It must be stressed again that none of these pieces of apparatus, short-wave, microwave or ultrasound, should be used by a patient or by anyone other than a fully qualified physiotherapist. Ultrasound in particular can seem very innocuous and the dancer may be tempted to apply it himself with very unfortunate results. Also there can be no excuse whatsoever for any physiotherapist, however busy, who allows a patient to apply the ultrasound himself, even when under partial supervision. Despite using a low wattage a poor application technique or use at a site overlying a very sensitive structure, such as a nerve, can produce damage.

INTERFERENTIAL THERAPY

Two medium frequency currents between 4000 and 4100 Hertz generate low frequency impulses between 0 and 100 Hertz in the area in which the medium frequency currents are superimposed. At this site they produce an interference pattern.

Depending on the low frequency current wavelength produced the result can be analgesic (pain killing), can stimulate muscle contractions or can increase the blood supply. The selected results can be used to make the active form of treatment, e.g. exercises, more easily carried out by either pain relief or by stimulating muscles. The hyperaemic effect can be of value in increasing the rate of healing, including the stimulation of the healing process in stress fractures. In competent hands interferential therapy is safe and effective and can be used in the presence of buried metal. However, in the hands of the careless or unskilled it is at best useless and at worst can cause the patient considerable

discomfort; either by producing electric shocks by allowing the machine to surge or by causing the muscles to go into very painful spasms by over-stimulation. Like the other machines it should not be used by the untrained person.

FARADISM

This is the direct stimulation of the nerve endings in the muscle itself by the use of electric currents at the make and break phases in order to produce muscle contractions. Its use is re-educative, as by making a muscle or group of muscles contract the patient will appreciate in the conscious part of the brain not only the movement that is required but also the sensation engendered by the muscle contracture. This sensation is brought about by a combination of sensory responses to stretch in the muscle tendons and by proprioceptors affected by joint movements. The patient must be encouraged to reinforce the contraction by voluntarily copying the contraction produced by the stimulating current. The stimulation can be decreased and then discontinued in due course but the patient will still be able to reproduce the contraction actively. It is only by active contraction of a muscle that it can be significantly strengthened. Mere passive contraction by faradism alone has little effect in strengthening muscles. Its commonest use is in faradic foot baths where, try how he may, the average patient with poorly functioning intrinsics is quite unable to voluntarily produce the desired movements. Once the patient 'gets the feel' of what should be happening by using faradic stimulation he can then begin to reproduce the same contraction voluntarily. It is important that the patient realises that for it to be effective he must work *with* the stimulating current; little benefit will accrue if he remains completely passive.

Faradism can be of help in initiating muscle contractions in other areas of inhibition, e.g. the quadriceps after a knee operation. Here as elsewhere it is re-educative and not a definitive treatment. Many dancers find it advantageous to own their own small faradic machine, enabling them to carry out regular faradic foot baths in order to keep the intrinsic muscles working efficiently and under control. It is surprising how easy it is to lose the conscious control of these muscles to the point that, however much the dancer puts in mental effort and tries to get them to work, there seems to be a complete loss of continuity between brain and muscle. This is probably because from an evolutionary point of view these muscles are on their way out as we no longer use the feet for gripping, as do the apes. It is in the maintenance of conscious control that the faradic machine plays a vital role.

In passing, it must be said that faradic stimulation does not produce weight loss, reduction of fat in selected areas or redistribution of fat. There are machines sold commercially to the public which claim just these benefits. They are expensive and quite useless for their alleged purposes.

TRANSCUTANEOUS NERVE STIUMULATION (TNS BUT TENS IN THE USA)

This is carried out by a very small battery-operated machine which can be worn on the belt or carried in a pocket. Electrodes at the end of wires are stuck to the skin and apply small electric currents in order to stimulate the nerves and relieve pain. (Mode of action – It is thought to work by closing a neuro-electrical 'gate' in the spinal cord, thus preventing pain impulses from ascending the spinal cord past this point and hence failing to reach the level of consciousness. An alternative theory is that it works by stimulating the production of endorphins. These are analgesic substances which occur naturally within the body. Recently they have been arousing a great deal of interest and have been referred to as naturally produced morphine-like substances. The action of the TNS may be a combination of these two theories.) By its repeated use it can gradually produce longer periods of pain relief, leading in the end in many cases to the complete relief of pain, enabling the TNS machine to be discarded. As the electrodes are stuck onto the skin, there is no invasion of the body and it has no attendant risks.

ACUPUNCTURE

This probably works in a similar fashion to TNS. However, because of the possibility of the transference of viruses such as hepatitis or even AIDS, if the needles that are used are not completely sterile, it is less safe than TNS.

ACUPRESSURE

This is by the external application of pressure to the acupuncture points. It works in a similar manner but is probably less effective. As it is non-invasive it is safer than acupuncture and carries no risk of infection.

MASSAGE

This is undoubtedly the oldest of all remedial treatments and was certainly being used more than 3000 years ago. Even without being looked upon as a definite treatment, massage is instinctively used by both man and animals who will naturally tend to rub a painful area.

Effects of Massage
1. Reflex –
   By stimulation of the peripheral receptors which transmit impulses to the spinal cord and brain to produce sensations of pleasure or relaxation. The relaxation is both of muscle and of mental tension.

2. Mechanical –
   a) It increases blood circulation by assisting the return of blood and lymph if the massage is applied with the greatest pressure towards the centre of the body.
   b) It can produce intra-muscular motion and may be effective in stretching adhesions between muscle fibres.

It is very important to remember that massage cannot build up muscle strength, nor can it dissipate fat. Overall, apart from producing a pleasurable relaxation, the effects are minimal. However, with care, it is quite harmless.

Contra-indications
Massage must be avoided in local infections and in any case of thrombo-phlebitis or suspected thrombo-phlebitis.

MOBILISATIONS

This is a term used for gentle, non-violent passive movements of joints. It is applied to areas of the spine as well as in the more peripheral joints. The useful results are produced by a gentle repetitive stretching of capsules and ligaments which will gradually diminish or abolish the painful impulses being transmitted from nerve endings within those structures. These impulses are often reflexly causing muscle spasm so a secondary benefit of mobilisations is the relief of this spasm. The mobilisations (also called Maitland mobilisations) are applied by oscillating passive movements without forceful techniques. In the spine their use is very much safer and has a much more localised effect than the violent manipulations used by osteopaths amd chiropractors.

MANIPULATIONS

This term (together with expressions such as Thrust Techniques and Grade V) is used to describe a forceful passive movement of small amplitude and high velocity. Skilful manipulation can relieve specific stiffness or subtly relocate a joint. When used carefully it can be most useful as part of a treatment. Over-use of manipulation can produce an instability over time, if exercises for stabilisation and proprioception are not included. As with all forms of therapy, if skilfully applied, manipulation has its place in the treatment of dancers.

STRETCHING

Stretching can be passive, assisted active or completely active. As has already been mentioned, stretching is effective if the tissues to be stretched are warm (see **Section 2.5** Deep Heating, p. 95). To be most effective, the stretch should be prolonged and steady rather than intermittent or frequent, short-term stretches. Any stretch has to be applied with care in order to avoid damage to the tissues. If tissues are torn during stretching, then healing has to take place. As was described in **Section 2.1**, all healing is by scar tissue, i.e. fibrous tissue. With the passage of time scar tissue tends to contract and this may well make the tightness, which the stretching was originally aimed to relieve, worse than before the stretching started. Certainly any forcible stretching can only be harmful and will tend to be totally counter-productive.

The aim of any stretching is to gain an elongation of the tight tissues without any bleeding into the tissues. This can only be produced gradually over a period and must never be rushed. After an injury, the tissues, even though apparently healed, can still be very sensitive in the early stages and may respond very badly to stretching. This can lead to further contracture rather than to the desired stretch. It is important, therefore, that following injury stretching does not take place until the appropriate time in the convalescent period which will tend to be later, rather than sooner. It is quite impossible to lay down any general time scale and it is here that the advice of a physiotherapist experienced in the treatment of sports and dance injuries is invaluable.

A certain flexibility is a prerequisite for dance. Entrance requirements to vocational schools include a natural, genetic flexibility rather than a tightly knit physique. Hypermobility (discussed on p. 67) at the extreme end needs to be handled with care and stabilised, but the tighter physique will require stretching more or less during different stages of development. (We are thinking about the lengthening of muscle here to allow joints further range of movement, not bony structures like the foot.)

Light, short stretching aims to lengthen the muscle/tendon unit contributing to warm-up and mobility in preparation for exercise. Heavier, longer stretching aims to elongate the connective tissue layers within the muscle, the muscle fibres, tendon and joint capsule/ligament, thereby permanently increasing the possible range of movement. It should be understood that strengthening of the opposing muscle to the one being stretched should take place as part of the same regime in order to use the gained range of movement. The range of a muscle group consists of active range (as in performing a relevé lent) and passive range which will be more (as in the 'throw' of a grand battement). The greater the difference between the two, the more vulnerable the dancer is. In fact it is unwise to gain extra range of motion over which there is not sufficient control.

The range of motion at a joint is restricted by:
• bone and joint structure
• tightness of connective tissue within the muscle
• muscle tension.
Bone structure cannot be changed significantly but over time soft tissues can be lengthened.

Static stretching is an effective way to stretch and requires moving slowly into the end of comfortable range and into strain (not pain). If the stretch is held for more than ten seconds the muscle is felt to 'give', tension release and the stretch can progress further into range. This process can be continued for several minutes.

Muscles are protected from injury by stretch receptors. Delicate muscle tissue, blood vessels and nerves would tear easily if not protected by the nervous system and its receptors. Throughout the contractile muscle belly sensors called muscle spindles are located, constantly monitoring the length of the muscle and the rate of change in length. The muscle spindle (under microscope, shaped like a spindle) is made up of specialised fibres called intrafusal fibres, which are sensory in action, monitoring the muscle shortening. They lie parallel to the extrafusal fibres, which are the fibres which contract to shorten the muscle. Nerve fibres relay messages from the spindle to the spinal cord and brain, on stretch. The stretch reflex is the quick response to sudden stretch. The central nervous system, if alerted to any sudden or harmful stretch, relays a message to the muscle (extrafusal fibres) to contract and the muscle is saved from overstretch. These events take literally milliseconds.

In a slow, static stretch the activity of muscle spindles is overcome by stretching into discomfort and waiting until subtle relaxation is felt as the muscle 'gives'. More range is then gained to discomfort and resistance when again the tension created by spindle activity gently releases.

A muscle will only gain length when tension is released and it relaxes. Breathing techniques can enhance a relaxed state of mind and body and therefore facilitate muscle elongation. As in yoga, controlled, rhythmic breathing can concentrate the mind and bring about a feeling of calm. As described above, the moving into the end of range brings about a resistance and tension in the muscle. While pausing to adjust over three or four breathing cycles, concentrating on relaxing during the exhalations, the sensation of increasing length should feel good. Further stretch is attempted on the subsequent exhalations. Breathing, as in yoga, should be through the nose filling the lower lobes of the lungs and expanding the ribs.

Imagery also can also enhance the stretch. Just imagine the anatomy of the muscle and the lengthening of the muscle fibres, can induce further length.

Nerves, muscles and joints function better when warm and so it is important to be fully warmed up before a heavy stretching. Soft tissues have a viscosity. When chewing gum is warm it becomes pliable and stretches easily but when cold it is brittle and breaks easily. When muscle and connective tissue has been warmed up it can be eased into deep stretch. When nerves are warm they activate well and reflexes are safely alerted. A cold muscle feels uncomfortable and resistant to stretch and protective reflexes are slow. The best time to stretch is after class when the body is thoroughly warm. There is less time available for a systematic stretch after barre.

Static stretching is probably the simplest way to teach the dancer to stretch safely and independently, and develop real sensitivity as to what the body needs and how far to push. It is unwise for students to stretch each other. Control, knowledge and manual skill are lacking and it often leads to accidents.

In the physiotherapy department **contract/relax techniques** are employed to relax and lengthen tight, overworked muscles. If the target muscle is moved into its maximum length and then contracted maximally against resistance for a count of about ten seconds, physiologically a greater release is induced and there-fore a greater stretch can be achieved. Again the dis-advantage here is the level of skill required.

Repetitive ballistic stretches should be avoided, even though many dance moves are ballistic in nature. Repeated bouncing into a hamstring stretch will not lengthen the muscle, but rather stimulate the firing of muscle spindles. If the body is cold the sudden stretches involved can cause injury. If however, choreography includes repeated ballistic movements, the warm-up should conclude with similar exercises in preparation.

A word of caution needs to be added here regarding stretching into the nervous system. If, for example, a hamstring stretch brings on pins and needles in the foot (of a healthy youngster) it means that the nervous system is being compromised. The sciatic nerve on stretch can only partially relay its nerve impulses. The sensation is unpleasant and sometimes brings on a feeling of nausea. It also interferes temporarily with nerve function – never to be recommended, and especially not in those about to use finely tuned control in dance. The most compromising positions approach the test position for the nervous system – the 'slump position' (see Fig. 2.7). The spine and hip are flexed, the knee is extended and the ankle is dorsiflexed. In a static hamstring stretch which mimics this, decreasing spinal flexion, plantarflexing the ankle and placing a towel under the knee can still achieve an effective hamstring stretch without interfering with nerves. Also the straight leg raise can stretch into a nerve when the hip is flexed, adducted and internally rotated, and the ankle is dorsiflexed. In this position pointe the foot, slightly turn out and ease the leg outside the hip line to lessen the strain on the sciatic nerve.

Lastly, hard-working muscles need regular stretching for recovery. It is believed that stretching inhibits immediate and delayed muscle soreness.

2.6 Straight Leg Raise Test. The therapist is testing the integrity of the nervous system by taking the lower limb into hip flexion and adduction, knee extension and ankle dorsiflexion

2.7 Slump Test. Again the integrity of the nervous system is tested, this time with added spinal flexion. These tests are done with care and are for examination and treatment purposes. In routine stretching dancers should not push vigorously into nerve compromising positions causing tingling or numbness

2.8 The spine is flexed over the extended knee and dorsiflexed ankle. The more adducted and internally rotated the hip is, the more compromised the nervous system. To be discouraged

2.9 Care must be taken here that the leg is not internally rotated or adducted

Passive stretching is, as its name implies, carried out entirely by the therapist. Active stretching is that carried out by patient or dancer alone. Assisted active stretching is a combination of stretch applied by the physiotherapist and by the patient. Again it must be emphasised that the dancer must be aware of what he is trying to achieve and the best way to go about it. The essential points are:

1. the dancer must be warm;
2. *gentle* stretching should be carried out after the pre-class warm-up and again during the course of class once the muscles are really warm, e.g. at the end of barre;
3. the stretch should be steady and prolonged and not forcible;
4. sudden forcible stretches, jerking, bouncing and similar stretching effects are undesirable and usually counter-productive;
5. a weak muscle should never be stretched. Stretching in this case must be deferred until the muscle has been adequately strengthened. Stretching must always be accompanied by exercises to strengthen the muscles;
6. Stretching must be in the longitudinal direction of the fibres in the tissue being stretched. Stretching across the fibres achieves nothing and may cause tearing. Stretching of tight areas is frequently not best carried out in the direction of the apparent tightness. Consideration must be given to what particular structures are causing the tightness and in which direction their fibres run. Only then can the stretch be carried out in the correct direction. A joint which seems tight in one particular direction (e.g. tightness of turn-out at the hip) may need individual stretching programmes in two or more different directions in order to obtain the desired increase in mobility.

Specifically, two of the worst things that can still be found happening from time to time is seeing a dancer, commonly a student, lying in the frog position with someone standing on their knees trying to push them apart and down to the floor. Quite apart from the damage that this is going to do to the soft tissues, the turn-out in the frog position bears no relation at all to the turn-out at the hips when the legs and hips are straight in the working position (see **Section 5.8**). The other abomination is to see a girl student with her fore-feet (toes and metatarsal region) under a piano or radiator leaning back in order to 'improve' her pointe. There are, unfortunately, still some older teachers around who advocate this as the only method of improving the pointe. These two different actions can be at best useless and at worst actively harmful. They will certainly produce no benefit on either turn-out or pointe.

EXERCISES: THEIR VALUE

In both dance and sports injuries, a suitable programme of exercises is by far and away the most important part of treatment and rehabilitation. All earlier physiotherapy treatments that have been described, although effective in many conditions and aiding the healing processes, cannot in themselves in any way produce a full return to normal function and strength. Only exercises can strengthen muscles. Only exercises can help to mobilise joints satisfactorily and permanently. Those treating dancers, as well as dancers themselves, must realise the importance of proper exercise programmes. If treatment is confined merely to something easy and quick to relieve the current symptoms and pain, this will leave any underlying weakness or weaknesses that have developed as a result of the injury or have been the cause of the injury to remain uncorrected. As a result the injury is likely to recur or further injuries at other sites will be likely to occur.

After any sort of injury the muscles involved in that part, as well as more distant groups, are going to weaken. This is the natural response of the body when muscles are not used for however brief a period. Every injury will increase the weakening and as the weakening itself increases, so will the liability to further injuries.

THE AIM OF EXERCISE

Cardio-respiratory Fitness
Any form of general exercise benefits the cardio-vascular and respiratory systems. It produces what is known as cardio-respiratory fitness, i.e. it stimulates and strengthens the heart, the general circulation, the respiratory capacity and the way the body can deal with metabolites (the by-products of tissue metabolism which are increased in exercise). Hence it produces an increase in the person's tolerance of exercise. In order to increase cardio-respiratory fitness, exercise must be taken daily to such an extent that the person becomes out of breath and the heart rate increases. With the increase in heart rate there is also an increase in the capacity of the heart so that the volume of blood pushed out on each contraction is increased. The trained heart will be able to push out a far greater volume of blood on each stroke than the untrained heart. In order to achieve cardio-respiratory fitness the best forms of exercise are swimming, rowing, cycling, either on a normal bicycle or using a static bicycle, cross country skiing, either actual or using a cross trainer machine, running or even very brisk walking. Although running and jogging are popular they do have some serious drawbacks. For most people the running will inevitably mean doing so on the pavements or on the road. This, despite the best of running shoes, produces repeated jarring and leads to problems with the back, knees, feet and ankles. It is better if the running can be carried out on grass. If not, one of the other forms of exercise is far less likely to cause injury.

While preparing for performances the dancer through repetition and demanding rehearsals will gradually increase exercise tolerance specific to the piece. It is recognised that increased aerobic fitness increases the efficiency of the heart, the circulation and the body's use of oxygen. Dancers cross-train using gym equipment to enhance their own fitness which is more anaerobic and specific to dance.

Increase to Muscle Strength
Exercise is essential to strengthen the skeletal muscles in the body. Exercise in this form may be directed at certain muscle groups that the dancer or sportsman wishes particularly to strengthen or it may be a more general strengthening programme. It is important to emphasise that not only should muscle groups be

strong, but they must also be balanced. It is obviously unhelpful to have a group of muscles on one side of the body much stronger than the same group on the other. There is a normal tendency for this to happen because most people have a preferred side for working and this side will therefore usually have more exercise for the muscle groups concerned.

Increase of Mobility and Joint Range
Exercises in dancers and certain sportsmen are designed to increase mobility and joint range. This is, of course, accompanied by stretching of the soft tissues. However, pure stretching does not necessarily or effectively increase the range of movements of the joints. It is equally important if not more important to exercise the muscles groups controlling the movement of a joint in order to strengthen them. Only too frequently a dancer will think that he has some restriction at a joint whereas an examination of the range of movements will show that the range is in fact full, but the dancer is unable to use the available range of movement because the controlling muscles are not strong enough. Therefore in addition to pure mobilisation exercises, attention has to be given to strengthening the groups of muscles controlling the joint so that the full range of movement can be used with complete muscle control throughout its range.

TYPES OF EXERCISE

Passive Exercises
These have very little place as far as sportsmen and dancers are concerned. Passive exercises are where a joint or part is moved by another person in order to maintain full mobility in a joint. This is applicable particularly where there has been paralysis of a limb. Passive exercises are undertaken in order to prevent contractures occurring around a joint. Passive exercises do nothing to strengthen the muscles concerned.

Active Exercises
Active exercises are those which are carried out by the dancer and they entail an active contraction of the groups of muscles concerned. This contraction can be either isometric, when the muscle is contracted hard but the actual movement is prevented due to increasing resistance being applied, or the contraction can be isotonic, where the resistance remains constant but the joint moves. Only active exercises can increase muscle strength. Normally, resistance in some form is required and the common method of applying this resistance is to use weights. Early in the training programme the resistance may merely be gravity, particularly following an operation. But soon the dancer will need to use some weights or other form of resistance. Occasionally the resistance may be provided by the physiotherapist

who is supervising treatment if it is following an injury. The resistance can take two forms – very heavy resistance where the patient is only able to exercise the muscle against this resistance for a relatively few number of contractions. These are referred to as high resistance low repetition exercises. The alternative is to have a relatively low resistance (in using a weight this will often be somewhere between one and four kilograms) with a far greater number of contractions or movements. These are low resistance high repetition exercises. They are preferable and probably more effective at building up muscle strength than the high resistance low repetition exercises which used to be favoured a decade or two ago.

It is now generally recognised that work with very heavy weights can produce actual muscle damage, increase the rate of wear within the joints themselves and can predispose to the development of osteo-arthritis. It can produce an unnatural and undesirable increase in muscle bulk. It is less effective in producing muscle strength than the low resistance high repetition method.

Active Assisted Exercises

This is a form of combination exercise where, although the patient is actively contracting the muscle, he is also receiving some assistance from the physiotherapist. This can be particularly helpful in the early days following an injury or after an operation when even the resistance of gravity can be more than the muscle can contend with, yet the physiotherapist does not want an exercise with gravity totally eliminated. Similarly the faradic machine, by initiating a contraction which is reinforced by the patient's own efforts, can help to produce a far more satisfactory muscle response. Exercises for individual muscles groups and the methods by which they are carried out will be considered in detail in **Section 4**.

EXERCISE TRAINING

In the dancer, exercise training is aimed at strengthening various groups of muscles in which strength is required but which may have been neglected during ordinary classes due to the way that the classes themselves have been structured, or due to the type of dance which is predominantly filling the dancer's working day. Basically it must be realised that the muscle groups have two main functions. There is that which everybody appreciates, i.e. the muscles are required in order to move the different parts of the body and the limbs. However, equally important and frequently neither recognised or given enough attention is the requirement that the muscles must also produce stability in both trunk and limbs. Without complete stability in the supporting parts, the working parts cannot achieve their best results. This strength and stability has to be achieved throughout the whole organism, starting at the centre and working outwards. Any area that is neglected will prevent the whole from working satisfactorily. The effects of weakness in particular areas will be discussed in **Section 5**. However, a few general considerations can be dealt with here.

In the presence of muscle groups there are several different effects. Firstly, in the weak groups, if they are trying to stabilise an area which is supporting a working part, they will tend to tire rapidly. They will then go into spasm. This spasm will spill over as tension and affect other areas, including the working areas, thus impairing the performance of whatever action is taking place. Secondly, because of the weakness in the supporting area, there will be a feeling of insecurity and this insecurity will itself cause tension in the working area and prevent proper relaxation of the antagonistic muscle groups, interfering with the fluidity of the movements (see **Section 1.3** Muscle Contraction, p. 20). Thirdly, the weakness will generally bring about a limitation of range of movement. This is because the weakness prevents complete control of the joints and, without this control, a full relaxation of the muscles opposing a movement cannot be achieved and hence there will be an interference with the full range of movements at the joint or joints.

Only too frequently dancers may be trying to stretch areas which they consider are tight when in reality there is no genuine tightness present and the lack of adequate range of movement is merely due to weakness of the muscle groups controlling that part. Taken overall, a dancer who appears tight in the joints is far more likely to be in need of strengthening than stretching. It is obviously vital in the initial stages to determine which actual cause is present so that the appropriate series of exercises can be worked out.

The other important aspect of exercise training is to realise and fully comprehend *the importance of balance* between the various muscle groups. Any imbalance can only lead to instability with its attendant problems. Only too often one sees dancers who have quite rightly felt that they are weak in one particular area and have been given exercises for that area without any exercises being given to the opposing groups or the synergistic groups. As a result, a pre-existing imbalance can be aggravated and the situation made worse. It is not exercise and muscle build-up as such which has been at fault but merely the programme which has been devised for that particular dancer. It is also important to realise that the weakness may be in groups of muscles somewhat removed from the area where the dancer feels that there is a problem, or even where the casual observer thinks the problem lies. This is particularly seen where a dancer may be having difficulties or even injuries around the hip region and although receiving treatment and exercise around that area, the feet can be completely neglected. They may in fact have been the initial cause of the problem and be requiring a great deal of work in order to strengthen them up and give support at the bottom end of the pillar.

In doing exercises to strengthen muscles, there are a whole variety of methods that can be employed. Gym work is convenient with specifically and safely designed equipment. Otherwise, exercises can be done using free weights, normally in the region of two to five kilograms. Pilates mat work requires no actual weights, but can be extremely demanding and the weight of the limbs against gravity is all that is necessary.

If weights are used, this can be done in two ways. Using a lower weight with a higher number of repetitions is felt to be best for dancers unless muscle bulk needs to be increased. The muscles must be exercised to fatigue and it is this exercising to fatigue which is the essential part of the training programme to strengthen the muscles. When exercising to strengthen muscles it is absolutely essential that the muscles are worked throughout their effective range. They must be able to exert full power through the full range of movement possible at the joint they control. In other words the exercise regime must be directed at achieving work against resistance through the arc from full extension to full flexion.

We see a different picture when considering isometric and isotonic exercises as the effects of these cannot be equated with each other. Isometric exercises are those which are carried out with the muscle remaining at the same length but the resistance varying. Isotonic exercises are those carried out where the length of the muscle alters but the resistance remains constant. It has been shown by experiment that if an exercise programme is made up using isotonic exercises only, then the benefits achieved are not transferable and the person will continue to perform best at the isotonic type of exercise on which he trained. Similarly an isometric programme will not produce an equal improvement in isotonic performance. This shows that it is important therefore to build up an exercise programme of a combination of both isometric and isotonic exercises.

Concern is often expressed by female dancers about the possible adverse effects of exercise programmes on muscle bulk. The normal female endocrine system will not achieve a noticable increase in muscle bulk; rather, muscle will be delineated with a good strengthening regime. Coupled with regular aerobic exercise, the dancer can only benefit.

FATIGUE

It is worth repeating that in order to increase muscle strength significantly the muscle has to be exercised to the point of fatigue. If a muscle is exercised well within its capabilities, it has, as it were, no incentive to become

stronger. (Physiologists thoroughly disapprove of the way the last statement was framed, implying as it does that muscles or other tissues have independent thought processes or psyches of their own!) In order to strengthen a muscle it is necessary to work it to the point where it tires.

What is meant by fatigue? It has been defined as the inability to carry out the assigned task in the assigned manner under specific conditions known to the subject as a result of prior activity. However, this is a behavioural definition. Physiologically, the point of fatigue is very much more difficult to measure. It may be done by measurement of the maximum aerobic capacity after which the oxygen consumption does not increase despite an increased performance of work. This extra work is anaerobic and the onset of fatigue will quickly result in a failure to continue the work at that intensity. Alternatively, electrical activity can be measured electromyographically during a maximal isometric contraction. When the electrical activity increases at the time that the mechanical force is decreasing, this shows that despite a continuing full effort by the subject, fatigue is occurring in that muscle.

Unfortunately, both of these methods of determining fatigue can really only be carried out in the laboratory and as a result the physiotherapist has to push the dancer, or the dancer has to push himself, to continue with the programme of exercises until it is felt that genuine fatigue of the muscle is occurring.

Medical and Surgical Treatments

In dance injuries as well as sports injuries, the role of the orthopaedic surgeon or sports physician is largely one of diagnosis. Most treatment is conservative (i.e. non-operative) and will be applied by the dance physiotherapist. The orthopaedic surgeon is there to examine the patient and make an accurate diagnosis of the underlying problem and to exclude fractures or other significant injuries which might need special treatment; then, in conjunction with the physiotherapist, to devise a programme of treatment and rehabilitation, including technical correction, that is most suitable for that patient with that particular injury. Every patient and every injury is slightly different and needs to be assessed carefully. There are, however, some treatments that can only be administered by the orthopaedic surgeon.

PAIN AND PAIN CONTROL

The perception of pain is essential for the well-being of any individual. Very rarely a person congenitally cannot to feel pain and there are also some diseases in which this ability is lost. As a result skin and soft tissues become damaged without the person being aware of it and joints can be severely damaged.

It is obvious that some pains are trivial e.g. a headache following a party the previous evening. Abdominal, chest or persistent headaches etc. should be investigated by the appropriate physician. Otherwise a dancer complaining of musculo-skeletal pain falls within the remit of the physiotherapist or sports physician. When first seen a thorough assessment should be carried out. In most cases this will lead to the necessary physical treatment.

It is important to remember that the site of the pain may not always be the site of the cause. As an example, in children a complaint of knee pain may well be caused by a problem in the hip joint, which may be due to a slipped upper femoral epiphysis. This is potentially a crippling condition and it is vital that it is not missed in the early stages. Unusually an adult with an arthritic hip may complain only of knee pain. It is also worth repeating that even if the site of the pain is the same as the site of the injury the actual cause may be far removed. For example, a tight turn-out can commonly cause injuries in the knees or feet. This applies particularly if the turn-out is being forced at the feet (overturned feet).

As an adjunct to physical therapies, medication may be required. However the use of painkillers should not be used merely to allow the dancer to perform when without the pain relief dancing would be impossible. This is the path to escalating injuries. Also be careful with the use of simple analgesics for headaches. If they are used constantly then the analgesic can itself be the cause of chronic daily headaches.

THE ANALGESIC (PAIN) LADDER

This term was introduced by the World Health Organisation (WHO) as an aid for the prescription of analgesics. (An analgesic is a pain-relieving drug.) The pain ladder introduces drugs in a progressive fashion.

Step 1

These are simple analgesics which can be bought over the counter (i.e. without prescription). They include paracetamol and aspirin.

Paracetamol is the drug of choice. Although two 500 mg tablets may be sufficient for a temporary pain such as a headache, a more persistent pain would be better treated by regular doses of paracetamol every six hours in order to keep up the blood level of the drug. The maximum dose of eight 500 mg tablets in twenty-four hours should be adhered to. Overdoses of paracetamol can cause liver damage and death with as few as twenty tablets.

Aspirin is effective but is more likely to cause gastric problems such as indigestion or ulcers and bleeding. It has an anti-inflammatory effect. It is somewhat more effective at reducing a fever. **N.B. Aspirin must never be given to children under the age of eighteen**. Although the cause is unknown it has been found that aspirin in children has been associated with Reye's syndrome. This is a potentially fatal condition although it is rare. There is no treatment apart from supportive therapy, usually in an intensive care unit.

Paracetamol can be supplemented by the addition of a non-steroidal anti-inflammatory (NSAID). Ibuprofen (Nurofen) can be bought over the counter but other NSAIDs require a prescription. They should not be used as a substitute for paracetamol but as an adjunct. As their name suggests they reduce the inflammatory response. There is some evidence that they delay the healing of fractures for this reason. As both aspirin and NSAIDs can cause gastric irritation it is probably better not to combine these. Additionally, NSAIDS and aspirin can both aggravate asthma and should be avoided if possible in asthmatics or only taken on medical advice.

The use of anti-inflammatory gels such as voltarol or ibuprofen gels gently rubbed in to the painful area can be very helpful in soft tissue pain. They can penetrate surprisingly deeply and as a result, if oral NSAIDs are already being taken, there is some risk of overdosage.

Step 2

When the pain is not controlled by the measures outlined in Step 1, the addition of a weak opioid may be sufficient to be helpful. The commonly used drugs are codeine and dihydrocodeine the latter is slightly more potent. Both can cause constipation, nausea and vomiting or drowsiness. When one or other is used they should be in conjunction with the drugs being used in Step 1.

Combinations of paracetamol and codeine can be purchased over the counter as co-codamol and dihydrocodeine with paracetamol as co-dydramol. There are many other proprietory combinations but most will be more expensive and no more effective.

N.B. If taking a combination drug that contains paracetamol it is vital that paracetamol which might already be taken in Step 1 is discontinued.

Always read the label on the box or read the leaflet inside. If in any doubt ask the pharmacist. This advice also applies if you are taking any prescription medicines as interactions can be dangerous.

Step 3

When the pain is too severe to be controlled by the measures in Step 2, then stronger opiates such as morphine may be indicated. These are controlled drugs and can only be administered under the supervision of a registered medical practitioner. It is therefore unnecessary to enlarge upon them further.

The rules are:

- Take the smallest dose which is effective.
- Take advantage of the benefits of physical treatments such as physiotherapy, including massage, acupuncture, which many physiotherapists can provide, hot or cold packs etc. These may make the use of painkillers unnecessary.
- If the symptoms are not resolving rapidly, see a qualified health practitioner – a physiotherapist or medical practitioner with a knowledge of sports injuries.
- Never use an analgesic to mask pain merely to enable you to continue to dance, without proper advice. To do so can aggravate an injury, much delaying recovery or even ending a career.
- To repeat, always read the label. Treat drugs with respect. All drugs have potential side effects.

HYDROCORTISONE ACETATE AND SIMILAR PREPARATIONS

These drugs, which are given by injection, certainly have a limited application in the treatment of dance and sports injuries. Their action is by abolishing the inflammatory response but, because they are suspensions of the steroid, their action is entirely local. They have no general effects elsewhere in the body and they certainly produce none of the side effects that are brought about by steroids that are administered by mouth. In any case, the dose that is given in one injection of Hydrocortisone Acetate amounts to about one twelfth of the body's daily output of naturally occurring Hydrocortisone.

In order to be effective, Hydrocortisone Acetate, which is the insoluble form of Hydrocortisone and is the one used in the treatment of injuries, has to be placed at the exact area where the lesion to be treated lies. It may increase the pain locally for some twenty-four hours and is frequently given together with a local anaesthetic. Its main use is where an injury has become chronic, i.e. there is a very low grade inflammation still present and the healing process is incomplete. It is typically of value in conditions such as tennis elbow, chronic tenosynovitis and chronic tendonitis.

Contra-indications are as follows:

1. Hydrocortisone should *never* be used in an acute injury as it will totally stop the healing processes.
2. It should *never* be used if a fracture is suspected or possible, e.g. a stress fracture.
3. In relation to the large tendons (Achilles tendon, patellar tendon, etc.) it should be used with caution and probably only one injection given. It should never be given into the tendon itself but merely into the tissues surrounding the tendon. One of the reasons for the great caution here is that if the tendon itself is the site of damage, the presence of

the Hydrocortisone may abolish the healing process which is taking place and result in a complete rupture of the tendon. Similarly, if it is injected into the tendon rather than into the peritendinous structures, it can cause damage to the tendon and subsequent rupture.

4. It should never be given if the diagnosis is uncertain or for want of anything better to advise.
5. As far as dancers and sportsmen are concerned, Hydrocortisone should never be given into a joint. The indications for intra-articular steroids are usually confined to those people who have arthritic conditions of the joints and this is not normally found in dancers or sportsmen during their active careers. It should certainly not be given when the joint is merely recovering from an injury.
6. The administration of either a local anaesthetic, or of steroids particularly, merely to enable a dancer or sportsman to perform, can only be condemned. It is asking for an exacerbation of that injury with the conversion of what is possibly a minor injury to something that is major.

ORAL STEROIDS

In some quarters oral steroids (cortisone, prednisone, etc.) are administered for three or four days following an injury on the grounds that it reduces or prevents swelling.

However, it does this by suppressing the inflammatory processes in all their aspects and not just the swelling. As seen from **Section 2.1**, this will totally interfere with the early phases of the healing processes. While this may not matter if the injury is really trivial, if there is any significant tissue damage the delay in the onset of the healing processes can only be disadvantageous. Also by the suppression of these inflammatory processes the dancer may be encouraged to continue full activities with potentially serious or disastrous results.

A further complication is that by the administration of oral steroids the natural body production of its own steroids becomes suppressed, together with more widespread alterations in other hormone levels. The suppression of natural steroid production even for four or five days may lead to a much longer period of hormone imbalance before the body finally settles down into equilibrium again.

Use of oral steroids in dancers is unwise, unnecessary and can only be condemned.

OPERATIONS

Surgical operations should only be undertaken when there is a very specific indication, when an accurate diagnosis has been made and when conservative treatment has failed or is not indicated.

These statements may seem so obvious that they are not worth printing. However, far too many dancers are subjected to totally unnecessary surgery for a variety of reasons. On the part of the orthopaedic surgeon there may be a lack of knowledge about dance or sports injuries, leading to an inadequate or inaccurate diagnosis. The surgeon may opt for an operation because he lacks the knowledge and understanding to recommend the correct type of conservative treatment. An example of this is the totally unnecessary surgery which is so often undertaken to remove spurs or areas of calcification which may be seen on an X-ray but are irrelevant to the patient's symptoms. Before embarking on any operation there must be an absolute indication for surgery which must be understood by both the surgeon and by the patient.

Surgery sometimes appears to come about unnecessarily due to pressure from the dancer himself. Only too naturally, the dancer is anxious to get better and return to work as quickly as possible and surgery may appear to be the easiest and quickest way to achieve this end. The dancer may have been shown an X-ray which shows a spur and then, far more justifiably than the surgeon, has fallen into the trap of saying that that is something that should not be there, therefore it must be causing the symptoms, thus pressuring the surgeon, who may be a little reluctant, to carrying out an operation. Only too often, dancers are seen who have undergone surgery and in the longer run are no better as a result and often worse.

It should be realised by everybody that these little spurs and calcifications nearly always represent old minor damage to ligament and capsular attachments and they have formed merely as part of the healing process. Once they have reached that stage, they in themselves are very rarely the source of symptoms.

The other aspect which has to be remembered is that after any operation there is inevitably going to be a period where the dancer is unable to do anything other than rest while the wounds and tissues heal. During this time the muscles will weaken generally throughout the body and more so in the limb which had the surgery. He will then have a period where he gradually progresses back to work. Only too often, if the original cause for the symptoms had been treated simply, possibly with a short period of rest but certainly with progessive treatment including technical help if necessary, then resolution would have taken place without any form of surgery and usually far more quickly and completely.

Finally, it must always be remembered that any operation, however small, carries risks. The anaesthetic itself has a definite, though small, risk. Any wound that is made in the skin has a risk of infection. The post-operative complications include deep vein thromboses.

Although the percentage of patients who suffer from any of these complications is fortunately very small, the complications do exist and surgery should not be undertaken lightly or unnecessarily. Ignorance on the part of the orthopaedic surgeon is no excuse for surgery.

Use of Supports
The use of elasticated supports for the lumbar spine, knees and ankles should always be questioned in a dancer. Developing good core stability, biomechanics and proprioceptive feedback from the lumbar spine is the first consideration. Wearing a lower back support has not been proven to prevent injury. In fact any tight support over abdominals and the muscles of the lumbar spine is thought to detract from their activation, promoting reliance on an extrinsic prop rather than intrinsic control.

Wearing a back support for pas de deux class or rehearsal of a demanding lifting role may even encourage pushing further than you should, giving a false sense of security. Professional dancers often choose to use a neoprene 'back warmer' but if this provides too much support and is used constantly, it may make the lower back vulnerable. Dance students should be discouraged from using these so that the teacher instead is able to clearly monitor spinal posture and control.

If a specific back injury requires temporary immobilisation then a heavy back support may be recommended by the therapist, but the appropriate exercises should also be carried out to keep active the deep muscles of the spine and pelvis without strain on injured structures. The same goes for knee and ankle braces/supports. If a joint is habitually given added support, its own balance mechanisms are thought to deteriorate. Taping however, can give appropriate proprioceptive feedback maintaining awareness of the vulnerable area. It can be invaluable in the right scenario – working through a Grade 1 sprain – with balance and proprioception exercises given simultaneously.

2.6 The Prevention of Injury

Although the methods for the prevention of injury can be deduced when reading the other sections, the main factors in the prevention will be summarised.

The Development and Maintenance of Good Technique

As described in **Section 2.3**, the cause of dance injuries is faulty technique, therefore conversely if a good technique is developed and maintained, the chance of sustaining a dance injury is minimised. Of great help in maintaining a good technical level of dancing is regular attendance at a class run by a *competent and observant teacher*. As in all activities, whether mental or physical, it is only too easy for technique, the application of technique and mental attitudes to gradually deteriorate with the passage of time. Even serious self-appraisal and self-criticism may not be sufficient to prevent the development of errors and flaws in technique. However, by attending a really good class regularly, the chances of injury can be kept to a minimum.

The Development and Maintenance of Muscle Strength and Joint Mobility

In the prevention of injury, the importance of maintaining adequate muscle strength cannot be over-emphasised. However, it must also be stressed that this does not mean an over development of bulk such as one sees in weight lifters and in those people competing in the 'Mr Atlas' contests. Pure bulk does not necessarily equate with desirable strength. Over-bulky muscles can be a distinct disadvantage to a dancer for they not only look unsightly but also may make dance more difficult. For example, over-development around the shoulder girdle and arms, due to an excessive enthusiasm for weight lifting, can raise the centre of gravity of the body and make the dancer rather more unstable when he tries to balance. Additionally, bulky muscles can get in the way at the extremes of joint movement range.

Correct muscle balance is as important as muscle strength; firstly, between one side of the body and the other and one limb and the opposite limb and secondly, between the various groups which control the movements of a particular joint or joints. A good instance of this is the over-emphasis which is so often placed on building up the quadriceps muscles in the thigh to the neglect of the other groups in that region, i.e. the adductors, the hamstrings and the gluteals. The ill effects of muscle imbalance are mentioned elsewhere, particularly in **Sections 3** and **5**.

Joint mobility goes hand in hand with muscle strength. If the muscles controlling a joint are weak, then the joint will not be stabilised sufficiently for it to be used satisfactorily in its full range. Therefore in maintaining muscle strength and balance, joint mobility will also tend to be maintained. Also playing a very significant part in achieving the fullest possible mobility of a joint is the necessity to exercise the controlling muscle groups through the *full range* of their movement. For instance, the muscle group controlling extension of a joint must be able to act powerfully throughout the full range of movement, from full

flexion to full extension and not during only part of that range. In order to achieve this it is essential that any exercise programme is directed at providing a correct exercise pattern for that muscle group throughout this range. *Only when the muscles controlling the joint are strong, can the range then be increased to the anatomically full range by gentle graduated stretching*. Stretching must go hand in hand with an exercise programme to strengthen the muscle groups. A weak muscle must *never* be stretched.

The Preservation of Cardio-respiratory Fitness

This will normally occur as a result of any exercise programme that the dancer is carrying out in order to maintain his muscle strength and joint mobility. Any form of general exercise will have its effect on the cardio-vascular and respiratory systems in helping to maintain them in the peak of condition. However, during vacation periods it can be helpful if the dancer continues to do some form of exercise, not necessarily related to dance, to preserve fitness. This can take the form of swimming, cycling or walking which may be more appropriate during a holiday. As previously stated, in order to maintain cardio-respiratory fitness it is essential that the exercise is vigorous enough to make the person concerned short of breath. This will ensure that during these times the cardiac output is called upon to increase. It is this regular demand on the cardiovascular system which maintains it in a state of physiological fitness.

School holidays and half terms are rest periods for the hard-working dance student, but from a fitness point of view they are too long and so while technique can take a rest, basic fitness should not. Coming back to high-level work is easier if fitness is maintained.

SMOKING

There is much information in the media about the side effects of cigarette smoking and most countries in the world restrict smoking in offices and public places. Opera houses and dance studios also come under these constraints.

When a cigarette burns, the heat breaks down the tobacco to release its toxins. The most damaging products are:
- tar – a carcinogen (causes cancer)
- nicotine – addictive and as a stimulant increases heart rate and blood pressure
- carbon monoxide – reduces oxygen supplied to the body.

Nicotine

When cigarette smoke is inhaled nicotine is absorbed through the alveoli of the lungs into the bloodstream.

From there it flows to the brain and it is at this point it is responsible for the feelgood factor. Nicotine interacts with neurotransmitters stimulating brain activity, improving reaction time, ability to concentrate and you feel you can work better. Nicotine initially causes a rapid release of adrenaline which raises blood pressure and accelerates breathing and heart rate. Smokers use this to re-energise themselves throughout the day. The brain remembers the feelgood reward and drives the desire to repeat – and you are addicted. In time you develop a tolerance to these effects and you smoke only to satisfy withdrawal cravings.

Tar

This is a carcinogen (substance that causes cancer). It coats the lungs, reducing elasticity of the alveoli (air sacs) and resulting in less oxygen absorbed into the bloodstream. Tar irritates the mucous membranes which swell and also interferes with the cleansing mechanism of the lungs and the build up of phlegm in the airways increases resistance. Therefore breathing is affected and you cough in an effort to clear the build up of mucous.

Carbon Monoxide

This component in cigarette smoke reduces oxygen in the body. When oxygen leaves the lungs it is transported in the blood by attaching to the haemoglobin in the red blood cells. However if carbon monoxide is present it preferentially binds to haemoglobin instead, reducing levels of oxygen in the blood. The release of oxygen from blood to the cells that demand it, is also reduced. This affects the heart muscle (high oxygen demand) and the skeletal muscles. Oxygen is important for the functioning of all energy systems in the body. Any mechanism which interferes with oxygen transport and uptake interferes with energy production and therefore dance performance. Connective tissue also suffers. Collagen production is slowed down due to oxygen depletion and superficially is seen in sagging skin tone with early lines and wrinkles. Subcutaneously the healing of tissue is also affected with delayed healing time in ligaments and tendons. A slower recovery from injury can threaten a dancer's career.

Dancing requires optimal lung capacity but smoking depletes it. High-level exercise requires maximal oxygen uptake but smoking reduces it. The combined effects of airways resistance, lack of oxygen and increased blood pressure make for inefficient physiological function. The professional responsibility of keeping the body working at its highest possible capacity does not allow for an addiction that diminishes the performance.

Smoking damages blood vessels in general. Blood vessels in the heart, brain, skin and muscle are subject to narrowing, again affecting oxygen transport. Even the blood vessels to the penis can be affected eventually, resulting in erectile dysfunction.

Smoking depletes the body of vitamins C and E which are powerful anti-oxidants.

The immune system is the body's natural defence system that protects against infection from bacteria and viruses. Hard-working dancers have fragile immune systems to begin with and need carefully balanced lifestyles to cope with the rigours of the profession. Smoking damages the immune system making you vulnerable to colds and other illnesses. Working days and performances are lost, due to chest infections. This can prove expensive to all involved in the long run.

It has been suggested that the effects of smoking on bone may begin in adolescence, resulting in lower than normal peak bone mass. A female dancer who smokes on top of a less than balanced diet is inviting problems in both the near and distant future.

Smoking also increases fatigue levels during and after exercise. Due to decreased oxygen transport, a smoker's endurance is reduced and her physical performance does not improve compared to the non-smoker.

Dancers will say that smoking helps with weight control. Smoking is believed to increase metabolism and reduce appetite. Smoking also decreases the sense of taste and therefore foods are less enticing. Smoking is also part of a less than healthy lifestyle, when a breakfast of coffee and a cigarette are enough to get one started.

They may also say that it helps control stress, but in reality they are only staving off the withdrawal effects from nicotine. Within hours of the last cigarette, irritability and loss of concentration take over. The association between smoking and feeling calmer reinforces the habit.

Some Interesting Facts
- Within twenty minutes of the last cigarette your blood pressure and heart rate return to normal.
- Within eight hours oxygen levels in the bloodstream normalise and carbon monoxide levels go down.
- Within two days you can taste and smell better.
- Within three days your lung capacity improves, your airways relax and breathing is easier.
- Within two weeks your body will adjust to a lack of nicotine.
- Within three months your circulation and lung function improves.
- Within nine months your lungs can clean themselves again and risk of infection decreases.

Dancers who smoke have stained teeth and hands and to non-smokers the smell of smoke on hair and clothes is very strong. This is unattractive in a profession where people work physically closely. Smoking is expensive and, in a profession that is not generally highly paid, to calculate an annual saving is persuasive to stopping.

Dance teachers and all those in authority have a duty to lead by example. Dance teachers who smoke are imitated by their students. Principal dancers who smoke, although few and far between, endorse the habit in younger dancers. It is plain to see that dancers are easily inspired and lead astray by their elders, in spite of the overwhelming evidence that smoking is counter-productive to those who aspire to dancing for a living.

Good Nutrition

The maintenance of a satisfactory nutritional state is essential in the prevention of injury and also in the healing of injuries (see **Section 2.7**).

The Orthopaedic Assessment of the Dancer in the Prevention of Injury

One of the most important aspects in the prevention of dance injuries is in the assessment of students before they are accepted by professional schools. This could, with great advantage, be extended to an assessment of each dancer when they are first taken into a company.

The purpose of this orthopaedic examination is to determine whether there are any anatomical areas which are likely to cause physical problems during a dance training or, when assessing adults, whether there is anything that is going to cause any particular problem with different types of dance. Although there are occasionally physical aspects of a person which can preclude any satisfactory participation in dance, in most instances although someone may be unsuitable physically for certain forms of dance, for example classical ballet, there are other types of dance with which they would cope perfectly satisfactorily. A careful assessment can therefore be used to guide a young dancer along the right lines. The orthopaedic assessment can be a great help when a teacher has a student who is apparently finding difficulty with some of the technical aspects of the work. Frequently there is some physical aspect of the dancer which, although not very obvious, is sufficient to make certain areas of dance technique difficult to carry out correctly.

By the time students have got through all the preliminary auditions, and before attending for a final audition at a professional dance school, the auditioning panel will have rejected most of those applicants who are obviously unsuitable. Were the population to be examined orthopaedically at random with a view to their suitability for dance, then large numbers would be found to be unsuitable. However, in the professional schools the auditioning panels will have rejected most of those applicants who are physically unsuited to dance before they are actually sent for an orthopaedic assessment.

It is always important to remember that artistic talent can overcome many apparent physical problems. If a student does show great potential talent then it is usually right to give them the chance to dance by allowing them to start training. Their progress should be carefully monitored in order to determine whether they are overcoming these difficulties. In these circumstances it is very important that all the teachers and the student are fully aware of any potential physical problems that are present and which may cause technical difficulties or injury either during training or later in a professional career. The orthopaedic surgeon must, therefore, have two thoughts in his mind while doing the assessment – first, whether there is any physical problem which calls for an outright rejection, for example an established spondylolisthesis, and secondly, to note carefully those areas which are potential problem points. During the course of this assessment there may be some aspects which can be amenable to early help from the physiotherapist or teacher, usually in the form of special exercises to strengthen or mobilise a particular area or areas.

Fig. 2.10 is a reproduction of the card that we have used for many years for the orthopaedic assessment of both students and professional dancers.

It is largely self-explanatory. The presence of a tight trapezius is noted because this will affect head movements, particularly if there is some limitation of rotation was well as of lateral flexion. At the shoulders a discrepancy in level can be very suggestive of an underlying abnormality such as a scoliosis or leg length discrepancy. However, the majority of cases where the shoulders are at different levels is purely postural and possibly associated to some extent with the carrying of heavy bags on one or other side. (The old-fashioned school satchel had a great deal to commend it as it did mean that the loading of the shoulders was equal.) Under 'shoulder line' we are looking for those children who have their shoulders forward, thus appearing to narrow their chests. Although the braced-back shoulders of the old military stance was a very poor position, equally bad is the narrowing caused by shoulder girdles that have rotated forwards around the chest.

Winging of the scapula is indicative of upper trunk weakness. Frequently the scapulae stand out sufficiently to slip a hand between the medial border of the scapula and the chest wall. This is often part of a scapula rotation and due to some weakness of the latissimus dorsi, so that the slip to the inferior pole of the scapula does not act sufficiently to hold the scapula down. In improving the posture the scapula has to be held down, largely by the latissimum dorsi, and must not be braced backwards as that affects the general line of the shoulders.

Under gleno-humeral joint range we are looking at

ORTHOPAEDIC ASSESSMENT

Name .... Date of birth: .... Age: ....

Height: .... Weight: .... BMI: ....

Neck	ROM:	Tight trapezius:

Shoulder girdle	Asymmetry:	Glenohumeral joint range:
	Winged scapulae:	Wrists:
	Elbows:	

Pelvis	Level:	Asymmetry:

Spine	Scoliosis:	Kyphosis:
	Thoracic spine flex:	Thoracic spine extension:
	Thoracic spine rotation:	Thoracic spine side flex:
	Lumbar spine flex:	Lumbar spine extend:
	Lumbar spine side flex:	
	General view:	

Lower limb	R Hamstrings:	L Hamstrings:
	R Achilles:	L Achilles:

Knees	Hyperextension:	Genu valgus:
	Patellae:	Tibial bow:

Foot	Pointe: R L	Metatarsus: R L
	Ankle: R L	
	Rt big toe extension:	Lt big toe extension:
	Lesser toes:	Metatarsals:
	R midtarsal:	L midtarsal:
	R subtalar:	L subtalar:

Hips	Rotation extended: R ER:	R IR: L ER: L IR:
	Rotation flexed: R ER:	R IR: L ER: L IR:

General	Past injury:	Beighton:'
	Operations:	Growth:
	Investigations:	General health:

Other comments

Examiner Date:

2.10 Orthopaedic assessment

the combined abduction and flexion of the shoulders. This is of great importance in the boys as if there is some restriction they will be unable to lift a girl up above their heads without tilting backwards in the lumbar region of the spine. A fifth postion of the arms require a certain looseness but adaptions can be made as long as teachers are aware. Movements and control of the shoulders is more fully described in Section 1 under Upper Limbs (p. 9).

In the arms the presence of swayback elbows is looked for as well as hypermobile wrists as part of a general indication of the presence of hypermobility (see end of **Section 1**). Hypermobility in a dancer is a very potent cause of injury, as is mentioned elsewhere in this book. If a student or dancer is hypermobile they then have to work far harder at maintaining muscle strength in order to control the hypermobility of their joints.

In the wrists, particularly in boys, one is looking for any restriction of dorsiflexion as this can also cause problems when lifting.

The pelvis should be assessed to detect any difference in level of the anterior superior iliac spines. If there is a difference this is suggestive of a leg length discrepancy or a lumbar curvature. Similarly, an asymmetry calls for particular care in both back assessment and leg length measurement.

In the spine, the presence of a scoliosis or kyphosis is noted. In children, this orthopaedic assessment may be the first time that they have been looked at thoroughly by any medical practitioner so occasionally a hitherto undetected scoliosis is picked up and can be referred for treatment. A very mild scoliosis is no contra-indication to dancing, but in the younger student the parents should be warned that there is a possibility that the scoliosis will progress as part of the natural history of the condition and that the child will have to remain under observation. Dance training in no way aggravates a scoliosis. In fact, the opposite occurs and the extra exercise of dancing, coupled possibly with side shift exercises and other trunk exercises, can actually be beneficial in stopping the progress of a scoliosis or in reversing the condition. Measurements of the spinal movements is self explanatory. Any restriction must be noted and assessed to decide whether it is sufficient to prove a problem in dance. In particular look for any lower lumber stiffness, i.e. a stiff lower lumbar segment (see Fig. 3.35), or for segmental stiffness elsewhere.

The heading 'Achilles tendons' refers to tightness in the calf. Dancers always refer to tight Achilles tendons as do other sportsmen. In the calf the gastrocnemius and soleus muscles join together at their lower ends to form the Achilles tendon. It is this whole complex which makes for tightness and not the Achilles tendon alone. Any tightness in this area will, of course, prevent the

dancer going down into a good plié. Similarly, an assessment of the hamstrings for any tightness is important, particularly in girls. However, if the Achilles tendons and calf muscles and the hamstrings are very loose then the height of the jump becomes impaired, so too much looseness at these sites is a disadvantage in boys.

The jump will have been noted in the audition by the panel of teachers.

At the knees, the presence of hyperextension or swayback is observed. Similarly knock knees (genu valgus), although not a contra-indication if mild, to a dance career, are aesthetically unsightly and if marked will prove a problem The heading 'patellae' refers, in fact, to the presence of tibial torsion. When the feet are pointing straight forwards if there is any tibial torsion then the patellae will point inwards (the so-called squint patellae) and the amount of rotation is measured and noted. This is not a contraindicator but should be monitored.

The presence of a tibial bow, whether it affects the whole tibia or whether it is just the lower quarter, is assessed. A lower tibial bow will produce an angle at the ankle joint so that the plane through the ankle joint is not parallel to the knee and may produce foot and ankle problems if not monitored. As a result the dancer will tend to both roll and sickle with the problems that can be associated with these two factors.

The Beighton Scale is explained on p. 68 and in Fig. 1.96.

The stage of growth is noted.

Big toe extension is particularly important. In the student an early developing hallux rigidus can often be detected by noting the restriction which is already present in dorsiflexion at the 1st metatarsophalangeal joint. If there is significant restriction this is an important contra-indication to proceeding with a dance training. All forms of dance call for demi-pointe work and as the hallux rigidus progresses it becomes more and more difficult to get up onto a reasonable demi-pointe and certainly prevents the dancer getting up onto three-quarter pointe or performing a correct relevé.

'Lesser toes' refers to the presence of any lesser toe deformities, the relative toe lengths and metatarsal lengths. In order to obtain a good support with a foot on both demi-pointe and full pointe it is far more satisfactory to have an even length of metatarsals and of toes.

In the feet, the intrinsic muscles are important as they allow the dancer to obtain a good pointed foot with straight toes when they are working strongly. If the intrinsics are weak when the dancer pointes the foot the toes claw, due to the action of the long flexors.

The extension of the hip is important as tightness in the front of the hip causes a variety of problems. This is dealt with later in the book.

The measurement of hip rotation with the hip flexed to 90° is noted. The measurement of hip rotation with the hip in full extension is a far more important measurement and reflects the degree of turn-out which is present when the dancer is standing, which is, of course, the normal position during working. The turn-out in the frog position and its genuine irrelevance to the dancer is discussed in **Section 5.8** on restriction of turn-out at the hips. However, most dancers and teachers still look upon the frog position as one of the methods of assessing turn-out. It is not included on the card and education of teachers continues.

The other items on the form which have not been mentioned are really self-explanatory.

Even using a form such as this, the genuine assessment of the dancer certainly calls for a lot of experience. For example, when examining an area which seems to be tight, the general feel of the tissues will give an experienced examiner a very good idea of whether the dancer will be able to stretch out the area with exercise and good training. This is something which cannot be learnt from a book but only by practice, by seeing a large number of dancers and dance students and being able to follow their progress over the years.

2.7 Nutrition

Every member of the population requires an adequate standard of nutrition. This must give sufficient but not an excess of calories, the correct balance of protein, fat and carbohydrate and all the necessary minerals, vitamins and water. Without a correctly balanced diet the physiological mechanism of the body cannot function at the utmost peak of efficiency. Dancers and athletes are no different from ordinary members of the population in this respect. However, dancers have a disproportionately high number of food fads. They labour under a whole variety of misapprehensions. They are led astray by old wives' tales which are repeated, propagated and multiplied by their elders and by their colleagues. They are ready victims for any ill-informed advice that is proffered, whether in the printed form or verbally, which claims to enable them to reach or maintain their desired level of activity or give them boundless energy at the times they need it.

Unfortunately, these misapprehensions are aggravated by the fact that many dancers are either in relatively poorly paid employment or are out of work and have to exist on a very small amount of money. This does not help them to eat a sensible and satisfactory diet. In the professional dance schools, whether they be producing dancers hoping for a stage career or dance teachers, there should certainly be an emphasis on instruction in nutrition. This would best be carried out by a sympathetic dietician who could advise them, not only on the elementary basics of nutrition and diet, but would also help them to plan their daily eating so that it would fall within their limited budgets and yet provide all the essentials for a healthy existence. So many of the good books on the subject of diet and nutrition recommend foods that are beyond the financial reach of both students and professional dancers. A sensible and well-informed choice of food and meals not only provides adequate nutrition but also helps to prevent the dancer becoming either overweight or underweight. A good diet is important in maintaining the healing processes at their peak of efficiency and also helps to prevent injury by keeping the body in the best condition.

Nutritional Requirements

PROTEINS

These are required for muscle and tissue development and repair. They also provide essential amino acids which are needed for the normal metabolism in the body. Protein is found particularly in lean meat, poultry and fish. It also occurs in variable amounts in milk and dairy products including cheese, eggs and in some vegetables. Although the human body can convert carbohydrates and fats into most proteins and amino acids (amino acids are substances which are obtained from metabolism of protein) there are what is known as essential amino acids which the body is incapable of synthesising. These, therefore, have to be obtained directly from the diet. Although these can be found in certain vegetables, they are far more abundant in animal protein. Animal protein is frequently referred to as first-class protein. If the total diet is insufficient to provide enough amino acids, the body will start to break down its own proteins, which largely means the muscular tissue, in order to provide the amino acids that it requires. This can happen in people who diet injudiciously or embark upon a badly structured diet.

CARBOHYDRATES

These are required as an energy source. This group is divided into two, the simple carbohydrates such as glucose, cane sugar and other simple sugars and the complex carbohydrates such as starch and complex sugars. The simple carbohydrates can be absorbed and metabolised very rapidly whereas the complex carbohydrates take longer to absorb and metabolise and will therefore give a slower release of energy.

FATS

These provide a high energy source. (High energy means also high calories.) They are metabolised and used very much more slowly than the complex carbohydrates so their benefit as an energy source will be much longer term. Fats are a vital carrier for the fat soluble vitamins A and D.

VITAMINS

There is a daily minimum requirement for vitamins. While they are not a food as such, inasmuch as they do not provide energy, they are essential for the proper functioning of the body. Provided the minimum requirements are met, there is no evidence at all to show that boosting the intake by the use of vitamin supplements has any benefit. It certainly has no effect on enhancing performance or increasing endurance. An excessive intake of Vitamins A and D can be extremely harmful. The former can cause damage to the eyes and the latter upsets the calcium and phosphorous metabolism and balance. As sufficient intake is included in the diet, it is unwise to supplement these two vitamins.

At present there is no evidence that over-dosing with either the B complex vitamins or with Vitamin C has any harmful effects. Both are excreted in the urine if they are in excess. This is very obvious in the case of the B complex, as you will observe if you take a couple of Vitamin B tablets following which you will notice that your urine becomes a bright yellow. The only time when a large dose of Vitamin C *might* be helpful is at the onset of development of the common cold. Some research workers have produced possible evidence, although it is by no means conclusive, that if Vitamin C is taken at the rate of a gram a day, starting right at the commencement of common cold symptoms, the course of the disease is significantly shortened or even aborted. Although relatively expensive to buy, the dancer might feel that the chances of deriving benefit are worth the cost and they can certainly rest assured that they will come to no harm. There is, however, no evidence whatsoever that taking Vitamin C in large doses permanently has any preventive effect at all in respect of actually catching a cold.

Vitamin B12 is sometimes considered to be an aid to performance. There are some ignorant athletic trainers who demand that their athletes have an injection of Vitamin B12 prior to a performance. Although Vitamin B12 by injection certainly gives many people a feeling of well-being, there has, despite intensive investigations, been no evidence that this extra B12 enhances either the performance of intricate tasks or increases endurance or sprint activities. Its use in these circumstances cannot be condoned and is only another example of the ill-informed pressing for the unjustified use of some or other preparation. Every injection, breaching as it does the integrity of the skin surface, carries with it a very small risk, however minimal this risk might be, and the athlete and dancer should avoid foolish advice such as this.

MINERALS

There is a very long list of essential minerals that are required in the diet. Most of these are required in very small quantities and are adequately provided in the daily food intake. The only exceptions are iron and calcium, both of which can be very deficient in dancers. Iron, particularly, can be low in the female because of menstruation. However, as most female dancers are of exceptionally low weight, many of them do not menstruate or only irregularly and occasionally, so iron depletion may not be as marked even when there is a minimal intake in their diet. If there is any doubt at all, then the dancer should consult her doctor, as a simple blood test will rapidly show whether there is any anaemia present. This can readily be corrected with an iron supplement. The requirement is 18 mg daily. If a dancer is anaemic, she will certainly not be able to perform at her best. She will tend to feel tired and listless and be a ready candidate for injury and various infections. Incidentally, research has shown that dancers who weigh less than 45 kilograms do not menstruate and as far as some research has progressed at present in America, this seems to be a fairly critical figure.

The calcium requirement is 1200 mg daily. This can be obtained by drinking 4–5 glasses of milk each day. Otherwise a supplement will be necessary.

WATER AND HYDRATION

Water is the most essential ingredient to health and the human body is 50–70 per cent water. Dancers require adequate intake of fluid to compensate for losses during exercise. Optimal performance – concentration, quickness of mind and stamina over long periods depend on energy reserves and adequate hydration.

Water is necessary for:
- transportation of nutrients
- elimination of waste products
- temperature regulation – muscles produce heat and the body cools by sweat evaporation
- good digestion and a healthy bowel
- lubrication of joints and tissues

Dehydration causes a drop in blood volume, the heart has to work harder and this causes:
- early fatigue and lack of co-ordination
- muscle cramps, especially in the legs
- lethargy and dizziness
- nausea and vomiting
- decreased performance.

A sufficient intake is essential for the satisfactory physiological processes of the body. The amount of fluid required depends on the intensity and duration of exercise, temperature and individual needs. At least two

2.11 An aerobic work-out on a cross trainer while keeping up hydration

litres of fluid should be consumed per day and as drinking large quantities at a time is uncomfortable, it should be sipped in breaks during the day. Gone are the days when dance students lasted an hour and a half class without water. If you feel thirsty, you are already dehydrated and muscles have already suffered. There-fore dancers must be equipped with water bottles for class, rehearsal and performance. The colour of urine is an indication of hydration status – light coloured to clear means you are hydrated. Darker, concentrated urine means you are probably dehydrated.

The kidneys require an adequate output of water in order to be able to excrete the waste products of meta-bolism. If the body is short of water then the blood volume will decrease and this can interfere with the transportation of both nutrients and oxygen to the cells as well as delaying the removal of carbon dioxide and metabolites. Water is also essential for the regulation of body temperature which it does by the production of sweat. If dancers become dehydrated, fatigue of both the muscles and the body as a whole will set in much earlier and they will become liable to sustain injury. The dehydration can also cause cramps and heat stroke and exhaustion. Also, a failure to take enough fluid can make the dancer initially feel nauseated, even in the absence of the other effects of dehydration, and this nausea can itself do nothing to help performance.

When water is lost through sweating, salt is also lost. However, the salt is readily replaced with the diet, although heavy performances, particularly in hot working conditions, may call for the addition of salt. This is very adequately done by taking some extra salt at mealtimes and the use of salt tablets is unnecessary. In more normal conditions a pinch of salt added to weak squash is usually all that is required. This addition of salt is certainly a wise precaution as a lack of salt will lead to quite severe cramps. Sports drinks

can be useful in maintaining hydration. These are isotonic drinks – they have a similar carbohydrate and electroloyte concentration as the body's own fluids.

As a precaution, the dancer should take great care to prevent dehydration and should take plenty of water during the course of each twenty-four hours. The two litres a day mentioned above is recommended for all adults but exercise increases the requirement. Food provides a certain amount of water during its metabolism but additional fluid will be needed, the volume depending upon the ambient temperature and the degree of sweating. The fluid does not need to be taken as pure water but can be consumed as fruit squash, some fizzy drinks such as fizzy orangeade, lemonade or similar flavours. However, the various cola drinks, together with tea and coffee, should not be included in fluid replacement drinks as they all contain substances which act as diuretics. A diuretic acts directly on the kidney in order to increase the excretion of water, so consumption of these three items can increase fluid loss to a greater extent than it replaces it. Alcohol comes under the same heading as it also acts as a diuretic and can produce dehydration. It certainly provides some calories but should not be looked upon as a source of energy as it has depressant and sedative effects. However, a little alcohol after a performance may help the dancer to relax and to this end a glass of wine will do no harm.

Recently it has been suggested that tea and coffee can be counted as part of the daily requirement by every individual, but they should not be used for rehydration associated with exercise.

The presence of dehydration and proof of its correction can be effectively carried out by regular weighing. This is frequently done in top class athletics and sports. A deficiency of one litre of fluid will produce a weight loss of one kilogram. Weighing before and after a heavy performance or class, particu-larly in hot conditions, will give an accurate indication of the quantity of fluid replacement required.

The Daily Diet

In deciding what to eat each day, it is not particularly easy or helpful to think in terms of protein, carbo-hydrates, fats, vitamins, minerals and water. It is easier to produce a balanced set of meals by considering what are known as food groups and making certain that one has sufficient out of each of the four groups. These groups are as follows:

THE MEAT GROUP

Two portions daily (one portion is equivalent to two ounces of meat with the fat removed, or poultry or fish, or two eggs, or four ounces of cottage cheese).

THE CEREAL GROUP

Four portions daily. (One slice of bread, preferably wholemeal, or two ounces of cereals such as cornflakes, or pasta such as spaghetti makes up one portion.)

THE MILK GROUP

Three portions daily. (One portion is equivalent to about half a pint of milk or yoghurt both of which can be low fat or skimmed, or one and a half ounces of ordinary cheese.) This group provides the calcium as well as other nutrients.

THE VEGETABLE/FRUIT GROUP

Four portions daily. (One portion would be equivalent to a large helping of vegetables or one fruit such as an apple, orange, pear, etc.) The dark green leafy vegetables or orange vegetables such as carrots contain Vitamin A and one portion of these should be taken four times a week. The other vegetables, particularly citrus fruits such as oranges, contain Vitamin C.

When working out the meals for the day, try to take one portion from each group in each meal. If possible, try to eat three meals a day, rather than taking more portions of each group in fewer meals. In particular, try to avoid a large meal at the end of the day just before going to bed. The best method of cutting down on calories is to reduce the fat intake; for example, make certain that the meat is well trimmed, use skimmed milk and low fat yoghurt, and cottage cheese rather than normal cheese. Weight for weight, fat provides twice as many calories as either carbohydrate or protein, both of which provide the same amount of calories for a given weight. In planning your diet do not forget that calories equal energy and energy is required to carry out a full dance programme each day. Also, the body requires a minimum number of calories just to keep going, even if the person remains perfectly still for each 24 hours. The actual level of calories required varies from individual to individual and depends upon their own metabolic rate. The basal metabolic rate, which is that which occurs when the person is completely inactive, is greatly increased during any form of activity.

Pre-performance Intake

Although most dancers will determine for themselves what they can or cannot eat and drink before performances, there are certain guidelines which they should try to follow. First, they should make certain that they are well hydrated during the course of each day. This is best achieved by drinking small amounts fairly frequently and regularly. During a performance, particularly if it is energetic and there is a high temperature, sips of water can be taken regularly. By doing this, dehydration and excessive thirst can be avoided. Half a pint or a pint of fluid taken immediately before a performance is as likely to end up over the conductor as be satisfactorily absorbed by the body and the dancer should not have let himself get into such a situation as to need this quantity.

Avoid concentrated sweet fluids. These will be absorbed far more slowly and they do nothing to enhance the energy levels or activity. Even if carbohydrate is taken in a dilute form, such as a dilute glucose drink, the effect will be counter-productive during the course of the performance. If the glucose is taken in a dilute form it will certainly be absorbed rapidly but this will produce a peak of glucose in the blood stream, the physiological mechanisms of the body will be stimulated to deal with this peak and metabolise it and as a result there will be a sudden burst of insulin poured into the blood stream. This peak of blood sugar will then fall and there will be a trough below the normal level (Fig. 2.12). The dancer may therefore suddenly feel halfway through a performance that he is excessively tired due to this troughing effect. In order to ensure a satisfactory energy supply during the course of a performance, a small meal taken one and a half to three hours before the performance would be far more satisfactory. For energy requirements, this meal should contain complex carbohydrates such as starch. This can be readily supplied by eating a small pasta dish or a sandwich, followed by a little fruit. If taken well before the performance this will have been digested by the time the dancer wishes to start a pre-performance warm-up

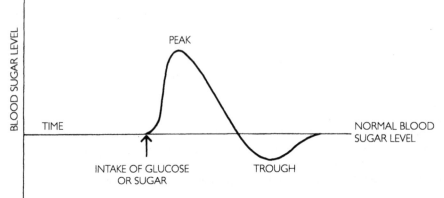

2.12 Peaking and troughing of the blood sugar levels following an intake of glucose, sugar or any other simple carbohydrate

but the energy supply will continue throughout the performance. Following a performance a large meal is not particularly satisfactory and, as was mentioned earlier, it is far better to try to provide for your food requirements by taking several small meals a day.

Having indicated some general guidelines for dancers to plan their diet and food intake, it is strongly recommended that if dancers have any particular concerns about weight or problems with food or diet, they should seek the advice of their doctor or a fully qualified dietician. A dietician will be able to help them to plan an appetising and nutritious diet which comes within their budget and would also fit in to their daily work programme.

In ensuring that their dancers performed at their best, management would be well advised to consider far more carefully the way they structured their dancers' day. They would obtain better results if they ensured that in the middle of the day each dancer had sufficient time to have an adequate meal without being pressurised to attend class in the morning, then only be given time to snatch a quick snack before being rushed into rehearsals. These should be arranged to allow those who are performing that evening to get a small meal well before the performance is due. While it may be thought that these are counsels of perfection, both management and dancers would be well rewarded by paying a little more attention to the physiological demands of the bodies upon which they both depend for their livelihoods.

2.8 Unexplained Under-performance Syndrome

Following a meeting at St Catherine's College, Oxford, Budgett et al. redefined so-called overtraining syndrome as Unexplained Underperformance Syndrome (UUPS). UUPS was originally defined by this Oxford group. It is frequently of insidious onset and may not be recognised for some considerable time. There may also be outside factors (social etc.) which can play a part in the development of the syndrome

It is a problem of which dancers, teachers and company managements need to be aware. Research in athletics has identified this particular fatigue syndrome in up to 10 per cent of elite endurance athletes.

Dancers are tired a lot of the time but still complete class each day and produce quality performances. If they do fatigue significantly, a two-week relative rest should allow recovery and a return to normal performance standards. In UUPS the fatigue and underperformance persist in spite of rest and are recognised by both teacher and dancer. The dancer feels under

par, depressed, constantly tired, sleep is disturbed and they wake unrefreshed; they lack energy, are emotional, irritable and anxious. The immune system is lowered and they suffer from minor infections and upper respiratory tract infections every three to four weeks.

According to the British Olympic Medical Centre the following have been reported in UUPS:
- fatigue and unexpected effort during training
- history of heavy training and competition (In dance terms, more intense classes/coaching/rehearsals and/or critical performances)
- frequent minor infections
- unexplained or unusually heavy stiff and/sore muscles
- mood disturbance
- change in expected sleep quality
- loss of energy
- loss of competitive drive
- loss of libido
- loss of appetite
- excessive sweating.

Research has shown endurance athletes to present with fatigue and underperformance with secondary mood changes. Power athletes and sprinters (dancers fall into this category) present primarily with mood changes, with a subsequent decline in performance.

If the syndrome is suspected the sports physician will do blood tests to eliminate other pathology. Often there is iron depletion. In dancers glycogen depletion due to poor diet and dehydration reduce the ability to recover or respond to heavy training. If diagnosed, the doctor will plan a recovery programme and refer to a nutritionist and psychologist. Recovery can take up to three months of light exercise, strict pacing and good nutrition with medication if necessary, to deal with depression and disturbed sleep. This a surprising length of time but it has been found that if the dancer tries to increase exercise too soon when feeling slightly better, fatigue sets in again.

Prevention requires a teacher or management to be aware of dancers' workloads, as a dancer will rarely turn down good challenging rôles. Dance students who also have part-time jobs to pay for training will not recover as quickly as those who can relax after rehearsing. Dietary habits, hydration, rest and pacing need to be observed by teachers or health professionals caring for professional dancers. Education on recovery strategies needs regular discussion.

Further reading
Budgett, R., Newsholme, E., Lehmann, M. et al. 'Redefining the Overtraining Syndrome as the Unexplained Underperformance Syndrome'. *British Journal of Sports Medicine* (2000), 34: 67–8.

Specific Injuries: Their Cause and Treatment

In this section we will describe the injuries commonly found in dancers, progressing systematically through the body rather than dealing with the injuries in the order in which they occur most commonly. .

In the discussion of injuries in this section, where necessary we describe the injury, the cause or causes of the injury and follow this with a description of the treatment and any complications which may occur that are relevant to the dancer. We have confined ourselves to discussing only those injuries which have some aspect which is of specific interest to dancers, e.g. the cause of the injury, some aspects of its treatment, etc.

In the description of the causes we hope that the dancer, dance teacher or therapist may be able to determine the possible reason why the patient should have sustained the injury. This will usually be associated with some aspect of their dance technique. The cause is particularly important when the injury is recurrent and during the course of treatment it is vital to eliminate or correct all possible causes.

Although weak areas, technical faults or anatomical problems may have existed for a long time without symptoms, it may take only a very small increase in work, a variation in technique or choreography or work on a raked stage, etc. to precipitate quite severe symptoms.

The section on treatment indicates the general lines that treatment should take but the details of application of the physiotherapy methods or surgical methods have been assumed to be known and understood by the physiotherapists or surgeons concerned with the patient. For those in doubt about treatment or for dancers who wonder whether the treatment that is costing a lot of money is relevant, reference can be made to **Sections 2.4** and **2.5**. Unfortunately dancers, like other athletes, are desperate to get better and back to performance or to continue performing without having to take time off. They are therefore particularly vulnerable to those who offer a quick cure (usually ineffective, particularly in the longer term). It is essential for dancers whose livelihood depends on returning to a full level of physical fitness to obtain the *correct* treatment, and that they attend for the fewest number of treatments and obtain proper value for their hard-earned money. However, it is must be emphasised in this context that the quick manipulation or the quick injection, is frequently far from being the most satisfactory method of obtaining

permanent relief. It may seem a speedy or cheap answer and may give short-term relief but it rarely produces a long-term cure. Far more commonly it will lead to recurrent injuries and problems, each of which may be more severe than the one before, so that finally the dancer ends up with an extended period off dancing, whereas a correct diagnosis followed by the correct treatment methods applied early would have prevented all the subsequent misery.

The section on special complications tries in each case to give some indication of the problem that can accompany a particular injury, either in the short or long term. Any factors affecting return to dancing are mentioned, together with any precautions which should be taken to prevent recurrences. Reference to these little sub-sections may aid the practitioner treating the patient in avoiding the less obvious or more remote pitfalls.

3.1 Sprain of the Lateral Ligament of the Ankle

The lateral ligament complex is made up of three sets of fibres. The commonest injury in dancers usually affects the anterior fibres, known as the anterior talo-fibular ligament (ATFL), which attaches the fibula and talus. This is stressed on inversion and plantarflexion. The middle fibres make up the calcaneofibular ligament, pass from the fibula to calcaneum and are stressed in pure inversion. The posterior fibres make up the posterior talo-fibular ligament. When the patient is initially seen it is very important to exclude a fracture of the lateral malleolus (lower end of the fibula) by X-rays (Fig. 3.1). A fracture of the 5th metatarsal is a commonly associated fracture (Fig. 3.2). It is also equally important to exclude a complete tear of the ligament. An ultrasound scan or an MRI scan with gadolinium will reveal full or partial tears in the ligament allowing for the appropriate treatment to follow an accident. It is important not to miss damage to the ligamentous fibres which allow the talus to rotate forwards in the ankle mortice. It is essential to test the 'anterior drawer' in the injured joint. The hindfoot is grasped firmly in one hand and the leg in the other and forward traction of the foot towards to the toes takes place, then it can be seen that the talus slides forwards in the ankle mortice and at the same time rotates slightly medially. If this type of

3.1 Spiral fracture of the lateral malleolus

3.2 A fracture (arrowed) of the base of the 5th metatarsal

instability is missed it leads to chronic problems for the dancer and the ankle remains permanently unstable.

There are three grades of ankle sprain.

- Grade 1 sprain: There is slight stretching of the ligament with possibly rupture of a few fibres but nothing severe. There is some pain and swelling. Walking without aids is possible but there is probably an inability to run or jog. The symptoms will usually settle in a few days with rest, some elevation and short periods of icing.
- Grade 2 sprain: There is partial tearing of the ligament. There is pain and swelling and probably bruising due to subcutaneous bleeding. Walking will be painful but usually possible.
- Grade 3 sprain: There is a complete tear of the ligament. Weight bearing may be difficult. Considerable swelling and bruising will be present. Instability (giving way) of the ankle may be experienced.

In all grades it is important that a dancer seeks advice from a health professional as soon after the injury as possible as early intervention may be required for the best results.

CAUSES

The lateral ligament of the ankle is always damaged by acute trauma. It follows an inversion injury. This is often a rather more complex injury where there is an element of inversion, an element of rotation, an element of excessive plantarflexion or, very rarely, dorsiflexion. In most injuries the actual direction of displacement is not purely in one direction or another. It commonly occurs when a dancer falls off pointe, or in boys during grand allegro. In boys it is usually the middle fibres (calcaneo-fibular ligament) which are affected, in girls it is usually the anterior fibres (anterior talo-fibular ligament). It seems that, almost as

commonly, the injury comes about in dancers in a manner which is totally unconnected with dancing – they may slip off a kerb, fall down stairs or suffer some other everyday mishap.

Predisposing or Contributory Causes

There are a whole variety of factors which may predispose to an injury of the lateral ligament. Probably the most important is a previous strain which has been inadequately rehabilitated. Weak feet (that is, the intrinsic muscles), weak ankle control, especially the peroneal group of muscles, and weak calf muscles producing a lack of control when landing from a jump are all common precursors of this injury. Lack of control of the turn-out allows the knee to turn in, the leg then goes out of alignment over the ankle so the weight is no longer correctly placed over the foot, resulting in a weight back situation (**Section 5.21**). As a result this makes the ankle unstable. Badly fitting shoes aggravate the problem. An unstable pelvis, producing either a lordotic spine or tucking in, combined as it usually is with weak trunk muscles, aggravates the instability at the lower end of the leg (**Section 5.6**). A similar effect is produced by faulty head posture or faulty jumps. Working with tension interferes with control, not only in this type of injury but also in most others. Poor floor surfaces are a frequent cause of problems, particularly if they lead to a bad take-off which will, of course, produce a bad landing.

TREATMENT

Initially, the dancer should remain non-weight bearing until fractures are excluded. The associated fractures are those of the lateral malleolus and the base of the 5th metatarsal. During this initial stage ice packs should be applied and the leg elevated and rested. With very minor strains, once diagnosed and more serious injury excluded, the dancer may continue limited work using an ankle support or taping. However, as in all other injuries, it is essential that an accurate diagnosis is made before the dancer is allowed to continue. The long term ill-effects of a mis-diagnosis cannot be over-emphasised.

Definitive Treatment

Icing, elevation and rest should be continued. The patient can be given ultrasound to the damaged and swollen ligament 48 hours after injury and should start non-weight bearing foot and ankle exercises with the leg in elevation. The muscle contraction and relaxation with the leg elevated helps to get the swelling down more rapidly. During this time elevation of the foot of the bed at night can be very beneficial in reducing swelling. This applies to all lower limb injuries. The exercises should be carried out for all muscle groups around the ankle and should be done with the foot

3.3 The use of the balancing board when sitting. The correct placement of the foot can be taught while sitting, in preparation for standing weight-bearing on the board

3.4 The use of the balancing board at the barre. This is an intermediate stage between sitting and standing freely, when the dancer still requires a little help with balance

3.5A The use of the balancing board standing without support. The dancer has not yet achieved the control of her hyperextended knee and, as can be seen in the photograph, is still pushing a great deal of her weight back on her heel

3.5B The position is correctly held. The balancing board is used to re-educate the postural reflexes which rapidly become ineffective following an injury or even a prolonged break from work

pointed, i.e. in full plantarflexion, and with the foot at a right-angle, i.e. in neutral. These two different positions are necessary in order to include all the peroneal muscles in the exercise programme. From the early stages of treatment the calf muscles should be kept well stretched as there is a tendency for them to shorten.. (See *Complications* below.) Intrinsic foot muscle exercises should be carried out as these muscles tend to waste very rapidly. During this period the patient can also spend a great deal of time doing general exercises for the rest of the lower limbs and trunk.

As the condition improves the patient passes through partial weight-bearing exercises and finally to full weight-bearing exercises. Balance and propriocetion exercise should start as soon as tolerated. Use of the balancing board in the later stages is very important. Its use can, however, start with the patient sitting, when these exercises will be non-weight bearing with the foot on the balancing board. They help to achieve mobility and also to give the patient the feel of all the ankle movements (Fig. 3.3). In partial weight-bearing the balancing board can be used at the barre (Fig. 3.4), with the dancer facing the barre with the hands supporting the body. Once the patient is fully weight-bearing then the balancing board exercises can progress to real challenge (Fig. 3.5).

At the time of the actual injury there is always damage to nerves and nerve endings within the ligaments and joint capsule unless the injury is minor.

These nerve endings are responsible for proprioception (appreciation of joint position) and loss of or interference with this enhances or is sometimes totally responsible for residual feelings of instability in the ankle. The dancer will feel insecure on the ankle, suspecting that it will give way at any moment. He will lack confidence in the joint when trying to dance or sometimes, if badly affected, even when walking. The balancing board is the most effective method in treating this and in re-educating the local postural and joint control reflexes.

Complications
Ankle sprains are probably the most inadequately treated of all dance and sports injuries. So often the dancer is dismissed with a bandage and told the injury will settle itself. Unless the injury is extremely trivial, this lack of adequate treatment will lead to chronic ankle problems with recurrent swelling, persistent pain and a feeling of instability of the ankle with lack of confidence. Adequate vigorous treatment is essential if this is to be avoided.

In almost all ankle injuries and certainly not in lateral ligament sprains only, the Achilles tendon (i.e. the calf muscles but always looked on by the dancers as the Achilles tendon alone) tightens within a few days of the injury. This tightening is almost always asymmetrical within the muscle so that later, when the dancer starts to perform a plié or a fondu, the foot is pulled into a rolling position (pronation) in order to

3.6 Testing for rightness of the Achilles tendon (actually the calf muscle/tendon complex). The foot must be correctly aligned with the leg and not inverted or everted. The flat of the hand is used to dorsiflex the whole foot while keeping the toes straight

3.7 Working on a slope to stretch the Achilles tendon/calf muscle. The feet must be kept parallel

achieve more depth. The tightening can be tested for by passively dorsiflexing the foot with the patella in line with the centre of the foot and pressure equally placed beneath the metatarsals with the flat of the hand (Fig. 3.6), taking care not to extend the toes dorsally above neutral. During this manoeuvre the tendency of the foot to go to one or other side can easily be detected. Also the tightness in the calf can be felt by the free hand of the examiner. The tightness is treated by massage to the whole length of the calf muscles from the ankle to the origins of the gastrocnemius just above the back of the knee. Passive stretching is carried out by the physiotherapist. (N.B. See the comments on stretching in **Section 2.5**, pp. 98–101). Later this stretching can be continued by the patient. In the final stages of rehabilitation a slope can be used by the patient (Fig. 3.7). A watch must he kept for a contracture of the lateral ligament due to scarring. This will require very gentle soft tissue work and stretching if necessary.

In a Grade 2 and 3 sprain the medial ligament may be painful as it undergoes a compression in inversion trauma This area also needs to be treated with soft tissue techniques.

The cuboid bone can also sublux in inversion sprains and this should also be checked (see Cuboid Subluxation p. 131).

3.2 Rupture of the Lateral Ligament of the Ankle

The causes are the same as for a sprain of the lateral ligament. It is essential that the diagnosis is made immediately following the injury. If missed, the consequences to the dancer are extremely serious. A complete rupture of the ligament or portion of the ligament, most commonly the anterior talo-fibular portion, requires surgical repair. If in doubt the injury can be confirmed or excluded by MRI scan. It is important not to miss the condition of anterior instability. This is caused by rupture of the anterior talo-fibular ligament and the anterior capsule of the ankle joint. Its presence can be demonstrated by drawing the talus forward in the ankle joint mortice. Normally, the talus should not slide anteriorly to any appreciable extent (compare with normal side). If there is instability, the talus (and whole foot below it) will move forward and probably also rotate slightly medially. This is known as the anterior drawer test. A late repair of a rupture leads to poor results compared with those following an immediate repair.

Rehabilitation, once the surgical treatment is completed, is the same as for a sprain of the lateral ligament of the ankle (**Section 3.1**).

3.3 Sprain of the Medial Ligament of the Ankle

This is uncommon in dancers. It is, however, very important to exclude a fracture of the medial malleolus or a complete rupture of the ligament, both of which require immediate orthopaedic treatment. Ligament rupture will certainly require surgery and a fracture of the medial malleolus, if it is more than just a crack, will probably require screwing back into place.

CAUSES

Commonly the injury occurs due to a bad landing with the weight mainly over the medial side of the foot and big toe. As a result the foot rolls and everts (over-pronates).

TREATMENT

This is similar to a sprain of the lateral ligament. Special attention must be paid to strengthening tibialis posterior, which inverts the ankle and the supports it medially, and to strengthening the peroneals.

Complications
See **Section 3.1**. Additionally, the tibialis posterior tendon may be traumatised and will need to be returned to full strength. If not, this produces a recurrent mild eversion strain by the rolling (pronation) which occurs. Also as a result of this rolling, the lateral ligament can become crushed by the impingement of the lateral malleolus and the talus.

3.4 Chronic Sprains of the Lateral and Medial Ligaments of the Ankle

CAUSES

These most commonly follow an acute sprain. A chronic sprain is the result of inadequate post-injury treatment, i.e. poor physiotherapy, the failure of the dancer to carry out instructions, or returning to work too soon after the injury – a danger with the free-lance dancer. However, a chronic sprain can also be produced gradually, without an acute phase, by faulty technique which allows incorrect weight-bearing on the foot.

TREATMENT

This is similar to that for the later stages of an acute sprain. However, there may be a great deal of scarring of the ligament and this may require extra attention from the physiotherapist. More effort will have to be put into the exercises for the various muscle groups. In this instance the weakness and wasting may well, and usually will, have spread to the muscles groups higher up the leg and even in the trunk. As a result of the chronic sprain, the dancer will have been working badly. The technique before the onset of symptoms may have been faulty, thus allowing a chronic sprain to occur, but even if not faulty before then, definite faults in technique will have set in as a result of the chronic sprain. This means that a great deal of time will have to be spent on correction.

3.5 Subluxation of the Peroneal Tendons

This is not very common in dancers. It usually follows an ankle sprain. The retinaculum (fibrous band) which holds the tendons in the groove behind and beneath the fibula becomes damaged. As a result the peroneal tendons can come out of their groove and slide across the lateral malleolus (the ankle bone on the outer side of the ankle). This can be both felt and seen on examination, particularly if the foot is actively dorsiflexed and everted. The dancer is aware of something slipping.

In the acute stage, treatment involves immobilisation in a plaster cast for about six weeks but unfortunately there is about a 50 per cent chance of recurrence. If the condition has become chronic where the sub-luxation occurs repeatedly then conservative treatment is most unlikely to be effective and surgical treatment becomes necessary.

The surgery can be directed at an attempt to repair or reconstruct the retinaculum but this is often ineffective. Another procedure is to deepen the groove in which the tendons run. This can work well but may leave rough edges against which the tendons will rub. There have been various sliding bone blocks devised but probably the easiest and most effective measure is to cut a flap of periosteum from the lateral malleolus with a thin layer of bone still attached deeply to it leaving a hinge posteriorly. This is then hinged posteriorly and attached with sutures behind the tendons forming a living block. Four to six weeks in plaster is required post-operatively. As in all procedures this should be followed by physiotherapy to mobilise and strengthen the ankle and muscle groups. Always, while a dancer has a part immobilised, the time should not be wasted and attention should be directed at keeping the rest of the body in condition with a suitable exercise programme. Rehab consists of strengthening and mobilising the talus, fibula and subtalar joint to fully recover the full depth of demi plié and height of three-quarter and full pointe.

3.6 Anterior Capsular Sprain of the Ankle

This injury may accompany either lateral or medial ligament sprains because of the hyperflexion element of the injuring force (plantarflexion). It is very important to note that injuries are rarely pure and localised and nearly always involve adjacent structures. The force applied is equally rarely purely inversional, eversional, etc. The treatment and complications of anterior capsular sprain are similar to that in lateral ligament and medial ligament sprains. However, an anterior capsular sprain is additionally complicated if swayback knees (hyperextended knees) (**Section 5.13**) are present and also if the weight is too far back when working (**Section 5.21**). Both these produce an excessive strain on the front of the ankle when on pointe and tension in front of the ankle in plié. The sprained ligament should be iced and ultrasounded and a protective taping applied to allow the dancer to continue working in some capacity with end range of plantarflexion restricted.

3.7 Fracture of the Lateral Malleolus

This fracture is caused by the same mechanism as a sprain of the lateral ligament. Usually, there is an inversion and rotation force, hence the actual fracture is most commonly spiral or oblique (Fig. 3.8). In most circumstances there is little displacement and complete reduction, even when displacement is severe, is usually easy and complete. If the trauma has been severe this fracture may also include a fracture of the medial malleolus and the posterior articular margin of the tibia, the degree of damage equating to the strength of the damaging force.

TREATMENT

This is standard orthopaedic care. Usually a plaster of Paris cast is applied for six weeks (or longer if a severe injury). Occasionally, if the fracture is minor, simple elastoplast strapping can be used but this is usually much less comfortable than a plaster cast. The strapping certainly does not imply that the dancer can continue

work. Sometimes an operation to fix the fracture internally with screws may be necessary.

During the period in plaster the dancer can, as in other injuries, continue to exercise all areas not immobilised in the cast. Not only will this keep the muscles strong but by promoting a good circulation will actually increase the rate of healing of the fracture within the cast.

Once out of plaster the muscle groups that have been inactive can be started on intensive exercises. Exercise will also be required to mobilise all the joints which have been kept immobile. Electrotherapy and ice for swelling and other therapeutic aids can also help. From here onwards the treatment pattern is similar to that following a sprained lateral ligament of the ankle (**Section 3.1**).

3.8 Fracture of the Medial Malleolus

This is caused by the opposite force to that causing a lateral malleolar fracture if it has occurred as an isolated fracture. As stated in **Section 3.7** it can also be associated with the severer degrees of lateral malleolar fracture. In the former situation (isolated fracture) it is usually oblique or spiral; in the latter situation, when associated with a lateral malleolar fracture, it is a transverse fracture as the medial malleolus is pulled off by the strain on the medial ligament (Fig. 3.9).

TREATMENT

This is standard orthopaedic treatment. Usually, medial malleolar fractures require internal fixation with a screw, though even so non-union remains common. However, this non-union takes place with the medial malleolus in

3.8 A spiral fracture of the lateral malleolus

3.9 A typical transverse fracture of the medial malleolus. There is also a fracture of the lateral malleolus present

the correct anatomical position and the sound fibrous union is usually sufficient to give total stability and is mostly painless. In the unusual circumstances where it remains painful a small bone graft may be required.

Further treatment – exercise regimes: treatment once the fracture has united and the general rehabilitation is as described above for a fracture of the lateral malleolus (**Section 3.7**) and the later stages of rehabilitation following lateral or medial ligament damage (**Sections 3.1** and **3.3**).

3.9 Osteochondral Fracture of the Dome of the Talus

This condition, which is a small chip fracture involving a portion of the articular cartilage and a small piece of underlying bone, occurs when the fragment is knocked out of the dome of the talus (where it forms part of the ankle joint) by a compression force (Fig. 3.10). Thus it occurs at the same time as a sprain of an ankle ligament or, more rarely, an ankle fracture. The osteochondral fracture may be difficult to demonstrate on an X-ray and as a result may not be found until very much later when, as a result of persistent ankle symptoms, further X-ray views are carried out and possibly an arthrogram. (This is an injection of air and radio-opaque dye into the joint.)

TREATMENT

If it is detected when fresh and if it has separated, then the fragment should either be removed if it is small, or else if it is larger, it should be pinned back into place. If it has not separated, then simple immobilisation may allow the fragment to heal in the correct position. Unfortunately and only too frequently the fragment, being deprived of its blood supply, separates at a later date and forms a loose body within the joint. The most important aspect of the condition is to think of the possibility if symptoms are persisting for longer than would be expected for the original injury.

3.10 Achilles Tendinopathy

The Achilles tendon does not have a sheath, so inflammatory conditions in this area affect either the loose fibrous tissues surrounding the tendon causing a peritendinitis, or changes within the tendon itself. or both. In the case of a tendon there may be small micro-tears within the substance of the tendon, larger partial tears or a degeneration described as tendinosis (see also Tendon Injuries p. 81).

CAUSES

Over-use can cause Achilles pain due to extra work following fatigue of muscle groups, or weakness of the feet, the gastrocnemius, the quadriceps, the hamstrings, or the gluteals or most or all of these. It is aggravated

3.10A An osteochondral fracture (arrowed) of the dome of the talus

3.10B An X-ray of a patient demonstrating an osteochondral fracture (arrowed)

3.10C An X-ray of a more extensive injury at the same site showing an osteochrondritis of the talus supero-medially and also long-standing damage to the medial malleolus. These types of changes within a joint can follow the injudicious injection of Hydrocortisone or other steroids into the joint. In the long term these changes result in severe osteo-arthritis of the joint by swayback (hyperextended) knees (**Section 5.13**), or by working with the weight too far back (**Section 5.21**). All these factors will cause overuse of the gastro-cnemius which has to do much of the work which should be carried out or aided by other muscle groups. The soleus is under-used in this situation because it does not cross behind the knee. The condition tends to be precipitated by a lack of work on three-quarter pointe in class. A muscle has to be worked throughout its full range in order to gain adequate strength. If sufficient work is not undertaken on three-quarter pointe in class, it means that the muscle will not be fully strong so when the foot has to actually work in and through three-quarter pointe, Achilles strain will frequently result. Three-quarter pointe is necessarily used on all jumps and landing and on going through the foot to rise on to pointe. If this is the only time that three-quarter pointe is in use, then the muscle will not gain sufficient strength to cope adequately.

Achilles tendinopathy may also be caused by tight-fitting shoes and ribbons which cut in; by shoes which are too small, causing a curling of the toes and pushing the weight back (**Section 5.21**); or shoes that are too wide and give no support to the forefoot, thus diminishing strength from the foot during jumps. Rolling with an unstable foot leads to the calf muscle not being worked in a balanced way. Pointing with a sickled in foot produces over-working of the inner (medial) side of the calf muscle and also of the medial hamstrings. Working with a sickled out foot also over-works the outer calf which in turn tends to produce stretching of the medial side of the front of the ankle (Fig. 3.11) and nipping of the insertion of the Achilles tendon. Anything which produces a tight pointe, such as an os trigonum or enlarged posterior tubercle of the talus, can precipitate an Achilles problem. Also, failing to stretch the calf properly when working i.e. getting the heels down in a demi plié when the range is available, may cause problems. Working on a raked stage can aggravate the effects of all these causes.

TREATMENT

Attention has to be paid to all possible causes of the condition with their elimination and correction (for example, strengthening other weak muscle groups). Biomechanics must be checked carefully for any abnormalities. Massage and stretching of the calf are required with exercises also for the dorsiflexors to balance the calf. If a degree of tendinosis is suspected, a programme of eccentric heel drops should be started and carefully monitored (see Figs 4.213–4.218).

Complications
When the pain is in the Achilles attachment at the heel the condition takes longer than when the tendinosis is

3.11A Sickling when on pointe

3.11B Sickling when in the air (fishing)

mid tendon. This called an enthesopathy (pain at a tendon attachment).

The tendon and calf must be stretched and worked evenly (medial versus lateral and right versus left) otherwise as soon as work is started againt postural balance is affected and therefore dance technique.

3.11 Rupture of the Achilles Tendon

Although micro-ruptures or small partial ruptures may occur in Achilles tendinopathy, we are dealing here with complete ruptures. Beware of missing a complete rupture and of labelling the condition as a partial rupture.

CAUSES

This will most commonly occur when the tendon is subjected to sudden unaccustomed stress. This may happen in the teacher who is out of training attempting to demonstrate a jump, particularly if not warmed up. In the dancer who is in a physically trained situation it is most commonly associated with an inadequate warm-up or by an unprecedented number of repetitions which call for explosive calf-muscle action. Frustratingly, sometimes the cause can be inexplicable.

DIAGNOSIS

Initially a gap can be felt in the tendon but, soon after the injury, local swelling may mask this and make diagnosis more difficult. Pain, swelling and an inability to stand unsupported on demi-pointe on the affected foot is an urgent indication for an orthopaedic surgical opinion. An ultrasound scan can confirm the diagnosis.

TREATMENT

This is by early (within twenty-four hours) repair of the rupture. Immobilisation in a simple plaster of Paris cast has been shown to give good results for a *partial* rupture *if the diagnosis is certain* and it may be treated successfully without surgery. After the surgery for a complete rupture the rehabilitation starts early with exercises for all other muscle groups. When the post-operative plaster is removed (usually at six weeks) the patient transfers to an aircaste boot with three wedges in the heel. Over a six-week period a wedge comes out every two weeks until it is time to start minimal pliés. An intensive programme of muscle strengthening for the whole lower limb will be required followed later by technical help. Initially everything feels tight but stretching must be gentle and progressive and always accompanied by strengthening exercises. It may well be up to six months before full work can be resumed, although some early class work can be used as part of a carefully devised rehabilitation programme. Even in the long term the calf muscle will always look slightly smaller than the other side and the Achilles tendon will be thickened because of the scar tissue formed in the healing process. As always, even while still in plaster, gym and Pilates exercises for the rest of the body can be continued.

Care must be taken during surgery as too tight a repair will cause shortening of the Achilles tendon; if the frayed tendon ends are not brought together sufficiently the tendon will be too long. A long tendon will result in poor elevation when jumping as well as other difficulties; a short one will limit the plié.

3.12 Achilles Tendon Bursitis

The Achilles tendon bursa lies between the tendon just above its insertion and the bone of the calcaneum (Fig. 3.12). It can become the site of inflammation with thickening and swelling if it is irritated.

CAUSES

It may be associated with an Achilles tendinopathy, especially with the overuse aspects of that condition.

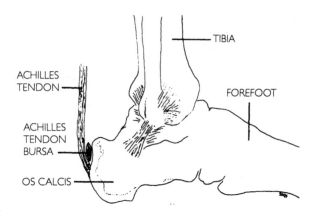

3.12 Diagram showing the site of the Achilles tendon bursa, which provides a cushion between the tendon and the heel bone (os calcis)

Calf length and strength must be attended to. Using pointe shoes that are too soft may contribute to the problem. It may occur alone in an overuse situation or from pressure over a prominence of the posterior part of the calcaneum (calcaneus altus).

TREATMENT

Ice and ultrasound may prove helpful. Elimination of the cause is required. Only very rarely should a Hydrocortisone injection be contemplated as the condition will most commonly settle without it.

3.13 Posterior Impingement at the Ankle

This is usually caused by the presence of an os trigonum or a large posterior tubercle of the talus. In most, if not all, cases an os trigonum represents a stress fracture of a large posterior tubercle of the talus (Fig. 3.13). The onset of the stress fracture may be the reason for the onset of symptoms. In many instances surgery may not be required. However, once symptoms have started they frequently do not settle satisfactorily with conservative treatment. Nevertheless conservative treatment should be undertaken conscientiously. Symptoms may also be precipitated by weakness after a growth spurt developing in a previously symptomless foot or calf. Sometimes after a long holiday coming straight back into class and rehearsals without a graded return to pointework etc. can precipitate problems. Sometimes coming back too soon after an illness e.g. an absence with influenza, will leave the dancer weakened. Symptoms may also be brought about by any situation which causes the dancer to work with the weight back (**Section 5.21**). The actual weakness may be far

3.13A Normal ankle
3.13B Large posterior tubercle of the talus
3.13C Os trigonum
3.13D Exostosis on the dorsum of the os calcis

removed from the ankle region, e.g. weak gluteals causing sitting in the hip and the weight being too far back. A differently fitting shoe may also start symptoms especially if the shoe is too small. In a student the symptoms may come gradually due to the slowly increasing range of plantarflexion.

Very occasionally similar impingement symptoms may be associated with an exostosis on the dorsum of the os calcis just behind the talo-calcaneal joint.

TREATMENT

Once symptoms have started, they may be impossible to relieve without surgery, but despite this every attempt should be made to alleviate the situation before surgery is undertaken, as sometimes conservative treatment can be successful. The treatment is directed at strengthening the foot with intrinsic foot muscle exercises, strengthening the quadriceps, adductors and gluteals to eliminate any overworking by the calf muscles and technical help to correct any faulty weight transmission.

Only if conservative treatment fails should surgery be considered. In this case removal of the os trigonum or enlarged posterior tubercle of the talus will be required. The approach surgically should be through the medial side of the ankle. A lateral approach interferes with the peroneal tendons and their sheaths, greatly prolonging the convalescence. Immediately post-operatively exercises must be started to both passively and actively encourage plantarflexion or pointing as this was the movement which was limited before the operation. A few days after the operation gentle non-weight bearing dorsiflexion should be commenced actively or assisted actively but not using any passive forcing. When the foot and ankle can be dorsiflexed to neutral then gradual weight bearing can be commenced. Once the wound is healed much more active weight-bearing and dorsiflexion should be encouraged including some pliés, with the dancer supporting himself on the barre. Intrinsic foot exercises can be started even before removal of the sutures. As progress continues, ankle strengthening exercises, the balancing board and slope walking can be started. The more distant groups of muscles must not be neglected.

Complications

For six months or more post-operatively there will be a tendency for the scarring behind the ankle to contract. A very careful watch must be kept for this and gentle stretching must be continued for a long time. Early contractures will be shown by a decreasing depth of demi-pliés.

Inadequate post-operative physiotherapy and/or inadequate technical correction can interfere with early improvement in pointe following the operation as well as allowing a gradual decrease in depth of plié. The long-term follow-up is too frequently neglected.

3.14 Anterior Impingement of the Ankle

As explained in 'The Ankle and Foot' in **Section 1** (p. 13) the talocrural joint functions as a mortice and tenon joint. As the dancer's ankle plantarflexes into the pointe position the talus moves forwards in the mortise. As the ankle dorsiflexes into a plié the talus moves backwards. The limiting factor in dorsiflexion is the Achilles tendon and calf complex and in plantarflexion, the anterior capsule and dorsiflexor tendons.

In dancers, especially those doing high levels of pointe work and jumps, the calf can become extremely tight with a significant muscle imbalance between flexors (plantarflexors) and extensors (dorsiflexors). Muscle imbalance around the ankle can cause joint misalignment and in this instance the talus is squeezed forward where it jams, with its normal backwards excursion disturbed. When the talus sits anteriorly it causes several problems. The most common is an anterior impingement between the upper surface of the neck of the talus and the lower end of the tibia in a plié or fondu. Landing from jumps is painful and compensation causes problems higher up.

An 'exostosis' or spur can develop on the anterior tibial margin and is identified on X-ray. This may develop following an untreated ankle.

DIAGNOSIS

In the neutral position the head of the talus is palpated and when compared to the unaffected side, may be found to sit further forward. The ankle joint on mobilisation is restricted. The calf and peroneals are tight and congested. The anterior compartment is also tense. The head of the fibula be may stiff on the affected side in which case it will also need mobilising.

TREATMENT

The calf requires soft tissue mobilisation and stretching. The joint requires mobilisation techniques with AP glides of the talus. Manipulation may relocate the talus and normal movement is restored with mobilisation with movement (MWMs) in the fondu position. Sometimes taping (see Taping Techniques p. 198) can help stabilise the ankle immediately post-treatment but the dancer must continue a calf-stretching regime and dorsiflexion exercises to rebalance forces about the ankle.

Proprioception exercises should always be included. Adverse neural tension should be checked and calf stretches in SLR should be included.

Complications
Sometimes the anterior position of the talus can disturb the deep peroneal nerve at the anterior ankle causing nerve pain, pins and needles or numbness at the first webspace.

3.15 Tibialis Posterior Tendinopathy and Tenosynovitis

CAUSES

This is caused by incorrect weight-bearing (**Sections 5.18** and **5.21**). It is particularly aggravated by correcting rolling at the ankle instead of carrying out the correction higher up the leg. Correcting at the ankle produces tension aggravated by weak intrinsic muscles, especially when associated with an oblique line of the metatarsal heads (Fig. 3.14), or during pointework with old shoes or badly fitting shoes, or failure to hold the turn-out correctly, or a combination of these factors. The condition is made worse by working on a raked stage and on slippery floor surfaces.

TREATMENT

Ultrasound and ice can be helpful. Intrinsic foot muscle exercises are always necessary. General strengthening of all groups around the ankle and of the groups higher up the leg should be carried out. A considerable

3.14 An oblique line of the lesser metatarsal heads

amount of technical correction to the turned-out hip/knee/foot is necessary to address an over-pronating foot, and the shoes must be checked. Taping can help with proprioception encouraging correct biomechanics of the ankle and foot.

Complications
The condition can be very slow to settle and it is difficult to treat satisfactorily. It will tend to niggle on for a long time and a great deal of supportive treatment is required. The jumping section of class work must be carefully regulated during rehabilitation.

3.16 Flexor Hallucis Longus Tendinopathy and Tenosynovitis

This condition is an irritation and or inflammation which can affect either the tendon or its surrounding sheath or, most commonly, both elements. Problems can occur anywhere along its length from the proximal end where the muscle fibres pass into the tendon to its insertion into the base of the distal phalanx of the great toe.

There is one condition which is exclusive to the flexor hallucis longus and its tendon and this occurs at the musculo-tendinous junction. In this particular muscle the fleshy fibres extend distally as far as the level of the back of the ankle joint. The tendon sheath, which extends past the ankle and through the foot and contains the actual tendon, commences just distally to the line of the ankle joint. As a result of this anatomical arrangement, the situation sometimes arises where full dorsiflexion of the great toe at the metatarso-phalangeal and inter-phalangeal joints pulls not only the tendon but also some of the fleshy part of the muscle (in dancers this can be hypertrophied), where it is joining the tendon, into the tube of the tendon sheath. If this happens recurrently it can lead to local swelling at the musculo-tendinous junction where it is being pulled in and out of the tendon sheath. A clicking can be felt and heard and is called 'triggering'. Symptoms of pain may be persistent at this site in which case surgery to split open the proximal portion of the tendon sheath will relieve the symptoms.

CAUSES

This condition is caused by incorrect weight-bearing on the foot (**Section 5.21**). It may also arise from a direct blow, a not infrequent cause, or by a cutting pressure from badly-fitting shoes. Weakness of the first inter-osseus muscle may aggravate or cause the condition.

TREATMENT

Ice and ultrasound to any swelling over the tendon on the medial ankle and into the foot, can help. Rest and FHL stretches (see pp. 91–101) can help settle the condition along withcalf massage, stretching and intrinsic foot muscle exercises. The intrinsics in this condition are usually very weak and cannot extend the interphalangeal joint of the great toe fully. At the same time the first space (between the 1st and 2nd metatarsals) opens out due to the weakness of the first interosseous. Strengthening of the intrinsics helps to close this space and allows the interphalangeal joint of the great toe to extend, permitting the weight to be brought to the correct position from having been too far back (**Section 5.21**). Strengthening the abductor hallucis (p. 192) will also help stabilise the medial longitudinal arch of the foot and the big toe. While the strengthening process is going on, taping the hallux to correct alignment can help. Alternatively a toe spacer can be use between first and second toes.

Complications
The condition is usually very slow to settle and treatment and technical correction may be required for a prolonged period.

3.17 Extensor Hallucis Longus Tendonitis

This may occur at any level of the tendon.

CAUSES

Direct blows are not uncommon or drawstring on pointe shoes may cut across the tendon. Rolling is a very potent cause as is also weight back with the toes clawed (**Sections 5.18** and **5.19**). In this situation the extensor hallucis longus tendon tends to become

shortened. Weakness of the intrinsics prevents proper extension of the great toe when working. Even when the toe is not being clawed, the weight being too far back may also cause the toes to repeatedly lift off the ground and hence tend to shorten the extensor hallucis longus. A high longitudinal arch where the plantar surface never touches the floor, tends to lift the great toe off the floor. Cutting from the block or vamp of the shoe may cause a tendonitis distally. Coming up on to pointe and working there with bent toes (knuckling) can cause the situation, particularly if it is associated with sickling outwards.

TREATMENT

Ice and ultrasound with intrinsic foot exercises are started at once. Taping the great toe to try to keep the interphalangeal joint straight or using a toe spacer with correction of the underlying cause are all required. Sometimes a hydrocortisone injection can clear up a chronic problem.

Complications
The condition can be difficult to get settled. Inspection of everyday shoes should be undertaken as unsuitable daily footwear can delay or prevent resolution. If it followed a direct blow, there may be other damaged tissues to treat. A developing stress fracture of the 2nd metatarsal may confuse matters by appearing to cause pain along the extensor hallucis longus tendon.

3.18 Stress Fractures of the Metatarsals

See also **Section 2.2**, p. 80.

The affected metatarsals are commonly the 2nd and 3rd. Occasionally the 4th or 5th metatarsals may be the site of the stress fracture. In dancers it is very rarely the 1st metatarsal unless the technique is very poor or the choreographic circumstances are very unusual. Fracture in the 2nd or 3rd metatarsal is usually mid shaft (Fig. 3.15), but a basal stress fracture in the 2nd metatarsal is not uncommon. Being a superficial bone, diagnosis is straightforward with local warmth, tenderness and swelling being easily detected.

CAUSES

Discrepancy of metatarsal length, for example, where there is a long 2nd metatarsal or short 1st metatarsal (Fig. 3.16) or occasionally a long 3rd metatarsal. Long toes and weak forefeet predispose to a basal fracture of the 2nd metatarsal. A predisposition anatomically is greatly aggravated by weak intrinsic muscles. Dancing on concrete or solid wood floors and other surfaces

3.15 X-ray of a stress fracture of the 2nd metatarsal shaft showing healing with plentiful callus (new bone)

3.16 Short 1st metatarsal in relation to the 2nd metatarsal. In this instance the 2nd and 3rd metatarsals are of equal length

without any elasticity or spring may fairly rapidly produce a crop of stress fractures in a class or company. A sudden increase in heavy workload, especially if a lot of pointe work or jumps are required, may produce a stress fracture. This is often seen where there is a sudden move from corps de ballet to principal or possibly, more commonly, the transition from part-time student with three or four classes a week to that of full-time student with classes all day. Badly-fitting shoes or worn-out shoes with soft blocks can also be a predisposing factor. Frequently when the discomfort starts, the dancer will move to wider-fitting shoes, assuming that the shoe itself is causing the pain. This means that the forefoot will have even less support and the situation will be aggravated.

Weak intrinsic muscles leading to dropping of the lesser metatarsal heads can cause a stress fracture because of the additional load placed on the metatarsal. The presence of even a moderate degree of hallux rigidus (degenerative arthritis of the great toe joint, see **Section 3.25**) will cause incorrect weight placement (**Section 5.21**), because the dancer cannot rise correctly through the foot as a result of the limited movements in the 1st metatarso-phalangeal joint. The 5th metatarsal is a special case, and a stress fracture often starts here as a complication of a severe sprain of the lateral ligament because the secondary weakness of ankle control, particularly laterally, i.e. from the peronei, places extra weight transmission through the 5th metatarsal. This tends to be brought about by a too early return to dancing following a lateral ligament sprain. There are also technical causes of which incorrect

weight transmission is the commonest – rolling, sickling outwards, over turning or failing to hold the turn-out, working with clawed toes and working with the weight too far back, which aggravates weak intrinsics (incorrect weight placement; **Section 5.21**).

TREATMENT

Rest is required to allow the fracture to unite. During this period, give exercises to strengthen all deficient groups and particularly intrinsic foot muscle exercises – lumbricals, interrossei and abductor hallucis. Correct the cause where possible (anatomical aberrations may not be correctable but a strong forefoot will lessen the stress on the bone).

Complications

The most commonly seen complication is an interference with healing due to an ill-advised injection of Hydrocortisone by someone who has failed to make the initial diagnosis and thinks that he is merely dealing with a soft tissue lesion. Oral anti-inflammatories in full doses will also very markedly slow healing by their suppression of the inflammatory response which is a vital part of the healing process (see **Section 2.1**). It is extremely important to note that X-ray evidence of a stress fracture will not appear for at least ten to fourteen days after the onset of symptoms. Although a bone scan would show a developing stress fracture, it should be perfectly possible to make the diagnosis with a fair degree of certainty on clinical grounds. The metatarsal bones are extremely superficial and the presence of local warmth, swelling and tenderness which is very well localised to the bone should cause little difficulty in enabling the examiner to come to the correct diagnosis.

3.19 Osteochondritis of the Head of the 2nd or 3rd Metatarsal

This is a condition which occurs in childhood. It is probably caused by trauma to the metatarsal head. As a result of this, changes occur in the head of the metatarsal and the articular surface begins to collapse. It is seen not only in dancers but also in sprinters and other athletic children. The diagnosis can be made clinically because of localised thickening and tenderness at the metatarsophalangeal joint. The diagnosis is confirmed by X-ray, which shows an alteration in structure of the metatarsal head and early or even late collapse of the articular surface (Fig. 3.17).

TREATMENT

If the condition is seen early when collapse of the articular surface is still only minor, then surgery should

3.17 Osteochondritis of the 2nd metatarsal head (X-ray)

be undertaken. The neck of the metatarsal can be opened and the articular surface elevated to its proper position and the head packed with bone chips, which can be obtained from the metatarsal shaft. This is followed by protected weight-bearing until consolidation takes place. Rehabilitation will necessitate faradic foot baths and intrinsic muscle exercises to strengthen the forefoot which will have weakened during the period of convalescence. However, during convalescence the dancer must spend a considerable amount of time exercising all other groups.

Unfortunately, cases usually present very late. When the patient is first seen with pain it may be found that not only is there marked thickening and tenderness around the metatarsal head and metatarso-phalangeal joint but that there is marked restriction of movement in the affected joint, particularly shown by a greatly decreased range of dorsiflexion. This will be causing problems on demi-pointe work. At this stage X-rays will show that the articular surface has been completely flattened and the metatarsal head broadened, sometimes with some osteophytic formation. Treatment is again surgical but it is impossible to restore the normal anatomy. Instead, the proximal half of the proximal phalanx of the toe is excised in order to produce a pseudarthrosis and restore the range of dorsiflexion of the toe. At the same time it may be necessary to trim any large osteophytes from the metatarsal head as occasionally they are sufficiently prominent to cause local pressure. If, however, there is no evidence that they are going to cause any local pressure, then they should be left alone. Treatment in the form of faradic foot baths, intrinsic muscle exercises, together with

active and passive exercises for the toes, can start as soon as the wound is healed. The results are usually very satisfactory. The shortening of the affected toe does not hamper the dance performance in any way.

3.20 Cuboid Subluxation

The cuboid is regarded as the keystone to the stability of the lateral longitudinal arch. This is composed of the calcaneus, cuboid and metatarsals 4 and 5 (see p. 15). The calcaneocuboid joint is the lateral component of the mid-tarsal joint. When a dancer works in an over-pronated foot position in turn-out, the mid-tarsal joint unlocks. The associated abduction here causes the cuboid to move inferiorly – sublux downwards. Marshall and Hamilton (1994) suggest that the classical dancer's relevé 'in the valgus position of the forefoot' predisposes them to cuboid subluxation. Rising from a pronated position and remaining too far over the 1st toe prevents the mid-tarsal joint from stabilising in a strong three-quarter or full pointe position. The cuboid is vulnerable in this position. The dancer will complain of pain over the lateral border of the foot. There may be a slight hollow over the cuboid on the dorsum of the foot. The more prominent cuboid can be felt on the plantar surface.

Plantarflexion and inversion sprains to the lateral foot or ankle are also thought to cause a cuboid subluxation and therefore should be checked.

TREATMENT

Manual techniques are necessary here to reduce the subluxation. Either manipulation or the 'cuboid squeeze' as recommended by Marshall and Hamilton are successful after the surrounding soft tissues have been released. A cuboid pad and taping are recommended for support after the first treatment (see p. 201).

If extensor digitorum brevis has lost a portion of its bulk over the affected cuboid, extension exercises for the outer toes can recover this.

The angle of turn-out should be corrected and intrinsic foot muscle exercises taught if necessary. Pointe shoes should be checked for size and block shape in case the foot is being pushed on to the inside of the shoe platform.

For further reading:
Marshall, P. and Hamilton, W. 'Cuboid subluxation in ballet dancers'. *American Journal of Sports Medicine* (March 1992), 20 (2) 169–75.

3.21 Plantar Fascial Strain

The plantar fascia lies in the sole of the foot, covered only by fat and skin. It is a very strong, thick, inelastic band of tissue which is attached to the medial tubercle on the heel bone at the back, and runs forward to divide into slips which attach to the proximal phalanx of each toe (Fig. 3.18). Lifting the toes tensions the fascia. It supports the longitudinal arches but weak intrinsic muscles make it vulnerable to strain.

3.18 The plantar aroneurosis (plantar fascia)

CALCANEUM

CAUSES

This is often due to chronic irritation from excessive pronation, resulting in microtears to the plantar fascia, often at its origin at the heel. If ignored and allowed to progress the problem can become very debilitating. This condition can arise with weak feet, particularly when associated with a high longitudinal arch. It is aggravated by wearing shoes that are too short which weakens the foot. It occasionally arises when a female dancer wears unaccustomed very high heels and then stands in these shoes for a very long period.

TREATMENT

In the initial stages, ice, ultrasound, and foot exercises are most effective. If the condition is chronic with thickening, hydrocortisone injection under ultrasound guidance can sometime be the only resort if the dancer has tried rest and conservative treatment. Strengthening of all the intrinsic muscles and technical correction is necessary to prevent recurrence.

Taping can help to alleviate pain by supporting the longitudinal arch (see p. 199).

3.22 Capsular Strains of 1st Metatarso-phalangeal Joint

CAUSES

Direct violence, e.g. stubbing the toe, or landing badly. The condition tends to be commoner in boys. Another prime cause of symptoms is repeated technical faults, particularly if they give a twist to the toe, for example rolling (Fig. 3.19) and all its causes (see **Section 5.18**) and, of course, sickling. The condition tends to be very much worse if there is a short 1st metatarsal, or conversely, a long 2nd metatarsal which produces a similar overall mechanical effect. Shoes that are too short cause the great toe to claw up. The presence of a hallux valgus will cause joint strain because, in rises, as the weight comes over the toes, there is a further valgus strain placed on the great toe and on the medial aspect of the joint. In the presence of a weak first interosseous muscle with a palpable gap between the 1st and 2nd

metatarsal heads, even in a case where there is not a congenital metatarsus primus varus, the situation would be greatly aggravated, as would also be the case where there is general weakness of the intrinsics.

In both situations, most of the weight is going through the great toe joint rather than correctly down through the centre of the foot. Shoes that are too wide give no support at all. There is certainly a general inclination, when there is any sort of toe discomfort, for the dancer to go into a wider fitting and this, of course, makes matters worse. Worn-out pointe shoes will also stress the great toe joint greatly. A painful toe, for example an ingrowing toenail, painful corns or verrucae will all cause a weight shift. In many instances the strain may be isolated to the medial ligament and capsule of the metatarso-phalangeal joint. When symptoms at this joint are troublesome there will often be restriction of movements and the clinical appear-

3.19A Rolling with a twist of the big toe. From the front
3.19B From the side

ance of a hallux rigidus. However, mobility will return when the capsular strain has been treated adequately.

TREATMENT

Ice, ultrasound in water and intrinsic muscle exercises are all helpful. Strapping of the great toe to help to maintain alignment or a toe spacer can help while treatment is in progress. The dancer can also carry out hot and cold contrast baths himself because frequently this condition tends to be rather more resistant to treatment if the circulation is not particularly good in the toes and feet. The shoes should be checked carefully, including outdoor shoes. Frequently traction on the great toe, to ensure the correct alignment and to gently stretch any tightness, accompanied by passive movements, can be very beneficial.

Complications

Poor circulation makes the condition slower to settle and much more difficult to treat. Usually there is a technical fault associated with this condition and this will lead to other injuries if the technical aspects are not very carefully checked. Any underlying tendency to hallux rigidus will be greatly aggravated. The condition may also cause a sesamoiditis if it persists or is not fully treated, or if it is of long standing. It is often not at all easy to obtain full resolution of the condition because it so frequently follows bad working habits which can be very difficult to eradicate adequately. An example of this is working with the weight back (**Section 5.21**).

3.23 Sesamoiditis

Beneath the head of the 1st metatarsal lie two small bones within the tendons to the great toe (Fig. 3.20). They are known as the medial and lateral sesamoids. They are exactly like a small version of the patella or knee cap, which is a sesamoid bone lying within the tendon formed from the quadriceps muscle on its way down to be inserted into the tibia. The patella is so large that it has a name of its own, whereas the two sesamoids under the 1st metatarsal head are named the tibial (inner) or fibular (outer) sesamoid. They are small, each being the size of a small bean. In normal walking and running they take the load and pressure beneath the metatarsal head and help to distribute it and also protect the tendons which would otherwise be subjected to direct pressure.

They are surprisingly free of trouble considering the great forces transmitted through them and their vulnerable position.

Occasionally one or both can be bruised becoming inflamed and painful so that weight bearing is

3.20A The sesamoid bones lying beneath the 1st metatarsal head. The X-ray is taken from above looking through the foot

3.20B Here the X-ray is taken looking along the sole of the foot

extremely uncomfortable, this condition being known as sesamoiditis. Very rarely a sesamoid can be fractured as a result of direct trauma. A fracture must be differentiated from a bipartite or tripartite sesamoid, which is a congenital condition when a sesamoid is in two or three separate parts from birth. A similar condition can occur in the patella. Sesamoiditis presents with local pain and sometimes swelling. Tenderness is localised to beneath the head of the 1st metatarsal. Passive dorsiflexion of the toe with pressure applied beneath the 1st metatarsal head makes the tenderness worse.

CAUSES

Sesamoiditis is precipitated by direct trauma usually brought about by a bad landing. Sometimes prolonged work on a hard surface will cause the condition. A weak big toe may make the sesamoids vulnerable.

TREATMENT

Sesamoiditis is frequently extremely slow to settle. Patience on the part of the dancer and the therapist is the most important factor.

For local treatment ice and ultrasound can be used. Felt padding to temporarily relieve pressure from beneath the 1st metatarsal head can be helpful. A podiatrist may be helpful in creating a slim inner sole for flat and point shoes which can off load a recovering sesamoid.

Only too often it is just the passage of time, frequently very many months, which allows the symptoms to subside.

Surgery has nothing to offer. Excision of the sesamoid more often than not leaves permanent residual tenderness. To risk surgery on the small chance of gaining relief is unwise. With patience the symptoms will always settle.

3.24 Hallux Valgus and Bunions

CAUSES

Probably the commonest cause seen in dancers is where there is a congenital metatarsus primus varus which produces a secondary hallux valgus (Fig. 3.21). Later in life a hallux valgus (Fig. 3.22) can appear following the use of very poor footwear or if the dancer as a child is put on pointe far too early when the feet are not strong enough. It can also be caused by very prolonged rolling or by weak forefeet (i.e. when the intrinsics are very weak).

There must, however, be an underlying mild hallux valgus deformity before these other latter causes will produce ill-effects and an aggravation of the already slight valgus posture. Overall it is surprising how

3.22 A severe hallux valgus in the right foot. Note the overriding second toe. Sometimes the big toe comes over the top of the second toe. The left foot has been improved in appearance by a Keller's operation. This shortens the big toe moderately. There is a marked decrease in one's power of movement so the operation is not suitable for the dancer who is still working.

frequently a very severe valgus deformity is seen which causes little or no symptoms.

TREATMENT

In the situation where there is a congenital metatarsus primus varus a Hohmann's osteotomy of the 1st metatarsal produces a very satisfactory result (Fig. 3.23). This corrective operation does not interfere at all with the capsule or ligaments of the 1st metatarsophalangeal joint and therefore does not lead to any stiffness if it is carried out correctly. It should ideally be undertaken in the mid teens. If the deformity is fairly marked, then it should almost certainly be carried out even in the absence of symptoms at that time. This also applies if there is a strong family history of bunions. After about the mid to late twenties or possibly the early thirties, a Hohmann's operation is usually contra-indicated, because the alteration in mechanics of the foot are not accommodated well by a foot of greater age and it may leave a painful foot with tenderness, particularly under the lesser metatarsal heads.

In the case of a hallux valgus without a metatarsus primus varus, operation in active professional dancers is contra-indicated and no radical surgery should be undertaken before they have retired from performing. However, in a teacher, they will usually cope perfectly satisfactorily following the standard Keller's operation (Fig. 3.24). If the bunion area becomes repeatedly infected, then it is possible to carry out a subcapsular excision of the bony osteophyte with a careful reconstruction of the medial capsule. The operation, however, may occasionally lead to some restriction of movements and it should not be carried out unless there is very definite indication for surgery. This

3.21A A metatarsus primus varus with a mild secondary hallux valgus developing
3.21B An X-ray of the same foot

3.24 Diagram of a Keller's operation which is carried out either for a hallux valgus and bunions or for a hallux rigidus (osteo-arthritis of the 1st metatarso-phalangeal joint)

indication is largely repeated episodes of inflammation or infection and a risk of underlying bony involvement. The operation must be done open so that the soft tissues can be identified clearly and preserved. One of the most important aspects of this operation is the accurate reconstruction of the medial capsule. If this is not done then a rapidly increasing valgus deformity will follow this type of procedure. To carry out the operation through a very small incision and blindly grind off the prominent bone is totally irresponsible and can only be condemned. Only too frequently the capsule is severely damaged and there is certainly no opportunity for its reconstruction.

Conservative treatment in hallux valgus and bunions is directed at care of the bunion area. Use of a felt ring pad can relieve local pressure over the bunion. Sometimes a wedge between the first and second toes can be helpful to support the great toe. However, this occasionally has the disadvantage that the pressure is transmitted to the lesser toes which causes them to start to drift into valgus. Faradic foot baths and intrinsic muscle exercises can also help by strengthening the control of the toes.

Complications
Recurrent blistering. This can lead to inflammation and infection of the actual bunions which in occasional cases can progress to bony involvement.

3.23 Hohmann's operation. The shaded section in the first diagram shows the area of bone removed. The second shows the displacement of the 1st metatarsal head towards the 2nd metatarsal and the positioning head securely on the bone peg formed at the end of the shaft. This is the subject of the X-ray. The projecting corner of bone at the medial end of the metatarsal shaft becomes absorbed and remodelled during union of the osteotomy and subsequent consolidation

3.25 Hallux Rigidus

This is a condition where osteoarthritis (degenerative arthritis) occurs in the metatarso-phalangeal joint of the great toe. It derives its name because as the condition progresses the toe joint becomes stiffer and eventually fixed or rigid. The condition starts in childhood and is first evidenced by limitation of movement, mainly dorsiflexion at the great toe joint. At that stage there are rarely any X-ray changes, although there may be some sclerosis of the epiphysis at the base of the proximal phalanx of the great toe. Even later, when movements have become markedly restricted, the changes seen on an X-ray are often relatively mild and advanced radiological changes are only apparent when the toe joint is severely affected and very stiff.

CAUSES

The cause is probably genetic because the condition is not usually associated with trauma and is bilateral. However, like any other joint, if there has been some significant damage to the joint, arthritis may follow. This latter type of hallux rigidus can start at any time in life depending upon when the episode of trauma occurred. The condition, whatever the cause, is unfortunately progressive. The range of movement slowly decreases and because of the limitation of dorsiflexion, it causes various technical problems. These are largely associated with the difficulty or impossibility in achieving correct weight placement (**Section 5.21**).

TREATMENT

Progress can be slowed and symptoms alleviated by gentle traction on the great toe joint to decrease the amount of stiffness and shortening in the soft tissues, by gentle active and passive exercises and, of course, by strengthening the intrinsic muscles in the forefoot. It is advisable to tell the dancer not to force three-quarter pointe as trying to get up too high tends to make the condition worse rather than better. The dancer should be guided on how high to go by the degree of pain

experienced. Some pain is inevitable in the very nature of the condition but it should not be extreme. If symptoms persist despite conservative treatment and particularly if the stiffening of the great toe is causing other technical problems and other injuries, then surgery should be considered. For a dancer this may be in the form of a replacement of the base of the proximal phalanx of the great toe (Figs 3.25 A and B). JH has had success using the silastic replacement but has not tried some of the newer protheses. In any case it is really a last resort operation. An alternative procedure suggested by Dr Boni Rietveld is an osteotomy of the proximal end of the proximal phalanx. This makes use of the range of plantarflexion movement, which is much less restricted than dorsiflexion. In the operation at the osteotomy site the distal part of the proximal phalanx is angled dorsally. This transfers the residual range of total joint movement to a more useful range in dorsiflexion but limits plantarflexion which matters little to the dancer, as long as there is sufficient for a proper pointe to be achieved. Care must therefore be taken to avoid too much dorsiflexion at the osteotomy site. However as hallux rigidus is a progressive condition the beneficial effects of this operation is limited in duration.

Surgery should not be undertaken in a student. The life of the replacement is limited, though variable. It is probably wrong to allow students to embark upon what will become a very brief professional career at an age when they would be better channelling their energies into some other job for the future. When the silastic joint fails it can be removed. This leaves the toe somewhat shortened and greatly decreased in power in jumps, relevés, etc. This latter state is, however, a situation which is perfectly satisfactory for normal life and probably for most dance teachers. In a professional dancer the extra working years which the silastic

3.25A Silastic replacement of the base of the proximal phalanx of the big toe

3.25B On pointe following the replacement

replacement will have allowed will be greatly welcomed. It is impossible to forecast pre-operatively how long the prosthesis might last but certainly dancers should be warned that it is not going to last them the rest of their anticipated stage career unless they are already of somewhat mature years.

But *beware*! The diagnosis of hallux rigidus may be made when there is only an *apparent* stiffness of the great toe joint. A stiff great toe needs careful assessment as, when the patient is first seen, there may appear to be a very genuine restriction of movement in the great toe joint but often the stiffness is only temporary. This is not a genuine hallux rigidus. The situation can be brought about by working badly and repeatedly traumatising the first metatarso-phalangeal joint. This is seen particularly in rolling when the weight is repeatedly transmitted at an angle through the metatarso-phalangeal joint. The joint itself can become swollen, painful and stiff as a result. However, with adequate local treatment and correction of the technical fault, the range of movement can be satisfactorily restored. Obviously, X-rays of the toe will show that there is no bony abnormality present and no evidence of any degenerative arthritis.

Complications
The complications arise from the technical faults which result from the alteration of weight bearing line due to the dancer working away from or off the painful great toe(s). Usually one side is more severely affected by the symptoms of pain and stiffness than the other.

3.26 Ingrowing Toenail

CAUSES

This occasionally appears to be congenital. The child is seen with very curved great toenails with the sides tending to go vertically down into the flesh. This type of nail is certainly predisposed to ingrowing. However, in the main, ingrowing toenails are brought about by over-tight or unsuitable footwear. The shoes should be checked and this check must include everyday footwear.

TREATMENT

In the early stages lifting the corner of the nail and putting a little animal wool (not cotton wool) under the corners may be sufficient to stop the nail ingrowing. Also the nail should be cut straight across and the corner should not be removed. If at the same time the cause of the condition is removed, then usually no further treatment is necessary. If, however, the ingrowing persists then a wedge resection of the border of the nail is usually sufficient, provided great care is

taken to remove the corner of the nailbed. A radical operation with total obliteration of the nailbed is rarely necessary. Occasionally after wedge resection a small spike of nail will regrow but this is easily trimmed and is normally painless.

3.27 Corns and Callosities

CAUSES

These are really an occupational hazard in dancers. However, they may be greatly aggravated by 'knuckling' when on pointe and by badly-fitting pointe shoes.

TREATMENT

Corns and callosities must certainly be treated with respect and care in order to avoid infection. Good quality professional chiropody is required rather than self-trimming with razor blades or similar implements, when the likelihood of infection would be very much greater. All causes must be eliminated as much as possible.

3.28 Areas of Calcification, etc.

CAUSES

These spurs etc. usually represent areas of previous injury. They are part of the healing process during which time the damaged tissue undergoes partial repair by ossification or calcification. They frequently occur when the soft tissue damage has taken place at a bony junction. For example, if a portion of ligament or capsule is pulled away from the bone this exposes underlying raw bone, bone cells spill out so, as healing takes place, it is accompanied by a little spike of new bone. These spurs are normally coincidental X-ray findings, in other words an X-ray is taken because of a complaint of pain and on the films one, or frequently more, of these little spurs are seen. However, it cannot be over-emphasised that their presence does not mean that they are the cause of the patient's symptoms. In fact they very rarely indeed cause symptoms themselves and removal of spurs, scraping of calcification on tendons and other miscellaneous and dubious procedures are totally unnecessary. This type of surgery is usually carried out because the true cause of the symptoms has not been determined or investigated or because conservative treatment has been inadequate or incompetent.

As a result, the dancer has an unnecessary anaesthetic and operation. The subsequent enforced period of rest may sometimes be a curative factor, giving the illusion that the surgery was the correct procedure. However, only too often, after the convalescence and when the dancer returns to work, the symptoms of which he was complaining before the operation recur because the underlying cause has not been corrected. In these circumstances the symptoms are very often worse because the dancer is weaker, further injuries then occur elsewhere, possibly leading to even more surgery with the underlying causes still uncorrected.

TREATMENT

Only very rarely indeed, a spur may impinge during joint movements and justify excision. This is unusual but even in these circumstances it is vital to correct any underlying faults (see 3.13 Posterior Impingement of the Ankle and 3.14 Anterior Impingement of the Ankle).

3.29 Stress Fractures of the Fibula

These commonly occur some 8 to 12 cm above the tip of the lateral malleolus. There is well-localised warmth, tenderness and thickening. There should be no real difficulty in making a clinical diagnosis (Fig. 3.26).

CAUSES

The main cause of fibula stress fractures is sickling outwards and pronation in the over-turned out position. This is frequently associated with weak feet. It is certainly aggravated by lower tibial bowing, which seems to be common in oriental dancers. This makes it particularly difficult to strengthen the inner sides of the thighs and the lateral part of the foot (see **Section 5.16**). Failing to hold the turn-out at the hips causes stress in the lower leg. Wrong blocks in pointe shoes can cause faulty weight alignment. Untreated ankle sprains can be followed by the development of a stress fracture

3.26 X-ray of a healing stress fracture of the fibula with callus (new bone) formation

and, as a corollary of this, the stress fracture may accompany the development of a chronic sprain.

TREATMENT

Work should be reduced until the patient can do this altered programme totally pain-free. If this cannot be achieved then the dancer will have to be off for a short period. Locally, the area should be iced. At the same time as the reduced dancing a great deal of effort should be made to strengthen all weak muscle groups. Particularly important is the re-education of technique as this condition is basically an injury due to faulty technique. If there is an underlying anatomical variation such as a lower tibial bow, then the technique should be improved to the greatest possible extent and time given to helping the dancer to work within it.

Complications

Untreated, the stress fracture may rarely progress to a complete fracture.

3.30 Shin Pain and Tibial Stress Fractures

Shin pain is common in dancers and it is important to diagnose the exact structure involved and, wherever possible, the cause. Dancers talk about 'shin splints' but that is often a blanket term to describe pain in the lower leg. In runners it is used to describe pain along the medial border of the tibia but if treatment is going to be effective diagnosis and explanation to the patient should be precise.

Pain in the shin area can be attributed to:
1) Bone stress reaction that may progress to fracture.
2) Inflammation and pain where muscles insert, especially along the medial border of the tibia.
3) Compartment syndrome where muscles swell with overuse and inflammation (see **Section 3.31**).

Bone Stress Reaction and Stress Fracture

Bones react to strain. They first develop a stress reaction in the cortex by becoming denser *and thicker* to withstand the strain, and this can be seen in X-rays where the white cortex of the bone has become thicker. This is known as stress thickening. If the strain increases beyond that point and continues, the bone starts to weaken and a stress fracture results. The dancer reports pain that has come on gradually and gets worse with exercise, especially jumping. If there is pain on walking and or pain at night, and on examination there is localised tenderness, an investigation should be done to fully diagnose, predict healing time and guide treatment.

3.27 Stress fractures of the tibiae. These are nearly symmetrical. In the tibia very little new bone is seen on the X-rays during the healing process

3.28A and B Lower tibial bows

These stress fractures are commonly at the junction of the upper two-thirds and lower third on the medial border of the tibia and about mid-shaft on the anterior border (Fig. 3.27). They may occasionally occur high at the junction of the upper third and lower two-thirds. Stress fractures may occur as a result of the tibial shape, for example – bowing and the level of a bow (Fig 3.28).

It has been reported that most stress fractures in other athletes occur on the medial border with localised tenderness on the bone. In dancers however, the stressing of the anterior border appears to be more prevalent. The anterior cortex of the tibia becomes tender at the junction of the middle and distal third. The pain is diffuse and dull and is made worse with exercise. If the dancer has ignored the symptoms for weeks or months there will be a palpable lump of periosteal thickening. In this case the first investigation to be done is an X-ray which may reveal 'the dreaded black line' – a horizontal black line marring the white cortex. *Most will heal with prolonged rest.* Some of these progress to non-union and therefore need to be managed carefully.

In an attempt to explain why stress fractures occur in this location it is necessary to consider the anatomy of the tibia. It is the second longest bone in the body and transmits force downwards through the talus to the foot and upwards through the knee to the femur. The tibia is triangular in cross section and has three borders and three surfaces. The anterior border and medial surface are subcutaneous and commonly known as the shin. Attaching the interosseous (lateral) border to that of the

fibula is the interosseous membrane. The muscles of the leg are divided into three groups. The anterior group (dorsiflexors) arise from the interosseous surfaces and membrane of the tibia and fibula and make up the anterior compartment. The posterior compartment is composed of the plantarflexors arising from the posterior aspect of the tibia, fibula and interosseous membrane. The lateral compartment is composed of the evertors arising from the fibula. While several muscles and a good blood supply support the posterior cortex, this is not the case in the anterior cortex which has less blood supply for regeneration and healing. When the calf muscles of the dancer contract, tension is exerted on the anterior cortex causing a tensile strain from the forwards bowing effect, and a compression strain on the posterior surface. This is known as the 'bow phenomenon'. Dancers are subject to muscle imbalance between the overused plantarflexors and the less emphasised dorsiflexors due to demands of technique. If this imbalance is not monitored, the tibia is at risk. These physiological effects can be combined with other risk factors that together can cause the high risk anterior cortex fracture.

Risk factors

a) Sudden increase in jumping.
   If workload suddenly rises, the shock-absorbing structures of the body do not have time to adapt and strengthen to cope with the strain. When fatigued the musculoskeletal system performs less well

(technique suffers too) and muscles neither adequately generate force nor absorb high forces sufficiently and bone suffers.

b) Hard floors

If dancers who normally work on sprung floors, work on hard floors for a period of time, for example on tour, a stress reaction in the tibia can result. The ground reaction force is the return force the dancer absorbs on landing. (For every force there is an equal and opposite force.) The dancer absorbs this shock through the muscles of the feet and the calves, quadriceps and gluteal muscles by the plié and in the back. As the foot meets the floor the equal and opposite force upwards is absorbed by the foot first, the ankle and then the tibia. If the floor is sufficiently sprung some of the force on landing is absorbed by the floor. The absorbed energy is transferred to heat up the floor. (Energy can be neither created nor destroyed.)

c) Weak feet

In classical dance the ballet shoe provides no cushioning as in the trainer. The foot needs to be strong with excellent proprioception. It will only develop that strength if it is used biomechanically correctly. The intrinsic muscles of the forefoot and toes provide the last push off and first force attenuation on landing. It is the strong foot that also silences the landing. Shock absorption from below protects the tibia above.

d) Lack of fitness

Poor general conditioning will increase the strain on all structures – bone, joints, muscles and tendons. Lack of aerobic fitness means earlier fatigue, loss of technical precision and consequent strain.

e) Menstrual disturbance

In females with amenorrhoea and lowered bone density bones are at risk. The muscles of dancers with eating disorders may also lack necessary strength to absorb strain.

f) Shoes

It is accepted that dance shoes contribute very little to shock absorption. However if shoes are slightly too small (short or narrow) the ability of the foot to work efficiently is disturbed. The intrinsic muscles of the foot are restricted and their eccentric control is lost. Even professional dancers' shoes, boots and layers worn within them should be checked.

g) Posture

It is highly unlikely that a professional dancer has got so far with incorrect posture (not impossible) but younger dancers at vocational schools with high workloads require careful assessment. When the weight is too far back the forefoot does not develop the strength it requires, especially for jumping.

An X-ray will not show abnormalities until *at least*

3.29 An isotope bone scan showing a 'hot spot' where a stress fracture is developing at the junction of the middle and lower third of the tibia

three weeks after onset of symptoms and often longer. Even then changes may be too subtle to be easily seen. An isotope bone scan can show early changes and uptake, but no specificity to fracture (Fig. 3.29). *In a bone an alternative diagnosis to that of a stress fracture would be very rare in this age group.* A CT scan is much more specific and allows visualisation of the fracture line. An MRI scan may be used but is less effective than CT. These investigations are more expensive. They are rarely necessary in a dancer.

Sports physicians regularly manage these injuries and have access to the latest research. In tandem, physiotherapists assess for and correct biomechanical problems. Rheumatologists are the specialists in bone metabolism and bone density and consultation with a specialist dealing with professional athletes may be recommended. In professional football certain drugs which enhance bone healing/bone density are being trialled but these are not yet widely used. Conservative treatment for a stress fracture of the anterior cortex requires at least six months' rest and until radiological complete union has been proven, return to training should not be advised. If symptoms persist then an orthopaedic opinion should be sought. Surgical options are a last resort for a dancer, require a protracted lay-off and are not guaranteed. Interferential therapy and magnetic coils have been used but there is no con-vincing evidence that they are helpful but they are not harmful.

Instead, prevention is the first line of action. Students at vocational schools should be educated to seek advice early for musculoskeletal problems and professional dancers too require careful monitoring of work levels and other risk factors.

Complications

A stress fracture may be misdiagnosed as anterior compartment syndrome but the localised nature of the

3.30A A stress fracture in the tibia

3.30B The stress fracture has become an acute complete fracture. In this case it was caused when the patient jumped down the last few steps when hurrying to catch a train. A not-dissimilar type of jump could have occurred during a performance

clinical findings should prevent this. However, if the stress fractures are multiple confusion is more likely. In these circumstances at least some of the fractures should be visible on an X-ray. If allowed to progress the stress fracture may gradually develop into a complete fracture of the tibia (Fig. 3.30). In this case union is desperately slow and may take a year or more. The only exception to this would be the case when a dancer was undertaking a big jump which produced a sudden acute fracture at the level of the stress fracture. In these circumstances, if the stress fracture had not passed through too great a proportion of the shaft diameter, union could be expected to be at the same rate as a 'normal' type of fracture occurring as the result of a sudden acute injury, i.e. some three to four months to achieve complete union.

3.31 Anterior Compartment Syndrome

The anterior compartment of the shin is bounded by the two bones, the tibia and fibula; by the interosseous membrane which is a very strong fibrous sheet of tissue lying between these two bones, joining them together; and then superficially by the deep fascia (Fig. 3.31). None of these structures are stretchable and it is this non-stretchability which accounts for the problems

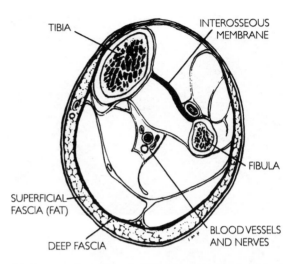

3.31 Cross-section of a leg in the upper third showing the fascial compartments

which occur in anterior compartment syndrome. If there is any swelling (which can arise from injury or other causes) within the anterior compartment, there will necessarily be a rise in pressure because of the non-stretchability of the structures encasing the anterior compartment. This rise in pressure will cause increasing pain, often known as shin splints. If the swelling becomes excessive, the rise in pressure within the tissue can become sufficient to interfere with or completely obstruct the blood flow, in which event the tissues within the compartment will then die from lack of oxygen. This situation, where there is greatly increased pressure, is a surgical emergency and urgent decompression of the anterior compartment syndrome is required before necrosis (death) of the tissues takes place. Fortunately, an anterior compartment of this degree of severity is rare and the condition does not usually progress beyond the milder, early stages.

CAUSES

The commonest cause is unaccustomed exercise or extra exercise of the muscle groups within the anterior compartment (anterior tibial muscle and extensors to the toes). The extra exercise produces swelling of the muscle bellies (as will happen with any sudden extra excessive use of muscles) and this causes the symptoms of shin splints. The weight back situation will also cause extra tension in these muscle groups (**Section 5.21**). Weak feet produce a similar over-work of the muscles. Over-tight ribbons, by constricting the lower leg, may interfere with circulation superficially and restrict movement. This can produce an irritation of the tendons of the tibialis anterior and of the toe extensors, producing a mild degree of anterior compartment syndrome. Short shoes, by causing

3.32 Both photographs illustrate rolling at the feet and ankles. Also shown is the beginning of the tension which develops in the front of the ankle

hamstrings, adductors and gluteals, all of which are more likely to be relatively weak in a dancer who has shin splints. The strengthening of these other groups will facilitate the technical correction which will be required. Also advise the dancer to sleep with the foot of the bed elevated by about 25 cm. It is sensible to elevate the legs between classes and without shoes if the condition is not severe enough to warrant total rest from work. Massage can be helpful, although it is time-consuming. Faradism under pressure in elevation can be effective in more severe cases, although it is very painful. Tight Achilles tendons, if temporary, should not be neglected in the treatment programme. (See **Section 5.15**.)

Complications

Muscle necrosis may occur if the condition is severe and remains undiagnosed, thereby not giving the patient the benefit of surgical decompression. A diagnosis of a stress fracture in the tibia may be missed as it can also arise from the same cause as the shin splints or, alternatively, a stress fracture may be mis-diagnosed as an anterior compartment syndrome. It is incorrect to call a developing stress fracture 'shin splints'.

3.32 Calf Muscle Tears and Cramps

Injuries to both gastrocnemius and soleus are common. An acute strain to gastrocnemius typically occurs on take off for a jump or sudden eccentric overstretch. A sudden acute, stabbing or tearing is felt in the medial gastrocnemius muscle belly or at the musculotendinous junction. Testing for strength and stretch is carried out with the knee extended. Soleus is also subject to strain especially if the foot pronates. Again the medial fibres are vulnerable to strain. Testing is carried out with the knee flexed.

A grade 1 strain is sharp at the time but the dancer is able to continue. It can take ten to twelve days to get back to dancing. In a grade 2 strain the dancer cannot continue and the injury will take up to three weeks to heal. A grade 3 injury will be a tear at the musculo-tendinous junction with severe pain and possibly requiring surgery or a plaster cast.

TREATMENT

A heel raise will take an element of strain off the calf. The treatment is described in the general section on the treatment of muscle tears (**Section 2.2** Muscle Tears, p. 83).

clawing of the toes, have a similar effect. Rolling will cause over-work of the anterior compartment muscles. If the dancer is observed in class, the great prominence of the tendons can be seen (Fig. 3.32). A similar effect can be brought about by a tight Achilles tendon restricting the plié. Anterior compartment syndrome, usually very mild, is common in first year full-time students and also during a growth spurt. Often during periods of stress, muscle tension causes the dancer to grip the floor unnecessarily with the toes.

TREATMENT

Provided the condition is not severe enough to place the circulation in jeopardy, conservative treatment is effective. Treatment should be carried out with the leg in elevation, using ice and interferential from the ankle to the groin to stimulate the circulation and venous return. (Make sure the knee is supported at the back as should be the situation in all treatments of any lower limb condition). Exercises are given to strengthen all the other groups including the feet, calf, quadriceps,

Complications

If calf pain is variable in location and difficult to pinpoint with a history of calf cramps, spinal involvement should be suspected. Neural structures should be tested with the slump test. In the older dancer with a history of spinal problems the lumbar spine should always be checked.

Calf muscle tears are particularly prone to contracture. This is in part from the scarring but also in part from the inherent tendency of the calf muscle and Achilles tendon complex to tighten up far more rapidly than might be expected. Calf muscle strains may present as pain behind the knee and may be mis-diagnosed as a hamstring problem or a knee injury. Remember that the two heads of the gastrocnemius are inserted in the lower end of the femur and therefore pass behind the knee joint.

3.33 Anterior Knee Pain

This is a term that is used to describe pain involving the patello-femoral joint. Students and younger dancers are more vulnerable to varying muscular forces through this joint with growth and with exploring the rigours of a developing technique. The patella may be seen to track laterally as well as proximally as the knee is 'pulled up' by the quadriceps. The patella may also be tilted laterally due to overtight lateral structures. Maltracking between the back of the patella and the anterior surface of the femoral condyles causes friction, resulting in swelling, pain and further loss of proprioception and control of the knee.

CAUSES

Muscle imbalance involving the quadriceps muscles with overused vastus lateralis (along with tensor fascia latae and tight iliotibial band) and under-activated vastus medialis, cause the patella to track laterally in its femoral groove. This causes pain and swelling increasing with exercise. The causes are structural and technical. Hyperextended knees are vulnerable if allowed to lock back in extension, and overturning the feet in turn-out will encourage muscle imbalance.

TREATMENT

Massage and stretching to overtight, overworked muscles is required and if necessary, patellar mobilisation. McConnell taping can stimulate vastus medialis activation and relieve pain in the early stages of treatment. Exercises to activate vastus medialis and the adductors will counteract lateral forces. Technical correction for hyperextended knees and control of turn-out is a must, to relieve debilitating symptoms.

3.34 Tight Tensor Fasciae Latae (TFL)

CAUSES

This is usually brought about by muscle imbalance in the thigh when the medial side muscles are weak (less strong – it can happen in strong legs and it is the imbalance which is the vital clue). Here the lateral side, including the TFL, is overused. In extreme cases the overuse is easily visible, with heavy outer thighs and less muscle on the inner side, including an underdeveloped vastus medialis. However, it can still occur with little obvious outward developmental difference. In these cases the difference in muscle tension can be felt on palpation. During examination, close observation of the patella will show that it moves laterally as well as proximally during an isometric quadriceps contraction. This is diagnostic of lateral/medial muscle imbalance, provided the knee is otherwise structurally sound. The young dancer with knock knees will be vulnerable to lateral forces and classical ballet will only increase the strain on the knees.

The demands of classical ballet on the flexors and abductors of the hip encourage development of muscle imbalance where the more superficial muscles become dominant and the deeper stabilising muscles function less. This is frequently seen in professional dancers. TFL is a flexor, abductor and internal rotator of the hip.

A tight TFL can impose anterior rotatory forces on the ilium, disturbing the sacroiliac joint, its ligaments and also the lumbar spine. It tensions the ilotibial band which in turn tensions its patellar attachments, disturbing the articulation of the patello-femoral joint. The hip joint is affected and an anterior impingement will ensue if the situation is not corrected. An overused TFL will often accompany over dominant upper gluteal muscles and tight deep turn-out muscles, especially piriformis and underused psoas, iliacus and lower gluteus maximus. Tightness of tensor fasciae latae prevents proper adjustments of the pelvis and transference of weight over one leg.

TREATMENT

Deep massage release to TFL and the ITB is necessary to decrease lateral forces. Postural and turnout control correction must be started along with an exercise regime for under active muscles. Stabilisation of the pelvis is a basic requirement and if this is insufficient, hip and groin problems will follow.

Conservative treatment is preferred at all times. Correction of muscle imbalance is complex and time is needed for analysis and education of the dancer who must also be convinced of the logic involved and committed to working differently.

Surgery in the form of lateral release is not to be recommended.

3.35 Patellar Tendinopathy

This usually occurs at the patello-tendinous junction. Pain here is due to strain at this junction between the tendon and the inferior pole of the patella where it attaches (see Fig. 3.33).

CAUSES

This is also called 'jumpers' knee'. The commonest cause of patellar tendinopathy is imbalance of the quadriceps between the medial and lateral components, giving rise to an unequal pull on the patellar tendon. Jumping puts added strain through this structure which will react with pain and thickening. It is often associated with rolling (**Section 5.18**) or with over-turning (**Section 5.7**) or with having the body weight too far back (**Section 5.21**). It is also frequently associated with an over-development of the lateral side of the thigh. In the presence of tight Achilles tendons and/or weak feet, when the dancer lands he cannot absorb the shock at the feet and the patellar tendon has to take the strain. Sticky surfaces can also cause strain in this area on any sort of twisting due to the increased friction between the foot and the floor.

A period of rapid growth may produce temporary inadequacy of the quadriceps and this can induce tendon problems. Inadequacy of the quadriceps can also be produced by pushing back on a swayback knee. In this instance it may be coupled with lateral/medial imbalance, both of these contributing to the patellar tendinopathy. In the weight back situation (**Section 5.21**), the extensor reflex is not stimulated because the main weight is on the back of the heel pad and not

towards the front of the heel pad. Pressure at the latter point will stimulate a much more effective quadriceps contraction. Tightness at the front of the hip (**Section 5.9**) prevents a satisfactory quadriceps activation. Tight hamstrings (**Section 5.12**) – often associated with growth – may precipitate patellar tendon problems because of inhibition of the quadriceps action by the tight hamstrings. Finally, kneeling routines may produce tendon problems and this is often associated with an infra-patellar bursitis.

TREATMENT

Local treatment starts with ice, particularly if there is any swelling, and then proceeds to ultrasound And massage of overtight structures. There then has to be a correction of any muscle imbalance. This is often helped by vastus medialis exercises to reinforce active contraction. If the fascia lata area is tight, benefit cannot be achieved by attempts to strengthen or correct imbalance of muscles without first massaging the fascia lata and the tensor fasciae latae muscle followed by stretching. There is also a need for careful examination for any of the causes outlined above and their elimination. Without this taking place local treatment will be ineffective.

Complications
Tendons do not heal easily and when the condition becomes chronic it is called tendinosis. This is described in 'Tendon Injuries' in **Section 2.2**, p. 81). The current definitive conservative treatment for chronic thickening and pain in the patellar tendon is a regime of eccentric squats on a decline slope. This is prescribed by a therapist along with restricted work and no jumping. The regime includes adding weights to the exercise to challenge the tendon and it can take 3 months for recovery.

3.36 Osgood Schlatter's Disease

The tibial tubercle is the bony bump just below the knee joint at the front of the tibia. In adolescence it is called an apophysis, a bony process which is not yet fully joined to its bone. Instead, it is attached by cartilage which will be fully ossified at maturity. The patellar tendon inserts on to the tibial tubercle, transmitting the forces of the quadriceps here to extend the tibia on the femur at the knee joint. When the strain on this attachment is too high the tubercle or tuberosity becomes inflamed, swollen and painful. This is called an apophysitis. Like the epiphysis, ossification takes place until the tubercle is firmly attached. This occurs when maturity is reached and no further growth

3.33 Site of a patellar tendinopathy

takes place. The apophysis does not take part in increasing the length of the bone like the epiphysis, and there are several of these small apophyseal areas around the body, usually where tendons attach.

CAUSES

Osgood Schlatter's disease is probably most commonly produced by relative weakness of the quadriceps muscle, often associated with a period of rapid growth. This weakness results in a jerking pull on the lower tendon attachment rather than an even controlled pull. On initial examination, the quadriceps frequently do not appear to be weak, hence the term relative weakness. This relative weakness takes into account the level of activity which is being carried out by the person suffering from Osgood Schlatter's disease. It is most common in children who are keen on games, sports and other activities. During adolescence the strength of the quadriceps may not be quite up to the effort which is being demanded of them and this then results in the uneven pulling on the tendon and subsequent apophysitis.

TREATMENT

The dancer should rest off activity if the condition is very painful and there is marked tenderness over the tibial tubercle. This area may be swollen and warm. During this time the dancer should concentrate on exercises and build up the quadriceps muscles as well as the adductors, gluteals and hamstrings. Correct any imbalance and also any tendency to push back on the knee. Technical correction may also be of value here. As the acute pain settles, the student can return gradually to class and dancing.

Sometimes it is only jumping that needs to be avoided, so when the jumping section commences, the student can complete a floor exercise programme.

Complications

Usually this is a transitory problem, which with patience and guidance will eventually pass.

The actual bony tubercle can become permanently enlarged if a lot of strenuous activity is continued despite the warnings of pain. This enlargement is not in itself of great significance. However, girls find it unsightly. In boys, should they be called on to kneel much, it can produce a painful area purely because of the mechanical prominence. Sometimes the treatment of Osgood Schlatter's Disease can be difficult, as continued rapid growth may prevent the patient catching up sufficiently with the strengthening routines to match the growth rate.

3.37 Chondromalacia Patellae

This name is often loosely applied to non specific anterior knee pain. Chondromalacia patellae is, however, a very definite entity and the term should, if possible, only be applied when there are actual changes in the articular cartilage on the retro-patellar surface. This cartilage becomes yellowed in patches, it softens, frays and then wears away. A true, well-established chondromalacia patellae can be a precursor of patello-femoral osteoarthritis. It is far preferable to avoid using the term loosely and just accept calling the symptoms anterior knee pain. We would accept that dancers, like any other patient, do like the sound of a name that implies an actual diagnosis.

CAUSES

Most commonly this is incorrect tracking of the patella (i.e. muscle imbalance in the quadriceps complex) especially when associated with overall weakness of the quadriceps muscles. It is therefore common after a growth spurt which will have caused relative weakness of the muscles, hence its frequency during adolescence and the teens. Tightness in the fronts of the hips can cause tight quadriceps. In the presence of tight Achilles tendons, the knee tends to be the main shock absorber and this aggravates the condition. Anterior knee pain is more commonly seen in runners, gymnasts and dancers than other types of athlete. These three groups all have a very high repetition of particular movements. It is also more common in the presence of swayback knees. It may occasionally be precipitated by a direct blow on the patella. However, in this situation it should not be confused with an osteo-chondral fracture. This is an acute fracture occurring in the bone just beneath the articular cartilage and will often break out a small fragment of bone together with the over-lying cartilage. Chondromalacia patellae is of more gradual onset and, following a blow on the patella, bruising of the retro-patellar cartilage can take place and this can then lead to the chondromalacia.

TREATMENT

Local treatment comprises soft tissue massage and appropriate patellar mobilisation. However a suitable exercise programme is by far the most important aspect of treatment. Exercises should be directed towards re-balancing muscles, quadriceps strengthening and also strengthening of any other weak muscle groups, particularly hamstrings, adductors, gluteals and calves, stretching any tightness in the front of the hips and also the quadriceps themselves and the calf if they are tight. A small heel (three-quarters of an inch – 2 cm) can prevent the weight being pushed back too far in the presence of swayback knees and similarly a lift inside a ballet shoe. This, using orthopaedic felt temporarily placed there until the muscle strengthens, can be very helpful. Once the symptoms have improved these aids should be discarded. Checking technical faults is, as always, of the greatest importance.

Complications
True chondromalacia patellae is very persistent and can be difficult to treat if it is long established, although if caught early, treatment is very much easier. An arthroscopy may be required, if only to confirm the genuine diagnosis. Surgery is to be discouraged. A lateral release operation merely aggravates muscle weakness and hence the imbalance is increased, even if there is some faulty patella tracking. A lateral release should only follow a muscle strengthening programme when it has been demonstrated that there is a true tightness in the lateral capsule which cannot be stretched out.

3.38 Capsular Strains of the Knee

These may occur anywhere around the knee but are rather more common posteriorly.

CAUSES
Forced hyperextension of the knee is probably the commonest cause and in these cases it may also be associated with a strain of one or both heads of the gastrocnemius. This can occur in many dance steps; for example, landing from cabriole with the weight on the heel, snapping the knee backwards. Frequently there is a significant amount of bruising and swelling associated with this injury.

TREATMENT
Locally ice and electrotherapy are used to decrease the swelling. The dancer should definitely be off until settled. During this stage strengthening exercises should be undertaken, paying particular attention to the hamstrings which protect the back of the knee.

3.39 Injury of the Medial Ligament of the Knee

CAUSES
Tears are usually caused by a faulty landing or collision or a fall, which may be precipitated by sticky floors. *Sprains* are caused by faulty landings and bad floor surfaces, i.e. much the same as events and conditions that can cause a tear but when the force is less.

They are also seen in unusual choreography with which the dancer is not familiar and in jumping off various stage props. Sickled feet greatly increase the possibilities of a bad landing and injuries of various types to the inner side of the knee. Anything which produces tiredness in the dancer, e.g. over-rehearsal, particularly on solid floors, can make the injury more likely to occur.

TREATMENT
Tears are an urgent orthopaedic problem and will require surgery if complete. In lesser cases, immobilisation is required unless the damage is very minor. The later stages of the rehabilitation, when surgery is complete and the tear has healed, are the same as for a sprain, as follows.

For *sprains*, local use of ice and ultrasound are indicated. The dancer should be off dancing unless the injury is very minor. Exercises are particularly important during the rehabilitation period with special attention to the quadriceps – vastus medialis and the adductors. Correct action of the foot, with a build-up of intrinsic muscles and correct weight distribution to prevent pronation is particularly important. Care should be taken to eliminate any tendency to overturn the feet, which always puts an excessive strain on the medial side of the knee. As in any knee injury, the muscle build-up will have to extend up to the gluteals and trunk and technical correction will also have to look at these areas. Any pre-existing fault which may not have caused symptoms or injuries before this ligament sprain, will certainly aggravate the medial side of the knee once it has been the site of an injury of any sort.

3.40 Injury of the Lateral Ligament of the Knee

Injuries here are uncommon in dancers and usually only occur as a result of direct violence, e.g. collisions and falls. If the rupture is complete, the lateral popliteal nerve may also be severely and permanently damaged. The injury is one requiring urgent orthopaedic care. The rehabilitation is similar to that given to the medial ligament sprains.

3.41 Injuries of the Cruciate Ligaments of the Knee

Trauma to the cruciate ligaments in dance is usually caused by landing badly (out of alignment) or by the foot slipping and the knee being forced out of position.

In football it is a contact injury. When the tibia is externally rotated and the knee is forced into the valgus position (the knee falls inward in relation to foot and hip) the supporting muscles can give way and the knee sinks into full flexion. This mechanism of injury can rupture the anterior cruciate, partially tear the medial collateral ligament and tear the medial meniscus. Therefore in this type of injury, each of the triad require investigation.

After a bad fall like this there will be immediate swelling, and testing of the anterior cruciate (Lachman test, anterior draw test, pivot shift test) will be positive along with testing the medial collateral ligament. The history is enough to predict the injury, but if there is any doubt an MRI scan should be done to reveal fully the extent of damage. A dancer will require surgery for anterior cruciate ligament (ACL) because of the complex stresses on the joint in dance. Over the last ten years these operations have considerably improved and athletes and dancers are returning to performance.

The cruciate ligaments stabilise the backwards/ forwards movement between tibia and femur, and the collateral ligaments stabilise the side to side movement. The meniscal cartilages act as shock absorbers, help align the joint surfaces during activity and minimise stress to the articular cartilage that covers and protects them. These friction-free surfaces allow for the gliding, rolling, spinning action during knee movement.

The anterior cruciate ligament is the primary restraint to anterior displacement of the tibia on the femur, and if ruptured is reconstructed with a graft.

Surgeons will choose from three options of graft. The central one-third of the patellar tendon can be safely harvested along with bone blocks at either end. These allow for secure fixing to femur and tibia with successful healing. The second option is to use the gracilis and semitendinosis (hamstring) in the recon-struction. These tendons can be removed safely from the opposite knee, are doubled over to create a new 'ligament' which is anchored with screws. The knee can survive without these two long, thin muscles and this option avoids disturbing the exposed patellar tendon. This option may be preferred for male dancers who kneel and jump. The third option is using an allograft – a patellar tendon graft from a donated tissue bank. This avoids harvesting from the patient. The orthopaedic surgeon will advise the patient according to the patient's needs, his or her own experience and expertise, and current evidence. There are continual advances in the treatment of ACL injuries. During the reconstruction surgery the medial collateral ligament will also be repaired along with the medial meniscus if they have also suffered damage.

The rehabilitation after this operation requires hard work from both patient and physiotherapist with patience, planning and goal setting. Use of gym, Pilates, pool and coaching in the studio contribute to a varied rehab formula. Each surgeon will have a treat-ment protocol divided into phases according to healing times and goals. The dancer will achieve full range of movement and strength, learning over a nine-month period how to manage the reconstruction in his or her chosen genre. Returning as quickly as possible to full function is always the aim but it is worthwhile taking the cautious route to fully consolidate proprioception and technique rather than taking any risks.

The ACL is not only a stabiliser but also contributes to the proprioception of the knee. Mechanoreceptors within the ligament contribute to fine control of tension in the ligament during knee function. There-fore a reconstruction is not going restore the joint's former properties – it will feel and function differently. A classical dancer with 60° or more external rotation at the hip will demand less stress from an operated knee and rehabilitation must take this into account. The 'new' knee will always require more warm-up and preparation for demanding work, and as long as this is accepted, the dancer should be able to reach and even surpass former levels of performance.

Posterior cruciate ligament damage is rare in dancers.

3.42 Damage to the Medial Meniscus of the Knee

The meniscus may be torn to a varying extent ranging from a minor tag to a full length tear or a total avulsion of the meniscus from its peripheral attachment. The problems arise in the longer term (after the initial symptoms of the original tear have subsided) because the torn fragment can catch in the joint, causing giving way or locking of the knee.

CAUSES

The tear takes place because the meniscus becomes trapped between the femoral condyle and the tibial plateau during rotation on a bent knee. There is no doubt that, by repeated malfunctions of the knee, tears can occur gradually and without immediate symptoms. This has been shown by the observation of a meniscal tear on arthroscopic examination when there has been no history of an acute episode. Frequently the symp-toms can be relatively minor some long time before a final acute episode, the latter of which is probably caused by the tearing of the last portion of an already developing tear. The situation is aggravated or caused by over-turning the feet, by weakness of the adductors and the vastus medialis, together with their associated postural muscles, and finally by a muscular imbalance causing lack of control of the knee. Weak adductors will not hold the leg correctly under the body when on one leg, thus increasing the strain on the medial side of the knee. In addition, the weak adductors will not control the turn-out at the hip, aggravating any overturning at the foot. When carrying the working leg through from front to side and especially also to the back, the pelvis will not be stabilised and controlled in relation to the supporting leg and will also swing round, causing a rotation at the knee and a secondary overturning at the supporting foot, as the leg above the foot rotates inwards (Fig. 3.34). Isolated technical faults such as rolling may contribute to meniscal tears. Ligament laxity can also be a contributory factor, hence swayback knees can be prone to cartilage tears, especially as they are so often associated with weak thigh muscles.

TREATMENT

A tear *per se* does not necessarily require surgery unless it is causing symptoms, i.e. locking or giving way or restriction of movements. If symptoms are present, removal of the torn portion is required and through an arthroscopy as little as possible of the normal meniscus is removed. However, correction of the causes outlined above coupled with a muscle strengthening programme and a gradual return to full work, will frequently remove the need for surgery at that stage. If surgery is undertaken, the same programme of rehabilitation will be required with even more strengthening work

because of the increased muscle weakness following even an arthroscopic procedure. In all cases, thorough technical investigation and correction is required. In post-operative care, immobilisation is avoided as it prevents an early and effective muscle build-up programme, particularly in the vastus medialis. Persistent or recurrent swelling can slow progress and needs treatment with ice, elevation and an increase in controlled exercises. Exercise programmes for knee rehabilitation are laborious and repetitive and require consistency and acceptance.

Pre-operatively, time spent on a regime of exercises to strengthen all relevant groups and rehearsals of the post-operative exercises can payoff in significantly reducing rehabilitation time.

3.43 Damage to the Lateral Meniscus of the Knee

This type of damage is the same as that which affects the medial meniscus. Lateral meniscus tears are relatively more common in dancing than in other types of sport, although the medial meniscus is, even in dancers, more often damaged than the lateral.

CAUSES

In dancers the lateral meniscus tear is commonly of gradual onset from repeated minor trauma rather than presenting as an acute tear, as happens in medial

3.34A Over-turning the supporting leg here is an unstable position and puts a strain on the supporting knee. The adductors cannot engage and the trunk is weak

3.34B As the leg lifts into arabesque the dancer relies even more on the barre

3.34C Again the supporting leg is compromised. Here the working leg is held too far back and the supporting knee and foot (with flattened medial arch) take the strain

meniscus damage where the chronic type injury is less common. The tear of the lateral meniscus can be brought about by a failure to control turn-out correctly the foot is rolled and the fascia lata is tight. This failure will also include the adductors. The more the dancer overturns the more the lateral structures grip – biceps femoris, tensor fascia latae and vastus lateralis. The iliotibial band tightens and the lateral meniscus is compressed causing a possible degenerative tear.

TREATMENT

This is similar to that for the medial meniscus, calling for an MRI scan and arthroscopic examination and partial menisectomy. However, with lateral meniscus damage the technical faults are often somewhat different from those occurring in medial meniscus injury but they need just as careful assessment and correction.

3.44 Ruptures of the Quadriceps Tendon or the Patellar Tendon or Fracture of the Patella

These injuries can be considered together because the causes are the same. In each case there is a disruption of the extensor mechanism occurring between the lower part of the muscle bellies of the quadriceps muscle and the insertion into the tibial tubercle. The three levels at which this disruption can take place are at the quadriceps tendon just above the patella, through the patella itself producing a transverse fracture of the patella, or through the patellar tendon between the patella and the tibial tuberosity. Ruptures of the patellar tendon or transverse fractures of the patella occur in a younger age group, whereas ruptures of the quadriceps tendon usually occur slightly later in life.

CAUSES

All these injuries occur because of a sudden explosive contraction of the quadriceps muscle, particularly in someone who is not at the peak of training, although a technical mistake or faulty jump can produce a similar effect. The extremely strong and uncontrolled muscle contraction causes the rupture by pulling the fibres of the tendon apart. In the case of the patella fracture this pull also produces a snap back of the patella onto the femoral condyles, breaking the patella transversely across. In all three injuries the contraction of the muscle will continue to pull the proximal part up the thigh, producing a gap at the site of the rupture. Each injury is followed by an immediate and very great swelling due to an extensive haemorrhage. If examined shortly after the injury the blood is still liquid and it is usually possible to feel the actual gap. However, if some time has elapsed the blood may have started to clot and certainly if it is a day or two later the gap may be difficult to palpate.

When examined immediately after the accident the dancer can be asked to lift the leg up straight. If he cannot do so, then a rupture should be strongly suspected. In other conditions affecting the knee, even though fairly serious, the dancer is usually able with an effort to lift the leg up straight because, in the early stage, inhibition of quadriceps muscle may not yet have taken place. If some time has elapsed this inhibition does occur even though there is no disruption of the extensor mechanism and the patient will be unable to lift his leg. These tendon ruptures or patellar fractures are all acute orthopaedic emergencies requiring immediate surgical repair. Failure to recognise the injury or to suspect it and refer for an orthopaedic opinion can make the difference between the dancer being able eventually to return to a full dancing career or otherwise. If there is a delay this will usually spell the end of any return to dancing or any sort of active sport at a competitive level.

TREATMENT

This is by surgical repair and each surgeon will have a strict and detailed protocol to follow. During the post-operative phase an exercise programme can be devised to keep the rest of the body in as good a condition as possible. Even while the knee is immobilised isometric contractions for the muscle groups on the affected leg can be commenced. Once the knee is ready to be moved intensive exercises should be started in order to build up the muscle groups and to mobilise the knee.

3.45 Quadriceps Muscle Strains and Tears

These have been dealt with in general in the section on muscle injuries (**Section 2.2** Muscle Tears, p. 83). However, it is particularly important in injuries at this site to ensure that the correct medial/lateral balance between the parts of the quadriceps muscles is restored during the treatment period.

Complications
These are associated with a failure to restore this medial/lateral balance with its associated problems, which have been described under various earlier headings.

3.46 Adductor Muscle Strains and Tears

The adductor muscles are probably the commonest site of muscle damage. Usually the tears occur in the proximal (upper) part of the adductor complex and are brought about by a sudden over-stretching such as may happen in forcing splits sitting in 2nd position. If the tenderness is very high and close to the bone of the pelvis an X-ray should be taken as sometimes the bony origin is avulsed together with a small piece of bone. The importance of this is that if early stretching is carried out then the injured area will be irritated and further bone cells will be shed into the haematoma (collection of blood) in the damaged area. At the time of the initial avulsion, as the bone has been exposed, there will already have been some spillage of bone-forming cells. Extra irritation will only encourage the conversion of the haematoma into a mass of bone instead of allowing the absorption of the blood and repair with the minimum of scar tissue.

CAUSES

As mentioned, the splits in 2nd position or any forcible abduction strain can cause the damage. As in any muscle injury it is far more common in the (physically) under-trained dancer or in the (technically) badly trained dancer. The injury can range from a mild strain to large muscle tears.

TREATMENT

Locally – ice and rest are required in the early stages together with electrotherapy. Strengthening exercises should commence as soon as the initial swelling has started to settle (not earlier than forty-eight hours because it can take this long for the bleeding to stop). The exercises should start gently and, if the damage is extensive, assisted active exercises may be required before progressing to exercises against gravity. The early use of resistance is contra-indicated as in all muscle tears.

The treatment is initially aimed at:
1. absorption of the blood;
2. healing with minimum of scar tissue;
3. strengthening the muscle concentrically;
4. stretching out to lengthen the scar tissue;
5. final stage rehab with eccentric exercise and changes in speed of contraction.

Stretching should not start until good muscle tone is restored (this is part of a protective mechanism and can help to prevent re-tearing). Stretching is aimed at preventing the scar tissue shortening. It should only be carried out at the end of the session of local treatment and exercise and when the patient is warm. The dancer should be taught stretches which will be incorporated in an exercise regime to be continued even after returning to full dancing in order to retain length and strength.

3.47 Groin Strains

These can affect several muscles in the groin area. It is more important to isolate the cause of the injury rather than to worry about which particular muscle has been strained. The commonest site is the origin of the rectus femoris and the sartorius.

CAUSES

Groin strains are usually brought about by faulty posture technique. There may, in fact, be no actual muscle weakness but the faulty technique encourages the use of the wrong muscles and hence their strain, especially in the repetitive nature of dance.

Instability of the pelvis means that the groin muscles, rectus femoris, sartorius and the adductors do not have a stable origin from which to control the lower limb. Tucking under (posteriorly tilted pelvis) disturbs the posture of the lumbar spine (flexes it), the function of the gluteal muscles and the hip flexors. An anteriorly tilted pelvis means the abdominal muscles are not functioning well and the lumbar spine is unsupported. The length of the hamstrings, quadriceps, the fascia lata and the adductors should be assessed. Rapid growth affects these and an appropriate stretching regime is required (see **Section 2.5** Stretching, p. 98).

During stages of growth it is unwise to overload the hip flexors with over repetition of challenging exercises like relevé lent to the front and second position. There is a fine line between loading muscles and straining. With different stages of growth in the same class a teacher's task is not easy.

Foot function and biomechanics as well as shoulder placement and port de bras influence posture and the dancer should be examined globally as well as specific-ally. Postural stability during movement must be assessed. The adjustment of weight over one leg must be clearly understood. Adjustment too far over the supporting leg encourages 'sitting' in the hip and under adjustment causes tension and compensatory faults.

It is important that iliopsoas functions well and is not inhibited by overuse of the superficial hip flexors – rectus femoris, sartorius and tensor fascia latae. Rebalancing the hip flexors requires analysis and exercises tailored to stimulate psoas and iliacus and inhibit and stretch TFL, rectus femoris and sartorius.

Changing established postural and movement patterns takes time and patience.

If any groin pain is persistent check that this is not a referred pain from a back injury. In teenagers, look out for glandular fever developing, in which case they may also be complaining of some tiredness and lassitude without anything more definite to indicate the presence of a virus infection.

TREATMENT

Usually the local damage is not severe and swelling only occasionally occurs. Locally, ultrasound (which is usually best applied with the area on stretch) is normally all that is required. The exercise programme is the most important part of treatment and must embrace technical correction. In this condition, the planning of the exercise regime and the technical correction must be very closely allied. One cannot be followed later by the other but must proceed in parallel from the beginning of treatment. (Unlike many other conditions when the technical correction can start towards the end of the treatment programme.)

3.48 Hip Impingement

This causes a deep groin pain brought on by flexion which is restricted, and medial rotation. This is a common groin pain in young active adults, especially dancers who will complain of pain and catching at the front of the hip in devant and second position en l'air.

In flexion of the hip joint the head of the femur should rotate posteriorly in its socket. In extension the femoral head will rotate forwards. In the neutral position the head of the femur points slightly anteriorly. In external rotation it moves forwards even more towards the anterior of the joint and its capsule. With a dancer's repeated movements turned out and to the side and also to the back, the deep turn-out muscles become tight and short together with the posterior joint capsule. The front of the joint – its anterior capsule and anterior hip muscles become stretched. The posteriorly tilted pelvis further exacerbates the problem. Working in a 'tucked-under' (hip extension) position turned out, stretches and destabilises the joint further. To aggravate the situation dancers often walk in turn-out and so the hip joint is given no respite. (Barbara Fewster, Principal of the Royal Ballet School, called this 'plying their trade' and discouraged it.) Dancers frequently stretch their hip flexors and any discomfort in the groin makes them feel they should stretch even more. This imbalance about the hip joint inhibits the normal rotation within the joint and slowly problems become apparent. The femoral head stays forwards in the acetabulum and movements become restricted with a distinct catch in certain positions. As dancers manage to avoid discomfort and compensate while dancing, the problem is often ignored. They talk about 'my sticky hip' and do not seek help until the movement patterns are deep seated and complex to solve.

When examining the pathology of the hip joint it is important to consider the movements of the head of the femur within the acetabulum. In flexion the head of the femur rotates about a coronal axis but also glides posteriorly in its socket. In extension it glides anteriorly. In the neutral position the head of the femur points slightly anteriorly. In external rotation it moves forwards even more towards the anterior of the joint and its capsule. In hip abduction the head of femur glides downwards and inwards in the acetabulum.

When the hip is fully externally rotated, the femoral neck will impinge against the posterior margin of the acetabulum. If attempts are made to force the turn-out further, there would be a tendency to slightly lever the femoral head out of the acetabulum anteriorly. This may happen particularly in those with lax ligaments and capsule e.g. some degree of hypermobility. Laxity is common (even inevitable by selection) in dancers even in the absence of true hypermobility. This recurrent lifting, though not a true subluxation, probably causes some damage in the long term to the labrum and capsular attachments and possible formation of osteophytes/spurs.

3.49 Hamstring Strains and Tears

These may be anything from mild strains to large tears and can occur at any level. As in the adductors, damage can occur at the origin avulsing the bony attachment and sometimes pulling off a piece of bone. If the tenderness is high up in the hamstrings, then an X-ray should be taken in order to show whether there has been some bony avulsion or not. The potential complications of bony avulsion are those which have already been described for the same event occurring in the adductors.

CAUSES

The injury commonly occurs during unwise stretching, particularly when the dancer is cold. Faulty technique frequently causes the damage, particularly when the weight is back and the dancer is sitting in the hip while the working leg is raised, as in a grand battement, penché arabesque, or even with the leg raised in 2nd position. In these circumstances the upper part of the hamstring tends to be injured. This basically comes about because when the dancer is sitting in the hip with the weight back, all the other muscle groups around the hip fail to work correctly so that the upper hamstring remains unprotected. Added to this, when the weight is back the hamstrings are themselves not being worked correctly and are therefore not in a state to tolerate stretch well. Over-turning causes the lateral hamstring to over-work and this also produces under-use of the medial hamstrings, which are then unprepared for sudden stretch. A false sense of warmth can be encouraged by the use of plastic trousers or other impermeable dance wear. These make the skin feel falsely warm and commonly this is not reflected by an increased blood supply more deeply. Therefore working in the plastic covering, particularly if any stretching is being undertaken, can produce damaging results. Additionally, these types of garments produce a marked increase in sweating which is unable to evaporate through the plastic. When the garment is removed for class or performance, the sudden increase in evap-oration produces a marked local fall in temperature and this chilling makes the muscle more prone to injury.

TREATMENT

Locally, ice should be applied if there is swelling or evidence of bleeding. Electrotherapy can be used to reduce both swelling and pain. Once the pain and swelling are settling, an exercise programme should be commenced and this programme should also embrace the allied muscle groups such as the adductors, gluteals and quadriceps, as well as ensuring that the hamstring muscle complex is itself functioning correctly. Stretching should start gently and proceed in a manner similar to that described for the adductors. Treatment of injuries at the upper end of the hamstrings can be difficult and prolonged. Extensive technical help is required if the injury is chronic, recurrent or of long-standing.

Complications

Hamstring tendinopathy occurs when the hamstring tendon at the ischium is injured, fails to heal and becomes chronically painful. Following the general rules of conservative treatment for tendinosis the hamstring is put through an eccentric exercise regime which is gradually loaded. This condition is more likely in the more experienced dancer.

3.50 Clicking Hip

CAUSES

This is, as in other joints, usually of no significance and harmless. A click at the front of the hip is caused by the psoas tendon as it passes over the hip joint. The click at the side of the hip is caused by the tight band of fascia lata slipping backwards and forwards over the greater trochanter. The greatest problem results when the dancer, usually a student, repeatedly reproduces the click deliberately thereby irritating the tissues involved

leading to local swelling. These rapidly settle with reassurance and avoidance as much as possible of movements producing the click, when the local deep (not visible) swelling will rapidly disappear. The tight fasca lata requires massage and stretching.

3.51 Perthes Disease and Slipped Upper Femoral Epiphysis

These two conditions are only included because the dance teacher may be the first person to notice a limp in a student or be aware of complaints of hip/knee pain. They are not particularly associated with dance or sporting activities as a cause. The rarity is under-lined by the fact that in thirty-five years at the Royal Ballet and other ballet schools JH never saw either of these conditions in any of the students.

Perthes Disease presents usually between the ages of five and ten years old. A limp will be noticed but not usually associated with pain. If this persists for more than a few days the child should be referred to their GP. In this condition the head of the femur softens due to loss of some of its blood supply and in the longer term and untreated can become misshapen. It is rare, affecting about one child in 10,000 and is four times more common in boys. The cause of the interference with the blood supply is unknown. Diagnosis is made by X-ray examination.

A slipped upper femoral epiphysis occurs in somewhere between thirty and sixty per 100,000 children in the age group ten to seventeen with a peak at thirteen in boys and eleven and a half in girls. It is three times more common in boys. Its cause may be minor trauma or there may be a hormonal basis. The presenting symptom is pain, more often in the knee than in the hip (referred pain). A child with knee pain *must* have the hip examined, not to do so is clinical negligence. Movements may be slightly limited and painful. The condition is an orthopaedic emergency and requires urgent referral. Diagnosis is by X-rays. In early cases the films may not show an obvious slip although there are other radiological signs so the condition should not be missed. Good results depend on early diagnosis and treatment.

3.52 Trochanteric Bursitis

CAUSES

This condition is commonly caused by pulling too hard with the gluteal muscles when working on the turn-out, especially if the dancer also 'tucks under' at the same time. this case, the tensor fasciae latae muscle and the fascia lata itself will increase the pressure on the distal part of the gluteal tendon and insertion. It is sometimes associated with a clicking hip when the tendon of the fascia lata is clicked recurrently over the greater trochanter.

TREATMENT

Local treatment is by ultrasound and interferential. Usually the dancer will benefit from 48 hours or so of rest and then a gradual return with any technical correction that may be required.

Complications
The bursitis can become very painful if it is not treated and particularly if any underlying technical problem is not detected and eliminated. If there has been tightness of the fascia lata there will usually be some accompanying quadriceps and adductor weakness which will need special attention to build them up.

3.53 Buttock Pain

CAUSES

Buttock pain may be produced by sciatic nerve root irritation in which case the pain may radiate lower down the thigh or leg or it may be merely localised to the buttock, producing muscle spasm at that site. Locally within the buttock the pain can be produced by tension in the small hip rotators, although even in these circumstances, the sciatic nerve as it passes by these small rotators may be irritated, specifically piriformis muscle. This may produce some radiation of pain to the thigh. The picture may be confused as to whether the primary origin of the pain is within the buttock or whether it is a referred pain down the sciatic nerve due to nerve root pressure in the lumbar spine. This may be a disc prolapse or facet joint inflammation .producing buttock pain with a very well localised tenderness within the buttock due to secondary muscle spasm. Classical ballet dancers, however, often become accustomed to tight gluteal muscles from overwork – gluteus medius and the deep external rotators. Technical faults frequently lead to buttock pain, either because of misuse of the lower back or by a failure to hold the turn-out adequately.

TREATMENT

It is important to determine the cause before starting treatment so that the cause itself and not merely the effect should be treated. If the pain is due to tension in the small rotators, i.e. a genuine local cause, the local treatment should be directed at release of the muscle spasm.

Classical ballet dancers should include a stretching regime for the deep rotator muscles as well as deep tissue work using a spiky ball. Internal rotation positions should be used to counteract constant turned out choreography.

Again posture and pelvic stabilisation should be examined. Working within the limits of hip external rotation is a requirement before muscle balance can be achieved.

3.54 Sacroiliac Strain

Because of the rotatory forces through the pelvis in dance with high legs, the sacroiliac joints are the site of strains especially in the more flexible dancer. Although the sacroiliac joint (SIJ) motion is minimal pain is thought to arise from the stretching the ligaments surrounding the joint. The pain is usually below L5, one sided. The ilium can rotate anteriorly and posteriorly on the sacrum (only 2.5°) and translate upwards and downwards (0.7 mm). In a normal pelvis the anterior superior iliac spines will be symmetrical, as will the posterior superior iliac spines. The symphysis pubis will also be symmetrical. Any asymmetry with pain over the SIJ indicates a dysfunction.

A common scenario in a dancer is a tight psoas and rectus femoris causing a unilateral anterior rotation of the ilium resulting in pain over the SIJ. The dancer may complain of catching at the front of the hip as well as back pain.

The piriformis muscle is the only muscle passing over the SIJ. When it is overly tight in a ballet dancer it exerts a debilitating strain on the joint.

A fall on the ischium can cause an upslip of the ilium on the sacrum which may need manipulation to resolve.

TREATMENT

Soft tissue techniques, manipulation and muscle energy techniques are used to successfully treat this area. Stabilising exercises for transversus abdominis and multifidus should be an integral part of recovery.

Complications
Pain over the SIJ can be referred from the lumbar spine. A facet joint strain, a developing stress fracture or a lumbar disc lesion can refer to the area.

3.55 Strain of the Muscles inserted into the Iliac Crest

These will produce local tenderness and there is no real difficulty in the diagnosis. Quadratus lumborum is one of these. It side flexes and extends the lumbar spine and is intrinsic to the arabesque. Sometimes pain, tenderness and bruising occur along the iliac crest when starting double work. Supporting and directing the girl, the boy holds the pelvis around the iliac crests but when not strong enough tends to clutch inadequately.

3.56 Interspinous Ligament Damage

These are the ligaments that lie between each spinous process in the posterior part of the individual vertebra.

CAUSES

Hyper-flexion may sprain an interspinous ligament and even produce tearing if very forceful. Hyper-extension can cause an impingement of adjacent spinous processes with a crushing of the interspinous ligament. This is particularly likely to occur in the dancer who fails to pull up the legs and trunk properly before starting a back bend and as a result will produce a localised hyper-extension at one level (Fig. 3.35). Sometimes a movement ends with a fast backbend with no time to pull up. Weakness of the back muscles may fail to control flexion, particularly when the flexion movement is rapid and this carried out repeatedly may cause a sprain of the interspinous ligament.

TREATMENT

Locally, ultrasound can be used and is more effective when applied with the spine slightly flexed so as to open up the interspinous area. It is best applied with the patient curled up on the side. The condition is often slow

3.35 Kinking in the lumbar region on a back bend. This is due to the dancer failing to pull up the legs and the trunk (i.e. she does not have the feeling of lengthening both areas) before starting to bend backwards. This photograph also shows the presence of a stiff lower lumbar segment

to settle due to the poor blood supply to the ligament. A considerable amount of work must be done on strengthening the trunk muscles in order to control movements properly and to prevent flexion and extension occurring principally at one or two levels alone.

The so called 'kissing spine' is an impingement of the spinous processes at one level. It produces a crushing of the interspinous ligament as mentioned above, with localised pain and tenderness. Surgery to excise the ligament and parts of the adjacent spinous processes must be avoided.

3.57 Facet Joint Strains

These joints are small synovial joints in the posterior bony complex of each vertebra and like similar joints elsewhere can be subject to sprains and strains. The injury is produced by uncontrolled movements, particularly when these become asymmetrical. Capsular tears and avulsions can take place. It occurs most commonly during jumping.

DIAGNOSIS

Deep tenderness at the side of a lumbar vertebra or on both sides if the condition is bilateral, and pain on hyper-extension with a tilt to one side as well as backwards, is very suggestive of a facet joint problem. Similarly, pain may be caused on flexion if there is also combined with this a tilt to one or other side. This will tend to stretch the synovium and capsule of the facet joint. It is important to exclude a stress fracture as the symptoms and signs are similar.

TREATMENT

Local treatment to relieve pain and muscle spasm is required and this should be accompanied by a period of rest from dancing. As the initial pain settles, an exercise programme can be commenced. This should be directed at strengthening the trunk muscles, correction of any asymmetrical working and also, and very importantly, at strengthening the control of the turn-out, particularly when the dancer is en l'air. In these circumstances the turn-out can only be held by the muscles working correctly. Those dancers who depend upon friction of their feet on the floor to hold the turn-out are particularly prone to this type of injury, as well as many other injuries at other levels.

If the condition is long-standing, it is occasionally necessary to inject the facet joint with a steroid. This should, however, only be necessary occasionally as most patients will have settled with normal conservative treatment. If an injection is to be carried out, then ideally it should be done under CT scan control so that the exact location of the point of the needle can be visualised prior to injecting the steroid.

Complications
A facet joint inflamed by injury can produce a referred sciatic-type pain because the sciatic nerve roots run closely past the facet joints at each level. This condition can to a certain extent mimic a lumbar disc lesion from which it must be differentiated. Facet joint pain is provoked by extension while disc lesions more on flexion. MRI can clarify the diagnosis.

3.58 Lumbar Disc Prolapse

Damage to the lumbar disc in the form of prolapse, dessication and narrowing or disc bulge is common in professional dancers. It is not surprising with the spinal movement and lifting by men required in dance. The outer third of the posterior annulus fibrosus has a nerve supply and is most vulnerable to a combination of axial rotation and forward flexion. An annular tear provokes an inflammatory response with widespread muscle spasm. Repeated torsional injury to the annulus fibrosus can result in radial fissures and eventually the nuclear material can herniate through these weakened areas – the disc prolapse. In the acute stages, especially when there is sciatic nerve root involvement, the treatment is a routine physiotherapy problem. However, once the dancer is in the recovery phase, considerable attention is paid to stabilising the trunk, gluteal and lower limb muscles with particular emphasis on the

correction of any technical and lifting faults. In an attempt to avoid surgery, an epidural injection of steroid can be very helpful.

The attention to posture and stabilisation in the student years is with the prevention in mind of these serious problems in later careers.

3.59 Stress Fractures of the Lumbar Vertebrae

These occur in the pars interarticularis, most commonly at the L.4 and L.5 levels. Although the fracture may be unilateral, it is more commonly bilateral, affecting both partes interaticulares at that particular level (Fig. 3.36). The condition can occur at any age from early student days through to mature adult life. If the stress fracture is not detected early, the fracture can gradually widen and separate so that the vertebral body and the whole spine above will slowly slip forward, leaving the posterior bony ring with the spinous process and inferior articular facet behind. Once this has started to occur, there is no chance of the fracture uniting. This condition with a forward slip is known as a spondylolisthesis (Fig. 3.37).

CAUSES

The most important single cause of stress fractures is lack of stabilisation and activation of the deep abdominal muscles. The two major precipitating factors are a lordotic posture in order to try to give more external rotation (turn-out) at the hips and over-turning (**Sections 5.6** and **5.7**).

3.36 A stress fracture (arrowed) in the pars interarticularis of the 5th lumbar vertebra

3.37 An X-ray of a spondylolisthesis. The 4th lumbar vertebra has slipped forwards on the body of the 5th lumbar vertebra. The single arrow indicates the mal-alignment of the posterior margins of the two vertebral bodies. In this instance there is a forward slip of about 1 cm. The double arrow shows the defect in the bone which started as a stress fracture (vide Fig. 3.36)

In particular these faults produce an excessive amount of movement (flexion, extension, lateral flexion and rotation) at one single level instead of having the movement evenly distributed throughout the lumbar spine. The greatest stress occurs at the point where the lumbar spine is attached to the pelvis at the lumbo-sacral junction L5/S1 or at L4/L5.

DIAGNOSIS

Clinically the dancer will present with low back pain associated with muscle spasm and tenderness at the sides of the affected vertebra, about a centimetre or two from the mid line. These signs are very suggestive of stressing at this level, or the next stage of deterioration when there is an actual stress fracture present. An early diagnosis is extremely important. The presence of a fracture should be strongly suspected when local treatment and trunk exercises do not rapidly abolish the muscle spasm. The diagnosis can be confirmed by oblique X-rays of the lumbar spine, *but* X-ray changes will not usually be present for some one to two months, or even longer, from the time of onset of symptoms. Hence if a fracture is suspected and if X-rays appear normal, an isotope bone scan should be undertaken. This will show a 'hot spot' at the fracture site in the early days of its development. If necessary, due to persistence of symptoms, there should be no hesitation in repeating the scan a few weeks later. A CT scan or an MRI scan might be necessary.

TREATMENT

A patient with a stress fracture requires immediate rest for the worst symptoms to settle. An initial exercise programme is started to activate deep stabilisers of the trunk. These are in the form of an individual pro-gramme of low-grade floor exercises to be carried out by the dancer. Supplementation of Pilates exercises adds variety and monitoring of a student is wise in the early rehabilitation. It must be impressed upon the dancer that fractures do not heal if they are moved and to 'try out' the back to see if it still hurts in an arabesque, must be avoided. Use of a back support for the first month can be reassuring and after six to eight weeks the dancer can start barre with low legs concentrating on pelvis and trunk placement.

On starting class work, although the back will be protected by the temporary support, the legs must be kept low and port de bras limited with flexion and extension trunk movements kept to the thoracic spine. When the corset is discarded for class, care must still be exercised to limit the range of flexion and extension until strength builds up satisfactorily. From the time class is commenced a careful watch must be kept for *the original technical fault which precipitated the injury*. The muscular build-up and rehabilitation will take at

least two months before the dancer can gradually increase work towards a full and normal class.

During the four-month period, during which it is hoped that union of the stress fracture will take place, trunk muscle exercises are continued. Exercises involving the shoulder girdle and all the muscles of the lower limbs are naturally included. It is essential that during this four-month healing period the dancer does nothing that puts the spine through excessive movement or under stress. Even sitting and resting positions must be supported in the neutral position. The extreme stresses on the spine of jumping and landing in open positions are reserved for the very end stages of rehabilitation.

The management as suggested above is for the ideal situation where there is daily physiotherapy or medical cover. This occurs mainly in professional companies and professional schools. In other cases when the dancer can only be followed up intermittently, a plaster-of-Paris jacket should be applied for four months. During this time the patient should be encouraged to exercise all limb muscles. When pain-free in the plaster, the dancer may return to some limited barre work, keeping the legs low. When the plaster cast is finally removed, a tempor-ary corset should be fitted. Rehabilitation then continues as above.

3.60 Thoracic Pain

This can occur at various levels from the mid thoracic region upwards. It is frequently acutely painful and often produces girdle pain, i.e. pain radiating around the chest wall, sometimes as far as the sternum. Even more frequently, the pain radiates to the scapula area of the back.

CAUSES

It is usually brought on by working with tension in the upper trunk, shoulder girdle or neck and is often associated with weakness of the muscles, not only in these areas but also in the lower back and in the muscle groups controlling turn-out. The two latter areas – lower back and turn-out – when weak, not only make dancers feel insecure while working and thus increase tension higher, but will also encourage rotation of one or other side of the upper trunk in relation to the lower trunk and pelvis. In these dancers the upper body weight is incorrectly placed. Thoraic pain may also be associated with swayback knees. The thoracic spine should naturally be a gentle convex curve but in classical ballet this part of the spine can, in faulty placement, extend throwing the ribs up and out at the front.

The shoulder girdle is complex and its correct placement relies on placement of the thoracic spine and vice versa.

In boys it can also be associated with incorrect lifting. Over-development of the shoulder girdle in boys due to ill-advised weight training can produce similar effects because of the relatively weaker and often neglected lower trunk. The mass of muscle at the top of the trunk makes balance more difficult and, when jumping, the upper trunk can frequently be observed from the side to be back behind an imaginary line passing through the centre of gravity and down through the greater trochanters.

TREATMENT

Acute dorsal pain can usually be relieved by Maitland mobilisations but it is vital to remember that this method of pain relief is only the beginning of treatment and not an end in itself. Once the acute pain has been relieved, by mobilisations, manipulation, massage to overlying spinal muscles and/or by electrotherapy the cause will have to be investigated – usually a technical fault – and eliminated and any necessary strengthening exercises at various levels will have to be instituted.

Spinal posture will need to be corrected, then shoulder girdle placement and port de bras. Among commonly neglected technical faults is incorrect arm placement. Breathing patterns will require checking and rib movements with lateral expansion facilitated.

3.61 Acute Torticollis

This is a condition where, because of pain, the head is tilted to one side. It is also known as acute wry neck and is often referred to by patients as a crick in the neck.

CAUSES

It is quite common in adolescence and is not necessarily associated with dance. In dancers, whether students or professionals, it is often precipitated by trunk instability and by a tendency to sit in one or other hip, because young dancers are usually predominantly right or left sided (right or left handed). With training, this predominance of one side or another is decreased when dancing though it often remains to a greater or lesser extent. Most dancers never achieve a complete equalisation. They nearly all have a preferred side on which to work.

Dancers often wake with this in the morning, having simply slept in an awkward position.

TREATMENT

The use of antinflammatories can be useful. Treatment should be gentle and sometimes mobilising the problem joint can make it more painful.

Massage is particularly useful in this condition and often some neck traction will help to give initial relief.

3.62 Shoulder and Arm Problems

Shoulder dislocation or subluxation is relatively common in adolescent male dancers who have a degree of hypermobility. The history of the more common anterior dislocation is usually one of forced abduction and external rotation. Recurrence of dislocations can lead to shoulder instability. Damage to the glenoid labrum is a complication which must be diagnosed. An arthroscopy should be considered to investigate this as MRI scans do not always show the labrum accurately enough.

Boys enjoy high resistance gym work but attention must also be given to scapular rhythm and fine positioning control. Given the time and the attention shoulders can be well stabilised as well as strengthed.

A supraspinatus tendonitis or sub-acromial bursitis can occur in boys, following a lot of lifting. Frequently, a local injection of steroid will relieve these two conditions.

The important aspect in dancers is that, if surgical repair is necessary, then the method used must be one which does not limit shoulder movements. To this end, the coracoid transfer operation (Bristow or Bonnin operation) is the best choice, producing as it does complete stability without any limitation of external rotation as always occurs in the Putti-Platt or Bankart procedures.

Other upper limb injuries usually follow a fall or similar trauma and are not really dance injuries but merely injuries which happen to occur in a dancer. They are all treated by standard orthopaedic measures. The only important point worth making is that during treatment (plaster of Paris, etc.) the dancer can work out or have worked out for him a programme of general exercise to keep the rest of the body as fit as possible.

Strengthening Exercises

In this section we describe a variety of straightforward exercises which can be performed by any dancer or student (or anyone else) who wishes to strengthen up various portions of the body. The photographs should be studied in conjunction with the captions before embarking upon each exercise. In some cases there are several exercises which are graduated according to difficulty and strength required, so start with the easiest. It is important to carry out each exercise accurately. They all need to be performed slowly with the body or limb under full control the whole time. The various groups of muscles being exercised must be kept firmly tightened throughout the exercise, e.g. in a lifting exercise the muscles can be made to work just as hard during the controlled lowering phase as when lifting, thus utilising the time taken to best advantage. There should be complete relaxation between each cycle of an exercise, e.g. tighten, lift, hold, lower, relax and then repeat. If this relaxation is omitted then the muscle may go into cramp. A good routine is to count five slowly for each phase of the cycle – tighten (5), lift slowly (5), hold (5), lower (5), relax (5).

The dancer and student can with benefit take a comprehensive selection of exercises and put them into a regular daily routine. The strengthening achieved will go a long way toward helping in injury prevention.

These exercises are not designed to improve cardio-respiratory fitness, although they will have a slight beneficial effect. A different type of exercise programme will be required additionally for this, e.g.
swimming, cycling, etc. Exercises are specific in their end result. 'Taking exercise' as such will not produce all-round fitness and strength of all areas. A specific programme needs to be devised to meet the requirements of the individual. These exercises are mainly devised to be an adjunct to class (or other forms of exercise for non-dancers) and are not an alternative.

We have tried to select a cross-section of exercises which should be readily understood and correctly performed without confusion as to purpose or method of performance. They are obviously only a very small number of the possible variations but may provide some help to the dancer who wishes to avoid the time and expense of visiting a physiotherapist to be taught exercises. However, if in doubt as to whether you are in fact doing the exercise correctly then some competent professional help would be advisable. If an exercise seems particularly easy and effortless you may be doing it incorrectly.

Remember:
1. All the exercises must be carried out slowly and under full control. Do not bounce.
2. Always try to tighten the muscles being exercised that little bit more especially during a 'hold phase'.
3. Repeat the exercise with the other side of the body or the other limb. A weaker group may require more repetitions than its counterpart but even so do not neglect the 'good side'.

4.1   4.2

4.3   4.4

4.1 4.2 4.3 4.4
Abdominal exercises for the straight muscle fibres (rectus abdominis). These are carried out by means of sit-ups. The knees are flexed to prevent the lumbar spine from becoming lordotic. The shoulder girdle must not do the main bulk of the work. The abdominal muscles must be used as hard on the way down as on the way up

4.5   4.6

4.5 4.6 4.7
This is the *incorrect* way to do abdominal exercises. Lifting legs straight produces a lumbar hyperextension (lordosis) and can lead to lumbar back strains. The figures clearly show the marked lordosis that can be produced. In Fig. 4.7 the hand under the lumbar spine is merely to demonstrate the large gap between the spine and the floor

4.7

4.8

4.9

4.8 4.9
Abdominal exercises for the straight fibres requiring more control and a more powerful use of the muscles

4.10

4.11

4.10 4.11
Abdominal exercises for the cross fibres (exernal and internal oblique muscles). The basic starting poisition is as for sit-ups. The twisting motion begins as soon as the movement is initiated. Do alternate sides, working first one and then the other

4.12

4.13

4.14

4.15

4.12 4.13 4.14 4.15
Exercises for the back extensor muscles. Start lying with the shoulder blades pulled down and the buttocks held firmly. Then, while the arms are kept in contact with the floor, the head and shoulders are lifted by the back extensors. They are not pushed up by the arms. The waist is pulled in during the exercise

4.16

4.17

4.18

4.16 4.17 4.18
Exercises for the back extensor muscles – a progression from the previous exercise. The shoulder blades are pulled down to prevent neck tension. The waist is pulled in. The buttocks are held tightly

4.19

4.20

4.21

4.22

4.19 4.20 4.21 4.22
Exercises for the back extensor muscles – a progression from the previous exercise. The same rules apply. The exercise requires more powerful use of the muscles

4.23

4.24

4.25

4.23 4.24 4.25
Exercises for the back extensor muscles – very much more advanced. The same rules apply. Repeat the exercise using alternate arms

4.28

4.26

4.27

4.26 4.27 4.28
Exercises for the back extensor muscles with some rotation. Repeat on the other side. The same rules apply as for previous extensor exercises. Fig. 4.28 shows a side view of the exercise

4.29
Exercises for the back exensor muscles with some rotation,.
more advanced with the arm out. Repeat on the other side.
The same rules apply as before.

There are many other exercises for the extensor muscles
of the back but these particular exercises have been devised
for people without equipment

4.29

4.30

4.31

4.32

4.30   4.31   4.32
Simple side exercises standing. Care must be taken not to twist the pelvis and the wait. The waist must be pulled in during the
exercises and must be pulled in harder on the way up. Do the exercise on alternate sides. Do not bounce

4.33

4.34

4.35

4.36

4.33 4.34 4.35 4.36

Exercises for strengthening the lateral trunk muscles (lateral flexors). Start with the right arm above the head, waist pulled in. Bend over to the left. Bring the left arm up until nearly parallel to the right arm. Slowly stand up straight with both arms above the head. Lower the right arm. Repeat exercise bending over to the right. Keep waist well pulled in throughout the exercise, pulled in harder when coming up. Also pull shoulder blades down when coming up otherwise shoulders will tend to become elevated

4.37

4.38

4.37 4.38
Exercises for strengthening lateral trunk muscles. A progression from the previous exercise. The lower elbow and forearm are used for balance only and not for total support. Pull waist in well. The legs and trunk must be kept lined up. Repeat the exercise the same number of times on the other side

4.39

4.40

4.39 4.40
Exercises for strengthening the lateral trunk muscles. A further progression from the previous exercises. The legs must be kept lined up with the trunk and pressed together. They should also have the feeling of being 'lengthened', that is, pushed distally away from the trunk to avoid bunching up of the lateral flexor muscles. Keep the waist (the abdominal muscles) well pulled in during the exercise

4.41 4.42 4.43 4.44 4.45 4.46 4.47 4.48 4.49
Quadriceps exercises. The same exercise seen from the side and from the front in two different dancers. Fig. 4.49 shows well that the vastus medialis is contracting very firmly. The hip, knee-cap and the centre of the foot must be kept lined up. The pelvis is kept square with the weight equally on both buttocks. The knee is allowed to flex slightly over a pillow during the relaxation phase. The trunk must lean back away from the leg because it leaves the hip more free. Repeat with the other leg

4.41

4.42

4.43   4.44

4.45

4.46

4.48

4.49

4.50   4.51

4.52   4.53

4.50 4.51 4.52 4.53

Exercises for strengthening the adductor muscles in the thigh. The upper leg is flexed at the hip to a right-angle (90°) in order to allow the lower leg which is being exercised freedom to move. The upper leg must be supported in order to keep the pelvis square with the floor – it must not rotate either forwards or backwards. This support may be a folded pillow as in Figs 4.50 and 4.51 or stool as in Figs 4.52 and 4.53, or even a low bed. Support the head on the elbow. The exercising leg must be kept with the knee-cap pointing forwards throughout the exercise. Do not pull the leg into the hip when lifting it; feel that the leg is lengthened. Pull in the abdominal muscles. Repeat with the other leg

4.54 4.55
The same exercise from above

4.54   4.55

4.56   4.57   4/58   4.59

4.56   4.57   4.58   4.59
Adductor muscle exercises. Slightly more difficult exercises than the foregoing. The leg is carried forward and lifted

4.60   4.61   4.62
Adductor muscle exercises.
Similar to the last exercise but
the leg is carried backwards and
then lifted

4.60   4.61   4.62

4.63   4.64   4.65   4.66   4.67   4.68   4.69   4.70   4.71   4.72   4.73   4.74   4.75   4.76   4.77   4.78   4.79
Exercises for the gluteal muscles (abductors). This exercise is carried out lying on the side with the underneath leg bent at hip
and knee. The back is kept straight. The top leg must be kept lined up with the trunk. The knee-cap must face forwards. Lift the leg
stretching it downwards, i.e. a feeling of lengthening the leg. Carry out the exercise slowly. Control the lowering of the leg as well
as the lifting

4.63   4.64   4.65   4.66

4.67

4.68

4.69

4.70

4.71

4.72

4.73

4.74

4.75

4.76

4.77

4.78

4.79

4.80

4.81

4.82

4.80   4.81   4.82

Exercises for hip extensors (gluteus maximus). Straight leg. The leg must be lined up with the trunk. Pelvis must not be twisted or move. This is purely a leg movement. The pillow is to keep the lumbar spine as flat as possible. Carry out with alternate legs

4.83

4.84

4.85

4.83   4.84   4.85   4.86

Hip extensor exercises. Progression from the previous exercise. Start straight. When the leg is elevated take it out to the side in abduction and then across the other leg into adduction and then back to the mid-line. Pelvis *must* be kept flat and *must not twist*

4.86

4.87　　　　　　　　　　　　4.88　　　　　　　　　　　　4.89

4.87　4.88　4.89
Hamstring exercises. Start lying flat. The legs must be lined up with the trunk. Flex the knee without any rotation of the thigh. The heel lines up with the centre of the buttocks on the same side

4.90　　　　　　　　　　　　　　　　4.91

4.90　4.91　4.92
Hamstring exercises. Side view. Keep the gluteal (buttock) muscles held tightly during the exercises in order to prevent the hip flexing

4.92

4.93   4.94

4.95   4.96

4.93   4.94   4.95   4.96
Peroneal muscle exercises. These are better done with the knee extended. Carry out the exercise first in some degree of plantarflexion (not full plantarflexion, i.e. not with the foot fully pointed) and repeat with the foot and ankle at a right-angle.

4.97

4.98

4.99

4.97   4.98   4.99
Intrinsic muscle exercises. Fig. 4.97 shows the dancer's right foot working. Fig. 4.98 shows the left foot working. Fig. 4.99 shows both feet working

4.100

4.100
Calf muscle and Achilles tendon stretch. Keep the foot flat on the floor, the heel down and the knee straight. Stretch gently

Further Exercise for the Abdominal Muscles

These are stabilisation exercises for the trunk. The spine and pelvis are held still and the lower limbs are used to challenge the abdominal obliques, transverses abdominis and the back muscles in their role as stabilisers.

4.101

4.102

4.101   4.102
The spine and pelvis are held in neutral, the shoulders are held down and breathing is from a sideways movement of the ribs, with neck tension-free

4.103
The pelvis is overly tucked under

4.104
Having established the initial poisiton of spine and pelvis the knee is allowed to fall out to the side 45° and return without rocking the pelvis towards the working side. The deep abdominals and lumbar spine muscles are challenged

4.105

4.106

4.105 4.106
From the start position the thigh is lifted with the pelvis stabilised. The foot is returned to the floor with no movement in the trunk

4.107
Lifting the first leg, then the second holding the spine and pelvis still. If the lumbar spine arches, the neutral spine should be flattened to begin with until enough control is acquired to control the neutral

4.108
Different combinations challenge the spine more

4.109
Starting position with arms and hips at 90°. The shoulders are held down by latissimus dorsi and the deep abdominals are activated

4.110
The right leg extends as the right arm is raised. The lower the extending leg, the more the pelvis is challenged

4.111   4.112   4.113

4.111   4.112   4.113
Similar exercises are performed lying along the foam roller to make them even more challenging

4.114

The initial position is four-point kneeling with spine and pelvis in the neutral position. The shoulders are held down, the scapulae are flat – a challenging position for the young shoulder girdle

4.115

The left knee is taken towards the chest without posterior rotation of the pelvis. The abdominal and lumbar spine stabilisation remains engaged

4.116

4.117

4.118

4.116 4.117 4.118
The left knee is swept through to a low parallel arabesque

4.119

The opposite arm to leg can be lifted without change to pelvis and spine. The left weight-bearing shoulder must be strong enough to stabilise and trunk control must be mastered before progressing to this exercise

4.120

4.121

4.120
The abdominal exercise for rectus abdominis. The spine is flat on the floor with the tranversus also engaged with the lower abdomen flat

4.121
Taking the left elbow towards the right knee engages the oblique fibres

4.122

4.123

4.122
Initial position: lying on the right side in a straight line with legs parallel

4.123
Sliding the left hand down towards the knee with pressure through the right arm activates the left obliques. The latissimus dorsi controls the shoulder girdle

4.124

4.125

4.124 4.125
Further exercises for the side flexors, this time lifting the lower limbs

4.126

4.127

4.128

4.129

4.130

4.131

4.132

4.126 4.127 4.128 4.129 4.130 4.131 4.132

The lateral flexors – the obliques and spinal flexors – are exercised here. Eccentric contraction on the opposite side to the side flexion, and concentrically on the way up. The trunk is held square throughout with lower abdominals engaged

4.133

In four-point kneeling the shoulder girdle is stabilised well with the scapulae flat, neither retracted nor protracted

4.134

Incorrect. Here the scapulae are winging

4.135

In this position the shoulders are held down and scapulae are held flat against the chest wall.

In all positions the deep abdominal should not be forgotten

4.136

When one arm is taken out the other shoulder girdle is challenged. This dancer is finding it difficult to keep the shoulder girdle square and the right shoulder stabilisers in control

4.137

The arm is taken up, demanding more extension in the thoracic spine

4.138
The exercise starts from a square position with shoulders held down. The head is turned 45° to the right. The spine is lengthened and a back bend is taken from the thoracic spine. The mid spinal extensors and latissimus dorsi are strongly activated, therefore these exercises are performed carefully with few repetitions

4.139
One arm up can challenge further

4.140
These are followed by a stretch

4.141
Stretch for the lumbar spine

Exercises for Latissimus Dorsi and Spinal Extensors

4.142
The start position is with forehead on the floor and deep abdominals engaged

4.143
The shoulders are placed in the activated position of upright posture

4.144
The arms are lifted with latissimus dorsi engaged to hold the shoulders down

4.145
The head is lifted retaining length through the back of the neck

4.146
The thoracic spine extends with lower abdominals engaged

Exercises for Shoulder Stabilisation

4.147

4.148

4.147
Start position is square with elbows into the sides and palms up

4.148
The palms are taken to the side (externally rotating at the shoulder) and the scapular muscles can be felt with latissimus dorsi

4.149

4.150

4.149 4.150
The same exercise using the resistance of a rubber exercise band

4.151

4.152

4.151 4.152
Rotating the thoracic spine (lumbar spine and pelvis held still) mobilises and relaxes the muscles in the mid spine

Press-ups: The Mainstay of the Male Dancer

4.153

4.154

4.155

4.156

4.157

4.153 4.154 4.155 4.156 4.157
Start with the hands at chest level and weight on the toes. With the shoulders abducted and internally rotated the pectoral muscles are challenged further

4.158

4.159

4.158   4.159
These are subtle exercises for the deep rotators of the hip. The hips are flexed with knees at 90° and feet in line with the spine. The knee is gently opened with no contraction of gluteus maximus or tensor fascia latae. Instead the deep rotators are activated

4.160

4.161

4.160   4.161
The hips here are in the standing position and the same exercise as that shown in 4.158–4.159 is performed

4.162

4.162
This is a good stretch for the left deep gluteal muscles

Exercises for the Adductors

4.163

4.164

4.163   4.164
Lying on the side and lifting the leg underneath turned out, activates the right adductor group.

    Alternatively the left leg can be placed on a cushion at 90° hip and knee, parallel. The trunk must be held square and the shoulders down

4.165
The adductors can be isolated here
squeezing the soft ball

4.166
An adductor stretch

Quadriceps Exercises

4.167

4.168

4.167   4.168
The knee extends over a rolled-up towel to engage vastus medialis

4.169

4.170

4.169   4.170
A controlled extension of the knee, here using a light ankle weight. Add a 30° external rotation to reinforce vastus medialis, the inside quadriceps which stabilises the patella

Exercises for the Hamstrings

4.171
The start position. The lower abdominals are active. The shoulders are down

4.172
The knee is flexed as far as possible with the pelvis and spine stabilised

4.173
The knee is taken to 90° with the foot pointed

4.174
The knee is lifted

4.175
The knee is extended and then lowered

4.176 The same exercise can be done with a light ankle weight for more resistance

4.177

4.178

4.179

4.180

4.177 4.178 4.179 4.180

Exercises for the gluteus maximus. The leg is circled feeling the lower portion of the gluteal muscle. A light ankle weight can also be used

Foot and Ankle Exercises

4.181

4.182

4.183

4.181   4.182   4.183
The well-pointed foot. The arch of the foot is strong, the posterior ankle is not overly compressed and the toes are held straight. The toes are not curled but ready to land from a jump. The foot is functional, not just visually attractive

4.184
Doming exercise for the foot. Exercise for the intrinsic muscles of the foot, especially the lumbricals

4.185
The extensor hallucis longus lifts the big toe

4.186
Using the rubber band the big toe flexors point from the MTP joint, keeping the toe straight

4.187
The abductor hallucis gives the big toe strength and stability and helps support the medial arch. The big toe should be able to move inwards and outwards with control

4.188
The dorsal interossei spread the toes

4.189
The plantar interossei bring the toes together and here the lumbrical muscles flex the MTP joints but keep the toes straight

4.190

4.191

4.192

4.190 4.191 4.192
The peroneal muscles are exercised with ankle at 90° as well as plantarflexed

4.193

4.194

4.193 4.194
A light ankle weight can be added to the previous exercise

4.195 4.196
The tibialis posterior is exercised here by inverting the foot

4.197
With more plantarflexion the tibialis anterior, which tends to be dominant, works less

4.198 4.199
After exercise the calves are stretched thoroughly with a flexed knee for soleus and extended for gastrocnemius

Balance Exercises

4.200
Various exercises can be given on a wobble board

4.201
Balancing on a foam block tests the foot and ankle as well as the posture above

4.202
Various uneven surfaces can challenge classical positions

4.203   4.204
Here the right foot and ankle are challenged to hold correct positioning while the left leg moves against the resistance of the rubber band

4.205
While simple positions are practised balancing on the wobble board, progress can be made to advanced exercises

Eccentric Exercises for the Patellar Tendon

4.206   4.207   4.208

4.209   4.210   4.211

4.212

4.206   4.207   4.208   4.209   4.210   4.211   4.212
These strengthen the quadriceps eccentrically

Eccentric Exercises for the Achilles Tendon

4.213

4.214

4.215

4.216

4.217

4.218

4.213 4.214 4.215 4.216 4.217 4.218
These strengthen the calf muscles eccentrically

Taping Techniques

4.219   4.220   4.221

4.222   4.223   4.224

4.225   4.226   4.227

4.228

4.129   4.220   4.221   4.222   4.223   4.224   4.225   4.226   4.227   4.228
Taping for hallux valgus strain

4.229   4.230   4.231   4.232   4.233   4.234   4.235   4.236   4.237   4.238   4.239   4.240   4.241   4.242   4.243

Taping for plantar fascia strain but also for any strain where the medial arch requires support

4.244 4.245 4.246

4.247 4.248 4.249

4.250

4.244 4.245 4.246 4.247 4.248 4.249 4.250
Taping to stabilise the anterior talus

Taping to stabilise the cuboid or support a lateral midfoot sprain (without pad)

4.251
A pad is placed under the cuboid

4.252

4.253

4.254

4.255

Technical Faults and Anatomical Variations: Their Causes, Consequences and Treatment

All forms of treatment are relatively pointless without complete correction of any fault in technique

Technical faults may arise for various reasons. They can occur as a result of the anatomical structure of the body, for example, restriction of turn-out being limited by the bony and soft tissue configuration around the hips. They may arise because of bad teaching or equally because the student does not take on corrections intelligently. Once a faulty technique has been learned it becomes extremely difficult to correct. Therefore poor teaching in the early days of a student's life may continue its effects throughout his professional career. Unfortunately, these faults will tend to increase with the passage of time, particularly if the dancer is working in a situation where there are no reasonable classes with good correction from experienced teachers.

All dance injuries arise from technical faults

Accidents outside the dancer's control, cannot be classed as dance injuries. It should also be understood that, in general, technical faults can be minor but, despite that, can produce major problems for the dancer, either in the treatment of the injury required or more often in the prevention of recurrences of the same injury. In general a major fault is unlikely to pass uncorrected except in the most inadequate of teaching situations. Certainly the most important difference between the good teacher and the indifferent teacher is the ability to recognise subtle flaws in technique and to correct accurately. A good teacher will not allow a student to progress to more difficult and demanding work until he has mastered the basics. An effective teacher must have 'a good eye' for line, sensing balance and stability. A 'good eye' can be developed with a knowledge of anatomy and biomechanics along side an extensive knowledge of classical technique and what it feels like. Teachers must understand the importance of technical faults in their relation to both primary and recurrent injuries in dancers.

It must also be pointed out that even in the case of a non-dancing injury, when the dancer starts to return to class he may develop technical faults in compensation, particularly if he has returned to class too early before rehabilitation is complete.

Frequently one technical fault leads to another and therefore do not occur in isolation and this calls for a very careful assessment of the dancer. The chain of events needs to be recognised and the cause corrected.

Coaching classes involving technical correction are an essential part of the rehabilitation of an injured dancer, even if the injury is only minor. A dancer presenting with an injury should be technically assessed. Referral to a coaching session should usually form part of the treatment process. These coaching classes are best carried out on a one-to-one or one-to-two or at most three basis. Adequate technical correction is difficult with more than three in a class. There is no doubt that regular individual assessments of all students, with a particular eye for correct technique, would play an important part in the prevention of injuries.

Repetition of movements and movement patterns in dance must be taught accurately. The more complicated these patterns of movement become, the more important it is to take time to ensure that they are learned correctly from the beginning. Short cuts will never lead to satisfactory results. Dance teaching is a form of co-ordination training which develops pre-programmed automatic multi-neuro-muscular patterns. The pre-programming is developed within the brain. It is automatic because much of it does not in the end require conscious thought. It is multi-muscular because many different muscle groups are used in order to produce the desired series of movements. These pre-programmed automatic multi-muscular patterns are known as engrams. (**Section 1.3** Neuro-muscular Co-ordination and Engrams, p. 21.)

It requires constant *exact* repetitions in order to produce an engram so that conscious thought is not given to individual muscles or movements. Proprio-ceptive feedback gives both sub-conscious and conscious monitoring of the movement and it is this which gives the conscious mind the knowledge of whether the movement was carried out successfully or not. These automatic engrams can only be developed by voluntary repetition of the precise programme *without any variation at all from one repetition to the next*. This must be done *extremely accurately*, otherwise the input of information will vary on each occasion and the engram cannot be developed. *It follows therefore that initially the pattern must be slow enough to be accurate.* An engram allows a complicated movement to be performed far more rapidly than would be possible if conscious thought of each part of the pattern of movement were required. It is important also to realise that at the same time as the movements are occurring, the engram will also produce an inhibition of *unwanted* movements. This inhibition is an essential part of the regulation of co-ordination. Inhibition cannot be produced directly and consciously. It is only achieved by regular, active repetition of the pattern of desired movements. Co-ordination of the most rapid, complex and skilful actions is automated by engrams rather than by a voluntary controlled series of movements.

The activation of the engram(s) is voluntary and under conscious control. In learning exercise patterns and in learning dance technique, or any other movement technique, accuracy is absolutely vital in order to develop the correct engram. If inaccuracies are allowed during the development of technique, this will produce 'bad habits' and these inaccuracies or 'bad habits' will

themselves become an engram. Once this has taken place the modification of the engram will be extremely difficult and will usually call for that portion of the technique to be learned again from scratch. Hence the importance of learning any complex series of movements accurately from the start. As previously stated, in order to achieve accuracy the pattern will have to be learned slowly, and the number of repetitions required to produce a really well developed engram is almost innumerable. However, this is not as bad as it sounds because an action is usually made up of a series of engrams. It is the sum of the engrams which produces the final result. The initiation of an engram is under voluntary and conscious control, although the constituent parts of the engram are themselves not by that stage under direct voluntary control. What the mind does is to select the stored engrams and put them together in order to produce the desired result.

Individual Technical Faults

5.1 Discrepancy in Shoulder Level

This is often brought about by weakness of one side. As a result of this weakness there can be an over-compensation so that the weaker shoulder is held higher or, conversely, without this compensation the shoulder that is weaker may be lower (Fig. 5.1). Only careful examination will demonstrate which pertains in a particular individual. Elevation of one side may also be brought about by unequal muscle tension caused by unbalanced weight distribution in the lower part of the body.

The presence of a scoliosis will usually cause elevation of a shoulder, particularly if the scoliosis is in the mid or upper dorsal region. The presence of a scoliosis should be eliminated as a cause of the shoulder elevation at the initial medical examination.

Leg length inequality may be reflected in differing shoulder heights as well as in a pelvic tilt.

Inequality of turn-out produces a swinging forwards of one side of the pelvis towards the opposite restricted side. The weight may settle more on one side than the other causing a one-sided trunk weakness and frequently an alteration in shoulder height on one side. Sitting in one hip will cause a similar picture.

The uneven shoulder level may follow an injury which has caused the dancer to take the weight off the painful side. This alteration can rapidly develop into a habit affecting also the pelvis, so that even when the injury is cured and the pain has disappeared, the postural alteration remains.

5.1 Discrepancy in shoulder level

One general cause of elevation of one shoulder is the habitual carrying on that side of heavy bags, frequently starting in students at a very early age. In schools children have to take all their school books for the day backwards and forwards each day. Dance students may additionally be carrying several changes of clothing as well as school books. Use of the old-fashioned school satchel or a rucksack worn correctly, taking the weight evenly on both shoulders, prevents the development of shoulder level inequality.

Postural bad habits are not corrected in schools and there is a great deal to be said for postural awareness and the school teacher who insisted that children sat correctly at their desks.

TREATMENT

An exercise programme is compiled to achieve the correction of any associated faults and this must be accompanied by constant postural correction. Underlying structural abnormalities may well call for referral for an orthopaedic opinion. If the shoulder level discrepancy is an isolated fault, it should be realised that its presence will have alter the weight-bearing line and an imbalance at the level of the lower trunk, the gluteals, the hamstrings, adductors, quadriceps and even in the lower leg. Therefore, the exercise regime should be directed at strengthening and balancing all these areas.

5.2 Tension around the Neck and Shoulders

This should be considered in two sections, (a) tension in the upper fibres of the trapezius and (b) tension in the pectoralis muscles. Both are caused by inaccurate placement of arms and/or inaccurate fixation of the scapulae. The former usually comes about because the arms are held too far back with the elbows behind the line of the shoulders. The arms may also be held too high. Problems can also occur if the arms are held forward in the correct position, but achieved by drawing the scapulae around the chest wall. Although this has the effect of flattening the scapulae against the chest wall, it does it by creating a great deal of tension in the pectoralis muscles as well as spasm in the trapezii.

The mechanism by which the arms are taken too far back is (a) by leading with the elbow rather than with the hand (Fig. 5.2) or (b) by over turning the feet, which causes the upper part of the trunk to sway backwards so that in obtaining a comfortable balance, the arms are taken backwards even more than the upper trunk (Fig. 5.3).

Weakness and instability of the lower trunk produces tension in the shoulder girdle because the feeling of insecurity produces an attempt at stability by tensing the upper trunk muscles.

Swayback knees which are pushed back cause the pelvis to tilt forward, the lumbar spine to become lordotic and in compensation the upper trunk goes backwards and this in turn alters the scapular fixation and scapular movements, producing increasing trapezius spasm.

A scoliosis, when present, always produces some tension to a variable degree during working. This is brought about because the compensatory curve above the scoliosis engenders some postural correction also, which then induces the tension. This postural compensation is often exaggerated as an attempt is made to put the centre of gravity over the base (i.e. the feet). In order to minimise tension, the best possible posture in the circumstances must be achieved. Corrections must start at the feet and legs and work upwards. Unless the base is correct it is impossible to achieve the best spinal position. The situation is often complicated by a pelvic tilt associated with the scoliosis, giving an apparent and sometimes a true leg length inequality.

A leg length inequality can produce a compensatory pelvic tilt, frequently leading to the development of tension higher in the back.

A kyphosis, or in its lesser degree, a rather more rounded thoracic spine than normal, can also lead to tension around the neck and shoulders. Its presence is really a contra-indication to a performing career in dance because there are no corrective measures. If at all marked, it is rarely if ever totally postural, although a bad posture can exaggerate the kyphotic appearance. The commonest underlying cause is Scheuermann's disease in adolescence. This is an osteochondritis of the growth plates at the upper and lower parts of each vertebral body. When the Scheuermann's disease finally settles with the cessation of growth, it may have left each of the vertebral bodies slightly wedge-shaped, narrower anteriorly, thus producing a forward curve of the spine (see **Section 5.5**).

Sometimes, and particularly during growth spurts, a child can apparently become mildly kyphotic but this is

5.2 Leading with the elbows and arms too far back. The dancer is also failing to hold her turn-out correctly. The tension in the neck muscle can be seen

5.3 The elbow drops and the control of the shoulder girdle no longer comes from a strong back and stable trunk correctable with suitable exercises and attention to posture and is, in any case, usually self-correcting.

TREATMENT

Treatment of the tension is by correction of the underlying fault. Often pain is present in the muscles concerned and frequently there is chest pain caused by spasm of the pectorals in particular, as well as being referred from the origins of the trapezius at the spinous processes and interspinous ligaments. Where there is muscle pain, initial treatment may be directed at relief of the muscle spasm and pain by the physiotherapist using massage and electrotherapy. In most causes of tension and especially in those with a scoliosis, breathing exercises should be taught. Upper chest breathers need education to use the whole chest and the diaphragm. Scoliotics need instruction to encourage the equal expansion of both sides of the chest as there is always a tendency for someone with a scoliosis to use the side of the chest on the convex aspect of the curve more than the other side of the chest. As a result, there is a gradual further collapse of the chest on the concave side and an increase in the postural component of the scoliosis. Also, in aiding correction as far as possible of the scoliosis, very significant benefit can be obtained by a suitable exercise programme to strengthen the muscles. In this context attention should be paid to the muscle groups in the legs. Frequently there is weakness of more than one group, resulting in an incorrect weight placement down at that level. Without correction here, a less satisfactory result will be obtained in the back and the chest.

5.3 Rib Injuries

In dancers injury to the lower ribs and/or costal cartilages is relatively common. It happens in vocational schools where students are learning partnering work, and to professionals attempting difficult partnered choreography. The male directs the movement by controlling the female pelvis. Mostly this is done by grasping the iliac crests with the whole hand. Lifting when possible is also around the pelvis, but if the grip slips his hands approach her lower ribs. At no point should he grab or grasp her trunk, but when this does happen fingers catch the oblique muscles anterolaterally, and the costal cartilages.

The costal cartilages are flattened bars of cartilage attached to the anterior ends of the ribs and extend up and forwards towards the sternum. The first seven pairs connect to the sternum, the eighth, ninth and tenth to the one above and the lowest two are short, ending in the muscular wall of the abdomen.

The cartilage can be disrupted with bruising to the surrounding tissue. A finger can cause a hernia in muscle which extremely painful. If a rib is affected more laterally the rib and its intercostal muscle will be bruised. Breathing deeply is painful along with extension and rotatory movements. The area should be carefully examined and if a rib fracture is suspected, an X-ray should be performed to confirm this. It will be two months before any partnering can be recommenced – well after all movement and palpation are pain-free. Taping to support the affected ribs can give some relief and reassurance, allowing some classwork to be continued. The taping should be removed at the end of the working day otherwise lung function can be impaired with the possible development of a chest infection.

Pas de deux technique requires careful teaching to avoid accidents. The use of the male's hands and the balance of arm, shoulder, back and thigh strength need to be understood in order to spread the strain. Core stability in the female is paramount or her trunk cannot be controlled by the male.

5.4 Scoliosis

This is a lateral curvature of a segment of the spine. This curvature is accompanied by a marked rotational element with the vertebrae rotating towards the concavity (Fig. 5.4). If it is very marked then aesthetically a professional career will be difficult. Therefore in the assessment of dancers the examiner is looking for relatively mild degrees of scoliosis which may not be immediately apparent on initial observation. The area affected by the curvature in the scoliosis is stiffer than normal. As most scolioses are in the thoracic spine, this in itself is frequently not of major importance if the scoliosis is only mild. However, in the lumbar region, the accompanying stiffness can make the whole spine too stiff to allow the movements required for ballet. The lumbar spine must have a good range of movement in flexion, extension and side flexion.

In the majority of cases the cause of a scoliosis is totally unknown. This is called an idiopathic scoliosis. Rarely nowadays a scoliosis is due to paralysis of a group or groups of muscles.

If the presence of a scoliosis is suspected, the student should be referred to an orthopaedic surgeon for an opinion. There are many different forms of treatment which can help the condition and may well be indicated in the individual case. If the scoliosis is mild, benefit can frequently be obtained by suitable exercises. Sometimes the use of an electrical muscle stimulator worn at night can bring about very marked

5.4 An X-ray of a scoliosis with the measurement lines drawn in. Here there is a 20° dorsal scoliosis and a 12° lumbar scoliosis. A scoliosis at a single level is more common. It is usually in the dorsal region of the spine

improvement in the degree of curvature. In more severe cases, mechanical bracing or surgery may be required. Spinal manipulations and massage will not cure a scoliosis but can relieve a degree of stiffness in joints and tightness in muscles.

The presence of even a marked scoliosis is not a contra-indication in itself to the child undertaking ballet classes. Dancing can even be helpful in exercising the scoliotic areas and in strengthening the muscles. The exercise from the ballet classes will be in addition to side shift and other exercises which may have been prescribed by the orthopaedic surgeon looking after the child as a patient. There are professional dancers who have achieved success in spite of a marked scoliosis without undue stiffness, but they are unusual. Even if the young dancer can manage the technical aspects of ballet, the presence of an obvious scoliosis may prevent them at auditions for vocational schools and companies.

Even in mild scolioses, difficulty can be experienced in centralising the line of weight-bearing and usually the weight is to one side, i.e. towards the apparently shorter side. As a result, groin, adductor and low back strains are common. Frequently the hamstrings on one side are tighter than the other and this can lead to hamstring injuries. The tightness arises because of the frequent presence of a pelvic tilt associated with a scoliosis but, once established, the tight hamstrings will

themselves repeatedly exert a rotational pull on the pelvis (**Section 5.21**). Very often, on the looser hamstring side a swayback knee may develop, causing its own particular difficulties (**Section 5.13**).

Because of the rotational element of the scoliosis, difficulties may be experienced with arm positions, causing muscle tension and strains around the shoulder girdle in attempting to achieve correct arm placements. In addition, in a dorsal scoliosis, the rib cage on the two sides is different, that on the concave side being compressed and with a decrease in volume.

The presence of a mild scoliosis which is not obvious cosmetically, may be suspected if the student appears to have difficulty achieving correct head positions; if there is one shoulder higher than the other; if there is a pelvic tilt or prominence of one side of the pelvis; a forward rotation of the pelvis on one side; or if there is a leg length discrepancy. Any of these factors calls for a careful examination of the spine.

A scoliosis will become apparent around the age of twelve and should be referred for a specialist opinion. Early treatment is always best.

TREATMENT

Treatment of the actual scoliosis is an orthopaedic problem. Exercises can certainly be beneficial in strengthening the muscle groups to decrease as much as possible the postural elements of the curve. Side shift exercises are helpful. The use of an electrical muscle stimulator at night really falls within the sphere of the treatment which will be ordered by the orthopaedic surgeon under whose care the child is.

The rehabilitation programme should start by strengthening the feet and leg muscles and by ensuring that the position is correct. If the legs and feet are not correct then all attempts to strengthen and align the pelvis and trunk will be unsuccessful.

5.5 Kyphosis

This is a stiff, flexed thoracic spine. There is already a primary curve at this level (Fig. 5.5) and a kyphosis is an increase in the curve beyond the normal limit (Fig. 5.6). It may arise as a result of Scheuermann's disease in childhood when, due to the osteochondritis affecting the end plates at the top and bottom of each vertebral body, these become somewhat wedge-shaped, narrower anteriorly, thus resulting in a curve. Frequently, however, there is no apparent cause for the kyphosis.

The presence of a kyphosis is aesthetically displeasing, but functionally, any damage or injury is produced in the lumbar region. As a result of the forward curve in the thoracic region, a compensatory

SECONDARY
CURVE

PRIMARY
CURVE

SECONDARY
CURVE

PRIMARY
CURVE

5.6A Line drawing showing a kyphosis in the dorsal region with a compensatory lumbar lordosis below it

5.6B An X-ray of a severe kyphosis

5.5 Diagram showing the primary and secondary curves. In foetal life, the whole spine is curved forwards in the direction of the primary curve. The secondary curves in the neck and lumbar regions gradually develop after birth and are in the opposite direction to the primary curve

lordosis is inevitable (see **Section 5.6** for the associated problems). Additionally, the head and neck have to be extended more than normally in order to allow the person to look forward horizontally.

With the presence of either a scoliosis or a kyphosis the resulting loss in mobility in these regions decreases the shock absorption of the spine as a whole. As a result, injuries of all types in the lumbar region become more frequent and the lumbar spine is constantly at risk. In the presence of a kyphosis, which inevitably leads to a compensatory lordosis, additional strain is placed on the lumbar spine as the dancer attempts to assume the extended positions required by dance technique.

TREATMENT

There is no specific treatment for a structural kyphosis. However, the posture can be helped by strengthening exercises for the thoracic spine extensors as well as the

5.7 Three lordotic postures from the side

abdominal muscles to decrease as much as possible any postural component of the curve. Stretches for the pectoral muscles may also help. During treatment, the weight position must be corrected as far as possible. With the compensatory lordosis the pelvis will be tilted forward and as a result of this the weight will be pushed back. As the kyphosis is fixed, and therefore the lordosis in this case cannot be completely controlled, full correction of the weight position will not be possible.

Due to the frequency of lumbar spine injuries associated with kyphoses, much attention must be given to trunk strengthening exercises to try to provide the maximum possible protection for the lumbar region of the back (see **Section 5.6** Treatment, p. 210).

The rehabilitation programme should start by strengthening the feet and leg muscles and ensuring that the position is correct. If the legs and feet are incorrect, all attempts to strengthen and align the pelvis and trunk will be unavailing.

5.6 Lordosis

This is the name given to the posture when the lumbar spine is hyper-extended or, in other words, very much hollowed. There is normally a lumbar curve but in a lordosis this normal curve is greatly exaggerated (Fig. 5.7). It is a postural condition and can be corrected, i.e. it is not a fixed curve as is the case with the scoliosis and kyphosis described earlier. However, in the presence of a kyphosis in the dorsal spine, correction is difficult (Fig. 5.8). Similarly, a fixed pelvic tilt due to marked tightness in the front of the hips will produce a similar difficulty in correction (Fig. 5.9).

5.8 Kyphotic posture with correction of the compensatory lordosis (which is showin in Fig. 5.6A). As a result the head pokes forwards and the neck has to be hyperextended

5.9 Pelvic tilt due to tightness at the fronts of the hips and a secondary lordosis

CAUSES

1. Thoracic kyphosis (**Section 5.5**).
2. A forward pelvic tilt due to tightness in the front of the hips (**Section 5.9**).
3. Weakness of the abdominal muscles.
4. Weakness of the gluteals. (3 and 4 usually go together, although not invariably so.) Weakness of the hamstrings is also commonly associated with weak gluteals.

5. Working overturned-out at the feet in relation to the hips will produce a forward tilt of the pelvis (Fig. 5.10). This may be due to a genuine limitation of turn-out at the hips or a failure to hold the available turn-out (**Section 5.7**).

6. Weakness of the external rotators and adductors produces a failure to hold the turn-out and results in the same problem as 5 (**Section 5.10**).

7. Swayback knees produce a compensatory pelvic tilt and a lordosis (Fig. 5.11) in order to bring the line of weight-bearing through the feet. Having been displaced backwards by the swayback knees being pushed back, the line of weight-bearing must be brought forward in order to maintain balance (**Section 5.13**).

8. A tibial bow (**Section 5.16**) produces weight-bearing more laterally and this makes it difficult to get a hold on the inner sides of the thighs. This results in a situation similar to that associated with adductors which are weak (**Section 5.10**) but given the attention, can be corrected.

9. Weakness of the forefeet (**Section 5.19**) causes the weight to be pushed back with similar consequences to those associated with other causes for the weight being back (**Section 5.21**).

10. Any other technical fault which causes the weight to be taken too far back will produce a compensatory lordosis.

11. Working with the arms too far back causes the upper trunk to tilt backwards and this will produce a compensatory lordosis in order to bring the weight forward. It is often accompanied by a forward poking chin, which is also part of an attempt to maintain balance (Fig. 5.12).

12. Tight shoes produce curling of the toes with the consequence that the weight will be pushed back, producing a lordosis.

13. In some dancers there appears to be a naturally occurring lordosis which, although initially postural and theoretically therefore correctable, can in practice prove almost impossible to improve or fully correct. In some of these people the lordosis, which has been present since they started to walk, can become at least partly fixed as they approach maturity. It is then uncorrectable, even when they lie flat on their backs and pull their knees up to their chests. Normally this manoeuvre rotates the pelvis and flattens the lumbar spine. If this does not occur, then it can be accepted that there is at least a degree of lordosis which is uncorrectable as the necessary mobility is lacking. It must be emphasised that the aim is to achieve the *normal lumbar curve* and not to flatten this curve out when working. This is as undesirable as an exaggerated curve or lordosis. However, unless the spine is supple enough to be able to attain a degree of posterior tilt it is not possible for the dancer to work easily as forward flexion of the trunk in the lumbar region cannot take place and forward bending can only occur at the hips.

14. Tight hamstrings may also contribute to a lordosis (**Section 5.12**).

5.10 Over-turned feet producing a forward tilt of the pelvis

5.11 Swayback knees producing a compensatory pelvic tilt and a lordosis

5.12 Lordosis because the arms are too far back. This also produces a forward-poking chin

CONSEQUENCES

These are the same as the consequences of the weight back situation (**Section 5.21**).

TREATMENT

This must be by correcting the cause of the lordosis whether this be weakness of muscle groups, faulty technique producing lordosis secondarily, or an incorrect weight-bearing line.

The rehabilitation programme will certainly be based on a programme of trunk strengthening exercises, as well as strengthening and balancing the various muscle groups in the lower limbs.

The rehabilitation programme should start by strengthening the feet and leg muscles and ensuring that the position is correct. If the biomechanics of the legs and feet are not correct, all attempts to strengthen and align the pelvis and trunk and control the lordosis will be unsuccessful.

5.7 Over-Turning

By this it is meant that the foot and lower leg are being turned out (externally rotated) beyond the degree of turn-out available at the hip joint (Fig. 5.13). The over-turned foot may reflect either an anatomical limitation of the degree of turn-out required by ballet technique, or it may be due to a lack of correct muscular control of the turn-out, therefore producing an apparent restriction in turn-out at the hips, with over-turned feet. Only too frequently the degree of turn-out being demanded may be too great to be realistic. Therefore

5.13 Over-turned feet in relation to the hips

they tend to drop into the lordotic position, thus weakening the trunk muscles. Very few dancers have flat turn-out (90° within each hip allowing the feet to be flat turned out) and even if they do, they cannot work like this because of the difficulty in achieving correct balance.

Much more disastrous than any of the above is the method of teaching which demands a flat 180° turn-out at the feet, despite the fact that the hips may not approach anything like this degree of external rotation. The results of this method of teaching may be

1. A marked pelvic tilt forward with the development of a lordosis.
2. Weakening of the trunk muscles, particularly the abdominals.
3. An increased rate of injury in the lumbar spine, including stress fractures. (On average it takes a bad teacher eight months to so weaken a previously adequately strong dancer that the risk of a serious back injury is imminent.)
4. General sequential weakening of the various muscle groups from above downwards – the abdominals, the back extensors, the latissimus dorsi (as the shoulders are back), the glutei, the hamstrings (especially the lateral hamstrings), the adductors and the vastus medialis, the lateral part of the calf muscle and the lateral intrinsic muscles of the feet. This in total produces complete imbalance of the legs. Most of these muscle groups are required in order to hold the turn-out so their gradually increasing weakness brought about by being made to work grossly over turned, causes increasing difficulty in holding the available turn-out. This becomes especially notice-able when they leave the barre to start centre work. During barre work the dancer will grip the barre tightly to give support in the unattainable (at the hips) flat, turned out position. Teachers who demand this flat turn-out demonstrate their ignorance of the mechanics of the body. Teachers must accept complete responsibility for injuries to their students and take very seriously a recurrent injury, or more than one of the same in the class. The situation described above is not only a cause of injuries but prevents the development of a good technique.

Unfortunately, many teachers who insist on a flat turn-out at the feet believe that they are following the Russian method of teaching. This is a double mis-understanding of the situation. Firstly, and importantly, the body types that are reaching this stage of training in the elite schools of Eastern Europe are chosen for their facility. Secondly, the ground work leading up to this method of teaching is quite different and far more thorough. As a result the child will be more mobile and much stronger before a nearly flat turn-out is required of him or her.

In the West where the selection of correct body types is less rigorous and demanding than in the Russian schools, it is quite wrong to try to follow the Russian method with students here. Only a small proportion will be able to cope satisfactorily with this method. The best teaching will follow a tried and tested teaching method, but always making allowances and adaptions for the individual physique.

The schools have two choices: either a much more rigorous selection of the correct body type, plus adequate preparatory groundwork in the training, or else accepting less satisfactory bodies (but good dancers) with the accompanying knowledge that a flat turn-out cannot be achieved without a high injury rate. Schools cannot have it both ways and a little more insight into the whole of the Russian method instead of a superficial and partial knowledge would greatly help matters.

Although a student or dancer will usually over-turn on both sides, the over-turning may sometimes be confined to one side only. Even if both sides are over-turned, frequently or even usually the over-turning will not be symmetrical but one side will be forced out to a greater extent than the other. The ability to over-turn lies in the use of friction between the foot and the floor. This friction can be increased by the use of rosin. It is impossible to over-turn if the foot is not on the floor and therefore control is lost on pointe and in jumping.

CONSEQUENCES

1. *Rolling*. This puts a strain on the great toe tending to push it into a valgus position (Fig. 5.14). This can cause damage to the capsule and ligament of the medial side of the joint, aggravated by actual local pressure there, which will occur as the rolled foot is pressed on the floor. Any underlying valgus deformity will be increased by the rolling, especially during work on demi-pointe, during relevés and during pointe work (Fig. 5.15). In the latter, the rolling will change during the relevé into a sickled out position with the weight medially through the foot. The situation can be complicated by the presence of lower tibial bows or swayback knees. In both these instances, the natural weight-bearing line is back and at demi-pointe the foot will tend to be sickled outwards (Fig. 5.16), i.e. the foot has the weight on the outer side. As the relevé continues the direction of sickling changes to the opposite situation so that the weight is medially when they reach full pointe (Fig. 5.17). Therefore, the observer may be misled if the dancer is only seen on demi-pointe. For further complications of rolling see **Section 5.18**.

2. *Injuries of the 1st metatarso-phalangeal joint*. These come about mainly as a result of the rolling but may

5.14 Over-turned feet with rolling and a valgus strain on the big toe

5.15 Over-turned foot on demi-pointe with valgus pressure on the big toe

5.16A Sickling on demi-pointe with the weight being transmitted down the medial side of the foot. Doctors and physiotherapists would refer to this as sickling *out* but dancers would usually call it sickling *in* (because of the direction that the ankle goes as opposed to the direction the foot takes)
5.16B Sickling on demi-pointe with the weight being transmitted down the lateral side of the foot. This is a precursor to sickling in the opposite direction when on full pointe (see Fig. 5.15)

5.18 Here the foot and ankle are compromised with friction between the foot and the floor created in holding the position

5.17 Sickling on full pointe with the weight being transmitted down the medial side of the foot

occur even if the rolling is corrected or absent. The weight will still be back due to over turning, the use of the wrong muscles and the friction of the floor. The injury may be due to valgus strain or to rotation of the great toe (**Section 3.22**).

3. *Clawing of the toes and intrinsic muscle weakness.* This is caused by the weight being back and the failure of the muscles in the hip and thigh to hold the turn-out. The toes claw in an attempt to hold on at floor level and this increases intrinsic weakness due to their lack of proper use and function (**Section 5.19**).

4. *Stress fractures* in the tibia and fibula can occur, in part due to the lack of shock absorption by the weak feet and in part by the rotational twist transmitted down the over-turned leg (**Sections 3.29** and **3.30**).

5. *Anterior Compartment Syndrome* can be induced for similar reasons (**Section 3.31**).

6. *Tibialis posterior tenosynovitis* occurs because of an attempt to correct the rolled feet at the foot and ankle level instead of at the hips (**Section 3.15**).

7. *Injuries of the medial side of the knee.* These may be tears of the medial meniscus or sprains of the medial ligament, both of which will occur as a result of the twist at the knee (**Sections 3.39–3.42**).

8. *Chondromalacia patellae and patellar tendinopathy.* These are both induced or aggravated because the rotation at the knee brings about lateral tracking of the patella (**Section 3.35**).

9. *Overuse of lateral hamstrings.* This is induced by rotation at the knee. The unequal pull then exerted by the lateral and medial hamstrings leaves the lateral meniscus more likely to sustain an injury.

The imbalanced hamstrings are also more likely to be injured (**Section 3.49**).

10. *The adductors* weaken because they do not function fully in the over-turned position. The adductors become more prone to injury due to the lack of stability of the pelvis by their own weakness, especially during grands battements when either adductor may be injured, i.e. that on the supporting side or that on the working side (**Sections 5.10** and **3.46**).

11. *Lordosis.* This will occur in over-turning as the pelvis rotates forward in an attempt to increase the available turn-out at the hips. In most people, any flexion at the hip joints will increase the apparent degree of external rotation available (**Section 5.6**). Associated with this will be a tightening at the fronts of the hips which may be real or apparent. This is aggravated by over action of the quadriceps (but not the medialis) which are used to grip in a weight back situation. As the rectus femoris crosses the front of the hip, it will also add to the forces causing the pelvis to rotate forward.

12. *Groin strains.* These are common, as a direct result of the over-turning coupled with the associated muscle weakness (**Section 3.47**).

TREATMENT

Basically the dancer should avoid turning the feet out further than the available turn-out at the hips.

In a student who has been over-turning, any of the above complications may need individual treatment and the various weak muscle groups will certainly need a considerable programme of strengthening exercises. A great amount of technical correction will be required to undo the harm caused by the previous bad teaching.

5.8 Restriction of Turn-out at the Hips

Everybody has an anatomical limit to their range of external rotation of the hips (i.e. turn-out). This range cannot be exceeded. In the young student, limitation

5.19 Frog position in an audition

5.21A Assessing turn-out accurately with the leg over the end of the couch, keeping the hip being examined fully extended. The other leg is flexed out of the way

5.21B Measuring internal rotation

5.20A Frog position – very good

5.20B Hips extended (as in standing position) and fully turned out (externally rotated). This demonstrates very well the great discrepancy which frequently occurs between an asssssment of turn-out in the frog position and the true turn-out when the dancer is standing

5.20C Hips extended and internally rotated, showing that the total joint range in rotation is full but that most of it is in internal rotation

due to ligament tightness can be gradually improved by correct working and gentle judicious stretching. This is more likely to be achieved before puberty.

Apparent limitation may be due to tightness at the fronts of the hips (**Section 5.9**) or frequently by weakness of the muscles controlling the turn-out – the deep external rotators of the hip and the adductors (**Section 5.10**).

For classical dance the lower limit of external rotation at the hip is about 45°. Anything less will tend to produce greater or lesser problems. The method of measurement of turn-out is particularly important. Only too frequently, particularly in auditions, one sees children being put into the frog position (Fig. 5.19) under the misunderstanding that the degree of turn-out is being assessed. In most people, the frog position will appear to have a very much greater range of turn-out than actually exists when the hips are fully extended due to the ligament configuration around the hip. The following series of photographs show how misleading the frog position can be when assessing turn-out (Fig. 5.20). It is when the hips are extended, i.e. when the person is standing up straight with the legs in line with the trunk, that they are in their normal working position for dancing. The method for assessing the degree of turn-out at each hip is shown in the accompanying photographs (Fig. 5.21). The hip which is not being measured is flexed . Care must be taken to make certain that the hip which is being assessed is held in the extended position as, if it is allowed to flex even a small amount, the apparent degree of turn-out can be increased markedly. Using this method 45° of turn-out (external rotation) is an acceptable minimum because when working, the lumbar spine is never flat and there is some forward rotation of the pelvis. However, it gives an excellent base line measurement which can be replicated accurately.

It is possible to measure turn-out with the dancer lying on his face but the results can be misleading unless the dancer is placed correctly (see Figs 5.22 and 5.23). In this position it is easier for the dancer to drop the lumbar spine into the lordotic posture, thus producing flexion of the hip and an apparent increase in the turn-out. Care must be taken to control this for accuracy. (Those who use this method suggest that 60° of external rotation is the acceptable minimum.) This method is of course easier to use in a studio and can give a teacher an idea of facility or restriction, and any marked difference between external and internal rotation.

The problems associated with a restriction of turn-out are those dealt with under over-turning (**Section 5.7**).

TREATMENT

The muscles controlling turn-out (see **Section 1.3** The Hip, p. 32) must be strengthened in order to control and hold the best available amount of turn-out. Additionally, many other groups may also require strengthening, notably the trunk, the glutei and the feet. Posture, weight position and weight transference must be corrected. Gentle and progressive stretching can be carried out under controlled conditions once the strengthening programme is under way. Stretching must not take place in the presence of weak muscles. In stretching, attention must be given to any tightness in the fronts of the hips.

Muscles must be stretched in the line in which they work and function. This is not necessarily in the longitudinal line of the limb.

The common method used, in the vain hope that turn-out is being stretched, is sitting or lying in the frog

position. In this situation the hips are flexed, nearly always giving an apparent increase in turn-out range. More important, this is not the position in which the hips are working when the dancer is standing or moving when turned out. He does this with the hips extended, i.e. standing up straight, apart from when going down into a plié or fondu at which time the hips are flexing. Lying in frogs is not stretching the actual structures which are tight. *The end results of various structures being tight can be restriction of turn-out.* It is necessary to assess and define which of the various structures associated with the turn-out are tight and then to stretch these individually. *Frequently, this means that the stretch is not in the actual direction of turn-out.* For instance, if there is tightness at the front of the hip, it is a cross pull on these structures which causes a limitation of turn-out but the actual stretch of these tissues must be longitudinal to their fibres and not, in this instance, in the actual direction of turn-out. This would be unproductive.

Additionally, it is of great importance to note that a well stretched muscle (not over-stretched) will contract much more efficiently and strongly.

5.9 Tightness at the Fronts of the Hips

As this implies, there is restriction of full extension of the hip joint, extension meaning carrying the leg backwards in relation to the trunk.

It is assessed by the following method (Fig. 5.24).

The tightness may lie in any of the anterior structures. The most superficial is the rectus femoris portion of the quadriceps. The rectus femoris crosses the front of the hip joint. It and the other three

5.22 External rotation (turn-out)

5.23 Internal rotation (turn-in)

5.24A Assessing tightness at the front of the hip, this photograph shows the normal range required for a dancer

5.24B A tight hip with limited extension

components of the quadriceps can be part of a generalised tightness. Also superficially placed is the tensor faciae latae which will often be tight. Deeper, the restriction may be caused by the ilio-psoas. Restriction of external rotation or turn-out is an overall complication of tightness of the front of the hip. Additionally, pectineus and adductor brevis as well as the anterior capsule of the hip can all play a part in the tightness at the front of the joint.

CAUSES

Although the tightness frequently exists in its own right it may be precipitated or aggravated by any one of the following.
1. Lordosis, when the forward tilt of the pelvis will gradually lead to tightening of the anterior structures (**Section 5.6**).
2. Any technical or anatomical fault which causes a forward rotation of the pelvis resulting in a secondary shortening of the structures in the front of the hips. If long-standing it can progress to an actual tightness or contracture.
3. Tightness of the hamstrings will lead to a tendency to work with the knees very slightly flexed thus preventing the hip from fully straightening (**Section 5.12**).

EFFECTS

1. The production of a lordotic posture and all its associated problems (**Section 5.6**).
2. Restriction of turn-out. This may be brought about by two factors:
   (a) *actual limitation* as occurs when the ilio-psoas or other strictures which limit external rotation are tight, or
   (b) *apparent limitation* by prevention of the external rotators from acting effectively in turning out

TREATMENT

Initially this is by exercise of all the weakened muscle groups where applicable (trunk, hamstrings, adductors and gluteals, etc.). Then when all these groups are becoming stronger and alongside the continuing strengthening programme any tight groups or areas, e.g. tensor fasciae latae, hamstrings, quadriceps or adductors are stretched out gently.

In general, these stretching techniques of the different groups and structures should be well understood by the physiotherapist and so detailed descriptions have been omitted. However, it cannot be repeated often enough that stretching should be gentle and gradual and never forcible, great care being taken not to traumatise any tissues otherwise scarring and contracture will occur.

5.10 Weakness of Adductors

These are the muscles which pull the thighs together. They help to hold the turn-out position. In dance they need to be very strong as they are in opposition to the abductors. There has to be balance between opposind groups of muscles in order to produce stability. They are naturally, in the average person, rather a weak group and they can be weakened further by overstretching. Weakness can also have the opposite effect and lead to the adductors becoming tight.

CAUSES

The most important cause of weakness of the adductors is the execution of an incorrect technique.
1. Sitting in the hip.
2. Rolling (**Section 5.18**).

3. Weight too far back (**Section 5.21**).
4. Over-turning (**Section 5.7**).
5. Swayback knees (**Section 5.13**).
6. Weak forefeet preventing correct weight placement (**Section 5.19**).
7. Lordosis (frequently a postural fault in children which becomes a technical fault if the teacher fails to correct it) (**Section 5.6**).

TREATMENT

This is by exercising in order to strengthen the adductors. They should be stretched gently if tight, and technique should be corrected – all else is pointless if a fault in technique remains.

5.11 Quadriceps Insufficiency

This means weakness of the quadriceps complex (vastus medialis, vastus intermedius, vastus lateralis and rectus femoris). This weakness may be total weakness where all muscle groups in the body are weak; a relative weakness compared with other muscle groups; a differential weakness with one leg compared to the other; a weakness within the complex where one part is weak compared to the others. This latter occurs mainly and commonly where the vastus medialis is differentially weak compared with the other three components.

CAUSES

1. Swayback knees are a potent cause of quadriceps insufficiency in dancers because of a failure to pull up, which results in the weight being allowed to remain too far back. The dancer will then relax into the posterior capsule and the muscles do nothing to support the knee (**Section 5.13**).
2. Tight hamstrings which cause the dancer to work with slightly flexed knees will weaken the quadriceps by making them work inadequately. It is also frequently seen that some people walk and stand without ever fully extending the knees and this is particularly noticeable in women who wear very high heels (**Section 5.12**).
3. After even a minor knee injury the quadriceps will waste and weaken within two to three days so a special effort will be required to strengthen them again, together with other associated or affected muscle groups. In this context special care should be taken to ensure that the vastus medialis is built up and that the quadriceps strength is balanced out between the two legs.

RESULTS

1. Anterior knee pain (**Section 3.33**). Note particularly

that lack of balance between various muscles which make up the whole quadriceps (especially vastus medialis weakness) leads to lateral tracking of the patella.
2. An increased risk of knee injury, notably meniscal damage (**Section 3.42**). Also it can lead to rupture of the quadriceps tendon or the patellar tendon (**Section 3.44**). A teacher who suddenly demonstrates a step requiring an explosive contraction of the quadriceps, e.g. a big jump, is particularly at risk.
3. Weakness of the vastus medialis prevents full locking of the knee in extension (**Section 5.11**). This can lead to a decrease in use of and a tightening of the lateral hamstrings (**Section 5.12**).
4. Calf over-development will occur because the calf muscles are taking more of the load in landing and expending more force in jumping. This in turn can lead to an Achilles tendonitis (**Section 3.10**) and an anterior compartment syndrome (**Section 3.31**) as well as anterior foot strains.

TREATMENT

This is by strengthening exercises. Balancing out within the quadriceps is essential. This usually calls for extra work on strengthening the vastus medialis. This part of the quadriceps complex contracts effectively in the last 15° of extension (straightening) of the knee. Balancing out between the two legs is required. There should be correction of any technical fault which may have lead to the original weakness.

5.12 Tightness of the Hamstrings

CAUSES

1. The hamstrings can be naturally tight to the extent that many people cannot lift their legs with the knees straight to a 90° angle. As the hamstrings cross behind the knee flexion of the knee will allow full hip flexion to take place even in the presence of tight hamstrings. The flexion of the knee relaxes the hamstring muscles. As will be recalled from **Section 1** on Anatomy, the hamstrings act as hip extensors and knee flexors.
2. The hamstrings tend to tighten as a normal course of affairs during any growth spurt, as do all other muscle groups. This is because the bones grow during growth spurts more rapidly than the soft tissues. This tightening will ease up and the student will regain the previous flexibility once the growth spurt has stopped.
3. Working with the weight back from any of its many causes will tend to cause a forward rotation of the pelvis (**Section 5.21**). The knees tend to flex slightly

and the hamstrings then weaken and tighten. In particular, the lateral hamstrings tighten and weaken in this situation. Associated with the weakening and tightening of the hamstrings there are frequently weak quadriceps due to a failure to lock the knee. In over-turning, the hamstrings cannot be utilised to their full extent because the pelvis becomes tipped forwards. Also the twist at the knee will cause an imbalance between the medial and lateral hamstrings with differential weakening and tightening.

RESULTS

1. Any tightness will aggravate the weight back situation which may in itself have been the precipitating factor, so there can be a vicious circle of deterioration (**Section 5.21**).
2. Tightness, of course, predisposes to hamstring injuries, both pulls and tears (**Section 3.49**).
3. Unequal tightness (medial versus lateral) can aggravate rotational pulls on the knee when it is partly flexed and therefore predisposed to meniscal damage (**Sections 3.42** and **3.43**).
4. Like quadriceps insufficiency and weakness, tightness of the hamstrings will put an overload on the calf muscles with resulting muscle injuries and Achilles tendon problems. (**Sections 3.10** and **3.11**).
5. Hamstrings which are not activated correctly will lead to tightening of the tensor fasciae latae as this muscle tries to stabilise the pelvis. This overwork laterally will spread to the lateral quadriceps, and as a direct result of this, lateral tracking of the patella will occur and then anterior knee pain (**Section 3.33**). This lateral tracking cannot be fully corrected by merely quadriceps medialis exercises and build-

up without first dealing with hamstring tightness and weakness and stretching the tensor fasciae latae.

TREATMENT

Correct the underlying causes, e.g. weight placement and technique; strengthen all weak groups and gently stretch out the tight areas. As in other situations treatment will be ineffective if the technical faults remain uncorrected.

5.13 Swayback Knees

This name is given to knees which hyperextend beyond neutral (neutral is when the line between the thigh and the shin is 180°). Hyperextension from that point can be as much as 20° or even more (Fig. 5.25).

CAUSES

This hyperextension or swayback is a naturally occurring situation in anyone who is fairly loose-jointed and is within the range of normal variation from one individual to the next. It can however be aggravated by incorrect working.

The question is often raised as to whether ballet training causes swaybacks. This is almost certainly not the case. As such knees give a very pleasing line aesthetically in the working leg, students with swaybacks (among other attributes) will tend to be preferentially selected, as evidenced by the large number of dancers with swayback knees. However, having said that, there is no doubt that bad teachers may aggravate and increase the amount of swayback by allowing the dancer to push the knee back on the

5.25A Swayback knees, from the front

5.25B Swayback kneeds from the side

supporting leg instead of teaching him to pull up with the thighs and then keep the knee in neutral.

RESULTS

The most important feature of swayback knees is the creation of the weight back situation, together with all its problems which have been mentioned so repeatedly. Swayback knees are, together with weak forefeet, the most important and potent cause of the weight back situation (**Section 5.21**).

Weight back and swayback knees will lead to the adoption of a lordotic posture and working with the arm line too far back. Associated with these is a marked tendency for these dancers to be poor breathers, this weakness being related to the faulty trunk posture. They will be upper chest breathers and this will cause upper trunk tension.

TREATMENT

Exercises are given to strengthen all the weak groups which will be in particular the adductors, vastus medialis, hamstrings and gluteals. In the lower leg the deep calf muscles will be tight and weak and will need strengthening. Swaybacks are always associated with weak (often fexible) feet, so much attention needs to be paid to strengthening the intrinsic muscles.

Alongside this the trunk muscles, particularly the abdominals (transverse, cross and longitudinal fibres), the trunk extensors and latissimus dorsi need to be strengthened and the lordotic posture corrected. Breathing exercises using lateral expansion are necessary.

Only too often treatment and technical correction are confined to the knee region with total neglect of the feet and even more often of the trunk. In these cases the weight back will persist with a continuation of the dancer's problems often leading him to the wrong assumption that the treatment received was incorrect, whereas the true situation is that the treatment was not extensive or widespread enough to encompass the whole situation. Unfortunately, any condition that is only partially corrected due to insufficient or too localised treatment tends to lead the dancer to assume that any treatment received was wrong rather than inadequate.

TRAINING SWAYBACK KNEES

If the student with hyperextended knees is worked with the heels touching in first position she feels as if her knees are bent with little control. The swayback knee only feels straight and stable when it is locked into hyperextension with the heels well apart. This type of knee has to be trained slowly to engage the quadriceps, especially vastus medialis when the knee is straight – not only in hyperextension. Exercises sitting on the floor with outstretched legs and engaging the

quadriceps without allowing the heels to leave the floor, can stimulate this control. The student should be placed with the heels far enough apart, standing in first, to allow the quadriceps to function with stability in the knees, without locking back. As the knees become stronger the gap can close more.

If the adductors are used well, turn-out is retained but it is impossible to lock back into the knees. Locking back makes the femur turn in and the adductors relax. Control of the knees is then lost. There are no hard-and-fast rules as each physique should be worked to its own needs. In fifth position the hyperextended knee is even more unstable, but if the knee has been strengthened in earlier grades and is proprioceptively aware, the knee finds its stability patterns in more crossed positions.

5.14 Tight Calf Muscles

The gastrocnemius is the superficial calf muscle that takes its origin from the femoral condyles above the knee joint. It provides the dynamic, explosive force for jumping. The soleus arises from the posterior surface of the tibia and fibula and is more a postural muscle recruited to balance the body weight over the centre of the foot. Both muscles insert into the Achilles tendon which inserts into the calcaneus. These are the main plantarflexors of the ankle. These muscles tighten and restrict ankle movement for different reasons.

CAUSES

Because of the demands of classical ballet – pointe-work and jumping in the female roles and grand allegro in male work – the calf complex is often overworked and becomes shortened and tight if not systematically stretched and maintained.

It is thought that a minimum of 10° of dorsiflexion of the ankle with the knee extended is necessary to allow normal biomechanics of the foot.

Sometimes tightness accompanies swayback knees that are not corrected and efficient weight placement is disturbed. The weight is held too far back on the heels. Instead it should be distributed between the heel and forefoot with a controlled knee, or the calf complex cannot work properly. The calf becomes weaker and the opposing muscles of the shin (anterior compartment /dorsiflexors) overwork in an effort to pull the leg over the foot for balance. This can be seen in the tendons (tibialis anterior, extensor hallucis longus and extensor digitorum longus) standing out at the front of the ankle. Tension here inhibits the depth of the plié and the calf is never fully stretched. The swayback knee must be corrected (**Section 5.13**) if technique is to progress.

A sequel to this can be an anterior compartment syndrome (see **Section 3.31**) with an overworked group of muscles and serious consequences.

Shoes that are too short can lead to tightening of the calf because the toes curl – flex at the IP joints – thus the forefoot cannot weight-bear properly with strong, straight toes and efficient use of the intrinsic muscles. The weight is pushed back on to the heels again with tension at the front of the ankle. Shoe size should be checked regularly in young dancers, and even professionals should be fitted each year as the foot continues to change as the career progresses. Foot intrinsic exercises should also continue throughout.

The Achilles tendon can be irritated by tight calves, as can the Achilles bursa.

A period of working on a hard floor can overwork the calf complex, exacerbating all lower-limb problems (and severely depleting the ranks of a company in a short time).

Dancers do not realise their calves have become tight as it can happen slowly, and so they should all have a 'calf regime' as ongoing maintenance.

If the calf is tight, the landing from relevés and jumps is adversely affected. By over-pronating, unlocking the mid-tarsal joint and dorsiflexing the forefoot on the rearfoot, the plié deepens. However, from this position the foot cannot recover in time to push off effectively again. This disadvantaged situation predisposes the dancer to metatarsal and tibial stress, and tendon strain.

TREATMENT

The calf muscles must be stretched regularly with a flexed (to access soleus) and extended knee (to access gastrocnemius). This is convenient to do on a small 45° ramp supplied in the dance studio. Thirty-second

5.26 Stretching gastrocnemius   5.27 Stretching soleus

holds post-exercise are required to lengthen and aid recovery. Calves should be stretched and 'drained' at the end of the last rehearsal. Lying with the legs up the wall relieves and drains the calves of metabolites built up from exercise. Contrast baths for hot and cold (two minutes each, four times), and draining (ten minutes) at the end of the day can help. Massage to clear accumulated waste products of exercise from the calf can help. Stretching in straight leg raise can mobilise neural structures also, which should not be forgotten in attempts to return muscle to normal length.

Strengthening can be as simple as daily regime of heel raises for the calf and regular intrinsics exercises for the foot should be included (see exercises on p. 192).

5.15 Tight Achilles Tendons

Although this expression is in common usage what is, in fact, meant is tightness of the calf muscle and Achilles tendon complex and not just the tendon alone. Frequently the tightness is confined to the gastrocnemius muscle so that when the knee is flexed, allowing the gastrocnemius to relax, the ankle can be dorsiflexed freely, showing that the soleus is not tight. (Remember that the gastrocnemius takes its origin from the lower end of the femur and therefore crosses behind the knee, whereas the soleus muscle which lies deep to the gastrocnemius takes its origin below the knee joint.)

CAUSES

As with tight hamstrings the tightness can merely be part of a general tightness, although occasionally it may appear to be confined to the calf and Achilles tendon area. If this type of tightness is structural it can only be helped to a very limited extent.

Far more often the tightness which seems to be present when working is only apparent, so that when the foot and ankle are dorsiflexed passively a full range is obtained. Therefore this type of 'tightness' is due to faulty technique, usually associated with weakness of various muscle groups. It often accompanies swayback knees and weight back. When the weight is pushed onto the back of the heel instead of being distributed between the heel and the forefoot the calf muscles cannot work properly or be stretched out fully when weight-bearing. Weight back also tends to weaken the calf muscles and this can be accompanied by tension and tightening in them because of their lack of strength in a controlled relaxation situation.

If the weight is back the dancer cannot utilise the full depth of the plié. When trying to do so, visible tension is present in the dorsiflexors of the ankle and this can be seen to be obviously prominent at the front of the ankle in this case.

Shoes that are too short can lead to this happening because the toes are curled up, pushing the weight back. This happens to boys more than girls and may be the only cause of the weight back, without any other underlying anatomical or technical problem.

Anterior knee pain (**Section 3.33**) can be associated with a tightening of the calf and the Achilles tendon complex. This is primarily brought about by the weight being back, in which case the quadriceps are used as a brake when jumping rather than using the calf muscles and quadriceps equally. It is more common in boys because they are used to much bigger jumps. As the calf is under-used it will tend to tighten and this may then lead to an Achilles tendonitis (**Section 3.10**) as well as all the various problems described in the section on anterior knee pain (**Section 3.33**).

Achilles tendinopathy (**Section 3.10**) and Achilles bursitis (**Section 3.12**) are both frequently associated with tightness and/or weakness of the calf muscles (not only when there is anterior knee pain). Following on from this there can then develop anterior compartment syndrome (**Section 3.31**) and stress fractures of the tibia (**Section 3.30**). All these problems being greatly aggravated by solid floors.

TREATMENT

Strengthening first and then gentle stretching of the calf muscles must be carried out (the actual Achilles tendon cannot be stretched). The condition requires technical faults to be identified and corrected as much as or more than almost any other technical or anatomical problem. Together with its associated Achilles tendonitis and bursitis it is probably the commonest source of apparent treatment failures.

Tight Achilles Tendons and Jumping

A naturally tight calf and Achilles complex that allows only a shallow plié can be difficult to deal with if the teacher has unrealistic aims. These physiques often have a good, natural jump. However, the dancer with a short Achilles finds it difficult, if not impossible, to land with the heels down, as advocated by many texts and teaching courses. Recognising the physique is the first step. The second is to be sure that weight placement and posture are correct. The third is to observe closely the landing mechanics and shock absorption. If the landing is smooth and subsequent take-off unhindered, although the heel is not in contact with the floor throughout the landing, it is best to leave well alone and not interfere with a natural jump. It is demoralising for a student to read for three years in a report, 'Must get the heels down', and then progress to

a professional career never having 'got the heels down'. (If a report repeats itself it would suggest that the blame lies with the teacher.)

In the landing, trying to get the heels down pulls the weight over the back of the heel and overactivates the dorsiflexors of the shin in an effort to deepen the plié. Subsequent take-off is disturbed because after all you do not take off from the heel, you take off by pushing from the forefoot.

Improving eccentric strength of the foot can slow down the descent before the end of the plié is reached. This can help with timing and control and smooth out shock absorption problems. However, the mechanics of a movement may well be different if the structure is different – in this case a tight Achilles restricting a normal depth of plié.

5.16 Tibial Bow

Although the tibia has a natural mild curve, which is convex laterally, this can commonly be exaggerated when it is known as a tibial bow. The bow can affect the whole length of the tibia or, more usually, the lower third (Fig. 5.28).

CAUSES

This is an anatomical variation of normal growth. Other causes such as Vitamin D deficiency are extremely rare nowadays in affluent societies.

RESULTS

Most of the problems are brought about because the ankle joint is slightly angled in relation to the centre line of the leg (Fig. 5.29). As a natural result of this the foot is rolled when standing flat. Dancers have to work very much harder to hold the turn-out and not to over turn, otherwise this rolling becomes greatly exaggerated. They need to work conscientiously on the inner side of thigh exercises.

Stress injuries of the lower tibia and fibula (**Sections 3.29** and **3.30**) are more common as a result of the abnormal foot posture produced by the bow. In addition, soft tissue problems around the lower fibula occur.

When the foot is pointed it is sickled in naturally and this needs correction to line the foot up with the femur rather than sickling the foot outwards to improve the line. Similarly, when on demi-pointe the foot will tend to assume the same sickle position until corrected. On pointe the dancer finds it very hard to rise into the right position and may sickle in either direction, much depending upon toe length variations and foot strength or weakness. These latter factors contribute towards the

5.28A The whole tibial bow

5.28B The lower tibial bow

5.29 The lower tibial bow. The foot on the left of the photograph is aligned with the leg as a whole. The foot on the right is aligned with the lower end of the tibia and the ankle. In the presence of lower tibial bows the dancer has of necessity to work with the foot aligned with the leg

greater tendency for stress fractures of the 2nd metatarsal to occur (**Section 3.18**) with tibial bows. In the turned-out position the outwards bowing becomes a backwards bowing. Viewed from the side the weight looks as though it is back, but in fact this is only because of the leg shape. As long as weight placement through the foot is correct and spinal position is good, a satisfactory posture has been achieved.

TREATMENT

A great deal of exercise is required to strengthen the adductors, the gluteals and the hamstrings to give stability in the upper leg. Work is required to strengthen the calf muscle equally. Frequently there is, as a consequence of the faulty foot position, weakness of the lateral part of the calf which tends to be present because of the overwork of the medial portion. Exercise to strengthen the intrinsic muscles of the feet are essential. Accompanying this, technical help is required to gain the hold of the turn-out and adjust the weight-bearing line through the leg. Once that is achieved it will have to be followed with correction of the foot position to the optimum. The foot position correction cannot be carried out before the upper part of the leg is correct. Any attempts to do so merely compound the problem.

5.30A and B Showing the correct use of adductor and gluteal muscles

5.31 Correct use of turn-out

5.32 The foot naturally follows the line of the tibia – an unattractive line

5.33 The correctly adjusted line

5.34 The foot adjusts to correct the line

5.35A Lateral of a normal ankle
5.35B Lateral of an ankle with a large posterior tubercle of the talus
5.35C Lateral of an ankle with an os trigonum
5.35D Lateral of an ankle with an exostosis in the dorsum of the os calcis

5.17 Posterior Impingement at the Ankle Joint

This is means an interference with full plantarflexion at the joint due to a bony prominence impinging between the dorsum of the os calcis and the posterior articular margin of the tibia (Fig. 5.35). The causes for this are an os trigonum or a large posterior tubercle of the talus or, more rarely, a bony prominence or exostosis on the dorsum of the posterior part of the os calcis or finally an osteophyte on the posterior margin of the tibial articulas surface. This latter is an acquired prominence which comes as a result of repeated minor injuries and early degenerative change. The first three are situations with which the dancer is born and occur normally in a certain percentage of the population.

Although the os trigonum has been described by anatomists and given its own name as a separate little bone occurring at the back of the ankle in some 14–15 per cent of the population, studies of sections of the os trigonum, in cases where this has necessitated removal in dancers, suggest that at least some are in fact stress fractures which have occurred in the large posterior tubercle of the talus. It may well be that in every case the os trigonum is a stress fracture of the posterior tubercle and was not at birth a separate bone. However, as far as the dancer is concerned, whether or not this is the case is purely academic.

CAUSES

The symptoms are produced by the presence of a piece of bone interfering with the full rotation of the talus in the ankle mortice during plantarflexion. As the talus rotates towards the plantarflexed position (or full pointe) the heel bone or os calcis rises towards the posterior articular margin of the tibia. The bony prominence projecting beyond the posterior angle of the talus comes between the dorsum of the os calcis and the posterior articular margin of the tibia. When this happens the capsule and the underlying synovium will be squeezed between the two bony surfaces and these soft tissues are the source of the pain. When this local pressure is repeated local swelling develops and this is followed by thickening of the soft tissues. The symptoms will steadily increase and pointing of the foot becomes more difficult and painful.

Symptoms are unusual before the mid-teens. It is not until this time that the student has achieved the maximum natural point and therefore any further plantarflexion of the ankle is prevented by the bony block. Also about this time in a professional dance school the amount and pressure of work is increasing greatly. As a result the soft tissues do not have time to settle between one class and the next as would happen in students who were only doing one or two classes a week. The condition tends to be far more common in girls who are working for a far better pointed foot and who are dancing a lot of the time on pointe. However, in boys who are putting in efforts at big jumps or having to rise onto three-quarter pointe there may be a precipitation of symptoms. Before this stage in their career the amount and pressure of work has usually been insufficient for a full pointe to have been developed. It is only gradually that stretching of the soft tissues has occurred and has allowed maximum rotation of the talus into plantarflexion. Even when there is an os trigonum or similar bony prominence, in many instances, despite the mild limitation of full plantarflexion at the ankle joint, the mid-tarsal region will have been mobile enough to have produced compensation and a satisfactory pointing of the foot. In these instances symptoms do not usually develop.

SYMPTOMATOLOGY

1. Usually the dancer complains of a painful Achilles tendon and general discomfort behind the ankle and around the Achilles tendon area. This tends to increase with work and settles with rest.
2. Pain over the anterior and antero-lateral aspect of the ankle is also common and this may be accompanied by swelling. The attempts at improving the pointe throws a strain on the antero-lateral aspect of the ankle and the anterior capsule, hence the pain.
3. Recurrent calf muscle strains, usually around the region of the musculo-tendinous junction, are not uncommon and they may be accompanied by more or less pain around the Achilles tendon and the posterior part of the ankle (**Section 3.10**).
4. Sometimes the student will present with pain under the plantar aspect of the foot brought about by straining to pointe the foot. Very frequently the dancer will curl the toes in an effort to improve the pointe causing more congestion at the back of the ankle.
5. Only rarely do the dancers complain of very well localised pain at the back of the ankle joint itself.

Clinical examination will reveal localised tenderness at the back of the ankle joint and frequently the lump of the bony prominence can actually be felt. X-rays will show the presence of either a large posterior tubercle of the talus or an os trigonum or, far less commonly, a prominence on the dorsum of the posterior part of the os calcis. Occasionally a degenerative-type osteophyte will be seen. However, it is important to emphasise that the presence of any of these does not mean they are the cause of the patient's symptoms. Only too frequently the symptoms are precipitated by weakness of the intrinsics, by lack of proper control of the ankle and foot and by general weakness of the muscles around the lower leg and foot.

TREATMENT

Initially, every effort should be made to relieve the symptoms by conservative measures. Strengthening up the muscle groups and the intrinsic muscles together with local treatment such as interferential therapy may be sufficient. Only if this fails should an operation be considered in order to remove the prominent piece of bone (Fig. 5.36).

If operation is undertaken it is essential that the aftercare is treated seriously. The leg should be elevated until the swelling has settled. Early exercises are instituted both in order to retain the increased plantar-flexion or pointing that has been gained by the operation and also to prevent the scar tissue contracting at the back of the ankle which has been the site of the operation. Walking can be allowed as soon as the foot can be dorsiflexed to the neutral position but the walking should be limited and the foot kept well elevated in order to decrease any tendency for swelling. Once the stitches have been removed treatment should

5.36A An X-ray showing an os trigonum just about to impinge on the posterior articular margin of the lower end of the tibia. Remember that soft tissues (synovius and capsule in this case) are being trapped and squeezed between the two bones. These soft tissues cannot be seen on an X-ray

5.36B Os trigonum with the ankle in neutral dorsiflexion/plantarflexion showing the large distance between the os trigonum and the posterior articular margins of the lower end of the tibia. Comparison with Fig. 5.36A gives an excellent impression of the actual range of movement which occurs at the ankle joint (a hinge joint)

5.36C An X-ray of the same patient following removal of the os trigonum

5.37A Rolling, shown without a shoe

5.37B The effect on the foot is less obvious in a shoe although it still occurs to the same extent

be directed at reduction of any swelling, general strengthening of the intrinsic muscles of the foot and of all the muscle groups controlling the foot and ankle. The ankle joint should be actively mobilised during the whole phase of treatment but passive mobilisation should in general be avoided.

If the treatment has been efficiently carried out the dancer should be fit by the end of four weeks to start a gentle barre and work from there for a gradual return to class. During this period he will also need some technical help and correction. Even after the dancer has returned to full work a careful follow-up should be continued for a minimum of six months as during this period there is usually a tendency for some contraction to occur in the tissues at the back of the ankle and this will result in a gradual decrease in the depth of the plié. The follow-up is required in order to treat any suggestion of contracture by vigorous and active exercises and probably also some passive stretching. When stretching the foot in the plié it is extremely important that the posterior stretch is evenly applied and that one or other side is not allowed to become tight.

5.18 Rolling/Pronating

The nature of rolling is best seen in the accompanying photograph (Fig. 5.37).

CAUSES

1. Weak intrinsic muscles in the feet (**Section 5.19**) and weak lower leg muscles which can occur normally during a period of rapid growth make the occurrence of rolling almost inevitable. In this instance the rolling normally ceases after the growth spurt has ended.
2. Over-turning (**Section 5.7**). There is a very fine division between adequate turn out and over turning. Once the dancer has gone past the former and starts to over-turn then rolling at the foot is inevitable, producing many faults.
3. Incorrect teaching of placement and the resulting over turning can lead to rolling. Certainly rolling is a natural consequence of the weight back situation and it becomes a compensatory mechanism in trying to maintain balance (**Section 5.21**).
4. Failure to adjust to a raked stage may also lead to rolling.

RESULTS

1. The turn-out is not under correct control because when the foot is rolled the weight is back and as a result the muscles around the hip cannot be correctly held. There will also be a tendency for the dancer to adopt a lordotic posture (**Section 5.6**).
2. A strain is exerted on the inner (medial) side of the knee (**Sections 3.39** and **3.42**).
3. There is a lack of adequate function of the calf muscles and of the peronei. The tibialis anterior and tibialis posterior become more liable to strain. Tendonitis can be the end result, particularly in the tibialis posterior (**Section 3.15**).
4. Damage to the lateral ligament of the ankle can occur because it becomes crushed on the flat foot and stretched on the rise because on rising the foot will go in the opposite direction to the rolling in order to maintain balance (**Section 3.1**).
5. Strain of the structures along the medial border of the foot, strain of the longitudinal arch and of the plantar fascia in its medial part are all associated with rolling (**Section 3.21**).
6. Because the majority of the weight is taken on the medial part of the foot the great toe takes most of the strain. This causes sprains of the capsule of the lst metatarso-phalangeal joint (**Section 3.22**), sesamoiditis (**Section 3.23**) (these two little bones lie under the lst metatarsal head) and frequently a twist in the great toe which can finally end with a permanent rotation at the metatarso-phalangeal joint, and severe valgus strains occur, thus aggravating any tendency towards a hallux valgus deformity (**Sections 3.22** and **3.24**). In the longer term this valgus pressure (i.e. pressure from the medial side directed laterally) can cause some valgus deformities of all the toes and of the distal part of the forefoot.
7. Continued incorrect weight transference leads to stress fractures of the metatarsals – mainly the 2nd (**Section 3.18**).
8. The rolling will cause not only a valgus posture in the great toe but will also cause a flexion at the interphalangeal joint of the toe with a hyperextension at the metatarso-phalangeal joint and, following that, an increased tension in the extensor hallucis longus tendon and an extensor hallucis longus tendonitis (**Section 3.18**).

TREATMENT

Identification and correction of all the underlying technical faults and strengthening exercises for all the weakened muscle groups is essential. This can commonly require exercise regimes from the trunk downwards. Although the treatment is relatively easy it can be very time-consuming for the dancer but in the long term is a protective measure and will save a great deal of injury time in the future.

5.19 Weak Intrinsic Muscles of the Feet

These are the small muscles which maintain the transverse arch and allow the toes to be extended at the interphalangeal joints while they are being flexed at the metatarso-phalangeal joints. They also spread the toes and pull the toes together (adduction and abduction). When correctly used they prevent clawing of the toes.

RESULTS

1. Weak intrinsic muscles interefere with the correct transmission of weight through the foot, the result

of which is that the weight is almost entirely taken on the heel instead of being distributed between the forefoot and the heel (**Section 5.21**).

2. On pointe the toes cannot be held extended (straight) in the absence of strong intrinsic muscles and they will claw up in the shoes. At the extreme the dancer will be on pointe on the knuckles of the toes. This is known in America as 'knuckling'. Also on pointe the weight will be pushed back (**Section 5.21**) and as a result there is a greatly increased tension in the structures at the back of the ankle, notably producing an Achilles tendinopathy (**Section 3.10**) and bursitis (**Section 3.12**) and/or a tibialis posterior tendinopathy (**Section 3.15**), depending on the individual build of the dancer. A small os trigonum which would otherwise have been symptomless can start to cause pain and problems.

3. On jumps or landing or during relevés there is an incorrect weight transference through the foot because of the weakness of the forefoot. The landing will be heavy with little shock absorbance or eccentric strength and the weight will be back (**Section 5.21**). If a jump is started with the weight incorrectly placed the landing will also have an incorrect weight placement, frequently leading to shin (**Section 3.30**) and knee injuries (**Sections 3.33**, **3.38**, **3.39** and **3.42**).

TREATMENT

Intrinsic foot exercises and correction of technique, together with correction of weight placement, are the essentials of treatment. Inspect shoes in order to make sure that they are fitting well and giving adequate support. They must not be too wide or too short. The extra hard soles in some shoes, used by some dancers with weak intrinsics, prevents correct use of the feet in relevés as the dancer cannot go through the foot correctly in order to achieve the optimum position for pointe work. Therefore this type of shoe only aggravates the situation and makes the muscles and feet even weaker.

5.20 Variations in the Length of the Toes and of the Metatarsals

The ideal forefoot is one where the toes and metatarsals are all about the same length across the foot from the first toe. Inevitably the lateral side of the foot, i.e. the 4th and 5th toes and metatarsals, tend to be a little shorter but when this slope is not very marked the dancer has a foot that is stable on both demi-pointe and on full pointe. Considering the

5.38 Long 2nd metatarsal and 2nd toe. Here the situation is aggravated by the presence also of a short 1st metatarsal

metatarsals first, there can be considerable variations in length. It is quite common to have a 2nd metatarsals which is markedly longer than either the 1st or the 3rd (Fig. 5.38). Another fairly common variation is a very short 1st metatarsal (Fig. 5.39) with the lesser metatarsals much of a length. Another variation is where the lesser metatarsals shorten quite markedly progressively towards the 5th metatarsal, giving a sloping line of metatarsal heads (Fig. 5.40). In all these instances the dancer will have greater or lesser difficulty when on demi-pointe, the degree of difficulty depending upon the particular anatomical variation which is present.

As far as the toes themselves are concerned, the length of the toes may mirror what is happening at the metatarsals. However, one also sees variations in actual length of the toes even if the metatarsals themselves are of a fairly even length (Fig. 5.41). The commonest situation is where there is a long 2nd toe either with or without an accompanying long 2nd metatarsal. This gives the so-called 'classical foot' as is seen in most of the Greek statues and also, very frequently, in fifteenth-sixteenth- and seventeenth-century paintings. This is, however, no comfort to the dancer as discrepancies in toe lengths cause considerable problems when doing pointe work. A long 2nd toe is inevitably going to become flexed up during pointe work.

RESULTS

Discrepancies in metatarsal lengths cause marked unsteadiness and instability on demi-pointe. This can cause strains of either the medial or lateral sides of the foot and ankle (**Sections 3.1**, **3.3** and **3.4**) depending upon the nature of the metatarsal length discrepancy and the way in which the foot will tend to fall. On half-pointe the foot may be either sickled inwards or outwards in an attempt to gain stability (Fig. 5.41).

In toe length discrepancy on full pointe the problems tend to be associated more locally with the toes

5.39A A short 1st metatarsal

5.40A Sloping (oblique) line of metatarsal heads. This is a difficult foot on demi-pointe

5.40B Here the situation is made much worse by the dancer also having very short lesser toes. This foot is extremely difficult for both demi-pointe and pointe work

5.39B An X-ray showing the short 1st metatarsal

5.41 Long 2nd and 3rd toes. In this particular foot the first three metatarsals are much the same length, giving a very stable foot for demi-pointe despite the short 5th toe and metatarsals. On pointe work the larger 2nd and 3rd toes make it more difficult even though here the discrepancy in length between 1st and 2nd is not as great as frequently occurs

themselves and the difficulty in satisfactorily fitting the shoe into the blocks. Local damage to the toes can occur in the form of blistering and marked callosity formation (**Section 3.27**). Additionally, the foot itself can be somewhat unstable on pointe.

In both situations, but particularly in metatarsal length discrepancies, stress fractures of the longer metatarsal or metatarsals are very common (Fig. 5.42) (**Section 3.18**).

TREATMENT

A great deal of attention must be paid to strengthening the intrinsic muscles of the foot and to strengthening all the muscle groups controlling the foot and the ankle. A lot of technical help may be required in order to get the dancer adjusted to the optimum position on both demi-pointe and pointe. It is important to try and correct any tendency to sickling one way or the other.

5.42A Unequal metatarsal lengths – short 1st metatarsal; 2nd and 3rd metatarsals equal length; and 4th and 5 metatarsals very much shorter

5.42B Sickling, with weight being transmitted laterally

5.42C Sickling, with weight being transmitted medially

5.42D In best position achievable. When on demi-pointe, the weight is taken only on the 2nd and 3rd metatarsal heads with some support from the 1st and 4th toes and the 5th toe only just touching the floor

Working on a Raked Surface

Eastern European opera houses and schools often have raked stages and studios of various gradients. Visually for the audience the action on stage is enhanced and viewed more easily, but for the dancer the mechanics of posture have to change. Facing downstage the body weight is pulled forwards stimulating the use of the back of the legs – the hamstring and gluteal muscles – and the extensors of the spine. There is a certain necessary 'pulling back'.

Problems arise when teachers are accustomed to teaching on a rake and then tackle posture on a flat surface when the weight back situation is not to be encouraged. Instead a sensation of 'up and forwards' is more appropriate.

Sometimes standing in a fifth position, teachers have suggested that there is more weight through the back foot, but this is another adjustment more suited only for working on a raked surface.

5.21 Incorrect Weight Placement

This usually means that the weight is too far back. When weight transmission is correct the line runs down vertic-ally from the mastoid processes just behind the ears through the centres of the shoulder, hip, knee and ankle joints to join the sole at the anterior edge of the heel pad (Fig. 5.44). Occasionally a dancer will overcorrect and take the weight too far forward so that it passes through the balls of the feet and, in these instances, the heels are frequently slightly lifted from the ground.

5.43 Stress fracture of the 2nd metatarsal. Healed with plentiful callus (new bone) formation

5.44 Although weight bearing is distributed throughout the sole of the foot, the line of weight transmission from the centre of gravity of the dancer should pass through the heavy black line shown above

CAUSES

1. Lordosis (**Section 5.6**).
2. Kyphosis and a stiff thoracic spine produce a compensatory lordosis (**Section 5.6**) which tilts the pelvis and moves the weight back.
3. Scoliosis will frequently produce a pelvic tilt often accompanied by pelvic rotation (**Section 5.4**).
4. Tightness at the fronts of the hips (**Section 5.9**) produces a forward rotation of the pelvis and pushes the weight back on the legs.
5. Weak trunk muscles cause tension in the upper back muscles which on movement makes the upper trunk fall back as a result of the lack of control of the middle of the trunk. This is accompanied by prominence of the front of the rib cage and relaxation of the abdominal muscles. Frequently this is accompanied by upper chest breathing which aggravates the problem by producing even more tension in the upper back muscles, including the trapezius.
6. Weak abdominal muscles (transversus abdominis), gluteals, hamstrings and adductors (namely any muscle group which takes part in the stabilisation of the pelvis) can together or individually allow a pelvic tilt.
7. Over-turning of the feet associated with either a genuine limitation of the external rotation available in the hip or lack of muscle control of an adequate turn-out produces a forward tilt (**Section 5.7**).
8. Inappropriate muscle development. This may be produced either by faulty teaching or by heavy weight resisted exercises or by *overdoing* other activities such as gymnastics, riding or skating. While the latter two can be enjoyed, they may lead to over development of muscle groups unhelpful to dance.
9. Lack of control of hyper-extended knees (**Section 5.13**) due to locking back the knees causes relaxation of the muscle groups controlling the pelvis.
10. Tibial bowing (**Section 5.16**) because of its tendency to produce rolling when flat, and sickling when rising. The bowing alters the line of weight transmission from the centre of gravity.
11. Tight pointe renders the dancer incapable of rising correctly through the foot to achieve correct half and three-quarter pointe. The weight is therefore taken back. When jumping the tight pointe prevents the dancer going up through the foot or coming down through the foot correctly. They start the jump with the weight back and land with the weight back. This is a potent cause of anterior leg problems and stress injuries of metatarsals (see also **Section 5.18**).
12. Stiff big toe joints (**Section 3.25**) push the weight on to the outer sides of the feet when rising instead of taking it through the centre of the foot. As a result the weight is pushed back.
13. Sloping line of metatarsal heads also pushes the weight on to the outer side of the foot in a similar fashion to stiff big toe joints.
14. Weak intrinsic muscles of the feet accompanied by clawing of the toes pushes the weight back too far on the heels.
15. Tight shoes will produce clawing of the toes with similar results to 14.
16. Growth spurts cause a generalised decrease in muscular control. As a result any of these affected areas can cause the weight to be taken too far back whether the weakness be at the feet, in the trunk or anywhere in between.

CONSEQUENCES

1. Low back strains.
2. Stress fractures of the partes intra-articulares (**Section 3.59**).
3. Groin injuries (**Section 3.47**).
4. Buttock pain (**Section 3.53**).
5. Hamstring injuries at various levels (**Section 3.49**).
6. Adductor muscle injuries (**Section 3.46**).
7. Anterior knee pain (**Section 3.33**).
8. Strains of the back of the knee joint (**Section 3.38**)
9. Stress fractures of tibia and fibula (**Sections 3.29, 3.30**).
10. Anterior compartment syndrome (**Section 3.31**).
11. Calf injuries (**Section 3.32**).
12. Achilles tendinopathy (**Section 3.10**).
13. Extensor hallucis longus tendinopathy (**Section 3.16**).
14. Stress fractures of metatarsals (**Section 3.18**).
15. Weakening of the intrinsic muscles due to lack of proper use (**Section 5.19**).
16. Damage to big-toe joints (**Section 3.22**).

TREATMENT

This is really a misnomer because the weight back situation is not an injury. It is, however, one of the most common and important faults in the dancer and its correction is essential. This can only be achieved by first determining which cause or causes (often multiple) are producing the weight back state. Considerable effort and attention must then be paid to correcting and eliminating all these causes. Treatment may in fact be necessary but this will be aimed at any injuries which have arisen secondarily to the weight back situation. *As in all other cases of injury simple treatment of the injury alone, without any correction of the underlying technical fault, will be useless.*

Glossary of Ballet Terms

Arabesque The dancer is on one leg with the other stretched out behind parallel with or above the line of the floor while the arms can be held in a variety of positions in front of the body but largely in line with it (p. 63).

Battement tendu A beating with the working foot (p. 62).

Degagé Moving the weight from one foot to the other or from both feet to one foot. The centre of gravity of the body has to move from a line passing between the feet when standing on both feet, to a line passing through the supporting foot.

En Dedans Inward turning of the legs or arms.

En Dehors Outward turning of the legs or arms.

Gargouillards A jump from one foot to the other while at the same time carrying out a rapid rond de jambe en l'air (q.v.) with each leg.

Fifth Position Standing turned out with the heel of the front foot against the big toe of the other foot.

First Position Standing with feet turned out and heels together.

Fourth Position Standing turned out with one foot in front of the other and a distance between them.

Plié Flexing the knees and hips with the feet turned out and the heels kept on the ground (see p. 61).

Pointe Dancing on the tips of the toes. Starting from flat this goes through quarter pointe (à quart pointe), to half pointe (à demi pointe), to three-quarter pointe (à trois quarts pointe) and finally to full pointe (sur la pointe). Pointe work started in the early 19th century but until the 1860s blocked shoes were not used, although the Cossacks had danced in soft boots on pointe for centuries but usually with their toes bent under so that they were on their knuckles. (From The Concise Oxford Dictionary of Ballet) Some ill-trained dancers still incorrectly dance on their knuckles, which in the USA is known as 'knuckling' (p. 64).

Retiré Lifting the working foot up towards the knee.

Rond de jambe en l'air A circling motion of the working leg giving the appearance of the leg below the knee describing a circle (p. 63).

Saut A jump from both feet at once.

Second Position Standing with feet turned out and apart.

Tendu The foot is stretched out to the pointe position, usually with the toes touching the ground.

Third Position Standing with the heel of one foot in the instep of the other foot, both turned out.

Turn-out The feet are turned out towards 90° with the turn-out taking place at the hips (external rotation) (see p. 58).

For further reading about ballet terminology and basic elements, positions and movements there are two publications from the Royal Academy of Dance:

Dictionary of Classical Ballet Terminology, 3rd edition (2007), by Rhonda Ryman.

Foundations of Classical Ballet Technique (1997, reprinted 2008). This describes the basic elements, positions and movements in classical ballet.

Credits

Illustrations
Sarah K. Howse
Irene M. Prentice

Black and white photographs
Justin Howse

Colour photographs
Elaine Mayson (www.elainemaysonphotography.co.uk)
Ryoichi Hirano

Index

Lightning Source UK Ltd.
Milton Keynes UK
UKHW05f0759261018
331234UK00004B/27/P

9 780713 685329